PENS OF MANY COLOURS

A CANADIAN READER

THIRD EDITION

EVA C. KARPINSKI
Seneca College

NELSON EDUCATION

NELSON EDUCATION

Pens of Many Colours:
A Canadian Reader
Third Edition
by Eva C. Karpinski

Editorial Director and Publisher:
Evelyn Veitch

Acquisitions Editor:
Anne Williams

Marketing Manager:
Cara Yarzab

Developmental Editor:
Shefali Mehta

Managing Production Editor:
Susan Calvert

Production Coordinator:
Hedy Sellers

Copy Editor/Proofreader:
Alex Moore

Creative Director:
Angela Cluer

Cover Design:
Sonya V. Thursby,
Opus House Incorporated

Cover Image:
Joe Fleming/Archive Inc.

Compositor:
Carol Magee

Printer:
Digital Printer Center

National Library of Canada
Cataloguing in Publication Data

Main entry under title:
Pens of many colours

3rd ed.
Includes bibliographical
references and index.

ISBN 0-7747-3767-0

1. College readers.
2. Readers—Multiculturalism—
   Canada.
3. Multiculturalism—Canada—
   Literary collections.
   I. Karpinski, Eva C.

FC104.P45 2002   808'.0427
C2001-904030-X
F1035.A1P45 2002

PREFACE

Putting together the first edition of *Pens of Many Colours* in 1993, my partner Ian Lea and I tried to recognize a growing need among the reading audience to explore the areas outside of what used to be called the literary mainstream. The 1980s and 1990s have seriously put into question the centrality of culture that has been mostly white, European-based and male-dominated. The so-far marginalized or silenced groups of women, minority, Native, or immigrant writers have become vocal participants in a dialogue for a pluralistic society. Of primary importance in the process of revising cultural assumptions and traditional literary canons is the increasingly multi-ethnic and multicultural make-up of Canadian society. To reflect this changing reality, which is also the reality of our classrooms, we have to be prepared to respect our differences as well as to be able to learn from them and about them. It is hard to imagine a better first step than exposure to a mosaic of texts that embodies Canada's diverse voices.

Preparing the third edition of *Pens of Many Colours*, I have asked myself if the goals of this type of multicultural reader have remained the same almost ten years after the original inception of the project. The lessons we have learned from the 1990s, when more and more critical voices from different communities were raised against multiculturalism as a liberal "whitewash" and when we watched escalating racial tensions in cities and on the reserves, make us painfully aware that the "multicultural dream" of harmonious coexistence will forever elude us if we fail to confront racism as its major obstacle. In my own teaching practice, multicultural education has become anti-racist education. Moreover, if we extend our definitions of "culture" to include minoritized groups such as women, gay and lesbian people, people from rural areas, the poor, disabled, old, and so on, then education will also have to be anti-sexist and anti-homophobic, sensitive to articulations by people of all classes. The changes made in this edition reflect such a wider perspective on "culture" and the need for (multi)cultural literacy that moves beyond celebration of ethnicities toward an analysis of gender, race, and class relations in our society through the medium of writing.

As much as diversity remains an overriding theme of the book, *Pens of Many Colours*—faithful to its title—is also concerned with writing, literature, and rhetoric. On the one hand, the collection aims to give a realistic account of the historical and contemporary presence of diverse groups of people sharing the same social and geographical space and to recognize their contributions to Canadian life and letters. On the other hand, it offers models of diverse genres, styles, and rhetorical modes that allow the students to work on literary critical and analytical skills. I have been looking for texts that engage the reader not only thematically, but also through the high quality of writing. As a result, the book is a flexible tool that can be used as a cross-cultural thematic reader in sociology and gender oriented courses, but can also hold inherent interest for Canadian literature and English composition courses.

Out of the 53 titles included here, 28 are new selections, some by renowned authors. All readings have been grouped into discrete units with thematic boundaries loosely drawn around some organizing concepts. Consequently, readings can be re-contextualized, and used in a different order and for different purposes. I have added a new unit on work to broaden the thematic scope of the reader. Similarly, the apparatus of introductions and questions attached to the readings has been modified. Unit introductions are shorter, meant to ground a particular segment in its thematic context. Conversely, biographies preceding individual selections have been expanded, contributing more background information and some directions for interpretation. Topics for Discussion have been trimmed, but they now offer thematic, analytical, and comparative directions for thinking. As in the previous edition, an alternative Rhetorical Contents has been appended to facilitate the choice of rhetorical models. Finally, a Selected Bibliography of over 40 titles published in the last decade has been included at the end of the book. It includes Canadian anthologies of short stories, essays, autobiographies, and other writing related to multicultural, multi-ethnic, or immigrant experience, excluding, however, poetry anthologies and individual authors' collections (which have usually been acknowledged in the biographies preceding each reading).

Thus revamped and refreshed, *Pens of Many Colours* is being offered to the readers as a tool for promoting greater democratization in education by encouraging individual growth and understanding of ourselves and others. The overall vision of the book, its commitment to a multicultural perspective, fairly balanced representation of diverse racial, ethnic, or cultural groups, and strong support to anti-racist and anti-sexist struggle has been maintained

throughout. In fact, the text has been made more inclusive by bringing in voices of openly gay and lesbian writers. Ideally, any such revi-
sions of the curriculum should be accompanied by changes in our
teaching practices as well. Along with our willingness to work with
these new voices, we might try to open up to less conventional peda-
gogical procedures and ways of student self-expression. If we agree
that it is through "voice" that various experiences can enter the classroom, we must remember that it is not just the voices allowed in as
texts, but also the students' voices as well as the teacher's voice that
are engaged in this polyphonic exchange.

Class-testing the material included in both editions of *Pens*, discussing it with students and other teachers, and reading the invalu-
able comments of my reviewers, I have found out that readers'
responses can be unpredictable and far more complex than expected.
As teachers, we cannot forget that the same text read by different
people can produce denial and identification, silence and outspoken-
ness, resistance to being treated as victims or "native informants" and
empowerment through recognition. We should use such classroom
situations to try to get across the point that no single culture con-
trols signification. Instead of training students how to arrive at one
"correct" reading of a particular text, teachers and students in multicultural classrooms must constantly practise negotiating meaning.
We must remember that our own and students' interpretations are
strongly influenced by our different backgrounds and individual cir-
cumstances, and even if certain comments appear "unusual" or "ille-
gitimate," such comments may reveal a lot about the situatedness of
our knowledges and highlight some important differences that
would otherwise go unnoticed.

Research shows that exposure to diverse viewpoints and perspectives is beneficial to both students of mainstream backgrounds and
students of diverse backgrounds (even though this distinction is only
provisional as the same person can belong to either of these categories, depending on whether race, gender, ethnicity, class, sexuality,
or language are taken to be dominant factors). Multicultural texts
like *Pens of Many Colours* provide successful models of people moving across cultural boundaries; validate the experience of students of
diverse backgrounds and affirm their cultural identity; promote
mutual understanding and empathy; increase the awareness of the
complexity of Canadian society; and de-emphasize the dominant
culture view of history and introduce other perspectives on the historical and economic forces that have shaped Canada. As such, multicultural anthologies can be useful in anti-racism education.
However, teachers and students alike should be aware of the potential

dangers of the version of "multiculturalism" inherent in the very form and structure of a multicultural reader. Very often such textbooks are underwritten by the pseudo-egalitarian "we-are-all-the-same" type of philosophy or, alternately, by the orientalist or voyeuristic fascination with difference. Through their false "democratic" pretensions, these textual "mosaics" may create the context where real, material differences can easily be forgotten, and any claims to "uniqueness" can be diffused by a variety that is quantitative rather than qualitative. Therefore, to alleviate this intrinsic problem of the genre of multicultural reader, in *Pens of Many Colours* we have tried to avoid voice appropriation; to place mainstream voices alongside multicultural voices, thus refusing to "ghettoize" the latter or marginalize them as "other than"; and to remind the reader of the specificity of recorded oppression or privilege through introductions and questions attached to the readings.

I have decided to place in this Preface the above theoretical comments because I think that we need a forum for sharing our experiences of working with multicultural readers. We often work in isolation and stand alone with our doubts. It is my personal belief that every effort made to transform models of education so that they reflect a multicultural standpoint is necessary and desired today. Against the rhetoric of economic restraint that reduces teachers and students to less than subjects in the teaching/learning process, we must insist on humanizing the institutions of education. Embracing the idea of multicultural and anti-racist education is an important step towards this change.

As usual, many people have contributed their knowledge, intelligence, and enthusiasm to the preparation of this book. I would like to thank the editors at Nelson, Anne Williams, whose ideas have been most inspiring, and Shefali Mehta, who has been the most patient Developmental Editor; the reviewers, Maureen Coleman, who is recently retired from Sheridan College, Tamara Boness of Dawson College, Nigel Spencer of Champlain College, and especially Jane Drover of Mount Royal College, whose generous and insightful comments have sustained my faith in the project; and all my colleagues and students who have offered their suggestions and support.

Eva C. Karpinski
Seneca College and York University

CONTENTS

UNIT ONE:
FIRST CONTACT/BEGINNINGS/
MIGRATIONS

UNIT TWO:
CHALLENGES/RACISM/
DISCRIMINATION

UNIT THREE:
LANGUAGE/CULTURE/DISPLACEMENT

UNIT FOUR:
EDUCATION/DIFFERENCE/POWER

UNIT FIVE
GENDER/FAMILIES/RELATIONSHIPS

UNIT SIX:
WORK/POVERTY/CHOICES

UNIT SEVEN:
MAPS/PLACES/MEMORY

UNIT EIGHT:
BORDERS/IDENTITIES/SELVES

RHETORICAL CONTENTS

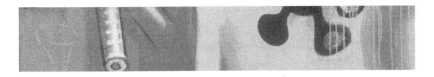

FIRST CONTACT/ BEGINNINGS/ MIGRATIONS

I N T R O D U C T I O N

The pieces in this unit are historically oriented and have been selected so as to convey a rich sense of intersecting histories of diverse racial and ethnic groups in Canada, from Native peoples, to Europeans, African Canadians, Asians, and others. The readings send us back to different historical periods, including pre-colonization, first contact between Native and white cultures, the

French-English conflict, the arrival of Blacks, different waves of immigration, and contemporary influx of refugees. Of the earliest literature documenting the period of exploration, trade, missionary expansion, and early colonial settlement, we have journals, letters, chronicles, reports, and other records—most of them intended to convey impressions from the "wilderness" to the "civilized world" back at home. We have records of Black slaves in Nova Scotia dating back to 1606. We also have rich literature of contact. In addition to Pauline Johnson's story, the texts by Native authors such as Pat Deiter-McArthur, Alootook Ipellie, Carol Geddes, or Jeannette Armstrong clearly demonstrate that the Eurocentric narrative of "discovery" must be discarded since the Americas had existed for thousands of years prior to European exploration. What the narratives of contact show is the devastating impact upon Native cultures of a colonizing force from the outside. Interestingly, different ethnic groups have their own stories of "first arrivals"—often mythical or legendary—such as tales of the Buddhist monks who drifted from China to the West Coast in the fifth and sixth centuries, the Irish legend of St. Brendan, or accounts of the Vikings' landing a thousand years ago.

The readings also introduce us to different geographies and changing motives for migrations. The motives for voyages to the "new world" have varied from imperial colonial ambition and greed, to enforced migration by slavery, to indentured service, transportation by charitable patrons, flight from persecution by authoritarian regimes, hunger, and economic pursuit of a better life. Finally, the naming of different "categories" of Canadians reflects the historical grounding of unequal power dynamics among First Nations, founding nations, immigrants, refugees, settlers, pioneers, and multicultural "others."

Margaret Atwood

Born in 1939 in Ottawa, Margaret Atwood is an internationally acclaimed author who lives in Toronto, Ontario. She has published over 50 books, including novels, short stories, poetry, children's books, and literary criticism. Her works have been translated into more than 20 languages. She has received many awards, including two Governor General's Awards, one for The Handmaid's Tale *(1985), which was made into a popular movie. Last year she won the prestigious Booker Prize in England, for her new novel* The Blind Assassin *(2000). Her most recent publications include the novel* Alias Grace *(1996), the published version of her lectures delivered at Oxford University, titled* Strange Things: The Malevolent North in Canadian Literature *(1995), and the volume of new poems called* Morning in the Burned House *(1996). Atwood's most famous essays were published in the book* Survival: A Thematic Guide to Canadian Literature *(1972), which was her attempt to identify the distinguishing marks and patterns of "Canadianness" in national literature, based mostly on English and French writers. Her discussion of "the immigrant novel" is limited to a very few examples.*

The poem "The Immigrants" is taken from her collection of poetry The Journals of Susanna Moodie *(1970), which is based on the life of the famous "pioneer" woman (see an excerpt from* Roughing It in the Bush *in the same unit). Atwood says that she was inspired to write her book while studying early colonial American writing at Harvard. As she says in the essay "Writing Susanna," "I'd got it into my head that we in Canada had been short-changed. We'd always been told—well, everyone knew—that Canadian literature, if any, was second-rate." Dreaming to life her version of Susanna Moodie, Atwood attempted to create a bridge spanning the past and the present of Canadian writing. It was also a reflection of Atwood's personal experience of what she presents as universal immigrant displacement: "She [Susanna] was appalled by the wilderness, I by the city, once upon a time. Both of us were far from home, both anxious, both scrabbling for cash, both under pressure. Both knew the space between what could be said safely and what needed to be withheld from speech. I said for her what she couldn't say, and she for me."*

The Immigrants

They are allowed to inherit
the sidewalks involved as palmlines, bricks
exhausted and soft, the deep
lawnsmells, orchards whorled
to the land's contours, the inflected weather

only to be told they are too poor
to keep it up, or someone
has noticed and wants to kill them; or the towns
pass laws which declare them obsolete.

I see them coming
up from the hold smelling of vomit,
infested, emaciated, their skins grey
with travel; as they step on shore

the old countries recede, become
perfect, thumbnail castles preserved
like gallstones in a glass bottle, the
towns dwindle upon the hillsides
in a light paperweight-clear.

They carry their carpetbags and trunks
with clothes, dishes, the family pictures;
they think they will make an order
like the old one, sow miniature orchards,
carve children and flocks out of wood

but always they are too poor, the sky
is flat, the green fruit shrivels
in the prairie sun, wood is for burning;
and if they go back, the towns

in time have crumbled, their tongues
stumble among awkward teeth, their ears
are filled with the sound of breaking glass.
I wish I could forget them
and so forget myself:

my mind is a wide pink map
across which move year after year
arrows and dotted lines, further and further,
people in railway cars

their heads stuck out of the windows
at stations, drinking milk or singing,
their features hidden with beards or shawls
day and night riding across an ocean of unknown
land to an unknown land.

TOPICS FOR DISCUSSION

1. How are the immigrants portrayed in the poem? What memories and dreams do they bring into their new country? How are the immigrants received by the people and the land where they wish to settle?

2. What images and metaphors does Atwood use to show common hardships and difficulties encountered by the immigrants?

3. Who is the "I" speaker of the poem? Why does she refer to the immigrants as "they"? How does she describe her relationship to the immigrants?

Pauline Johnson

*Pauline Johnson (Tekahionwake) was born in 1861 on the Six Nations
Reserve near Brantford, Ontario; she died in 1913. She was the daughter
of George Johnson, a Mohawk chief, and an English mother. After her
father's death, she started to make a living by writing poems for money and
began her career as a recitalist. She made herself a buckskin costume that
was supposed to look like the dress of an "Indian princess," and she recited
her dramatic poems to audiences first in southern Ontario, and later in
London, England, the United States, and most of Canada. Her performances on Native subjects could frighten audiences or move them to tears.
Exhausted from years of touring, she settled in Vancouver to devote herself to
full-time writing. She published several books of stories, poems, and essays
that earned her a reputation as a popular writer. She died of breast cancer
and is buried in Stanley Park, her favourite place in Vancouver. Often
romanticized for the taste of the reading public of her day, her narratives,
nonetheless, have a realistic edge and portray some of the conflicts emerging
at the point of contact between Native and white societies.*

The following story was first published in The Moccasin Maker
*(1913), a collection of magazine and newspaper articles and short stories.
"As It Was in the Beginning" can be read as an allegory of gender and race
relations under colonialism. On the surface, it is a melodramatic narrative
of love, betrayal, and revenge. On the symbolic level, through the figures of
the missionary and the fur trader, it captures the mechanisms of colonial
conquest involving the complicity between the Church's "civilizing" mission
and the economic interests of the imperial state. One of the central questions
of the story seems to be: How can Christianity be compatible with racism?
The framing sentence invites the reader to consider the consequences of contact from a gendered perspective, suggesting that for Native women the
process of colonization had meant double subjugation, as Natives and as
women. In fact, recent historical studies show that prior to colonization
Native women enjoyed greater autonomy, and that they resisted religious
conversion as forcing them into the European models of inferior, submissive
femininity and the patriarchal nuclear family.*

*For other narratives of contact, see Pat Deiter-McArthur (Unit Two)
and Alootook Ipellie (Unit Seven). It is particularly useful to relate Johnson's
life and times to Deiter-McArthur's description of the political climate coin-
ciding with the "second generation."*

As It Was in the Beginning

They account for it by the fact that I am a Redskin, but I am something else, too—I am a woman.

I remember the first time I saw him. He came up the trail with some Hudson's Bay trappers, and they stopped at the door of my father's tepee. He seemed even then, fourteen years ago, an old man; his hair seemed just as thin and white, his hands just as trembling and fleshless as they were a month since, when I saw him for what I pray his God is the last time.

My father sat in the tepee, polishing buffalo horns and smoking; my mother, wrapped in her blanket, crouched over her quill-work, on the buffalo-skin at his side; I was lounging at the doorway, idling, watching, as I always watched, the thin, distant line of sky and prairie, wondering, as I always wondered, what lay beyond it. Then he came, this gentle old man with his white hair and thin, pale face. He wore a long black coat, which I now know was the sign of his office, and he carried a black leather-covered book, which, in all the years I have known him, I have never seen him without.

The trappers explained to my father who he was, the Great Teacher, the heart's Medicine Man, the "Blackcoat" we had heard of, who brought peace where there was war, and the magic of whose black book brought greater things than all the Happy Hunting Grounds of our ancestors.

He told us many things that day, for he could speak the Cree tongue, and my father listened, and listened, and when at last they left us, my father said for him to come and sit within the tepee again.

He came, all the time he came, and my father welcomed him, but my mother always sat in silence at work with the quills; my mother never liked the Great "Blackcoat."

His stories fascinated me. I used to listen intently to the tale of the strange new place he called "heaven," of the gold crown, of the white dress, of the great music; and then he would tell of that other strange place—hell. My father and I hated it; we feared it, we dreamt of it, we trembled at it. Oh, if the "Blackcoat" would only cease to talk of it! Now I know he saw the effect upon us, and he used it as a whip to lash us into his new religion, but even then my mother must have known, for each time he left the tepee she would watch him going slowly away across the prairie; then when he disappeared into the far horizon she would laugh scornfully, and say:

"If the white man made this Blackcoat's hell, let him go to it. It is for the man who found it first. No hell for Indians, just Happy Hunting Grounds. Blackcoat can't scare me."

And then, after weeks had passed, one day as he stood at the tepee door he laid his white, old hand on my head and said to my father: "Give me this little girl, chief. Let me take her to the mission school; let me keep her, and teach her of the great God and His eternal heaven. She will grow to be a noble woman, and return perhaps to bring her people to the Christ."

My mother's eyes snapped. "No," she said. It was the first word she ever spoke to the "Blackcoat." My father sat and smoked. At the end of a half-hour he said:

"I am an old man, Blackcoat. I shall not leave the God of my fathers. I like not your strange God's ways—all of them. I like not His two new places for me when I am dead. Take the child, Blackcoat, and save her from hell."

The first grief of my life was when we reached the mission. They took my buckskin dress off, saying I was now a little Christian girl and must dress like all the white people at the mission. Oh, how I hated that stiff new calico dress and those leather shoes! But, little as I was, I said nothing, only thought of the time when I should be grown, and do as my mother did, and wear the buckskins and the blanket.

My next serious grief was when I began to speak the English, that they forbade me to use any Cree words whatsoever. The rule of the school was that any child heard using its native tongue must get a slight punishment. I never understood it, I cannot understand it now, why the use of my dear Cree tongue could be a matter for correction or an action deserving punishment.

She was strict, the matron of the school, but only justly so, for she had a heart and a face like her brother's, the "Blackcoat." I had long since ceased to call him that. The trappers at the post called him "St. Paul," because, they told me, of his self-sacrificing life, his kindly deeds, his rarely beautiful old face; so I, too, called him "St. Paul," though oftener "Father Paul," though he never liked the latter title, for he was a Protestant. But as I was his pet, his darling of the whole school, he let me speak of him as I would, knowing it was but my heart speaking in love. His sister was a widow, and mother to a laughing yellow-haired little boy of about my age, who was my constant playmate and who taught me much of English in his own childish way. I used to be fond of this child, just as I was fond of his mother and of his uncle, my "Father Paul," but as my girlhood passed away, as womanhood came upon me, I got strangely wearied of them all; I longed, oh, God, how I longed for the old wild life! It came with my womanhood, with my years.

What mattered it to me now that they had taught me all their ways?—their tricks of dress, their reading, their writing, their books. What mattered it that "Father Paul" loved me, that the traders at the post called me pretty, that I was a pet of all, from the factor to the poorest trapper in the service? I wanted my own people, my own old life, my blood called out for it, but they always said I must not return to my father's tepee. I heard them talk amongst themselves of keeping me away from pagan influences; they told each other that if I returned to the prairies, the tepees, I would degenerate, slip back to paganism, as other girls had done; marry, perhaps, with a pagan—and all their years of labor and teaching would be lost.

I said nothing, but I waited. And then one night the feeling overcame me. I was in the Hudson's Bay store when an Indian came in from the north with a large pack of buckskin. As they unrolled it a dash of its insinuating odor filled the store. I went over and leaned above the skins a second, then buried my face in them, swallowing, drinking the fragrance of them, that went to my head like wine. Oh, the wild wonder of that wood-smoked tan, the subtlety of it, the untamed smell of it! I drank it into my lungs, my innermost being was saturated with it, till my mind reeled and my heart seemed twisted with a physical agony. My childhood recollections rushed upon me, devoured me. I left the store in a strange, calm frenzy, and going rapidly to the mission house I confronted my Father Paul and demanded to be allowed to go "home," if only for a day. He received the request with the same refusal and the same gentle sigh that I had too often been greeted with, but *this* time the desire, the smoke-tan, the heart-ache, never lessened.

Night after night I would steal away by myself and go to the border of the village to watch the sun set in the foothills, to gaze at the far line of sky and prairie, to long and long for my father's lodge. And Laurence—always Laurence—my fair-haired, laughing, child playmate, would come calling and calling for me: "Esther, where are you? We miss you: come in, Esther, come in with me." And if I did not turn at once to him and follow, he would come and place his strong hands on my shoulders and laugh into my eyes and say, "Truant, truant, Esther; can't *we* make you happy?"

My old child playmate had vanished years ago. He was a tall, slender young man now, handsome as a young chief, but with laughing blue eyes, and always those yellow curls about his temples. He was my solace in my half-exile, my comrade, my brother, until one night it was, "Esther, Esther, can't *I* make you happy?"

I did not answer him; only looked out across the plains and thought of the tepees. He came close, close. He locked his arms about me, and with my face pressed up to his throat he stood silent. I felt the blood from my heart sweep to my very finger-tips. I loved him. Oh God, how I loved him! In a wild, blind instant it all came, just because he held me so and was whispering brokenly, "Don't leave me, don't leave me, Esther; *my* Esther, my child-love, my playmate, my girl-comrade, my little Cree sweetheart, will you go away to your people, or stay, stay for me, for my arms, as I have you now?"

No more, no more the tepees; no more the wild stretch of prairie, the intoxicating fragrance of the smoke-tanned buckskin; no more the bed of buffalo hide, the soft, silent moccasin; no more the dark faces of my people, the dulcet cadence of the sweet Cree tongue—only this man, this fair, proud, tender man who held me in his arms, in his heart. My soul prayed to his great white God, in that moment, that He let me have only this.

It was twilight when we re-entered the mission gate. We were both excited, feverish. Father Paul was reading evening prayers in the large room beyond the hallway; his soft, saint-like voice stole beyond the doors, like a benediction upon us. I went noiselessly upstairs to my own room and sat there undisturbed for hours.

The clock downstairs struck one, startling me from my dreams of happiness, and at the same moment a flash of light attracted me. My room was in an angle of the building, and my window looked almost directly down into those of Father Paul's study, into which at that instant he was entering, carrying a lamp. "Why, Laurence," I heard him exclaim, "what are you doing here? I thought, my boy, you were in bed hours ago."

"No, uncle, not in bed, but in dreamland," replied Laurence, arising from the window, where evidently he, too, had spent the night hours as I had done.

Father Paul fumbled about for a moment, found his large black book, which for once he seemed to have got separated from, and was turning to leave, when the curious circumstance of Laurence being there at so unusual an hour seemed to strike him anew. "Better go to sleep, my son," he said simply, then added curiously, "Has anything occurred to keep you up?"

Then Laurence spoke: "No, uncle, only—only, I'm happy, that's all."
Father Paul stood irresolute: Then: "It is—?"

"Esther," said Laurence quietly, but he was at the old man's side,
his hand was on the bent old shoulder, his eyes proud and appealing.

Father Paul set the lamp on the table, but, as usual, one hand
held that black book, the great text of his life. His face was paler
than I had ever seen it—graver.

"Tell of it," he requested.

I leaned far out of my window and watched them both. I listened with my very heart, for Laurence was telling him of me, of his
love, of the new-found joy of that night.

"You have said nothing of marriage to her?" asked Father Paul.

"Well—no; but she surely understands that—"

"Did you speak of *marriage?*" repeated Father Paul, with a harsh
ring in his voice that was new to me.

"No, uncle, but—"

"Very well, then; very well."

There was a brief silence. Laurence stood staring at the old man
as though he were a stranger; he watched him push a large chair up
to the table, slowly seat himself; then mechanically following his
movements, he dropped onto a lounge. The old man's head bent
low, but his eyes were bright and strangely fascinating. He began:

"Laurence, my boy, your future is the dearest thing to me of all
earthly interests. Why, you *can't* marry this girl—no, no, sit, sit until
I have finished," he added, with raised voice, as Laurence sprang up,
remonstrating. "I have long since decided that you marry well; for
instance, the Hudson's Bay factor's daughter."

Laurence broke into a fresh, rollicking laugh. "What, uncle," he
said, "little Ida McIntosh? Marry that little yellow-haired fluff ball,
that kitten, that pretty little dolly?"

"Stop," said Father Paul. Then, with a low, soft persuasiveness,
"She is *white*, Laurence."

My lover startled. "Why, uncle, what do you mean?" he faltered.

"Only this, my son: poor Esther comes of uncertain blood; would
it do for you—the missionary's nephew, and adopted son, you might
say—to marry the daughter of a pagan Indian? Her mother is hope-
lessly uncivilized; her father has a dash of French somewhere—half-
breed, you know, my boy, half-breed." Then, with still lower tone and
half-shut, crafty eyes, he added: "The blood is a bad, bad mixture, *you*
know that; you know, too, that I am very fond of the girl, poor dear
Esther. I have tried to separate her from evil pagan influences; she is
the daughter of the Church; I want her to have no other parent; but
you never can tell what lurks in *a caged animal that has once been wild.*

My whole heart is with the Indian people, my son; my whole heart, my whole life, has been devoted to bringing them to Christ, *but it is a different thing to marry with one of them.*"

His small old eyes were riveted on Laurence like a hawk's on a rat. My heart lay like ice in my bosom.

Laurence, speechless and white, stared at him breathlessly.

"Go away somewhere," the old man was urging, "to Winnipeg, Toronto, Montreal; forget her, then come back to Ida McIntosh. A union of the Church and the Hudson's Bay will mean great things, and may ultimately result in my life's ambition, the civilization of this entire tribe, that we have worked so long to bring to God."

I listened, sitting like one frozen. Could those words have been uttered by my venerable teacher, by him whom I revered as I would one of the saints in his own black book? Ah, there was no mistaking it. My white father, my life-long friend who pretended to love me, to care for my happiness, was urging the man I worshipped to forget me, to marry with the factor's daughter—because of what? Of my red skin; my good, old, honest pagan mother; my confiding French-Indian father. In a second all the care, the hollow love he had given me since my childhood, were as things that never existed. I hated that old mission priest as I hated his white man's hell. I hated his long, white hair; I hated his thin, white hands; I hated his body, his soul, his voice, his black book—oh, how I hated the very atmosphere of him!

Laurence sat motionless, his face buried in his hands, but the old man continued: "No, no; not the child of that pagan mother; you can't trust her, my son. What would you do with a wife who might any day break from you to return to her prairies and her buckskins? *You can't trust her.*" His eyes grew smaller, more glittering, more fascinating then, and leaning with an odd, secret sort of movement towards Laurence, he almost whispered. "Think of her silent ways, her noiseless step; the girl glides about like an apparition; her quick fingers, her wild longings—I don't know why, but with all my fondness for her, she reminds me sometimes of a strange—*snake.*"

Laurence shuddered, lifted his face, and said hoarsely: "You're right, uncle; perhaps I'd better not; I'll go away, I'll forget her, and then—well, then—yes, you are right, it *is* a different thing to marry one of them." The old man arose. His feeble fingers still clasped his black book; his soft white hair clung about his forehead like that of an Apostle; his eyes lost their peering, crafty expression; his bent shoulders resumed the dignity of a minister of the living God; he was the picture of what the traders called him—"St. Paul."

"Good-night, son," he said.

"Good-night, uncle, and thank you for bringing me to myself."

They were the last words I ever heard uttered by either that old arch-fiend or his weak, miserable kinsman. Father Paul turned and left the room. I watched his withered hand—the hand I had so often felt resting on my head in holy benediction—clasp the door-knob, turn it slowly then, with bowed head and his pale face rapt in thought, he left the room—left it with the mad venom of my hate pursuing him like the very Evil One he taught me of.

What were his years of kindness and care now? What did I care for his God, his heaven, his hell? He had robbed me of my native faith, of my parents, of my people, of this last, this life of love that would have made a great, good woman of me. God! How I hated him!

I crept to the closet in my dark little room. I felt for a bundle I had not looked at for years—yes, it was there, the buckskin dress I had worn as a little child when they brought me to the mission. I tucked it under my arm and descended the stairs noiselessly. I would look into the study and speak good-bye to Laurence; then I would—

I pushed open the door. He was lying on the couch where a short time previously he had sat, white and speechless, listening to Father Paul. I moved towards him softly. God in heaven, he was already asleep. As I bent over him the fullness of his perfect beauty impressed me for the first time; his slender form, his curving mouth that almost laughed even in sleep, his fair, tossed hair, his smooth, strong-pulsing throat. God! How I loved him!

Then there arose the picture of the factor's daughter. I hated her. I hated her baby face, her yellow hair, her whitish skin. "She shall not marry him," my soul said. "I will kill him first—kill his beautiful body, his lying, false heart." Something in my heart seemed to speak; it said over and over again, "Kill him, kill him; she will never have him then. Kill him. It will break Father Paul's heart and blight his life. He has killed the best of you, of your womanhood; kill *his* best, his pride, his hope—his sister's son, his nephew Laurence." But how? How?

What had that terrible old man said I was like? A *strange snake*. A snake? The idea wound itself about me like the very coils of a ser-pent. What was this in the beaded bag of my buckskin dress? This little thing rolled in tan that my mother had given me at parting with the words, "Don't touch much, but sometime maybe you want it!" Oh! I knew well enough what it was—a small flint arrow-head dipped in the venom of some *strange snake*.

I knelt beside him and laid my hot lips on his hand. I wor-shipped him, oh, how, how I worshipped him! Then again the vision of *her* baby face, *her* yellow hair—I scratched his wrist twice with the arrow-tip. A single drop of red blood oozed up; he stirred. I turned the lamp down and slipped out of the room—out of the house.

I dreamt nightly of the horrors of the white man's hell. Why did they teach me of it, only to fling me into it?

Last night as I crouched beside my mother on the buffalo-hide, Dan Henderson, the trapper, came in to smoke with my father. He said old Father Paul was bowed with grief, that with my disappearance I was suspected, but that there was no proof. Was it not merely a snake bite?

They account for it by the fact that I am a Redskin.

They seem to have forgotten I am a woman.

TOPICS FOR DISCUSSION

1. How has Johnson portrayed the incursion of missionaries into the Native community? What steps did the missionaries use to dispossess the Cree children of their identity? What stereotypes did they use to rationalize the "civilizing" mission?

2. For Esther, what does the betrayal by white religion consist of? What lesson does she learn at the mission about being "a Redskin" and "a woman"?

3. Despite its indictment of Christian hypocrisy, the story relies heavily on Christian symbolism. What symbolic meanings does "snake" have in Christian and Native traditions? How appropriate is the allusion to the Garden of Eden in the story's title?

Susanna Moodie

Susanna Moodie (1803-1885) emigrated from England in 1832 and settled in the Peterborough area of southern Ontario. Her experiences clearing the land and on a bush farm were described in Roughing It in the Bush *(1852). Her sister, Catharine Parr Traill, gave her version of similar experiences in* The Backwoods of Canada *(1836), based on letters she wrote to her relatives in England. Moodie and Traill were impoverished members of the English gentry who came to Canada to repair their fortunes; they found, however, that their cultural background had not prepared them well for the rigours of "bush farming" in the colonies. Both books were designed to inform and warn prospective English immigrants who might have been misguided by exaggerated claims of Canadian developers. Unlike her sister, Moodie was able to infuse her stories with a great deal of humour. In 1840, Moodie and her husband moved to Belleville, where she wrote the sketches collected in* Roughing It in the Bush, *as well as its sequel,* Life in the Clearings *(1853), and several novels. She was also an adept water colour painter who sold her flower illustrations to supplement her income from writing.*

*   *Roughing It in the Bush *was first published in England and the United States. The first Canadian edition appeared in 1872. The first edition included four chapters written by Susanna's husband and a number of poems, mostly by Susanna, along with some quotations and epigraphs, and some poems by her husband and her brother Samuel Strickland. "A Visit to Grosse Isle" offers a glimpse of early nineteenth-century arrivals in British North America. After a long and scary Atlantic crossing, new immigrants usually ended their journey at the port of Quebec. However, they had to make their first stop at Grosse Isle, where a medical officer gave an entry clearance. If any sick people were found aboard, everybody was put into quarantine on Grosse Isle. It is a place where many poor immigrants had died before reaching the land of their hopes. At the time of Moodie's story, the British and Irish comprised the largest groups of immigrants. The Irish were running away from poverty, hunger, and oppression by English colonial landlords back in their homeland. In particular, the great potato famine of the 1840s caused massive emigration from Ireland.*

A Visit to Grosse Isle

Alas! that man's stern spirit e'er should mar
A scene so pure—so exquisite as this.

The dreadful cholera was depopulating Quebec and Montreal, when our ship cast anchor off Grosse Isle, on the 30th of August, 1832, and we were boarded a few minutes after by the health-officers. One of these gentlemen—a little, shrivelled-up Frenchman—from his solemn aspect and attenuated figure, would have made no bad representative of him who sat upon the pale horse. He was the only grave Frenchman I had ever seen, and I naturally enough regarded him as a phenomenon. His companion—a fine-looking fair-haired Scotchman—though a little consequential in his manners, looked like one who in his own person could combat and vanquish all the evils which flesh is heir to. Such was the contrast between these doctors, that they would have formed very good emblems—one, of vigorous health; the other, of hopeless decay.

Our captain, a rude blunt north-country sailor possessing certainly not more politeness than might be expected in a bear, received his sprucely dressed visitors on the deck, and, with very little courtesy, abruptly bade them follow him down into the cabin.

The officials were no sooner seated, than glancing hastily round the place, they commenced the following dialogue:

"From what port, captain?"

Now the captain had a peculiar language of his own, from which he commonly expunged all the connecting links. Small words, such as "and" and "the," he contrived to dispense with altogether.

"Scotland—sailed from port o' Leith, bound for Quebec, Montreal—general cargo—seventy-two steerage, four cabin passengers—brig, ninety-two tons burden, crew eight hands." Here he produced his credentials, and handed them to the strangers. The Scotchman just glanced over the documents, and laid them on the table.

"Had you a good passage out?"

"Tedious, baffling winds, heavy fogs, detained three weeks on Banks, foul weather making Gulf, short of water, people out of provisions, steerage passengers starving."

"Any case of sickness or death on board?"

"All sound as crickets."

"Any births?" lisped the little Frenchman.

The captain screwed up his mouth, and after a moment's reflection he replied, "Births? Why, yes; now I think on't, gentlemen, we had one female on board, who produced three at a birth."

"That's uncommon," said the Scotch doctor, with an air of lively curiosity. "Are the children alive and well? I should like much to see them." He started up, and knocked his head, for he was very tall, against the ceiling. "Confound your low cribs! I have nearly dashed out my brains."

"A hard task, that," looked the captain to me. He did not speak, but I knew by his sarcastic grin what was uppermost in his thoughts. "The young ones all males—fine thriving fellows. Step upon the deck, Sam Frazer," turning to his steward: "bring them down for doctors to see." Sam vanished, with a knowing wink to his superior, and quickly returned, bearing in his arms three fat, chuckle-headed bull-terriers; the sagacious mother following close at his heels, and looking ready to give and take offence on the slightest provocation.

"Here, gentlemen, are the babies," said Frazer, depositing his burden on the floor. "They do credit to the nursing of the brindled slut."

The old tar laughed, chuckled, and rubbed his hands in an ecstasy of delight at the indignation and disappointment visible in the countenance of the Scotch Exculapius, who, angry as he was, wisely held his tongue. Not so the Frenchman; his rage scarcely knew bounds,—he danced in a state of most ludicrous excitement,—he shook his fist at our rough captain, and screamed at the top of his voice.

"Sacré, you bête! You tink us dog, ven you try to pass your puppies on us for babies?"

"Hout, man, don't be angry," said the Scotchman, stifling a laugh; "you see 'tis only a joke!"

"Joke! me no understand such joke. Bête!" returned the angry Frenchman, bestowing a savage kick on one of the unoffending pups which was frisking about his feet. The pup yelped; the slut barked and leaped furiously at the offender, and was only kept from biting him by Sam, who could scarcely hold her back for laughing; the captain was uproarious; the offended Frenchman alone maintained a severe and dignified aspect. The dogs were at length dismissed, and peace restored.

After some further questioning from the officials, a bible was required for the captain to take an oath. Mine was mislaid, and there was none at hand.

"Confound it!" muttered the old sailor, tossing over the papers in his desk; "that scoundrel, Sam, always stows my traps out of the way." Then taking up from the table a book which I had been reading, which happened to be *Voltaire's History of Charles XII.*, he presented it, with as grave an air as he could assume, to the Frenchman. Taking for granted that it was the volume required, the little doctor was too polite to open the book, the captain was duly sworn, and the party returned to the deck.

Here a new difficulty occurred, which nearly ended in serious quarrel. The gentlemen requested the old sailor to give them a few feet of old planking, to repair some damage which their boat had sustained the day before. This the captain could not do. They seemed to think his refusal intentional, and took it as a personal affront. In no very gentle tones, they ordered him instantly to prepare his boats, and put his passengers on them.

"Stiff breeze—short sea," returned the bluff old seaman; "great risk in making land—boats heavily laden with women and children will be swamped. Not a soul goes on shore this night."

"If you refuse to comply with our orders, we will report you to your authorities."

He turned upon his heel, and the medical men left the vessel in great disdain. We had every reason to be thankful for the firmness displayed by our rough commander. That same evening we saw eleven persons drowned, from another vessel close beside us, while attempting to make the shore.

By daybreak all was hurry and confusion on board the *Anne*. I watched boat after boat depart for the island, full of people and goods, and envied them the glorious privilege of once more standing firmly on the earth, after two long months of rocking and rolling at sea. How ardently we anticipate pleasure, which often ends in positive pain! Such was my case when at last indulged in the gratification so eagerly desired. As cabin passengers, we were not included in the general order of purification, but were only obliged to send our servant, with the clothes and bedding we had used during the voyage, on shore, to be washed.

The ship was soon emptied of all her live cargo. My husband went off with the boats, to reconnoitre the island, and I was left alone with my baby, in the otherwise empty vessel. Even Oscar, the captain's Scotch terrier, who had formed a devoted attachment to me during the voyage, forgot his allegiance, became possessed of the land mania, and was away with the rest. With the most intense desire to go on shore, I was doomed to look and long and envy every boatful of emigrants that glided past. Nor was this all; the ship was out of provisions, and I was condemned to undergo a rigid fast until the return of the boat, when the captain had promised a supply of fresh butter and bread. The vessel had been nine weeks at sea; the poor steerage passengers for the two last weeks had been out of food, and the captain had been obliged to feed them from the ship's stores. The promised bread was to be obtained from a small steam-boat, which plied daily between Quebec and the island, trans-porting convalescent emigrants and their goods in her upward trip, and provisions for the sick on her return.

How I reckoned on once more tasting bread and butter! The very thought of the treat in store served to sharpen my appetite, and render the long fast more irksome. I could now fully realise all Mrs. Bowdich's longings for English bread and butter, after her three years' travel through the burning African deserts, with her talented husband.

"When we arrived at the hotel at Plymouth," said she, "and were asked what refreshment we chose—'Tea, and home-made bread and butter,' was my instant reply. 'Brown bread, if you please, and plenty of it.' I never enjoyed any luxury like it. I was positively ashamed of asking the waiter to refill the plate. After the execrable messes, and the hard ship-biscuit, imagine the luxury of a good slice of English bread and butter!"

At home, I laughed heartily at the lively energy with which that charming woman of genius related this little incident in her eventful history,—but off Grosse Isle, I realised it all.

As the sun rose above the horizon, all these matter-of-fact cir-cumstances were gradually forgotten, and merged in the surpassing grandeur of the scene that rose majestically before me. The previous day had been dark and stormy; and a heavy fog had concealed the mountain chain, which forms the stupendous background to this sublime view, entirely from our sight. As the clouds rolled away from their grey, bald brows, and cast into denser shadow the vast forest belt that girdled them round, they loomed out like mighty giants—Titans of the earth, in all their rugged and awful beauty—a thrill of wonder and delight pervaded my mind. The spectacle floated dimly on my sight—my eyes were blinded with tears—blinded with the excess of beauty. I turned to the right and to the left, I looked up and down the glorious river; never had I beheld so many striking objects blended into one mighty whole! Nature had lavished all her noblest features in producing that enchanting scene.

The rocky isle in front, with its neat farm-houses at the eastern point, and its high bluff at the western extremity, crowned with the telegraph—the middle space occupied by tents and sheds for the cholera patients, and its wooded shores dotted over with motley groups—added greatly to the picturesque effect of the land scene. Then the broad, glittering river, covered with boats darting to and fro, conveying passengers from twenty-five vessels, of various size and tonnage, which rode at anchor, with their flag flying from the mast-head, gave an air of life and interest to the whole. Turning to the south side of the St. Lawrence, I was not less struck with its low fertile shores, white houses, and neat churches, whose slender spires and bright tin roofs shone like silver as they caught the first rays of the sun. As far as the eye could reach, a line of white buildings extended along the bank; their background formed by the purple hue of the dense, interminable forest. It was a scene unlike any I had ever beheld, and to which Britain contains no parallel. Mackenzie, an old Scotch dragoon, who was one of our passengers, when he rose in the morning, and saw the parish of St. Thomas for the first time, exclaimed—"Weel, it beats a'! Can thae white clouts be a'houses? They look like claes hung out to drie!" There was some truth in this odd comparison, and for some minutes, I could scarcely convince myself that the white patches scattered so thickly over the opposite shore could be the dwellings of a busy, lively population.

"What sublime views of the north side of the river those *habitans* of St. Thomas must enjoy," thought I. Perhaps familiarity with the scene has rendered them indifferent to its astonishing beauty.

Eastward, the view down the St. Lawrence towards the Gulf, is the finest of all, scarcely surpassed by anything in the world. Your eye follows the long range of lofty mountains until their blue summits are blended and lost in the blue of the sky. Some of these, partially cleared round the base, are sprinkled over with neat cottages and the green slopes, that spread around them are covered with flocks and herds. The surface of the splendid river is diversified with islands of every size and shape, some in wood, others partially cleared, and adorned with orchards and white farm-houses. As the early sun streamed upon the most prominent of these, leaving the others in deep shade, the effect was strangely novel and imposing. In more remote regions, where the forest has never yet echoed to the woodman's axe, or received the impress of civilisation, the first approach to the shore inspires a melancholy awe, which becomes painful in its intensity.

Land of vast hills and mighty streams,
The lofty sun that o'er thee beams
On fairer clime sheds not his ray,
When basking in the noon of day

Thy waters dance in silver light,
And o'er them frowning, dark as night,
Thy shadowy forests, soaring high,
Stretch forth beyond the aching eye,
And blend in distance with the sky.
And silence—awful silence broods
Profoundly o'er these solitudes;
Nought but the lapsing of the floods
Breaks the deep stillness of the woods;
A sense of desolation reigns
O'er these unpeopled forest plains,
Where sounds of the life ne'er wake a tone
Of cheerful praise round Nature's throne,
Man finds himself with God—alone.

My day-dreams were dispelled by the return of the boat, which brought my husband and the captain from the island.

"No bread," said the latter, shaking his head; "you must be content to starve a little longer. Provision-ship not in till four o'clock." My husband smiled at the look of blank disappointment with which I received these unwelcome tidings. "Never mind, I have news which will comfort you. The officer who commands the station sent a note to me by an orderly, inviting us to spend the afternoon with him. He promises to show us everything worthy of notice on the island. Captain —— claims acquaintance with me; but I have not the least recollection of him. Would you like to go?"

"Oh, by all means. I long to see the lovely island. It looks a perfect paradise at this distance."

The rough sailor-captain screwed his mouth on one side, and gave me one of his comical looks, but he said nothing until he assisted in placing me and the baby in the boat.

"Don't be too sanguine, Mrs. Moodie; many things look well at a distance which are bad enough when near."

I scarcely regarded the old sailor's warning. So eager was I to go on shore—to put my foot upon the soil of the new world for the first time—I was in no humour to listen to any depreciation of what seemed so beautiful.

It was four o'clock when we landed on the rocks, which the rays of an intensely scorching sun had rendered so hot that I could scarcely place my foot upon them. How the people without shoes bore it, I cannot imagine. Never shall I forget the extraordinary spectacle that met our sight the moment we passed the low range of bushes which formed a screen in front of the river. A crowd of many hundred Irish emigrants had been landed during the present and former day; and all this motley crew—men, women, and children, who were not confined by sickness to the sheds (which greatly resembled cattle-pens)—were employed in washing clothes, or spreading them out on the rocks and bushes to dry.

The men and boys were *in* the water, while the women, with their scanty garments tucked above their knees, were trampling their bedding in tubs, or in holes in the rocks, which the retiring tide had left half full of water. Those who did not possess washing-tubs, pails, or iron pots, or could not obtain access to a hole in the rocks, were running to and fro, screaming and scolding in no measured terms. The confusion of Babel was among them. All talkers and no hearers—each shouting and yelling in his or her uncouth dialect, and all accompanying their vociferations with violent and extraordinary gestures, quite incomprehensible to the uninitiated. We were literally stunned by the strife of tongues. I shrank, with feelings almost akin to fear, from the hard-featured, sun-burnt harpies, as they elbowed rudely past me.

I had heard and read much of savages, and have since seen, during my long residence in the bush, somewhat of uncivilised life; but the Indian is one of Nature's gentlemen—he never says or does a rude or vulgar thing. The vicious, uneducated barbarians who form the surplus of over-populous European countries, are far behind the wild man in delicacy of feeling or natural courtesy. The people who covered the island appeared perfectly destitute of shame, or even of a sense of common decency. Many were almost naked, still more but partially clothed. We turned in disgust from the revolting scene, but were unable to leave the spot until the captain had satisfied a noisy group of his own people, who were demanding a supply of stores.

And here I must observe that our passengers, who were chiefly honest Scotch labourers and mechanics from the vicinity of Edinburgh, and who while on board ship had conducted themselves with the greatest propriety, and appeared the most quiet, orderly set of people in the world, no sooner set foot upon the island than they became infected by the same spirit of insubordination and misrule, and were just as insolent and noisy as the rest.

While our captain was vainly endeavouring to satisfy the unreasonable demands of his rebellious people, Moodie had discovered a woodland path that led to the back of the island. Sheltered by some hazel-bushes from the intense heat of the sun, we sat down by the cool, gushing river, out of sight, but, alas! Not out of hearing of the noisy, riotous crowd. Could we have shut out the profane sounds which came to us on every breeze, how deeply should we have enjoyed an hour amid the tranquil beauties of that retired and lovely spot!

The rocky banks of the island were adorned with beautiful ever-greens, which sprang up spontaneously in every nook and crevice. I remarked many of our favourite garden shrubs among these wild-ings of nature. The fillagree, with its narrow, dark glossy-green leaves; the privet, with its modest white blossoms and purple berries; the lignum-vitae, with its strong resinous odour; the burnet-rose, and a great variety of elegant unknowns.

Here, the shores of the island and mainland, receding from each other, formed a small cove, overhung with lofty trees, clothed from the base to the summit with wild vines, that hung in graceful fes-toons from the topmost branches to the water's edge. The dark shadows of the mountains, thrown upon the water, as they towered to the height of some thousand feet above us, gave to the surface of the river an ebon hue. The sunbeams dancing through the thick, quivering foliage, fell in stars of gold, or long lines of dazzling brightness, upon the deep black waters, producing the most novel and beautiful effects. It was a scene over which the spirit of peace might brood in silent adoration; but how spoiled by the discordant yells of the filthy beings who were sullying the purity of the air and water with contaminating sights and sounds!

We were now joined by the sergeant, who very kindly brought us his capful of ripe plums and hazel-nuts, the growth of the island; a joyful present, but marred by a note from Captain ——, who had found that he had been mistaken in his supposed knowledge of us, and politely apologised for not being allowed by the health-officers to receive any emigrant beyond the bounds appointed for the per-formance of quarantine.

I was deeply disappointed, but my husband laughingly told me that I had seen enough of the island; and turning to the good-natured soldier, remarked, that "it could be no easy task to keep such wild savages in order."

"You may well say that, sir—but our night scenes far exceed those of the day. You would think they were incarnate devils; singing, drinking, dancing, shouting, and cutting antics that would surprise the leader of a circus. They have no shame—are under not restraint—nobody knows them here, and they think they can speak and act as they please; and they are such thieves that they rob one another of the little they possess. The healthy actually run the risk of taking the cholera by robbing the sick. If you have not hired one or two stout, honest fellows from among your fellow-passengers to guard your clothes while they are drying, you will never see half of them again. They are a sad set, sir, a sad set. We could, perhaps, manage the men; but the women, sir!—the women! Oh, sir!"

Anxious as we were to return to the ship, we were obliged to remain until sun-down in our retired nook. We were hungry, tired, and out of spirits; the mosquitoes swarmed in myriads around us, tormenting the poor baby, who, not at all pleased with her first visit to the new world, filled the air with cries; when the captain came to tell us that the boat was ready. It was a welcome sound. Forcing our way once more through the still squabbling crowd, we gained the landing-place. Here we encountered a boat, just landing a fresh cargo of lively savages from the Emerald Isle. One fellow, of gigantic proportions, whose long, tattered great-coat just reached below the middle of his bare red legs, and, like charity, hid the defects of his other garments, or perhaps concealed his want of them, leaped upon the rocks, and flourishing aloft his shilelagh, bounded and capered like a wild goat from his native mountains. "Whurrah! My boys!" he cried, "Shure we'll all be jontlemen!"

"Pull away, my lads!" said the captain. Then turning to me, "Well, Mrs. Moodie, I hope that you have had enough of Grosse Isle. But could you have witnessed the scenes that I did this morning—"

Here he was interrupted by the wife of the old Scotch Dragoon, Mackenzie, running down to the boat, and laying her hand familiarly upon his shoulder, "Captain, dinna forget."

"Forget what?"

She whispered something confidentially in his ear.

"Oh, ho! the brandy!" he responded aloud. "I should have thought, Mrs. Mackenzie, that you had had enough of *that same*, on yon island?"

"Aye, sic a place for *decent* folk," returned the drunken body, shaking her head. "One needs a drap o' comfort, captain, to keep up one's heart avá."

The captain set up one of his boisterous laughs, as he pushed the boat from the shore. "Hollo! Sam Frazer! steer in, we have forgotten the stores."

"I hope not, captain," said I: "I have been starving since daybreak."

"The bread, the butter, the beef, the onions and potatoes are here, sir," said honest Sam, particularising each article.

"All right; pull for the ship. Mrs. Moodie, we will have a glorious supper, and mind you don't dream of Grosse Isle."

In a few minutes we were again on board. Thus ended my first day's experience of the land of all our hopes.

OH! CAN YOU LEAVE YOUR NATIVE LAND?

A Canadian Song

Oh! can you leave your native land
 An exile's bride to be,
Your mother's home, and cheerful hearth,
 To tempt the main with me;
Across the wide and stormy sea
 To trace our foaming track,
And know the wave that heaves us on
 Will never bear us back?

And can you in Canadian woods
 With me the harvest bind,
Nor feel one lingering, sad regret
 For all you leave behind?
Can those dear hands, unused to toil,
 The woodman's wants supply,
Nor shrink beneath the chilly blast
 When wintry storms are nigh?

Amid the shades of forests dark,
 Our loved isle will appear
An Eden, whose delicious bloom
 Will make the wild more drear
And you in solitude will weep
 O'er scenes beloved in vain,
And pine away your life to view
 Once more your native plain.

Then pause, dear girl! ere those fond lips
 Your wanderer's fate decide;
My spirit spurns the selfish wish
 You must not be my bride.
But oh, that smile—those tearful eyes,
 My firmer purpose move—
Our hearts are one, and we will dare
 All perils thus to love!*

*This song has been set to a beautiful plaintive air, by my husband.

T O P I C S   F O R   D I S C U S S I O N

1. Discuss how the narrator caters to her readers' prejudices by employing ethnic and racial stereotypes of the French, the Scots, the Irish, and the Natives. What differences in rank and class among and within different groups are visible in her narrative?

2. Moodie's description of the grandeur and beauty of the island stands in sharp contrast with her reaction to the sight of the Irish immigrants. Explain what is meant by the warning that "many things look well at a distance which are bad enough when near."

3. Find examples of the comic effect—intended and unintended—in Moodie's account of her first exposure to the "new world."

Lyse Champagne

Lyse Champagne is a French Canadian born and raised in Ontario. She works for the federal government as a policy analyst and as a communication specialist. She also writes short stories, some of which have appeared in Room of One's Own *and the* Antigonish Review.

As a francophone Ontarian, she knows well the price of non-belonging to either English Canada or Quebec. Describing herself as perfectly bilingual and bicultural, she refuses to take sides in the national debate on the French-English question. Instead, she cherishes her location in-between, which helps her understand both sides rather than choosing one. From her vantage point, Lyse Champagne can notice what neither English-speaking nor French-speaking nationalists seem to be paying much attention to, namely, that the obsession with language excludes both Native Canadians and Canadians from other ethnic backgrounds.

The fragment reprinted here comes from her collection of essays, called Double Vision: Reflections of a Bicultural Canadian *(1990). Based on her own experience, she adds her personal voice to the old argument about the two solitudes not understanding each other. Her book promotes a double vision derived from inhabiting two cultures, whether they are French-English or a different combination. However, such a vision is not easy and requires a lot of personal effort and commitment to self-education, as well as the ability to live with compromise and contradiction.*

The fragment below raises the issue of different constructions of history from bits and pieces of the past preserved by different groups. Contrasting several facts and events from the history of Canada as seen by English Canadians and French Canadians, she shows how emphasizing or ignoring particular moments in the past serves to preserve a sense of collective identity and cultural continuity of each group. Memory of the past is crucial to survival, especially for a conquered people, whose versions of history are often marginalized or erased. Still, Lyse Champagne alerts us to the subjective nature of historical narratives and to the danger of separations that they create in the present.

Bits and Pieces of the Past

I don't know if history repeats itself but the history of a conquered people repeats itself *ad nauseam.*

First there is the act of conquest. The event that bisects the history of a conquered people into the glorious "before" and the terrible "after." Then there are the many small defeats that remind people of their great loss, of their continued disgrace. French Canadians are raised on this kind of history.

Contrast this with the history of the British Empire, a history of conquest too, but of conquerors not the conquered. A history of power, wealth, and influence.

Or with the history of Canada (as seen by English Canadians), a history of slow steady progress from colony to nation—as the eldest daughter of the Empire, then the Commonwealth—its emergence as a peace broker on the world scene. A history of evolution, not revolution.

Or with the history of our American neighbours, who went from colonial to superpower status in less than two hundred years. A history of manifest destiny.

I don't want to talk about the history that is actually taught in our schools or the ground-breaking research undertaken by our historians, but what we tend to remember about the past. The bits and pieces that we carry around in our heads and in our hearts. That are embedded in our culture.

Our past is not a neat package but a jumble of dates, events, places, and people. We can find bits and pieces of Canada's past in our monuments, traditions, ceremonies, and special holidays. We have woven them into legends, poems, stories, and songs, these bits and pieces are deeply rooted, emotionally charged, and immune to historical revision. Every nation has them, every culture.

History is a nation's childhood memories. Just as what we remember about our childhood says more about what we've become than what actually happened to us, what we remember about our history says more about the kind of nation we've become than what actually happened in the past. Only our childhood memories are not the same. Québec's memories are of an abused childhood, with Britain and then English Canada as the abusers.

Canada has not one history but many histories, some of which have been ignored, some of which have been overemphasized. By continuing to foster the two-founding-nations myth, we perpetuate a history that excludes more Canadians than it includes.

I know that history textbooks have changed radically since I went to school, that they now acknowledge our Native peoples and the role of immigrants in the building of this country, and that they highlight Canada's social evolution as well as its political development. But our continued obsession with linguistic duality undermines the way we look at the past, which in turn undermines the way we look at the future.

Let me share with you the bits and pieces of my people's past, bits and pieces that have survived in my mind and heart, in spite of two university degrees in history.

I'm not obsessed by the Conquest. It happened, I can't do anything to change it. But I do understand how it has shaped the history of my people into a catalogue of its many struggles to stay alive, to preserve its identity.

Although I went to school in Ontario, the history I remember is very different form the history English Ontarians remember. Instead of the arrival of the Loyalists, the Family Compact, clergy reserves, the War of 1812, William Lyon Mackenzie, the Fathers of Confederation, the building of the Canadian Pacific Railway, the settlement of the West, the Boer War, the Winnipeg Strike, the Depression, and the two world wars, I remember Samuel de Champlain, the seigneurial system, Jean Talon, the Acadian Deportation, the Plains of Abraham, Louis-Joseph Papineau, Lord Durham's report, the hanging of Louis Riel, the Manitoba Schools Question, Regulation 17, the conscription crisis, and the Asbestos strike.

First, the glorious "before," the history of New France.

Jacques Cartier and 1534 are the first two facts I remember. Where exactly Cartier landed or how many boats he had may or may not have been part of the lesson. But in my mind, I can still see the large cross with three *fleurs-de-lis* and a little scroll that read *le Roy de France*. A cross he supposedly erected to claim the land for France. There must have been a picture or drawing in my history book, since I can visualize it so clearly.

Samuel de Champlain is the next heroic figure, the founding of Québec in 1608 the next memorable date.

The various expeditions of the Recollets and later the Jesuits were explained in great detail, but the Indians they were trying to convert were mentioned only in passing. The role of Indians in opening up the fur trade was more than eclipsed by the tales of their "barbaric" torture of missionaries.

There wasn't that much emphasis on the fur trade, the focus being more on the growing settlement of New France. We learned about Louis Hébert, his wife, and their three children, the "first" farming family of New France. The founding of Montréal by de Maisonneuve in 1642. The bravery of Dollard des Ormeaux who died with all his men trying to defend Montréal (I found out later that he was attacked because he was trying to seize furs directly from the Iroquois).

We learned about *les filles de roi*, the young girls who came from France to marry the many single settlers in the new colony. Some had royal dowries, hence the term *the King's daughters*. I used to imagine how brave they were to leave their families and friends, to marry strangers in the wilds of New France. I had no way of knowing that many of these girls were orphaned or without means of support. That a marriage arranged by the state, even if it were in the wilds of New France, might have seemed a less scary alternative than a life of destitution.

I had visions of *seigneuries*, long and narrow, along the beautiful St. Lawerence, the stately *manoir du seigneur*, the modest church, the neat habitations of the *censitaires*. I don't know if this idyllic view of the seigneurial system was learned or imagined.

We learned about the various intendants, about the able management of Jean Talon who conducted the first census of the colony and the corruption of the last intendant, François Bigot.

The *coureurs de bois* and the *voyageurs* were mentioned only in passing. Perhaps the nuns thought they were too disreputable. We did not dwell on the adventures of des Groseilliers and Radisson, Jolliet and Marquette, La Salle, or La Vérendrye, although their exploits were praised for extending the frontiers of France's territory in North America.

The importance of religion in the colony was of course well documented. We read excerpts from the *Relations des jésuites*, recounted the martyrdom of de Brébeuf and Lalemant and their fellow missionaries, extolled the good deeds of the Ursulines in Québec and Montréal; there was plenty of material to inspire admiration among impressionable Catholic girls.

And there were many heroines for us to admire: Jeanne Mance who founded and ran a hospital in the struggling new settlement of Montréal. Marguerite Bourgeoys who founded the first Canadian

order, the Congrégation de Notre-Dame de Montréal, dedicated to
the teaching of young girls. Madeleine de Verchères who helped to
defend her family's *seigneurie* from the Iroquois until reinforcements
could come from Montréal.

This is the history the good nuns taught me. The emphasis was
on the glory of France and of the Catholic church. Then the glory
ended and the terrible "after" began. Although the Conquest marks
the official beginning of the terrible "after," it actually started with
the Acadian Deportation.

Most Canadians think the Deportation had an impact only on
the Acadians and their descendants. But the long-lasting legacy of
that cruel decision has been to colour the way most French
Canadians (not just Acadians) view the English, even though the
same fate did not await the *canadiens* on the shores of the St.
Lawrence. The Deportation was what the "big bad" English were
capable of. (Never mind the way the French treated Indians. I was
not aware of such contradictions then.)

The Deportation was the first in a long series of "wrongs" done
to my people. The history I was taught from that moment on
focused on these wrongs. It did not celebrate achievements. Our
only achievement was survival.

As in any history of a conquered people, the critical event was
the great catastrophe, the Conquest. Although the capitulation of
New France didn't happen for another year, the Conquest is most
identified with the battle of the Plains of Abraham on September
13, 1759, a battle that apparently lasted only fifteen minutes.

Fifteen minutes that changed things forever.

The Conquest is the "big bang" of our history, hurling fragments of the past into the orbit of the future, and forever altering
the chronicling of that past. From tales of glory to *la survivance*,
from physical survival in the wilderness to cultural survival under
the British.

I was taught to be grateful for the Quebec Act of 1774, which
recognized Roman Catholicism, the seigneurial system, and the
French civil code. To welcome the creation of Upper and Lower
Canada in 1791, which gave French Canada a territory all its own.
The War of 1812 was barely mentioned. We spent considerable
time on the *patriotes* and their leader, Louis-Joseph Papineau, and
on the rebellions in Lower Canada in 1837. William Lyon
Mackenzie and the rebellion in Upper Canada were more or less
ignored.

We dwelled on the Durham Report and its stated intention of
assimilating the French. Lord Durham's indictment of French
Canada as "an old and stationary society, in a new and progressive

world" was much quoted, along with his famous description of Upper and Lower Canada as "two nations warring in the bosom of a single state."

Confederation and the British North America Act of 1867 were not given great prominence. They were neither praised nor condemned. Confederation was sort of glossed over, not identified as the birth of Canada. I remember being surprised in 1967 with the fuss over the centennial. Since I thought Canada was more than three hundred years old, a centennial seemed a strange anniversary to be celebrating.

I don't remember exactly what I was taught about Louis Riel, only that his hanging inspired the same aversion the Acadian Deportation did. It was another example of what the "cruel" English could do—hang an innocent man who was fighting for a desperate cause. When I was in Winnipeg several years ago, standing in front of Riel's commemorative statue, an older man came up to me and said: "You know, if that guy hadn't had French blood in him, you never would have heard of him. And his statue wouldn't be standing here in this park."

In the history I was taught as a girl, Manitoba figured twice, in the Riel Rebellion and the Manitoba Schools Question. Although the issue was about separate schools (Manitoba wanted to abolish them), I remember it as a language question. Perhaps because separate schools in my mind were always French schools. In any event, the issue was given prominence as an example of what happened to minority rights in the rest of Canada.

French Canada's objection to participating in Britain's wars was another big theme. First, the Boer War in 1899, in which Canada participated against the wishes of Québec (although the regiments were made up of volunteers); but more particularly, the two world wars and the conscription crises they precipitated.

In Ontario, we didn't have a deportation to deplore, or a Louis Riel to mourn, but we had Regulation 17. When I was very little and heard adults discussing *le règlement 17* in hushed tones, I always wondered what they were talking about. For years, it was a mystery to me. At one point, I became convinced it was a combination of the Ten Commandments and the seven cardinal sins (the only two religious numbers I knew that added up to seventeen).

A history lesson eventually cleared up the mystery. Regulation 17 was the culmination of a gradual restriction of French as a language of instruction in Ontario schools, a process that had started as early as 1885, the year Riel was hanged. Passed in 1912, this regulation limited the use of French in schools to the first two years. There was much conflict and bitterness over this regulation, and an

Ottawa school board even closed its schools over the matter. But the regulation, which was amended in 1927 to allow teaching in French where the numbers warranted, remained on the books until 1947.

Not as earthshaking as the deportation of a people or the hanging of a hero, but it was a tragedy unique to French Ontario. *"Souvenez-vous du règlement dix-sept"* we were told as children. *"Souvenez-vous toujours du règlement dix-sept."*

This is the history I was taught as a child, a mixture of emotion and fact. It greatly influenced my sense of self, my sense of identity as a French Canadian. Although the emphasis may have changed, certainly the references to the religious aspects, I would venture to guess that the history taught in Québec primary schools today has many of the same elements I remember.

At university, I discovered a new kind of history, scientific and objective. We spent a lot of time demolishing historical myths, disproving schools of interpretation. The more I read and studied, the more I questioned the interpretations, the more enamoured with the "objectivity" of history I became. I never admitted to my professors what a struggle I had with the bits and pieces of the past that were in my head and heart. They surfaced at the most inopportune moments, sometimes inaccurate, even irrational, but very much intact. They created a tremendous bias that I constantly had to overcome.

As much as I would have liked to study for a Ph.D. in history, personal circumstances forced me back into the real world. With each passing year, the possibilities of working in my chosen field dimmed. I earned my living as a writer and researcher but not as a historian. The only contact I now have with history are the books I read.

My experience as a graduate student convinced me of the inherent subjectivity of history, a subjectivity I had experienced first hand as the descendant of a conquered people. Academic objectivity was no match for the bits and pieces of my past.

The issue of funding for Catholic schools in Ontario made me realize how these bits and pieces could short-circuit both my scholarly training and my political convictions.

I am not a practising Catholic. My son is not baptized, and he goes to a French public school. Yet when the Ontario government decided to extend funding to the last three years of Catholic high school (grades eleven, twelve, and thirteen), I "sided" with the Catholics.

Although I had personally rejected the separate school system for my own child, I believed separate schools were entitled to receive funding for all grades, just like the public schools. Raised as a Catholic myself, I had no trouble understanding why Catholics wanted to maintain a separate school system, why they believed religion was an integral part of education. Separation of church and state (in this case, keeping religion out of state-controlled schools) is a Protestant concept, not a Catholic one.

And yet, I shared the concern of other parents who believed that separate school systems are expensive and create unnecessary duplication. I also recognized that those of other faiths who believed religion was an integral part of education had to organize private schools that received no government funding. But the bits and pieces of my past, the fact that my mother had to pay to send us to Catholic high schools, that all French schools in Ontario were separate schools (which is no longer the case), won in the end and I supported the extended funding.

We can't change the bits and pieces of the past that we carry in our hearts and in our heads. They can't be "rewritten" the way a history text can be rewritten to reflect new research, new evidence, new interpretations. But we must be conscious of them in order to understand how they affect us, how they shape our opinions and decisions, political and otherwise.

We also have to realize that, as Canadians, we do not share the same bits and pieces of the past. And yet we are trying to build our future on these fragments, to enshrine them in our constitution.

Much has been said about the importance of history, of knowing the past. That those who cannot remember the past are condemned to repeat it (George Santayana). That the farther backward we can look, the farther forward we can see (Winston Churchill). I prefer what Ludwig Wittgenstein had to say about the present, that if we live in the present, we live in eternity. Since we cannot share the same past, let us at least live in the same present and work towards the same future.

We have to let go of the past—but in so doing, there is a danger. That Québec may let go of Canada, may consider the last 123 years as a period of occupation. Québec might start afresh, with a new past and a new future—and forever change the past and the future of Canada.

TOPICS FOR DISCUSSION

1. What point is Lyse Champagne trying to make by contrasting the history of French Canada with that of Britain, English

Canada, or the United States? Where conflicting versions of the past coexist side by side, what factors determine whose narratives become official?

2. What different concepts of history emerge from her essay?

3. Explain what is meant by "the inherent subjectivity of history." What specific examples in the text support the view of history as "a mixture of emotion and fact"?

4. Using Quebec as example, what is the importance of history for a particular nation, group, or community? What are the dangers?

Joy Mannette

Joy Mannette teaches in the Faculty of Education at York University in Toronto. In her research, she combines anti-racism education with African Canadian studies and Aboriginal studies. She has written on the history of Black Nova Scotians, on the education of Africans in the late twentieth century, and on racism towards the Natives in the Canadian criminal justice system. Her academic work challenges the perception of Canada as a benevolently multicultural and inclusive country.

"My Dearest Child" is a white mother's letter to her African Canadian child, in which she weaves together different threads of Canadian history linked through her ancestry (Acadian and Cape Breton Scottish-Irish) as well as through land sharing with Black Nova Scotians and the Mi'kmaq nation. On the father's side, her son inherits the tradition of South African anti-apartheid struggle.

Acadia refers to a region including today's Maritime provinces that for 150 years formed a French colony, New France. In 1755, the British began the Great Deportation (le Grand Dérangement) of Acadians, who were subsequently scattered along the eastern shores of the Atlantic (see references to the Acadian Deportation in Lyse Champagne's essay in this Unit). Although Mannette traces the history of Black Nova Scotians to Loyalists, the presence of Blacks in Nova Scotia can be documented as early as the beginning of the 17th century, when first slaves were brought to the colonies. Slaves were also brought to Quebec and Upper Canada, before slavery was abolished in 1834. With the exception of the well-publicized story of the Underground Railroad, which between the late 18th century and the American Civil War of 1865 had brought to southern Ontario hundreds of fugitive American Blacks, not many facts concerning the history of African Canadians are mentioned in mainstream historical textbooks. In Nova Scotia, on the outskirts of Halifax, Black Canadians founded a settlement known as Africville, which endured for 150 years, until in 1967 it was destroyed by the government's order to give way to a new development. No proper compensation was ever given to the original owners of this land.

Speculating on the possible intermarriage between her Acadian ancestors and the local Mi'kmaq people, Mannette refers to her volunteer involvement in the treaty trials of the late 1980s, which were to decide the legal status of promises and land guarantees given to the Natives by the British Crown. Ironically, here the intricate weave of history comes full circle again because the apartheid system of strict racial segregation was modeled on the reserve system introduced by the Government of Canada.

My Dearest Child

My dearest child,
How shall I tell the story of who you are? You are an African Canadian man-child. It is easy to speak of the "African" and of the "Canadian" but neither naming captures who you are. Indeed, you problematize the notion of "Canadian." Yet, in your little brown body and in your naming, Rakgwedi Manet Ramphore, you express something about the story of Canada. You are a Canadian citizen but you carry your own passport.

Who are you *puna* and what is your story? *Ra, man; kgwedi, moon—a state of being, not a noun.* You are named by *Nkono* as the ancestors proclaimed: "A boy child will take the name of the first Rakgwedi who was a pastoralist. You carry a strong spirit, *puna;* never forget that."

"What a beautiful name!" exclaims a skater at Toronto's Nathan Phillips Square, a man who embodies the Canadian ideal: tall, strong, fair-haired, blue-eyed and a good skater. More frequently the response is, "what a mouthful;" and "how do you say that." You let people call you "Rock" because you want to belong and don't understand what it means to be denied your name. You are only eight years old. You know you are "brown" and somehow "African" and you know that Mamma is "white"—well, sort of pinkish, actually. You sing "Oh, Canada" and "Kkosi sike'lele" but Pokémon is often more important. In grade three you are asked to do a unit on pioneers. You know, it's like Toronto's Black Creek Pioneer Village. You went on a trip there once with your daycare. What's this notion of "pioneer" got to do with more recent settlers of Canada? It's too prosperous, too land-bound, too ethnically exclusive, too "way back then." *Ntate* is a settler; Mamma is too; but "pioneer" has nothing to do with the way history lives in them and, so, in you.

In naming you Manet, Mamma reclaimed her patrilineal name from its nineteenth-century anglicization. You are Acadian, *puna.* Your *patrimoine*, through me, your mother, finds its place in a small village, Chezzetcook, on the eastern shore of Nova Scotia. About forty-five kilometres north of Halifax, this place of tides was a haven of Catholicism in a sea of Protestantism. It was French but only in the 1980s was it honoured by being named "acadien" by the Centre for Acadian Studies and the University of Moncton. There are Romas and Murphys, along with Mannettes, Bellefontaines, LaPierres, Fouchès, and Bonnevies. When I was a child, before Vatican II, a French homily and French hymns were sung in the epicentre of the *parroise*; but also on Christmas there was "mumming," when we disguised ourselves and roamed door to door, giggling and excited not to be uncovered.

But did I tell you too, *puna*, that we children also learned to call the Christmas treat of Brazil nuts, "nigger toes," and that we sorted our playmates with "eenie, meenie, mini, mo; catch a nigger by the toe?" Perhaps this explains why, in your words, Mamma "went on and on" at your Toronto daycare, when she found you and your playmates using "eenie, meenie, mini, mo; catch a tiger by the toe."

After midnight mass at a Chezzetcook Christmas, we used to go to my grandparents' home and eat paté—rabbit, salt pork and onions, cooked in bread dough and basted with drippings. Our land, the Mannette land, like that of our neighbours stretched form the Atlantic inlet to Porter's Lake—an anglo incursion—which the busy Acadian men dyked so that the sea would not come in. What was it about these Acadians and their dykes; their struggle against the sea both for land and on little boats? What was this attachment to the land; the peasant's dream of what was not possible across the water; the deep and sustaining bond with earth and water; and learning to tell the time by the moon, the plants and the tides? The little boats were curiously flat-bottomed and had room for only one man and one boy, so as to be able to navigate the estuaries at both low and high tides. We were the only known Acadians who ate sauerkraut, learned from our German neighbours. It is said that the cattle grazed on the saltmarshes. Your genealogy is too complicated, said the Acadian genealogist; not "laine pûre," as the Québeçois would have it, nor the Chezzetcook variation—"cocques pûres," perhaps.

The Mannette men were long livers. I remembers my great-grandfather, Grandad Fred, né Frédéric. He died in 1961 at age ninety-seven when I was nine years old. The nuns at the village school said, "Why should she go to the funeral; he was only her great-grandfather." I must have persisted because I remember following the coffin into the church and watching its descent into the damp ground in St. Anselm's graveyard, the only place where I now can find our name. You are the last of our Mannette bloodline, *puna*. Will you go back to the earth in that graveyard as Mannettes always have? Will you have to choose between the fog and damp of Chezzetcook, and the dust and calabash-red soil of Mohlakeng, the place of reeds, in South Africa? It is in Mohlakeng where lies *ntatemaholo*, your Sotho grandfather, for whom you were taught the rituals of soil and calling on the ancestors when you were but three years old.

My Acadian great-grandfather stood tall and spare and carried a walking stick to shoo away troublesome snakes. He shared his "humbugs" with me. I found him kind but my anglo grandmother, Hannah, said he was a hard man who sent his son, my grandfather, called "crooked Willie," out to work when he was seven years old. My anglo grandmother was full of aspirations for upward mobility and stories from her "black sheep" father, a charming and handsome alcoholic wife beater who sprang from minor gentry. His father was a magistrate. "Remember girl," he told Nanny, "there's lords and ladies in your family." Nanny, lonely and isolated, kept me apart from the Acadian neighbours and decried her husband's insufficient table manners. She rigourously instilled in Mamma a sense of being different and better than the Chezzetcook people. Is that why her daughters married anglo-Celtic men and welcomed their new naming, Spencer and Bell? As a university professor, Nanny would have believed I was following her lessons. As a young girl, *puna*, Mamma did, at the nunnish Mount Saint Vincent Academy. There I cohabited with the daughters of the Halifax Catholic elites. I came to despise where I came from and my nascent Acadian accent was shamed out of me. Yet, as a scholar, the more I moved "up," the more I was drawn back.

Crooked Willie was my grandfather, your great-grandfather, *puna*, whose mother, Marie Charlotte, had died giving life to a misshapen boy-child. The women, Mannette-by-marriage, losing their names and, thus, the sense of "mix," married and died young, usually in childbirth, after bearing about twelve children each, only half of whom survived infancy. There were the Mannette women, all named Marie—Honore, Celestine, Berthe—the men, all named Josephe—Etienne, Guillaume, Georges, Luc. Josephe William, my "Grampy," born in 1895, "the year of the white mice," he said; the year of the raising of the current Ste. Anselm's, whose architecture signals its communal significance. It is made of clay brick from the Chezzetcook mudflats, which also made its way to the fine homes and businesses of the building boom of 1870s downtown Halifax, following a fire which wiped out nearly all the clapboard edifices. My Grampy could turn his hand to anything but he could not read much more than the church bulletin and newspaper headlines—and that only much later when he taught himself in his seventies.

They were skilled, the Chezzetcook men, and they "went to market," exchanging animals, produce, and legendary Chezzetcook clams for the edification of the townspeople. Loading the ox-pulled wagon in the middle of the night, they travelled the rutted road to catch the first ferry from Dartmouth across the harbour to the Halifax City Market, where cousin Reggie Mannette's family now bring seasonal transplants from their greenhouses which go on to the pots and small green spaces of the city. And the children picked berries and flowers, mayflowers and blueberries, bringing on corrosive competition with our neighbours, the "coloured people" of Preston: "Never buy blueberries from coloured people, they pee on them first" was my first remembered association of "Black" with dirty.

You were born in Nova Scotia, *puna*; does that make you a Black Nova Scotian? Black Nova Scotian communities are not as long-standing as the Acadians, whose first church-recorded presence in Chezzetcook predates the Black Nova Scotian Preston settlement by at least thirty years. Black Loyalists, as they are now known, were publicly acknowledged as a group largely through the efforts of Sylvia Hamilton, who in 1983, on the bicentennial of the coming of the Loyalists to Nova Scotia, insisted that Black people were also part of that crucial migration from the fallen New England colonies. The Black Loyalists were free men and women "of colour," former slaves, to whom British commanders in the field had promised freedom of person and free land and provisions to any who would abandon their slave masters and cross behind the British lines to fight for the British cause. Is this not a "treaty," *puna*? Three thousand Black Nova Scotians—soldiers, pilots, reconnaissance men, wheelwrights, smiths, farmers, seamstresses, cooks, washerwomen— formed part of skilled immigrants to the colony. One third of the initial Loyalist migration the British loaded on ships, after the fall of New York in 1781, and brought to Nova Scotia. Black, free men and women built the towns and cleared the farms, changing forever Nova Scotia from British possession to colony and establishing the character of what, one hundred years later, became Canada.

Other Black people—the Jamaican Maroons, for example— went on to construct the Halifax Citadel and, held in high esteem by colonial authorities for their military prowess, were mustered into a regiment, in anticipation of Napoleonic incursions. The British were never able to defeat the Maroons militarily; rather, British commanders tricked them into a peace settlement and then forced them to relocate. However, the Maroons successfully agitated for removal from Nova Scotia, and in 1799 they were sent to Sierra Leone to put down the insurrection against the British of other Black Nova Scotians there. But I am getting ahead of myself, *puna*.

Settled on the poorest land, impossible even for subsistence farming, outside the boundaries of the white towns, the Black Loyalists found precarious freedom in the slave society. Emancipation came only two generations later, with the 1834 Act of Emancipation of the British Parliament. American raiders routinely sailed under sanguine British eyes into the coastal communities, reclaiming human property for their Republican masters. Black Nova Scotians were rendered a permanent but marginalized working class and refused entry to places of worship as well as schools. If permitted in Anglican churches—the state religion—Black Nova Scotians were consigned to the "slave galleries." One of these remains in Halifax's St. Paul's Church, built in 1749, where ironically, the imperial eagle shapes the pulpit and regimental banners laud the imperial triumphs, including the 1899 Boer War. The last Black/white racially segregated school closed in Nova Scotia in 1956, four years after Mamma was born, *puna*. Not to mention the Indian Residential School at Schubenacadie which was not closed until the 1970s. Elsewhere, Black Nova Scotians were even legally denied public entertainment as the largest Loyalist town, later Shelburne, banned "Negro frolics" in 1785.

Among the Black Nova Scotians came literate and worldly men—including several preachers, and the enterprising "Thomas Peters man" of Annapolis Royal. In the late 1780s, Thomas Peters worked his passage to London, where, together with the emancipationists at work for the Black Poor of that city, he petitioned the Crown for the fair enforcement of the proclamation that British commanders had made in the field during the Revolutionary War. They argued that freedom of person was meaningless without the means to sustain free life. The British promptly sent out to Halifax John Clarkson of the Society for the Propagation of the Gospel to organize the Sierra Leone relocation. Colonial authorities thwarted Clarkson at every turn, as landowners, alarmed at the potential loss of cheap Black labour, stymied Clarkson's efforts. But in January, 1791, two ships loaded with twelve hundred Black Nova Scotians embarked for Sierra Leone; for the "best and brightest" of the Black Nova Scotians, this signified leaving behind the unfulfilled promises of the "promised land," Nova Scotia; and looked ahead to their new dream: back to Africa.

They left behind decimated Black Nova Scotian communities, soon to be replenished with another empty imperial promise, during the War of 1812. For the Crown, Clarkson's Sierra Leone relocation was an expedient resolution of two colonial problems: to quell dissent in Nova Scotia, and to establish a British-allied Black commercial and military presence in West Africa. Today, in war-ravaged Sierra Leone, the "Kreo" of the Black Nova Scotian exodus are still distinguished from the Mende and other groups, in terms of language, custom and status.

Among those who sailed for Sierra Leone was Lydia Jackson. In the words of George Elliott Clarke, Black Nova Scotian poet, Lydia Jackson was "Black as stars, slaved and served, slaved and starved; in this rough land, cold and hard, water and rock were her guard." In Nova Scotia Lydia Jackson, "slave madonna," was owned by Dr. Buhlman. You can still see his fine town house in Lunenburg, *puna*, marked by a plaque, an important feature of this "Dutch" tourist site's walking tour. Lydia Jackson, unlettered Black Loyalist, had been abandoned by her husband upon arrival in Guysborough, and was then tricked into signing a thirty-nine-year Bill of Indenture, which was then sold to the good Lunenburg doctor. "And when she came to him, with the news [Buhlman's rapes had born fruit], he knew just what to do; he beat her; he beat her 'til she was black and blue and the poor child, he died when due." Hearing of Clarkson's relocation scheme, Lydia Jackson traveled overland some 150 kilometres to Halifax, presented herself to Clarkson and sought passage. Clarkson arranged for her court appearance, where the chicanery of the indenture was revealed and Lydia Jackson was declared a free woman. She also overrode Clarkson's admonition that all women who embarked on the voyage to Sierra Leone must have a man to assume responsibility for them.

Recorded in the Ste. Anselme parish register, 1761, the year of the Royal Proclamation, our first ancestor in Chezzetcook, one Georges Mannette; it is said that he and his brother made their way to Chezzetcook from fallen Louisbourg on Île Royale and that they had been soldiers. Along the way, Georges had acquired a Portuguese wife, Carlotta, probably likely Georges' kin, probably at the important fishing station, Ship Harbour in Guysborough, while more Mannettes, likely Georges' brothers, established themselves at nearby Larry's River were the only two Mannette root places known to Mamma, until just last year when I was told by a Trinidadian acquaintance that her cousin had married a Mannette—with the same anglicization of the name. Only two months ago, *puna*, Mamma came across a website which informed her that Ellie Mannette, also of Trinidad, is honoured as the twentieth century "father of the steel pan." These are more strands in the weave of who you are, *puna*. Another theory is that Chezzetcook was settled by returning Acadians who had hidden in the woods during the 1755 Grand Derangement.

Black people continued to go to and from Nova Scotia. By 1821, there were the Black Refugees and that year marked the departure of "100 Negroes" for Trinidad. Back and forth between Nova Scotia and New England, Black Nova Scotians carved routes that confound accepted national boundaries of the master narrative of North American history. In the burgeoning industrial centres of the northern United States, Black Nova Scotians sought the dignity and opportunities denied to them in Nova Scotia. The 1890s brought "mechanics" from the Caribbean to Halifax industries and the nationally vital coal and steel production of Cape Breton. In 1918, one third of Canada's wealth was generated in Cape Breton coal and steel. Yet today, in Sydney's Whitney Pier—an ethnic enclave separated from Sydney proper by the steel plant property— the Barbados flag flies proudly over the churchyard of the African Methodist Church on Hankard Street during the "Caribbean Picnic."

Organized into a racially segmented labour force at "the plant" and in "the pit," Black men were denied union membership during the great labour struggles of the 1910s and 1920s. Only much later, in the 1970s, Winston Ruck emerged as a union leader. Black women ran boarding houses and served hot dinners to plant workers from their homes, "conveniently" located next to the coke ovens. The racial hierarchy ensured that the closer to the plant you lived, the lower was your status. But in 1937, the famed champion of the back to Africa movement, Marcus Garvey, spoke to an impressive crowd in Whitney Pier. Today, the "coke ovens," home to 100 Black families, is one of Canada's worst ecological disasters. Again there is talk of "voluntary" relocation and destruction of the community.

Throughout Black Nova Scotia, in the late nineteenth and early twentieth centuries, Black women toiled "in service" and as "Saturday girls." "A dollar a day for back-breaking, sweat-soaked" labour, writes Nova Scotian poet Maxine Tynes. "Helen was some-body's 'girl,' some white lady's 'girl,' this never-married Black woman... What did my little girl mind know?...the secret whispers of lady talk...She died 'in service.'" On through the twentieth century, Black people continued to arrive to Nova Scotia as nurses, lawyers, physicians, teachers, from the Caribbean and Africa. Then, in the 1970s and 80s came the "international students," like your father, *puna*. Slapped with higher fees—a particularly onerous burden against "Third World" currencies. And the sleeping car porters followed the rails to Montreal, Winnipeg and northern American cities; sleeping car porter, the career ceiling for Black Nova Scotian men until the 1960s. Sometimes, the porters married into Black communities on their "routes;" sometimes they brought their wives home, "home to Africville."

Africville was destroyed by Halifax urban planners in the spirit of 1960s urban renewal. Ironically, *puna*, Mamma's 1967 Mount Saint Vincent Academy yearbook features a photo of "Mount girls" against the backdrop of a bulldozed Africville and the half-completed "new" bridge, the A. Murray McKay. Wedged among the city dump, the railway line and the prison, Africville was home to so many sleeping car porters. "Where the road ended, Africville began," stated the narrator of the NFB's *Remember Africville*. But Africville lives today in the Africville Genealogical Society; and at the annual August picnic at Seaview Park, which now marks that fallen Black space. People come from all over Canada and the US, come "home to Africville." As George Elliot Clarke put it, "Nova Scotia is such a hard place to stay."

Nineteen sixty eight saw the coming of the Black Panthers and the pinnacle of "Rocky's revolution." But that year also marks the denial of burial to a Black child in a white cemetery at St. Croix, Nova Scotia. Before Rosa Parks said "No" to the back of the bus, in New Glasgow, Mrs. Viola Desmond, a Halifax beautician, refused to sit in the "coloured" balcony of that town's cinema. No disrespect to Miss Rosa Parks but Mrs. Desmond said "no" too. Why, then, does the history of Black American resistance eclipse what Black people in Nova Scotia did, in the spirit of resistance, throughout the long history of their settler presence in Nova Scotia? In 1968, the Black Panthers in fact inspired panic and quick containment from the provincial fathers, in the form of the Nova Scotia Human Rights Commission; and in 1970, provincial funding was established for the Black United Front. Young Raoky Jones, who in his fifties was called to the Nova Scotia Bar, came home to Nova Scotia fresh from SNCC to work with youth in the Halifax city projects and help direct the fate of the people of Africville and of those moving from rural areas. Afro-ed, bearded, dashiki-ed, "Black and Proud," Rocky Jones scared the hell out of white folks who feared that "The chickens had come home to roost" in Nova Scotia. Predictably, people ignored Joan Jones, whom Mamma thinks is actually more "scary" to white privilege, *puna*.

The 1970s and 80s brought the rise of what Mamma calls the "Black Renaissance," an explosion of music, writing, art and community consciousness. It is the "little children [who] lead them." The Cultural Awareness Youth Groups (CAYG) were brought to life by young Trinidad-born David Woods, who had come to Nova Scotia at the age of twelve. Banned in some Metro Halifax schools—and where permitted relegated to "extra-curricular" status—the CAYG spawned *Four the Moment*, Delvina Bernard's a capella group. "Three Black and one white women—an appropriate balance," they modelled themselves on the American *Sweet Honey in the Rock*, and sang Langston Hughes' "Nothing Lights a Fire Like a Dream Deferred." "History singing," claimed Delvina when *Four the Moment* put to song the powerful poetics of George Elliott Clarke. Did you know, *puna*, that it was George Elliott Clarke who renamed Black Nova Scotians "Africadians"? A shock to Mamma's *Acadienne* sensibilities, it was still a powerful claim to place. *Four the Moment*, which went on to be a darling of the Canadian "definer" Peter Gzowski, made their debut at a 1981 "Smash the Klan" rally in downtown Halifax.

The KKK, *puna*, had a presence in rural Nova Scotia that dated back to the 1930s. It was the CAYG at Cole Harbour High School that fine-tuned Delvina Bernard's early race consciousness. Cole Harbour High School has gone on to Canadian notoriety as the site of late 1970s and early 1980s race struggles (named "race riots" by alarmist media). Did Mamma tell you, *puna*, that I taught there and coached the girls' basketball team from 1979 to 1981? Did I tell you that I "took a punch" during a racially charged fracas at a school dance there in 1980? Did I tell you, *puna*, that I quit teaching in 1981 because I could no longer be a white "gatekeeper." That is why my MA thesis and Ph.D. dissertation are on Black Nova Scotians?[1] In "Lullaby for Cole Harbour," *Four the Moment*, sing "How can they stop the tears about to fall, knowing that another child's innocence is lost? And how can they start to teach African ways, when buses are driving the children away?"

Black Nova Scotian communities continue to lose their future as the young venture forth to Montreal, Calgary, and Toronto. In search of the "promised land," they all too often become statistics of drugs and guns and men's violence. "I only know that it's a crime to take a life and lose your own," laments *Four the Moment*. And still, the young persist in staking the audacious claim to be Nova Scotian, and, thus, Canadian. This is an important point, *puna*. The way regional identity works is that you are Nova Scotian first and Canadian second. However, I have found, *puna*, that people in Toronto just don't get it. Furthermore, it is only central Canadians of a certain class or ethnic background who go around trying to define "Canadian identity;" the rest of us know who we are because we are rooted in a place and a time. That's part of the reason why the master narrative of Canadian history is so skewed and incomplete, *puna*: you've got all these academics of a certain class, ethnicity, and gender telling us the story of who we are. However, it's only the story of who they are, or who they want to be.

"You don't have to play the bagpipes to be Nova Scotian," asserts Sylvia Hamilton's searing NFB documentary *Speak It!* And Winston's girl, graduating university student Marlene Ruck, matter-of-factly stated at the 1989 Atlantic Association of Sociologists and Anthropologists Meeting that "we are strangers in our homeland…which sings of the contributions of the Celtic peoples." Stellar contributions to the British Crown and Canada have never conferred the rights and privileges of citizenship on Black Nova Scotians. The long lines of Black Loyalists, miners and steelworkers, "girls" and charladies; the World War I Black Battalion; the first "Canadian" recipient of the British Victoria Cross—Thomas Hall for valour in the Crimea; the Order of Canada for William P. Oliver; the Harry Jerome Award for Clothilda Yackumchuck; and other community service efforts, attest to these.

The wave of who you are becomes more intricate in the late 1980s. Mamma was then working at the University College of Cape Breton and was involved in pro-bona work during the Mi'kmaq Treaty Trials, which established that the *1752 Treaty* "of peace and friendship" between the British Crown and the Mi'kmaq Nation, had not been extinguished. Mamma's mother's people came from Cape Breton, *puna*, more displaced people, the Parkers, the Kennedys, and the MacNeils, of the Scottish highland clearances and the Irish potato famine. Mamma's mother, on hearing about my appointment, was happy I was "going home;" I knew better.

It's ironic, though, *puna*, that as I edit this writing, I am watching on television the funeral of forty-year-old John Morris Rankin. He was not only a brilliant musician, but a good man. Mamma remembers John Morris as just a "little fella," whose legs were too short for him to reach the pedals of the piano in the parlour of Uncle Dan's and Aunt Mary's farm house in Brook Village, Inverness County, Cape Breton, Nova Scotia. I can see and hear him still, along with the late, great fiddler, Dan R. MacDonald, his big stomach straining his white shirt. The music was magic, *puna.* You just had to dance. As my dear friend Elizabeth Beaton said of the mourning for the loss of John Morris, "Cape Bretoners still know how to pick their heroes." John Morris Rankin was a Canadian hero, *puna.* When I was a little girl, my family would travel by car each summer from Elliot Lake, Ontario, where my father worked in the uranium mines. First we would go to Boston and visit there with my mother's transplanted Cape Breton kin. For all of us, though, the best part of the holiday was going to Brook Village. It was on that farm that Mamma learned about taking the cows to pasture and feeding the chickens. Everybody worked on the farm. We always made it to Brook Village to make hay. The work teams of men went from field to field, farm to farm, and laboured from the time the morning milking was done 'til it was dark to get the hay in before the rain. I remember, too, *puna*, that after the supper dishes were done and the cows were taken to their night pasture, everybody would get cleaned up and dressed up and go to a "ceilidh" or dance—one for every night of the week, except Sundays at the Inverness County village halls. The Rankins were related in some way, I never knew just how, which is why I came to see and hear little John Morris.

However, my coming to Cape Breton in 1987 was in a different time and space. Also, when news of my relationship with your African father made the rounds, one of my students was quizzed in a Cape Breton job interview on how I could "lower myself" in that way. Nurses in the maternity ward of your birth gave pause once they saw your father. Strangers would exclaim in surprise, when they saw the baby (you) with me, "He's so beautiful!" I knew what they had expected. Actually, it was among Mi'kmaw people on the Eskasoni First Nation in Cape Breton that Mamma came to feel most at home. It was Eleanor Johnson who told me that "All you can really do is love them," as I agonized about the racism you would encounter, *puna*. I knew that Nova Scotia was no place to bring up a "Black" child. It's the "one drop rule," *puna*. Eleanor Johnson, who so despised the academic "cognitive tourists" who told stories about the Mi'kmaq, taught me so very much about how to teach Mi'kmaw people the book knowledge of the university. It was Marie Battiste, the first Mi'kmaw with a Ph.D., who organized a "party" for this *aglasiew* who knew so little about babies and how best to take care of them. For the Mi'kmaw, to celebrate a baby's birth before the fact was a strange white custom; so they organized a party. The men, including *ntate*, were shooed outside with the beer and the barbecue, and thirty or so Mi'kmaw women provided tea and food and talk, and wonderful baby stuff for you, *puna*. There was much punning and laughter, healing loving laughter, and you kicked vigorously. I think you liked it too. I was overwhelmed, and it wasn't just "hormones" that brought me to tears. Many of these Mi'kmaw women who had so little in material goods had brought you such lovely things and shared their baby wisdom with me through "telling-story," as Marie Battiste names it.

During the Treaty Trials, Sakeg Henderson had organized a group of us, Mi'kmaw and non-native, and we pored over the documents of the British Colonial Office, consulted with Elders, strategized with the lawyers, and attended court, unless we were teaching. It was these documents, the much-reviled record of imperial interest, that were touted in the court by an academic historian,

University of New Brunswick's Steven Patterson, as the "truth" of the treaty process. I wrote and delivered a stinging indictment of Patterson's historiography and the questionable ethics of his paid secondment to the Crown Attorney. In my *Making of the Expert Witness*, Mamma was shunned as "ungentlemanly" by other academics because I had not alerted Patterson to my work and invited him to debate! But, that, *puna*, is another story.

One of these documents revealed to me the 1754 translation efforts of a certain Jean Baptiste, a Mi'kmaq "Roman" convert, from a fishing community, "some leagues north of Halifax." Well, I knew that the only Catholic fishing community "some leagues north of Halifax" was Chezzetcook! When I consulted the genealogy of the first Acadian families of Chezzetcook, prepared by St. Anselm's Monsignor Melanson in the mid-twentieth century, I found that Jean Baptiste was our ancestor, the great-great-grandfather of Grampy's mother; we had always talked about Grandfather Murphy's and usually went there in August to pick blueberries. Monsignor' Melanson's labours also recorded that the first Catholic place of worship in Chezzetcook was known as the Mi'kmaq Chapel. Now, the Mi'kmaq Nation had been a Catholic nation since 1610, when Sagamow Membertou embraced Catholicism. Material history from the Nova Scotia Museum had also told us that the harbours of Nova Scotia's Eastern Shore were important summer and fall camping sites for the Mi'kmaq before they wintered inland, near Schubenacadie. There was much communal interdependence and friendship between the Mi'kmaq and the Acadians, bound as they both were in French allegiance, faith, and struggle against the English. There was much intermarriage as well. Of course there was Mi'kmaq blood among the first Acadian families of Chezzetcook! All I had to do was look in the mirror to recognize the "skinny-faced" Mi'kmaq prototype, with high cheek bones and prominent nose; the face of my Grampy; the face of his daughter, Adah, who believed herself unattractive so much of her life, in comparison with her round-faced, short-nosed sister. However, before I could recognize this in myself, I had to "see" this as a possibility. So, the weave of who you are is rich in skeins, *puna*.

What about *ntate, puna*? Sydney James Ramonametsi Ramphore—freedom fighter for Azania—Sotho and Tswana but taking his lineage from his father's Sotho line. Born into apartheid South Africa and carrying his English names, his parents sought to keep him safe from the 1970s student struggles, sending him to be educated by Irish monks in a Free State boarding school. They expected, as did Sydney, that education would be better there than Mohlakeng Township schooling. It was not. Your father says, "*thato ke lesedi*," education is light. And the light was fire, burning the schools, making the country ungovernable. The schools and their education for inferiority are where your father learned to be an expert gardener. At the 1976 Student Uprising (again, "the little children shall lead them") your father took a bullet and kept running: to stop is to die. Your father learned to be a cadre in APLA, took part in covert operations within the country to the sound of an oft-sung freedom song, "*Ntate, bana bashwa, Father, your children are dying.*" APLA was the armed wing of the Pan Africanist Congress, the infamous PAC whose motto was "One settler, one bullet." There is something to be learned there, *puna*, about pioneers.

The young man who took a bullet and kept running became a man. On the run, he crossed the Limpopo, hearing the crocodiles take cadres in silence: anything to thwart the Groot Crocodile.[2] In the camps, safe houses and prisons of front-line state, *ntate* finds the political organizations as deadly as the Boer. In the former Yugoslavia, he fine-tunes espionage. In Libya, he shows the mettle of *Afrique du Sud.* He joins cultural groups touring other African countries and Europe in order to gain support for the struggle. He was part of the PAC delegation to the United Nations in New York. This is your father, *ntate*, who speaks nine languages but not "standard" English, as he soon learned in a Canadian university. To stop is to die.

Ntate came to Canada as a political refugee. He said, "among the nations of the West, Canada had such a good reputation in its support of the struggle." *Ntate* came to get book knowledge and to find in Canada what is impossible in South Africa—a university degree. In his eighteen years in exile, *ntate* was determined to make something of himself so that "when South Africa is free," he might return as well-equipped to build as he then was to destroy. In Canada, he found the bitter pill of multiculturalism. "Multiculturalism is racism multiplied," your father says. Your father, who learned so much in nearly twenty years of exile, finds himself accused of plagiarism. How could he know so much, so well? when he tries to explain why *The Heart of Darkness* poses some problems for the African mind.

He hopes that a university education and Canadian citizenship will become other ways in which to engage in "the struggle." Public speaking, performance poetry, story-telling are more lines in the weave of "the struggle." Curiously, it is in Canada that *ntate* moves beyond the deadly divisions of South African politics. He learns to count the African National Congress' Mafika Ludidi as friend, as well as Jacob Motswaledi, burning with Black Consciousness Movement's passion. Remember, *puna*, Jacob, whom you, as a two-year-old, also called "*puna*," and who patiently took you everywhere you asked including South African poet, Don Mattera's Halifax reading in 1992? Mattera too is BCM, the powerful and parallel philosophy and practice of African empowerment, which is not modeled on that of Malcolm X, Martin Luther King, Jr. or Stokely Carmichael. I have to say that, *puna*, since so many people cannot believe that Bantu Steven Biko's thought is original.

For his first two years in Canada, *ntate* could not speak his language. There was no one who spoke any of his African languages, let alone Sesotho, and he could not telephone his family since in the past phone calls had brought the Boer harassing his mother nightly for months. Do you remember, *puna*, *ntate* telling you how *Rakadi Bopi* travelled to Zimbabwe to give the Ramphore ancestors' blessing to him before he came to Canada? *Ntate* came to see the political expediency of WUSC's[3] "throwing him" in the isolated University College of Cape Breton, both as a regional development initiative and as a barrier to exiled South Africans' political work. *Ntate*—revolutionary, poet, linguist, soldier, organic intellectual, sculptor, actor, musician, singer—"an African man, *puna*," he often said. However, the 1994 return to South Africa, as with so many cadres, was devastating; the South Africa of "the struggle" no longer exists. Your father did not know how to be in the "new" South Africa and became "homeless" again.

Ntate, who, in Audre Lorde's words, "was never meant to survive" plants the seed in an ostensibly barren *Acadienne* woman and, to our wonderment, the spirits sent you to us, *puna*. "We are making miracles," *ntate* said. Musing about why I had chosen to marry an African man and bear his child, one of my students said that it must have been this experience that shaped Mamma's race consciousness. "No," contradicted a Black student, "I think it's the other way around; it was her race consciousness that led her to marry an African man and bear his child." Actually, it's both, *puna*, for I never really understood racism until I had you.

For the first two years of your life, *ntate* was all of Africa to you, and he gave himself to your care. "You must bend the branch when it is green, *mma-rakgwedi*," he would say to me. He is your father who assisted your birth, confounding cultural taboo, to hold you warm from my body. He is your father who always had you in hands, a true African child. He is your father who urged baby (you), "Be like *tau*, the lion; be yourself, *puna*. Because *tau* know who he is." He is *ntate* who bathed you, changed you, fed you, sang to you freedom songs from the camps. Your favourite seemed to be a lament for Robert Sobukwe,[4] *Sobukwe, khaosi kokekhle...* In 1998, I took your picture, *puna*, as you stood outside Sobukwe's house on Robben Island. Remember, we took a hydrofoil boat there and, on the way, everyone was somewhat festive. On our return trip, there was silence, following the tour, led by one of *ntate's* cadres, who had been imprisoned there on Robben Island for four years. We have a picture of you with him outside the prison walls. He called you "a fine young man," and asked you to greet *ntate* for him when we got to Pretoria.

The Boers segregated all political prisoners from the general population but so feared the influence of Robert Sobukwe that they built a prison house for him, well removed from the main prison. It is said that Sobukwe was poisoned. The Boers put political prisoners on Robben Island, hoping, I suppose, that the dank Atlantic cold and gypsum quarry work would finish them off. *Madibha's*[5] eyesight was ruined working in that quarry. Nova Scotia's *Four the Moment* sing, "Dark crow caws bitter blue; yes, a bear brown, black and bitter blue; it's the only song, it knows how to use; for a nigger miner digging gypsum for the cash to fix his shoes." The weave comes full circle so many times, *puna*.

Ntate insisted that baby (you) have the best because these were things he could never have given to his first-born, your brother, *Molefe*, in Zimbabwe. You must have the best, because "you deserve," he said. He is your father, the African Canadian who turns his back on Canada, "the promised land." He decides that if he is to be challenged to show his papers in an airport lounge, it might as well be in South Africa. *Ntate* decides that the "empty smiles" of Canadians are to be avoided. *Ntate* dismisses the Americanization of Black Canadians, Black Caribbeans, Black Americans, and their rejection of Africa. "They are not conscious," he says. Your father comes to realize that in Canada, as in South Africa, he is still a "*kaffir*."

I have come to the end of the story, for now, *puna*. Where does this leave you, whose little brown body and naming so seriously disrupt what it means to be Canadian? I brought you to *Toronto, "the place of meeting,"* because I could not bring you up in South Africa; I was too afraid. Even now, on our visits, it is as if I can only breathe with relief when the plane touches down at Pearson Airport. Apartheid lives on in the "white country with a Black president," and the violence of apartheid is now unleashed everywhere, not just contained in the townships. But we both know, don't we *puna*, that Toronto is fraught with peril for a Black child? However, that will be your story to tell one day, should you so choose.

Ke a leboa,[6]

Mamma

ENDNOTES

1. *Making Something Happen: The Experiences of Black People in Nova Scotia, 1780–1900 (1984); Nova Scotia's Black Renaissance, 1968–1986 (1988).*
2. The name given to the State President, in Afrikaans, by freedom fighters.
3. World University Service of Canada.
4. Robert Sobukwe's profound philosophy led to the 1959 break with the ANC and the formation of the PAC. It was the PAC which organized the demonstration against the pass laws, which culminated in the infamous Sharpeville massacre of 1961 in which the South African police opened fire on the demonstrators, killing at least fifty and wounding about two hundred more. And, it is the date of the Sharpeville massacre, March 8, which the UN used to designate the International Day for the Elimination of Racism, so hypocritically observed in Canada.
5. The term of affectionate respect for Nelson Mandela who spent nineteen of his twenty-seven-year sentence on Robben Island and chose to celebrate the millenium there.
6. In Sesotho, this is the expression by which one gives thanks.

TOPICS FOR DISCUSSION

1. How does Joy Mannette put together different fragments of Canadian history in her letter? Why does she use the metaphor of weaving?

2. Why does the naming of her son—whom she defines as "an African Canadian man-child"—"seriously disrupt what it means to be Canadian"?

3. In the light of the author's personal history, what symbolic meaning does the name "Africadians" (coined by George Elliott Clarke) have for her?

4. Comment on the author's statement that "multiculturalism is racism multiplied."

Denise Chong

Denise Chong was raised in Prince George, British Columbia. She worked as an economist for the Department of Finance in Ottawa before becoming an economic advisor to Prime Minister Pierre Trudeau. Based on her family history, The Concubine's Children: Portrait of a Family Divided *(1994) received the City of Vancouver Prize and became a national best-seller. Chong has most recently published* The Girl in the Picture: The Kim Phuc Story *(1999), a biography of a Vietnamese girl whose terrifying photograph, showing her burned and running from her napalmed village, hastened the end of the Vietnam war in 1972.* The Concubine's Children *tells the story of Chong's maternal grandmother, May-ying, who was sold at the age of 17 as a concubine to Chan Sam, a man who had emigrated to "Gold Mountain" (North America) to support his wife and children left behind in China. Chong has done meticulous research, both in Canada and China, trying to make sense of her own family origins as well as of wider experiences of Chinese immigrants in Canada. The fragments reproduced below provide a background to the long history of exclusion and anti-Asian sentiments in Canadian immigration law and society. Between 1858, when the first Chinese gold miners arrived in Canada from San Francisco, and the 1960s, when all barriers to Chinese immigration to Canada were finally removed, the Canadian government had imposed several discriminatory policies on Chinese immigrants. The most important ones were withdrawal of voting rights from the Chinese; a head tax imposed as early as 1885; business and job restrictions (for example, the Chinese were barred from professions; they couldn't hold a liquor license or employ white females, etc.); finally, the 1923 Chinese Immigration Act. The Act almost completely banned Chinese immigration and imposed strict controlling measures on immigrants who were already here. Until the Act was lifted in 1947, the predominantly male Chinese population in Canada was prevented from bringing their wives or children to Gold Mountain. The Chinese communities actively resisted discrimination and countered racist stereotypes by developing a strong work ethic, encouraging education, self-sufficiency, political lobbying, and court challenges.*

For other personal documentation of the early treatment of Chinese immigrants, read Chinese Wall Writings *(Unit Six). Joy Kogawa's text from* Itsuka *(Unit Two) provides later examples of discrimination against Asian Canadians.*

from The Concubine's Children

It was early in 1924 by the western calendar when May-ying was married off. Her rebellion was useless; in the Confucian way of thinking, a girl has no authority of her own. She does as she is told. The choice was that or suicide. The village gossip would cast Auntie as the tyrant and May-ying as a girl wronged only if she took her own life, if her body were discovered floating near the stilt-houses over the Pearl River at the village's edge, or hanging from a beam in Auntie's house.

Auntie grew excited about helping May-ying make preparations to leave. She engaged a photographer to record May-ying's new identity. The photograph had to conform with the age on the false birth certificate. Perhaps feeling guilty that there would be no wedding biscuits to distribute to the villagers, no double-happiness cutouts to hang form the doorways of her house, Auntie hired a tailor to sew two *cheong sams* for May-ying as her going-away present. May-ying's outburst forgiven if not forgotten, Auntie reveled in repeating tales of Chinese men going to Gold Mountain and harvesting the money trees and coming home rich men with prestige. She imagined May-ying, once she came back to China, living in one of the large houses of the wealthy, where the rooftops are all that is visible over the wall around the compound. She imagined a harmonious household, where the man's first wife, instead of being jealous, encouraged concubinage. "She will choose you over the other concubines to serve her," said Auntie. "She will prefer you to occupy the master's bed, you will be the one to produce the sons."

A Chinese knows only one thing for certain: that danger and evil spirits lurk everywhere. According to Chinese belief, jade and gold are the only talismans, and the more they come handed down, the more power they have to bestow good luck. May-ying's dangling earrings had been worn by her mother. The pendant, a flawless baize-green jade inlaid in gold, had been retrieved from the coffin of her mother's mother, and was even more precious. She left Auntie's house as she had left her mother's, with these pieces sewn inside her clothing.

May-ying's outward journey began by sampan, hailed for among the many plying the Pearl River. After a day downstream, slowed by the crowd of boat people living on the river, she and the middleman accompanying her arrived in Canton. There, May-ying had her first glimpse of the ancient trading city, flagstoned lanes choked with shops selling everything from firecrackers and ready-made herb preparations to sandalwood and rattan. On the train trip from there to Hong Kong, she peered out the window as rice fields gave way to a city hinting of people with greater ambitions. The man delivered her to an address on Des Voeux Road, and another man there delivered her to the ship. The officers of the Blue Funnel Steamship Line found her papers in order, stamped them and accepted her for passage.

After eighteen days at sea, the ship steamed into the port of Vancouver. Mountains and sea seemed to diminish man's efforts at fashioning this young cityscape. Among the wide-eyed disembarking passengers was a tiny girl, who, but for her mature hairstyle, looked too young to have left home. Her birth certificate said she was born in Ladner, British Columbia. The fertile farmland of the Fraser Valley just outside Vancouver was dotted with Chinese laboring in the fields for white farmers. Presuming she was one of the new generation of Chinese born in Canada, immigration officials accepted her false papers, and the girl who had left her Chinese homeland as Leong May-ying was waved through as the woman Chung Gim-ching returning to her native Canada. "Such a pretty girl alone?" asked the interpreter. No, she was being met, she said, by her husband.

One Chinese man waiting for the passenger ship to dock at the pier at the foot of Granville Street stood out from the crowd by virtue of his nearly six-foot frame. He had a body that was all limbs, long even in his fingers, which gave his every gesture an elongated emphasis. A fedora graced his head, and he was attired in a custom-tailored three-piece gray suit. His shoes and wire-rimmed glasses were polished and his black hair meticulously combed to expose a high forehead, a physical trait the Chinese considered a sign of intelligence. He owned two suits—one gray, the other brown—and two fedoras. Believing one's appearance mirrored one's inner mind, his appearance today was, as always, immaculate. His manner, like his dress, was sober and serious. At thirty-seven, he was a year younger than the city of Vancouver.

A few Chinese were among the waiting crowd of whites, some of their faces familiar to Chan Sam. But he had no desire to squander time in conversation with someone to whom he had no loyalties. He returned to studying that day's *Chinese Times*, to a report of a speech given by a Canadian-born Chinese in Victoria calling for political reform in the homeland. He underlined the characters he did not know; in this way he added two or three new characters each day to his written vocabulary.

The dock scene was a marked contrast to what it had been like when Chan Sam himself had first stepped onto this same pier in 1913, eleven years earlier. Now, the Chinese dressed in western dress. Then, he was one of the few among his compatriots who had spilled off the packed freighter not in mandarin-collared jackets, pajama-like trousers and sandals. Chan Sam had arrived in a western tailored suit. But it had made no difference to his reception; along with the other arriving Chinese, he was herded into a dock-side low brick building to spend three months in quarantine behind barred windows and under guard. Despite their protests that they had already stood naked in a line for examination by the white doctor onboard ship, the men were fumigated with sulfur, and so were their belongings. Inside the packed and filthy "pigpen," as the Chinese called it, amid the noise from trains rumbling into the adjacent western terminus of the transcontinental railway, it had been hard for them to keep fast their belief in Gold Mountain's fairy tales, spun from men before them who'd gone to make their fortunes.

They were men from the delta of the Pearl River in Kwantung province, where seafarers were folk heroes. In the eighteenth century, Canton had been the only Chinese port open to foreigners. Ever since the arrival there of foreign traders offering to exchange opium from India for Chinese silk and tea, distant shores had meant adventure. In 1848, gold was truck in Sacramento, California, and the race was on across the Pacific to Gold Mountain. More Chinese left in 1862, in a second dash for gold up British Columbia's Fraser River to Barkerville. Many, when pushed off the better claims by white prospectors, stayed on to cook and wash clothes, and early Chinatowns sprang up and thrived. Anti-Chinese feelings intensified, and whites up and down North America's west coast began lobbying local governments—state, provincial, municipal—to stem the flow of arriving Chinese and to make it clear to those already there that they were unwelcome. In the 1870s and 1880s, there were limits on the number of incoming Chinese per boat, bans against hiring men with pigtail-length hair and against the use of poles to carry baskets. There were special taxes levied on the Chinese for school and policing, employment, laundry, shoes and even cigars. Worse was to come. Chinese were soon barred from becoming naturalized citizens, from owning land, from working on public works.

Such distaste for the Chinese presence did not deter white contractors who were looking for cheap labor to carve out the great transcontinental railways across the United States and Canada. Their governments bought their claim that the Chinese would work for much less and were more reliable than the available white labor, mostly Irish. Though many Chinese, assigned the most dangerous jobs, died building the railway, racist resentment sped along the newly built iron rails. Whites in the east railed against the inevitable eastward settlement of a race they condemned as alien, steeped in moral depravity and degradation.

The Chinese continued to arrive—fathers, uncles, sons and brothers of those who had come before. One was Chan Sam's father. His voyage from China to San Francisco was financed by his clan society in his home country. During his sojourn abroad, he met his own expenses and his wife's at home and still returned home for a visit every third year, three times in all. To further distinguish his name, he more than repaid his debt to his clan society by soliciting overseas donations to help build an ancestral hall.

Luck was with him in that he first landed in America before the United States Congress passed the historic Chinese Exclusion Act of 1882. That act gave in to the most fanatical of those lobbying against the Chinese presence and slammed the door shut to new arrivals. Only diplomats, certain scholars and import-export merchants holding temporary visas were to be allowed in. The effect was to condemn Chinese men already in the country to a life abroad without the possibility of their families joining them. The male-female ratio in Chinatowns, already primarily bachelor societies, would change only with the birth of their American-born children.

In 1888, Chan Sam's father was back in China cradling him, his firstborn child. That same year, Congress suddenly declared void all Certificates of Return, which had allowed previous sojourners to reenter the United States. Chan Sam's father was grateful that his years abroad had been fat. He had made ten times what he might have had he not gone, enough to buy some thirty *mau tin* (one *mau tin* equals less than one-sixth of an acre of cultivated land), enough to have a second child, a third and a fourth.

The only door to the mythical Gold Mountain that the Chinese could still pry open was Canada's. The Americans had posted guards at the border, lest any Chinese tried to sneak into the United States by way of Canada. But the Canadian government, aware that some Chinese saw it as a back door to the United States, sought to act in concert with the Americans. In 1885, it tried to put off the average Chinese laborer by imposing a fifty-dollar head tax upon entry. Merchants were exempted for fear they'd go south of the border. In 1904, in the same year that the United States extended its Exclusion Act indefinitely and broadened it to apply to Hawaii and the

Philippines, then American possessions, the Canadian government raised the head tax to five hundred dollars.

Chinese men were desperate enough to leave China that they found ways to raise such sums. In 1913, when Chan Sam crossed the Pacific, he was one of seven thousand coming to Canada that year, a new high. Such numbers dismayed even the Canadian Chinese Benevolent Association, headquartered in Victoria's Chinatown, Canada's oldest. That year, in an urgent circular to Kwangtung province that was posted in county magistrate offices, the Association painted a picture of the Chinese in Canada as job-less, hungry and cold: "In a nutshell, it is better not to come." The Association's fear was that the Canadian government would over-react to the growing number of arrivals by driving out those already here. Exclusion was the Association's worst nightmare.

In Chan Sam's time, the destination of choice was Vancouver's Chinatown. The community had boomed along with the city. But so too had anti-Chinese sentiment. Within the four to five square blocks of Vancouver's Chinatown, some three to four thousand Chinese, mostly men, lived and worked in virtual isolation from white society. No self-respecting white would be seen anywhere near Chinatown, believing it to be populated with shifty-eyed, pigtailed Chinamen of the Fu Manchu and Charlie Chan movies that would later show in North American movie houses. The appetite for painting the Chinese as villains grew when First World War veterans came home to a depressed economy. Newspapers and politicians alike pandered to public hysteria, accusing the Chinese of stealing jobs from Canadian fathers. Chinatowns were denounced as dirty and disease-ridden, as centers of gambling and crime. Vancouver's was depicted in local newspaper editorial cartoons as a congestion of rooming houses, of unmarked doorways to a labyrinth where lasciv-ious Chinamen smoked opium, lay with Chinese prostitutes, fed on rats and enslaved white girls. No one saw the contrasting truth, that there were, among the bachelors, a few upstanding families living there. These included the wives and children of the merchant class who could raise the money to pay for the five-hundred-dollar head tax on each family member, who could install them above their ground-floor businesses, and who could afford to send their children back to China for part of their education. Selling out their business was always an option too, if Canada got unbearably inhospitable, to pay for the family's passage home.

In 1923, the Canadian Chinese Benevolent Association's worst nightmare came true. That year, the Canadian Parliament went the way of the American Congress and passed its own exclusionary law. The date the Chinese Immigration Act went into effect—July 1, the day the nation's birthday is celebrated—the Chinese marked as "Humiliation Day." In reply to such hostility, many Chinese men went home for good. After ten years abroad, Chan Sam too could have abandoned his plan to sojourn abroad. But to do so would have led to a loss of face, for which he could not look himself in the mirror. Some might have called his pride a character flaw, except that showiness was almost expected of those coming back from Gold Mountain—a sign to others that the dream of riches abroad was still alive.

Chan Sam was lucky to find work immediately, despite the economic gloom that pervaded Vancouver. Still, there were almost always jobs for the Chinese, either in Chinatown, or else the menial, poorest-paying or the most dangerous jobs on a sawmill floor, a mine or a farm. Certainly the white owners of the sawmills along the Fraser River, the canneries on Burrard Inlet and the vegetable and pig farms just outside Vancouver saw the advantage of hiring Chinese foremen to find them cheap Chinese labor. What work a man got depended solely on his connections and how much money he had to set them in motion. In Chinatown, a job was both a privilege earned and a favor granted. Outside Chinatown, a man got nowhere without an "in" with a Chinese foreman.

If there was one Chinese law of the universe, it was loyalty to *gee gay yun*, to one's own people. In the homeland, it was to family, village and clan—sometimes one and the same. In the new world, where connections were spread more thinly, a man's demonstrable loyalties were to an extended family—to men not only from this own clan, but men from the same locale in China. If there were few from his clan, then the shared locale was extended to include men from the same county, or from a group of counties. Chan (also anglicized as Chen or Chin) was not among the more common surnames, like Wong, Lee or Mah, whose clan societies were well established in Chinatown at that time. A man without a clan association to help him get a job had to know where to go to be looked after by his own. Chan Sam found a foreman of the mill from his home county and got work as a sorter and a tie-up man, catching and bundling shingles coming off the line. He learned why it was work a white man avoided when a flying shingle severed the top of his middle finger.

He worked eleven-hour days, six days a week. The Chinese, only too grateful to have any work at all, were not complainers. At Chan Sam's mill, the Chinese were third on the pay scale behind whites and Hindus, earning a fraction of their pay. They paid room and board; others did not. Their bunkhouses were segregated from whites, and they were expected to survive on salted fish, soup and rice. Whenever Chan Sam tired of the abuse that came from the white man's mouth, he reminded himself that one week's wages could buy one *mau tin* in China. But expenses made it difficult to save. He cut costs by coming back to Chinatown on his one day off a week and during the off season, where he shared the rent on a bunk at a tenement complex. To cram in more bunks, rooms were crudely partitioned, windowless and no bigger than six feet by eight, with makeshift bunks three deep on each side. Like a game of musical beds, there were more bachelor men sharing the monthly rent than there were bunks.

The typical bachelor's entertainments were afflictions Chan Sam shunned. The ratio of men to women fell from twenty-five to one to ten to one within a decade of his arrival. But on the streets, the ratio was dramatically higher. "Decent" women—the merchants' wives—rarely ventured beyond the walls of their family home. A laborer, on the other side of the social chasm from a merchant, called a rooming house home and rarely even saw a woman or girl, unless he fraternized with the white prostitutes in the skid row area bordering Chinatown, or unless he frequented the tea houses, all of which employed waitresses. Chan Sam was faithful to his wife and policed himself on all matters of vice. He rarely even entered a gambling den and certainly never even passed by one on payday. He would take an occasional whiskey, but he regarded drinking, like gambling, to be addictive. Such moral caution and frugality enabled him to remit money to keep his wife at home, and within three years of living abroad, to send money home to repay his debt to the old lady and to start saving for his family's future.

He had been in Canada five years when he received news that his wife had died. Numb with sadness, he spent some of his savings to buy a ticket home. He would visit her grave and erect an ancestral tablet there, so that future generations could worship her soul. Bad news came on top of bad. He came home to find his brothers, both now married, deeply in debt. At first sorry that the *mau tin* had not been enough to meet their families' expenses, Chan Sam soon found out to his chagrin that they had also spent all the money he had remitted home instead of repaying the old lady for the traffic fee she had lent him. He admonished his brothers. "Your conduct is not good," he said. They asked him to lend them more money. Chan Sam pleaded that he could not on account of his plans to open a business upon his return to Canada.

He could be absent from Canada one year without having to again pay the head tax. Before the year in China was out, he did the sensible thing of taking a "replacement wife." Huangbo was plain, quiet, unassuming and kind. At twenty, she was old to be married off and happy to have her future provided for, if by a widowed man twelve years her senior. Chan Sam pledged to care for her as if she were his first wife. He asked her to be dutiful in helping work his share of the *mau tin*, in raising his deceased wife's daughter until marrying age and in keeping the home for an absent husband. When the time came for him to leave, she was pregnant; once back in Canada, he learned that their baby girl had not lived long.

In 1919, he and a couple of his bachelor friends opened a small storefront in Vancouver's Chinatown. They had rented space at the east end of the three long blocks of Pender Street, Chinatown's main artery, to sell miscellaneous Chinese dry goods, one of many shops that did the same. But their idea was to rely on the loyalty of the patronage of their own people, the moral contract that kept dozens of other storefronts in Chinatown in business. It provided an adequate income.

His brothers wrote to ask if they had best come to Canada. Chan Sam remained optimistic about life abroad: "It is not easy to save money, but making a living here is better than making a living by cultivation in the homeland." Without consulting him, the brothers sold the four water buffalo for their traffic fee money. Abruptly, exclusion came in 1923, and their plans to come had to be canceled. "You sold the only productive asset!" Chan Sam wrote his brothers when he found out what they had done. The *mau tin* that had not been lost to mounting debts were eventually unable to support two families. One brother decided to leave for a country that would have him. Using Chan Sam's name and the *mau tin* as collateral, he borrowed money from the bank and a rice shop to pay his passage and to start a business in Havana, Cuba. At the same time, he had Chan Sam lend him the same amount and more. Other than one miserly gold coin sent from Cuba to the wife and daughter he had left behind, the brother was never heard from again, leaving Chan Sam to clear up his bad debts.

The money that Chan Sam, feeling guilty for being duped himself, sent to his brother's abandoned wife left him anguishing about his own. He himself had to make a choice. The Canadian exclusion act required every Chinese in Canada, born there or abroad, to register with immigration authorities and to state whether they were staying or leaving. Prospects for Chan Sam's shop on Pender Street were not good; exclusion would choke Chinatown's growth. By day and night at the shop, his friends gathered to talk of the growing numbers registering to leave. For many, years, possibly decades of separation from their families stretched behind and ahead. Chan Sam did not know how much exile he himself could or ought to endure. Fighting loneliness, worry and homesickness, he lay awake nights wondering if his wife, Huangbo, and other villagers were still alive. He was thirty-six and had yet to father sons. The exclusion act allowed absences of two years, but spending money on a visit would only postpone the day he went home for good. He pondered a way to ease the pain of his solitary life: he decided to take another wife.

A friend of a friend knew someone returning to the homeland. "Can you find me a *chip see?*" Chan Sam asked. The request for a concubine was not unfamiliar among married Chinese men abroad. The wife in the village, the one chosen by their parents, was the "At-home Wife." The concubine, sent from China, joined the man abroad and the two lived together in the foreign country as man and wife. Those who wanted to observe western customs legalized it with a marriage certificate, but few saw the need, for within the Chinese notion of the family, the At-home Wife had her husband's first loyalties.

To bring his plan to fruition, Chan Sam needed money and the birth certificate of a Canadian-born Chinese about the same age as his imported concubine. In short order he was put in touch with an agent who dealt in "paper families." The agent bought and sold birth certificates of people already dead, of people who had left Canada with no intention to return or who, for a price, could be convinced to stay away. He offered Chan Sam the birth certificate of a woman born in Ladner, outside Vancouver. Nothing was said of what had become of her.

A decade earlier, Chan Sam's traffic fee had been seven hundred dollars. To acquire a concubine, the price was more than triple that. On top of the bride-price, most of that was the cost of the birth certificate and the fees of middlemen in Vancouver, Hong Kong and China. It was not the kind of money that a man like Chan Sam, a peasant minding a storefront, had.

The Blue Funnel Steamship stood dockside. The building known as the "pigpen" was boarded up, but it served to remind Chan Sam again of his first reception. He turned his attention to the arriving passengers as they began to disembark. He looked for a face that matched the photograph of May-ying.

He heard the murmurs of approval from other Chinese men before he himself caught sight of a porcelain doll come to life. He recognized the dangling earrings and the hairstyle, the chignons over the ears. He stepped forward into her path.

"I'm inviting you to *dim sum,*" Chan Sam told May-ying as they stood on the pier, having barely made their introductions. The teenaged girl strained to understand the thick peasant accent. She caught the words *dim sum*, a phrase borrowed from Canton's social custom of tea houses. She gave a quick smile and tried to hold back a laugh of girlish delight. Going to sip tea, she thought, was a kindly first gesture from this older man who was her new husband.

Chan Sam hailed one of the waiting taxis. He had decided before setting out on foot from Chinatown that they would take a taxi back. Usually he walked everywhere.

From the pier it was a short, ten-minute ride east along Pender Street to Chinatown. Their taxi skirted the city's financial district. Its tall stone buildings and the rhythmic flow of streetcars spoke of ordered calm. On the other side of the tram lines that ran between New Westminster and Vancouver, the western architecture suddenly gave way to a dense conglomeration of two- and three-story brick buildings bedecked with an assortment of awnings. Two tiny alley-ways off Pender, Canton and Shanghai Alleys, both of which had been privately developed, were congested with tall, narrow tene-ments, dozens of businesses, shops, restaurants, even a public bath and an opera house. May-ying was vaguely reminded of buildings she had seen in Canton.

They alighted from the taxi at the corner of Pender and Carrall, where Chinatown first began. The tidal waters of False Creek had left sludge along these shores that repulsed all other settles but the Chinese.

"We're going upstairs, over there," Chan Sam said, pointing to a second-story sign across the street. "Peking House," it said in Chinese; in English, "Pekin Chop Suey House." The ground floor was occupied by a boot-and-shoe shop and by a Chinese grocery store. The building was Victorian on three sides, but on the fourth side, overlooking Pender, its facade was Italianate, with curved arches and wrought-iron railings enclosing recessed balconies. In south China, the doors to these balconies would have been left open to circulate air in the day's heavy heat. Here they were closed.

May-ying followed Chan Sam through the crowd of men milling on the sidewalk. Some were leaning against the buildings or in doorways, some chatting to pass the time; many of the younger ones were smoking. All stared at the new face in town, that of the tiny young girl. All wondered at the mismatch: Chan Sam was tall, older; she was so short, and so young. They watched as the two of them climbed the wide stairway to the upper floors.

The owner of the tea house saw them come in and strode up. "*Ah* Chan Sam, *Sin-sang*," he said, using the title for a gentleman. "You are here!" His voice was too loud, even above the din of chatter from people sequestered behind half-curtains drawn across lines of wooden booths.

May-ying hoped the ebullient greeting hinted well at her husband's status in this new land. Chan Sam beamed; he was proud to introduce her. The owner led them to a booth adjoining a table where some staff were eating, outside the swinging doors to the kitchen. "Today is a special day," he said, " a day for a feast."

A waitress, a pretty girl perhaps not much older than May-ying, placed before them bamboo basket after basket of hot steamed morsels, rice dumplings of shrimp and minced pork, small porcelain dishes of bite-sized spareribs, stuffed bitter melon, dishes that could be found in tea houses in Canton. To wash it down, there was a choice of teas: jasmine, chrysanthemum or "six contentment," a mixture of several teas.

At the end of the meal, the owner parted the curtain and stood before them. "Everything taste all right?"

"Very tasty, very tasty." Chan Sam reached into his trouser pocket and made an elaborate gesture of reaching for money.

"No, no, put your money away." The owner slid onto the bench across from May-ying and poured a cup of tea for himself.

Then Chan Sam told her: "*Ah* May-ying, this gentleman is your new boss."

TOPICS FOR DISCUSSION

1. How does the excerpt from Chong's novel demonstrate that social and political history filters down and affects people on an individual level?

2. What are Chan Sam's values with regard to his family, his work ethic, and his community?

3. What do we learn from this excerpt about stratifications of gender, class, and race that operated both in traditional China and in Vancouver?

4. What is the author's method of constructing and reconstructing the characters and events from her family history? What is the tone of the narrator's voice?

Helga (Kutz-Harder) Mills

The real life stories collected in Helga (Kutz-Harder) Mills' reportage often have their source in unspeakable human suffering and misery that caused their subjects to flee their homelands and become refugees in Canada. The socio-political background of these personal experiences includes the Iranian Revolution of 1978, led by Ayatollah Khomeini. The revolution replaced the Shah's regime with Islamic government, establishing strict Moslem fundamentalist rule, followed by a period of religious dictatorship more brutal than the Shah's.

In 1978 in Afghanistan, a Soviet-backed military junta seized power, initiating the cycle of domestic violence and guerilla fighting that went on for ten years, until the Soviet troops were finally withdrawn. The civil war left the country devastated and depopulated, gradually submitting to the Taliban regime that imposed severe restrictions especially on women. From 1979, El Salvador, in Central America, has been the site of relentless battle between the U.S.-supported military government and the leftist popular movement. Thousands of people have been killed or "disappeared"; thousands have sought escape in refugee camps. Burundi, a small African country, formerly exploited by two successive colonial powers, Germany and Belgium, has been troubled by a long-term political instability which has its roots in ethnic conflicts. For years, it has been unable to escape the bloody civil war between the Hutu majority and the Tutsi ruling class. Somalia, an African republic uniting the former British and Italian colonies, is subject to both drought and flood, which places this country in the so-called "hunger belt." It has received international economic and technical assistance. Sri Lanka, formerly the British colony of Ceylon, has been wrecked since its independence in 1948 by the violent religious, linguistic and ethnic conflict between the majority Sinhalese Buddhists and the minority Tamil separatists. The politics of violence and terrorism is the island's everyday reality.

Over the years, Canada has been offering a safe haven to different groups of refugees running away from persecution based on race, religion, nationality, political opinion, or membership in a particular social or ethnic group. In 1993, Canada was also the first country to recognize gender persecution as legitimate reason to claim refugee status. Although women may be persecuted for the same reasons as men, they are often subjected to gender-related forms of persecution such as sexual violence and severe discrimination through restrictions on their personal freedom.

Breaking the Barriers:
Refugee Women in Canada

The stories of the refugee women I have met in Canada fill me with woe and wonder. The realities of their past sometimes defy my imagination. The courage with which they find their place in a settled society like Canada is awe-inspiring. Many of them have an aura of calm and beauty which masks the turmoil inside when they try to hold in tension the unbearable memories of the past, the spirit-defying obstacles of everyday life in a cold new country, and the tentative flame of hope which dares to believe that this is the place where their spirits can flourish.

Many of the refugee women are reluctant to talk of their past, sometimes because they are afraid of unleashing emotional despair which they may not be able to control, and sometimes because they need to bury some of the details in order to be accepted by their people here. Breaking the barriers within themselves requires as much courage as breaking the barriers between them and their new society. The stories which I have gathered here are tributes to this courage. They look inward and outward. They give us truth about ourselves, about us, and about the world in which we live together. The women and their stories are a gift to us.

YOUNG WOMAN FROM IRAN

A young Iranian man started the conversation: "Women in Iran suffer two times more than men." The young widow accompanying him continued the story. Because her husband wrote down his criticism of the government he was imprisoned. Because she was pregnant with his child, she, too, was imprisoned. When he died, the authorities freed her from prison, but she found herself imprisoned by a society which shunned her because of him. She had no right to study, no right to work, no way to survive and feed a child.

She was bitter about her past: "Women are half of a man, except when they have to go to prison the same as a man." She told me that many women with children fill the prisons, and many women are executed. Many children lose both parents and become the lost children of Iran, because "nobody is allowed to help them."

She arrived at a Canadian airport, carrying a small daughter and "horrible memories" of family members' executions, and religious repression, especially of women. Immigration officials treated her well and gave her a hearing only two days later. She came to the meeting tired and worried. She did not know what to do when the official thundered: "Why, why, why don't you go home where you belong? Why are you coming and stealing jobs from Canadians?" In her heart she cried: "I can't go home, I would rather be executed than treated like this. I can't stop crying." She needed to believe that she would be helped, not criticized for why she was where she was.

As a single mother she knew that first of all, she must find work. But before that, she must study French because she was in Montreal. She worried about a lot of things. What could she do with her little girl? How could she manage? How could she live if her baby became sick? She could find work in a factory, but how nice it would be to work at her own profession, even at a minimum wage.

She ended her conversation: "Women aren't refugees because of what they have done, but because of what their husbands have done." She bowed her head and, as her lustrous black hair fell over her shoulders, we wept, men and women alike. Will we ever know what keeps her going day after day?

YOUNG WOMAN FROM AFGHANISTAN

She was one of the privileged few who had ventured out of a tradition in which females are sequestered, to attend the university in Kabul. The times away from campus were still spent with women in whose company love and tradition and nurture were felt and passed on. Men were for marrying and for stability.

Then came the terror of war and the flight from danger. Her mother died in her homeland. One sister found her way to Germany. Other sisters found their way to Australia. She married a countryman along the way, and they came to Canada along with his five unmarried brothers. She and her baby daughter were the only females in the household, and she longed for women to turn to for guidance and cultural continuity.

At twenty-three she saw the advertisement for a youth training program available to anyone unemployed under the age of twenty-four. Toronto apartments are expensive, and a child needs toys and a bed and clothes and books and love. "If I don't take the program now I'll be too old for the age restriction, and when I leave my child with the sitter she cries and will not eat," she explained. At home, a mother or an aunt or sister could have helped. Here, a strange woman with strange customs cares for her child. She sobs over the telephone. I cannot solve her dilemma, but I can listen to her story.

She called again recently. She has moved to the suburbs, far away from public transportation, to be able to offer her child a garden to play in. Her loneliness and alienation are intensified. I wonder how long it will be before she walks with a sense of fulfilled promise.

YOUNG WOMAN FROM EL SALVADOR

A church heard about her fear of returning to El Salvador, and quickly agreed to sponsor her into Canada. She waited eleven months in Buffalo while the Canadian authorities read through the stacks of paper and signed the right ones before she could finally end her journey. The room they provided was so warm and welcoming, and she sank into some pillows, exhausted. Eventually the young man she had met along the way found her, and became her husband.

Like most new immigrants, their monthly income was minimal, unequal to the expectations she placed on herself as a good wife. In her understanding, that included serving expensive cuts of meat and spending the day at home to protect the timing of the evening meal. Meanwhile, her sponsors ate bean sprouts and granola, and watched her weekly allowance used up in apparently inappropriate grocery bills. They advised when they could, and in time the grocery bills got lower; so did her self-esteem as a wife. She learned how to fit into the Canadian economy, but felt she was betraying her cultural values.

How do any of us know which culture should be imposed on which? Will she eventually be a Canadian Salvadorean woman, or a Salvadorean Canadian woman? Either way, she may feel as if she has failed at being a good woman.

YOUNG WOMAN FROM BURUNDI

She had been a refugee in Africa for seven years, and was relieved when Canada selected her as a government sponsored refugee, along with her four small children. She came to Montreal, fluent in French and full of hope. Two children went to school, and two children went to daycare. She was one of the lucky ones; she got a job in a factory. Factory work itself was an unfamiliar experience. She began to sense that no one wanted to talk past her black face. She tried to realize what was happening around her: "I cried in the washroom, and nobody noticed my tears when I came out. I wondered why nobody cared about me until I realized that nobody cared about anybody. Nobody even said 'excuse me' when they stepped on a toe."

Machines frightened her, and she was transferred to a simpler one. It wasn't simple, though, to be working with men for the first time in her life. She finally decided to leave her job, and was amazed that the boss was sad. She realized with surprise that he thought she had been doing a good job. He never told her!

She stayed home for a while and worried about the other women. She had never been involved in collectives of any kind, but she knew they needed each other. She went to an International Centre and told them about her worries and how they could help each other. She filled out complicated forms to create a job to help other women, and got a grant for a new job. Now she works with women and helps them from her own experience in Canada. "All those women are slaves to their culture," she said. "They forget their own possibilities."

Can we ever fully understand why they are here? Can we learn from their experience? Can we understand them as individual women? Will we ever look at them without prejudice?

YOUNG WOMAN FROM SOMALIA

She was highly skilled in Somalia: a typist and telex computer operator. But after her husband disappeared (just one of thousands) her life changed, because in Somalia a working woman needs a male sponsor. At first her uncle sponsored her, but he disappeared, too. And so she was fired, with no place to go. "The war in Somalia is an anarchist war. It is a war on women," she said. Any woman between the ages of eighteen and forty is not safe from being forcibly removed to the army camps to be raped and violated. And that's only the beginning. If her husband finds out, he kills her for the shame of it all; if they know that he has found out, they kill him, too; if he goes into hiding instead, and she won't tell where he is, they kill her.

And so she escaped to Canada, aching because she left a young baby with her sister, who couldn't come to Canada, as protection for her sister: only a girl with a baby is safe from violation. And so she sacrificed her baby daughter to save her sister. Most of all she feels so alone because there are not enough Somalis in Canada to form the kind of community to which she needs to belong, in order to stand upright in the midst of the pain and the memory of the flesh and blood she left behind.

YOUNG TAMIL WOMAN FROM SRI LANKA

As a child she had heard stories of bombings from her mother. Then, one of the bombs killed her young husband, and she felt them in her soul when she realized that her unborn twins would never know their father. She was a high school teacher, and one extra-violent day her principal warned her to stay at home. Frozen with fear, three women watched while thugs ran to the back of the house with torches to burn it down—just because she was a Tamil. Only wit and the need to survive kept them moving to a temporary safe haven, a room 6'x10' for fifty people. "I still feel the scars of that burning," she said.

The nurse who helped her wash the twins asked: "When are you going home?" She remembers bursting into tears because she had no home to go to. They kept moving, sleeping with their clothes on and a bit of food nearby, ready to move when necessary. For three months they stayed in India, then they found their way to England, where a Canadian church heard about them and sponsored their move to Canada. They waited eleven more months before arriving at the welcoming church. One of the first comments from an unthinking person confused her: "You a refugee? Surely immigrant is more like it."

The sponsoring church is kind, but the trauma and depression remain. Holding her teaching skills in her memory, she wonders why only the men are easily given studying opportunities here in Canada. She shared some of her disappointments with us: "The cultural transition lies heavily on the women. The guilt for having left home is heavy." Beneath the warm smile and the classic beauty lies a lot of pain.

These refugee women will never forget the land of their birth. Without doubt, the scars of past traumas will also never be forgotten. Perhaps they did not know much about Canada before they arrived here. But now they know that Canada is their homeland.

They know that the peace and safety they have found in Canada will give them a chance to start a new life. Now they have an opportunity to develop their potential and contribute their talents to the land which gave them refuge.

T O P I C S   F O R   D I S C U S S I O N

1. What is the author's role in "Breaking the Barriers"? How objective is Kutz-Harder's approach to her subject? Whom is she trying to reach in her audience?

2. Why has the author chosen to concentrate on women? What gender-specific barriers do female refugees face in their homelands and in their adopted country? What predicament do they share with their male counterparts?

3. Explain the differences between immigrants and refugees. Consider the motives for their journey, their attitudes to the country of origin, to the new country, their vision of the future, difficulties and dilemmas encountered in their respective situations, etc.

4. In the global economy, what are the reasons for increasing migrations of people? Why are there so many refugees coming from the so-called Third World countries?

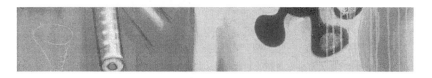

CHALLENGES/ RACISM/ DISCRIMINATION

INTRODUCTION

We live in a society where our experiences are racialized and where people of colour—like the girl in Himani Bannerji's story "The Other Family"—are forced to recognize themselves as "different" or "other." There are still inequalities and oppression due to race, gender, class, sexuality, the language spoken, religion, ability, or age. In order to confront the inherited history of white domination, we must realize that excluding "whiteness" from the concept of race makes "whiteness"—or the absence of colour—into a norm, a neutral state as opposed to "difference." In fact, "whiteness" is the colour of privilege in Canada, the privilege that pretends to be invisible. As the authors in this unit argue, racism and discrimination are not just individual abuses of power but rather systemic problems. They occur in a social and institutional context historically established so as to serve the interests of one group over those of others. Racism in Canada exists in many forms: from the "black-and-white" conflict, to the deeply entrenched racism against Native peoples, to anti-Semitism and anti-immigrant racism. Indeed, immigration appears to be a ground where Canadian racism surfaces again and again, against different groups, in different historical periods. As suggested by African Canadian, South Asian, and other critics of the official policy of multiculturalism, the liberal ideal of multicultural harmony started to be perceived in the 1990s as a cover-up for unresolved racial conflicts in our communities. Therefore, anti-racism education has an important role to play in unlearning stereotypes and bringing institutional changes in education, law, health care, social services, and other sectors of life in Canada.

Michelle La Flamme

Michelle La Flamme openly claims her identity as a mixed race woman (her mother is Métis and her father is Black). She has an M.A. degree in English. She was one of the first scholarship students in the Writing for Film and Television Program of Vancouver Film School. Prior to joining the school, she had taught creative writing in Vancouver, Spain, and Holland. She has worked in film and video, combining her love of words with her interest in visual storytelling. With extensive background in theatre and performance, La Flamme has been reading, performing, publishing, and recording her writing for over a decade. Her projects include It's a Hair Thing, *a documentary for the National Film Board, and* Rant, *a project for video. She has also produced many music videos.*

"Yo White Boy" is one of her pieces on a tape called Void to Voice *(released in 1994), combining dub poetry from artists of colour on the West Coast. Dub, which literally means "to double," is a genre derived from reggae that uses rhythm and repetition to voice the experiences of marginalized people. The poem below has been anthologized in the collection* Miscegenation Blues: Voices of Mixed Race Women, *edited by Carol Camper (1994). In "Yo White Boy" La Flamme uses various oppositional strategies to challenge racist stereotypes affecting the lives of women of colour and denaturalizes "whiteness" as an invisible privilege of the dominant culture.*

Yo White Boy

Yo white boy, Ya, you, are you talking to me?
Asking about my eth-nic-ity?
Wanna know where I am from?
Wondering why I am brown?
Wondering if I will live up to your idea of the exotic, the erotic,
Black, brown-skinned beauty with a grin?

Yo white boy, ya, you, are you talking to me?
Aunt Jemima, now ain't she sweet?

She's smiling through a vale of tears
Tears of syrup on your shirt
Poc-a-hon-tas in a Blood-stained buckskin mini-skirt…
Just for you, Ya just for you.

Yo white Boy
Ya, you, are you talking to me?
From you perception of SUPERIORITY?
Equating my darkness with sinful sexuality!

Yo White Boy
Ya, you, are you talking to me?
Hoping I'll feel shame for my silent pain,
Taking on the blame for my people's degradation?

Yo White Boy
Believing in God and trying to make me,
believe that GOD wants ME to be free!!

Yo White Boy
I don't buy your religion –
separating me from ALL MY RELATIONS

Yo white boy
Army fatigues and Nintendo games, can't you see?
I can't connect with playing "KILL THE OTHERS"
'cause the others are
the others are Me!!

Yo white Boy
Ya, you, are you listenin' ta me
I don't sell my sex for money,
it's your domination fantasy, that's not me!!

Yo White Boy
Ya, you, you talking to me,
Yer "Dry and Abstract" Point of View,
Is not what my mind is in to.

Yo white boy
Ya You!! Now I am talking to you –
Discover what the colour of your skin means?
Discover what wasn't written into history's scenes.

T O P I C S   F O R   D I S C U S S I O N

1. What stereotypes are evoked through the images of "brown-skinned beauty," Aunt Jemima, Pocahontas, etc.?

2. How does the poem foreground "white" as a colour and as the unmarked race? What are the connotations of "whiteness"?

Pat Deiter-McArthur (Day Woman)

Pat Deiter-McArthur (Day Woman) is a Cree. Deeply committed to Native history and rights, she has written two books: Dances of the Northern Plains *and* Games of the Plains Cree *(the former has been made into a video). She is a private consultant in ethno-historical research and training. She has worked with the Federation of Saskatchewan Indian Nations to raise Native consciousness, improve employment conditions, and foster the integrity of the Natives vis-à-vis the white-dominated Canadian establishment. Herself a member of the "fifth generation," she examines in the following excerpt the five generations of Native peoples' history since their initial contact with Europeans.*

Pat Deiter-McArthur's essay illustrates that the colonization of Native peoples in Canada was not a one-time process, but occurred in phases. Despite the fact that the British Crown had promised to respect the rights of Native peoples to the land and their culture, the Government of Canada after 1870 encouraged large numbers of bands to sign "treaties" through which the Natives exchanged their land for a reserve and some goods. Today there is still much controversy about the validity of the treaties. In the 1980s and 1990s, several legal challenges were launched with respect to Aboriginal land claims and treaty rights. Deiter-McArthur also mentions the Indian Act, which gave the Government power to control all aspects of Native life, including the right to determine who was and who was not "Indian." Perhaps this reference to the Indian Act explains the author's naming practices in the essay. She persistently uses the term "Indian" which, although imposed from without, is still the official legal designation of Native peoples in Canada. In contrast, "First Nations Peoples" is a self-designation adopted to remind the so-called "Founding Nations" (the French and the British) of the Aboriginal presence on this land. Another issue highlighted in the essay is that of Native education. As seen in Pauline Johnson's story in Unit One, religious conversion in mission schools was always accompanied by forced assimilation. The residential school system, run by the churches and later on by government, was a deliberate attempt at cultural genocide, trying to eliminate Native languages and cultures (see Basil Johnston's essay in Unit Three). Numerous cases of injustices such as physical punishment, torture, and abuse perpetrated in residential schools have recently been brought to public attention. Current controversies over First Nations land claims, aboriginal self-government, and the Indian Act prove that the legacy of colonialism and racism is still very much alive in the relationship between the Canadian government and Native peoples as well as in Canadian culture and consciousness.

Saskatchewan's Indian People— Five Generations

I t has been about five generations since Saskatchewan Indian people have had significant contact with European settlers. The First Generation strongly influenced by Europeans were the treaty-signers. The key characteristic of this generation was their ability to have some input into their future. They retained their tribal cultures but realized that they had to negotiate with the Europeans for the betterment of future generations. They did not give up their language or religion or the political structures of nationhood. They were perceived by government as an "alien" nation to be dealt with by treaty.

The Second Generation (1867–1910) of Indian people were the objects of legal oppression by the government. This generation lived under the absolute rule of an Indian agent, a government employee. Through the Indian Act, this generation was denied their religion, political rights, and freedom to travel off their reserves. A pass and permit system was strictly adhered to on the prairies; every Indian person required a pass to leave the reserve and a permit to sell any agricultural produce. All children were required to attend residential schools run by the churches. The goals of their schools were, first, to make Christians out of their students and to rid them of their pagan lifestyles and, second, to provide a vocational education.

Tuberculosis was a major killer of Indian people during this time and contributed to decimating their population in Saskatchewan to a low of five thousand in 1910. This generation was treated as wards and aliens of Canada.

The laws which served to oppress the second generation were in place until the early 1950s. The Third Generation (1910–1945) was greatly affected by these laws and schooling. This generation can be described as the lost generation. These people were psychologically oppressed. They rejected their Indianness but found that because of the laws for treaty Indians they could not enjoy the privileges accorded to whites. This third generation was our grandfather's generation. Many Indians at this time could speak their language but would not because of shame of their Indianness. They were still required by law to send their children to residential schools, to send their sick to Indian hospitals, and to abide by the Indian agent. They rarely had a sense of control over their own lives. This generation was considered wards of the government and denied citizenship.

Our father's time, the Fourth Generation since treaty-signing, can best be described as the generation of an Indian rebirth. This generation (1945–1980) is characterized by a movement of growing awareness—awareness that being Indian was okay and that Indian people from all tribes are united through their aboriginality, historical development, and special status.

This generation saw the rise of Indian and Native organizations across Canada, the return of traditional ceremonies, and an acknowledgement of the need to retain traditional languages and cultural ways.

Indian people of this generation were given the right to vote in 1960. The pass and permit system was abandoned in the late 1930s. In 1956, Indian children could attend either residential schools or the local public schools. However, the effects of this generation being raised within an institution and their parents being raised in the same way had a severe impact on these individuals. The residential school not only taught them to suppress their language but also to suppress their feelings and sense of individualism. The continued attack on Indian languages by residential schools left this generation with an ability to only understand their language, but many were not sufficiently fluent to call their Native language their first language.

During the sixties, there was a rise in Indian urbanization, a trend that continues today. This generation also contributed to an Indian baby boom that is estimated to be eight to ten years behind the non-Indian baby boomers. The federal and provincial vote allowed Indian people to legally consume alcohol. Alcoholism, suicides, and violent deaths were on the rise for this generation.

This was a period of experimentation by both the Indian communities and the government. Unfortunately, neither side was ready for each other. The intended government goal of assimilation was besieged with problems of racism, poverty, maladjustment, and cultural shock.

Today's Indian people are part of the Fifth Generation. The fifth generation is faced with choices: assimilation, integration, or separation. Indian people are now able to intermarry or assimilate with non-Indians without the loss of their Indian status. Indian leaders across Canada are seeking a separate and constitutionally recognized Indian government. Indian government is to provide its own services within Indian reserves. Integration allows Indian people to retain a sense of their cultural background while working and living within the larger society.

The fifth generation people are the first children since treaty-signing to be raised by their parents. Many of this generation are not able to understand a native language. Their first and only language is English. This generation is generally comfortable about their Indianness without strong prejudicial feelings to others. However, this generation is challenged to retain the meaning of Indian identity for their children.

TOPICS FOR DISCUSSION

1. What is the purpose of Pat Deiter-McArthur's essay? Who will make up her readership? How does she situate herself in relation to the facts presented? How effective is her method of presentation?

2. What challenges to Native people's identity are chronicled in her essay? What were the effects of contact with Europeans upon the Native population in each period she discusses?

3. What methods did white governments in Canada adopt in dealing with Native people? Find examples of assimilation, integration, separation, and annihilation as patterns of Native-white interactions described in the text. Can different patterns overlap?

4. In what ways does her argument challenge or supplement mainstream accounts of Native history?

Joy Kogawa

Joy Kogawa was born in Vancouver in 1935; she is a nisei, *a second-generation Japanese Canadian. After the attack on Pearl Harbor and the Japanese capture of Hong Kong in 1941, Japanese Canadian civilians were rounded up by the Canadian government, their possessions were auctioned off, and they were transported to internment camps away from the British Columbia coast. Kogawa and her family were evacuated to Slocan, B.C., and later to Alberta. After the war, she moved to Toronto, where she studied music and theology. The experience of the evacuation is reflected in much of Kogawa's work, especially in her celebrated novel* Obasan *(1981). The same theme has also recurred in her children's book* Naomi's Road *(1986). Kogawa has been active in the legal fight for redress from the government for the abuses committed against Japanese Canadians during World War II. She was made a Member of the Order of Canada. Joy Kogawa is also a poet, with five published volumes of poetry. Her work addresses issues of racial and cultural difference, persecution, and identity. Her latest novel,* The Rain Ascends *(1995), deals with another emotional issue, namely, sexual abuse of children by a Protestant clergyman.*

This fragment from her novel Itsuka *(1992), which is a sequel to* Obasan, *describes the apology made to Japanese Canadians in Parliament. At the end of the excerpt is a government document of "acknowledgement," formally stating Canada's responsibility. Commenting in an interview on the effects of the redress on the Japanese Canadian community, Joy Kogawa says, "What is healing for a community is more than just a solution of a political kind. What heals is a process of empowerment, the process that heals is one where there is a striving for and an attainment of mutuality" (in* Other Solitudes: Canadian Multicultural Fictions, *edited by Linda Hutcheon and Marion Richmond, 1990).* Itsuka *means "someday."*

from Itsuka

Dreams dreams dreams.

It begins in earliest infancy, this journey through the world's many borderlands. It proceeds through the day of the odourless fawn, past summer, into the mustier season of leaves, orchards, the harvest with its memories and dance. To be without history is to be unlived crystal, unused flesh; is to live the life of the unborn.

What I've wakened to in this new autumn day is hunger. My eyes are hungry. The palms of my hands are hungry for this square inch of space we are inhabiting today. Our bite-sized moment of life. I'm as small and as hungry as a newborn sparrow.
September 22, 1988. Ottawa.

Perhaps it's in the scheme of things that when life is most bleak, miracles break through. It's such a mystery. And so completely unexpected. I first heard about it last night. Last night was another lifetime ago.

I was still at *Bridge* when Aunt Emily called around seven. Dan had just called her. She immediately called Anna and me. She couldn't call any others because it's still completely confidential. All she said was "Come over immediately. I can't tell you why." I rushed up to the apartment and found her looking around abstractedly. She packed in silence, mechanically. We tried to sleep. We were up before the alarm. Anna, looking like a blimp, came by with Brian at 5:30 a.m., and we've been driving the four and a half hours along the 401 towards the cut-off at the Tweed highway. We're in a daze.

Our president, Mick Hayashi, Dan and others on the strategy team, unlike most of us, had felt something would have to happen following the American resolution, but over the many months and years they'd grown wary of false optimism. They did not communicate a word of hope to the rank and file. There had been so much debility and loss of morale when repeatedly, after promises of negotiations, there'd be a collapse in talks. Then suddenly, three weeks ago, the team was called to a Montreal hotel, and after a weekend of non-stop negotiating the unbelievable happened. An agreement was reached. There's to be a full acknowledgement of the injustices, individual compensation of $21,000 each to those affected (the Americans are to receive $20,000), a community fund and a race-relations foundation. It's a $350,000,000 package.

"All that? Just like that? But—was there no warning?"

The team was sworn to secrecy. They were told that if the news leaked out in any way, and if the Legion, for instance, objected, the whole thing could be jeopardized. Even now, everything could be stopped. Dan took his oath so seriously that he went north to an isolated cabin.

"It's a miracle. What happened, do you think?"

Brian thinks it's because it's election time. Plus they're copying the Americans, for sure. Maybe it's because of a few key people—like John Fraser, the Speaker of the House.

Young John Fraser, Aunt Emily tells us, was a child in Vancouver when we all disappeared. His father took him to the cenotaph in Stanley Park where Japanese Canadian veterans of the First World War were memorialized. "I fought beside those men," he told his son. John Fraser never forgot.

Whatever the reasons may or may not be, we're so used to pessimism that the fact of a settlement isn't really registering. Aunt Emily says she doesn't want to say another word until she's actually in the House and the papers are actually signed. Dan told her the whole thing is so precarious anything could still stop it.

"How do you think Nikki's going to react?" Anna asks.

"Publicly?" Aunt Emily says. "She'd be a fool to oppose it. And Nikki's no fool."

"Privately, she'll break out in a rash," Brian says.

Privately, I'm wondering if Nikki is still convinced the NJCL are greedy opportunists. Vultures, I think she called us. Could there be any truth in her statement that history will condemn us and vindicate her? That, I suppose, is something none of us can know. What we as a community decide to do from this day on will reveal who we are.

Brian is familiar with the route. We take a rest break at Tweed, get to Ottawa shortly after ten, check in to a friend's house on Gilmour Avenue near the Lord Elgin Hotel, collapse for a second on our beds. And now here we are in this city, the country's capital, the four of us, walking up to Parliament Hill under the blue-white September sky.

I think of the years of labour, the rally half a year ago that Aunt Emily missed—how we walked along in the drizzle and how I wasn't feeling a whisper of hope even though I was carrying the yellow ribbons of hope, and suddenly this unbelievable, this most astonishing day.

If I were a watcher in the skies, I might notice small antlike groupings of people walking up Parliament Hill this morning, up past the Centennial flame; up the wide walk and the steps and into the lobby of the Centre Block with its high vaulted ceiling. Dan flew up last night. Others from the strategy team are here with Mick Hayashi, plus some people from the Ottawa community. Only a few passes have been arranged since it's all such a secret. We hand over our cameras and notebooks at a desk, go down the marble hall, enter the high narrow gallery above the House of Commons and look down directly on the members of Parliament facing each other from their two tiers of benches. So few members present. The speaker is on a dais to our left. To our right is the public gallery, without a single person in it. The huge chamber seems almost empty. Just a handful from our community. So little flesh, but so many ghosts.

Mick Hayashi, Dan and all the main people plus a couple of senior citizens are on the side of the gallery facing the Prime Minister. A few other people from Ottawa, Aunt Emily, Brian, Anna and I sit in the opposite balcony. Anna waves a finger to our team. Below us are the people who lead the country. We can see the top of Prime Minister Mulroney's head from the back and, opposite him, Mr. Broadbent, leader of the New Democratic Party. The leader of the Liberal Party is not present.

11:00 a.m.

The Prime Minister stands. The magic of speech begins—this ritual thing that humans do, the washing of stains through the speaking of words.

"Mr. Speaker," the Prime Minister begins. "Nearly half a century ago, in the crisis of wartime, the Government of Canada wrongfully incarcerated, seized the property, and disenfranchised thousands of citizens of Japanese ancestry...." Even as I strain to hear and remember the many words, they are gone and speech is a trickster, slipping and sliding away. "To put things right," the Prime Minister says in his low voice. And again, "to put things right." And once more. "To put things right."

"Most of us in our own lives," he is saying, "have had occasion to regret certain things we have done. Error is an ingredient of humanity. So too is apology and forgiveness. We all have learned from personal experience that, as inadequate as apologies are, they are the only way we can cleanse the past so that we may, as best we can, in good conscience face the future...."

In the future I know we will look back on this moment as we stand and applaud. We'll remember how Ed Broadbent crossed the floor to shake the Prime Minister's hand and we'll see all this as a distant sun, a star, an asterisk in space to guide us through nights that yet must come. The children, the grandchildren, will know that certain things happened to their ancestors. And that these things were put right.

Sergio Marchi, the Liberal Party representative, is commending our president and community "for their never-ending determination and deep belief in the cause that they carried so well for so long. Today's resolution, no doubt, is a tribute to their sense of purpose, but it is also an appropriate response to those who continue to question the legitimacy and motivation of the leadership...."

I feel us wanting to jump up and cheer but we are contained. And as I look down I can see Mr. Broadbent, who was married to a nisei and knows our story from the inside. I'm glad to be on this side, facing him. He appears agitated, his hands shuffling papers, his eyes glancing up to where we sit. And then he rises and speaks and he's fighting to control his voice. "They, as Canadian citizens, had done no wrong," Mr. Broadbent says. "They had done no wrong...."

This feast of words is too wonderful, too sad, too joyful. I'm numb. Aunt Emily too is listening from some great slow distance of time and space. We are seated at a banquet table that was a hope for people yesterday and will feed us with hope tomorrow. The power of this hour is being stored now in our hearts as a promise fulfilled, a vision realized, and the healing rises up to us, the healing falls about us, over the countryside, here and there, today and tomorrow, touching the upturned faces filled with the waiting and longing of all the wordless years.

The speeches end and it's all going by so fast, so fast, and we're back in the west hallway, in a room where a small throng is gathering. The signing of the agreement is happening here and I catch just a glimpse of the Prime Minister again, no more or less real than any other person as he steps into the room. The TV cameras are directed upon him and our president, smiling, shaking hands, then sitting at a table, the strategy team standing behind. A flashing of lights and cameras clicking. And it's done.

Then, like a gathering swarm of bees, politicians, staff members, the NJCL vanguard in a block, TV crews and reporters all move down the hall, the wide stairs. We walk back down the middle of the Hill to the press conference on the other side of Rideau Street. Aunt Emily is sleep walking.

We can't get into the room where the press conference is and we go with the overflow, up the crowded elevator to a sixth-floor lounge and a television screen, then back down again into the world of microphones and cameras, and catch up with Dan and the others as they walk back up to the Parliament Buildings for a reception.

I want some way to slow down the day, but the waterfall refuses to be contained in a cup and we're swept along in the swift liquid hour, into a room with tables of food, glib words, glazed eyes, cameras flashing, and Aunt Emily is standing with Mr. Broadbent and she looks stunned and not altogether coherent.

"I feel I've just had a tumour removed," one of our friends from Ottawa says to me. "Can you believe it, Naomi?"

We're in a buzz of sounds whirring about.

"Let me congratulate you, Mick. I think you've created a vaccine."

"Yes?"

"Against fatigue. A vaccine against compassion fatigue."

Cedric, Morty, Marion and Ken have just flown up from Toronto and Cedric has the most joyful tearful smile I have ever seen. He comes rushing up to me and in all that crowd he takes me in his arms. "Watch out, world," he whispers. "The mouse has roared."

I laugh. I am whole. I am as complete as when I was a very young child. Marion puts her arms around us both. "God bless us every one," she says.

Aunt Emily and Dan are talking with a man from the Secretary of State who asks Aunt Emily, "How did you feel when you heard the apology?"

Aunt Emily is in a trance and can't reply. My aunt of the so many words. How does she feel as this day speeds by? How does the grass feel in the cool autumn air? How does the sky feel? And the community across the country as it hears the news today?

Ken says, "I finally feel that I'm a Canadian." You can hear the trembling in his voice.

Aunt Emily and I look at each other and smile. We've all said it over the years. "No, no, I'm Canadian. I'm a Canadian. A Canadian." Sometimes it's been a defiant statement, a demand, a proclamation of a right. And today, finally, finally, though we can hardly believe it, to be Canadian means what it hasn't meant before. Reconciliation. Liberation. Belongingness. Home.

Anna and Brian, Cedric, Morty, Aunt Emily and I walk back to Gilmour Avenue. We let ourselves smile. "Well?" Aunt Emily asks, looking up at the sky. That's all she can say.

We make some tea and catch the TV news on every channel we can find. We gasp when we see the official shots. By focusing on the Prime Minister and the MPs behind him, the camera makes the House seem packed, when in fact, it certainly wasn't—not that it mattered. There's a brief report on the radio that Nikki was contacted in Toronto. She said she was very happy about the announcement. We all applaud and toast Nikki with our cups of tea.

The Vancouver contingent phones and we go off to meet for supper. Someone is doing an interview with Mick outside the restaurant. We go in. Wait. Mick arrives. We eat. A few Ottawa people drop by. Then Cedric and I excuse ourselves and leave, ducking past a man taking pictures. We walk hand in hand out into the evening air, up Elgin Street, along Rideau, where strangers are standing at their bus stops, waiting for their many buses, walk past and up to the grounds of Parliament Hill again. We're walking off the stage of the day with its hovering of well-wishers and the great happy crush of the press—away from the speeches, the interviews, the congratulations, the shaking of hands at the restaurant, where some people are still looking at one another, pinching themselves, asking if it's true.

We're taking time, taking time to quieten this day, to bring it back from its already past. We're stretching it out on the canvas of the night air, shaking it out like a blanket to wear.

Oh Aunt Emily, Aunt Emily, is it not the happiest day of your life? I want to remember everything. Savour it all. Our frantic search for a safety pin for the tie on Anna's skirt. The man who honked his horn on Rideau Street and waved. The pattern of sand on the Centre Block steps. Mick, our brave president, with a hand in his hip pocket as he walked briskly ahead of us. I want to etch the day onto the permanent airwaves of memory, replay it over and over until it starts to seem real. Aunt Emily, I want to be able to see you for ever and ever the way you were this morning, walking happily, happily up the hill in your brown trenchcoat and your good walking shoes, my dear warrior aunt. I want to call all the ghosts back again to share this day that none of us can believe is happening.

In my pocket, I have the folded piece of paper that contains the government statement. I read the words again and I take them into my childhood home. I pile them like firelogs, one by one. I warm my limbs.

"As a people, Canadians commit themselves to the creation of a society that ensures equality and justice for all...."

I hand the paper to Cedric and he reads it aloud as we stand looking out over the shadowy trees and bushes on the slope, to the Ottawa River below. In a month's time the leaves of the trees will change colour, and then they will fall as they've been falling for ever, year after year, each leaf with its own tiny story twirling into every other ongoing tale.

This hill is not unlike the slope to the Old Man River near Granton, though it's steeper here and the river is more wide. Sixteen years ago I stood with my uncle on the Granton coulees in the coolness of a night like this, looking down at the ocean of grass, and he said, as he always did, "Umi no yo." It's like the sea.

It's like the sea tonight, Uncle. A busy bubbling trembling sea of the almost sighted and the sometimes blind, the swimmers, the drifters, and those who don't know how to swim. We are here together, and it's enough.

Sixteen years ago this month, my uncle died. And two years later, so did my Obasan. I'm thinking of them and of the rapids, the waterfalls, the eddies in the journey to the sea, and how today we've touched the sounds of the waves on the shore, the applause, the pulse of earth's heart still beating. And I'm thinking of Uncle's words and the words of an old man in Slocan.

"There is a time for crying," they said. "But itsuka, someday, the time for laughter will come."

This is the time, dear Uncle, dear Ojisan. The dramatics, the tears and cheers, have arrived in their own way in their own time. We have come to the hour when the telling leaps over the barricades and the dream enters day.

I can hear the waves from childhood rippling outwards to touch other children who wait for their lives. I can hear the voices, faint as the far-away sound of a distant, almost inaudible wind. It's the sound of the underground stream. It speaks through memory, through dream, through our hands, through our words, our arms, our trusting. I can hear the sound of the voice that frees, a light, steady, endless breath. I can hear the breath of life.

Thank you for this.

ACKNOWLEDGEMENT

As a people, Canadians commit themselves to the creation of a society that ensures equality and justice for all, regardless of race or ethnic origin.

During and after World War II, Canadians of Japanese ancestry, the majority of whom were citizens, suffered unprecedented actions taken by the Government of Canada against their community.

Despite perceived military necessities at the time, the forced removal and internment of Japanese Canadians during World War II and their deportation and expulsion following the war, was unjust. In retrospect, government policies of disenfranchisement, detention, confiscation and sale of private and community property, expulsion, deportation and restriction of movement, which continued after the war, were influenced by discriminatory attitudes. Japanese Canadians who were interned had their property liquidated and the proceeds of sale were used to pay for their own internment.

The acknowledgement of these injustices serves notice to all Canadians that the excesses of the past are condemned and that the principles of justice and equality in Canada are reaffirmed.

Therefore, the Government of Canada, on behalf of all Canadians, does hereby:

1) acknowledge that the treatment of Japanese Canadians during and after World War II was unjust and violated principles of human rights as they are understood today;

2) pledge to ensure, to the full extent that its powers allow, that such events will not happen again; and

3) recognize, with great respect, the fortitude and determination of Japanese Canadians who, despite great stress and hardship, retain their commitment and loyalty to Canada and contribute so richly to the development of the Canadian nation.

TOPICS FOR DISCUSSION

1. "To be without history is to be unlived crystal, unused flesh." How do these words refer to the narrator? Find other examples of Kogawa's use of figurative language to convey the "unspeakable."

2. In her narrative, Kogawa uses real figures like Brian Mulroney and Ed Broadbent. What is the effect of introducing historical personages into the fictional world of the novel?

3. "The washing of stains through the speaking of words" is what humans do, says Kogawa. What does she mean by "stains"? Why does she believe that "stains" might be washed clean by a public government apology?

4. One of the characters, Ken, says, "I finally feel I'm a Canadian." How did the meaning of being Canadian changed for Japanese Canadians on the day they received the apology?

5. How does Kogawa's text celebrate the sense of purpose in the Japanese-Canadian community? How do they view their responsibility toward the past and future generations?

6. Why has Kogawa included the government "Acknowledgement" at the end of this fiction?

Joanne Arnott

Born in 1960, Joanne Arnott is of mixed Native/non-Native ancestry, orig-
inally from Manitoba. She lives with her family on the West Coast and
works as a facilitator of workshops on unlearning racism and on mothering.
Her first collection of poetry, Wiles of Girlhood *(1991), won the Gerald*
Lampert Award of the League of Canadian Poets. My Grass Cradle
(1992), her second book of poems explores issues of mixed heritage. She is
best known for Breasting the Waves: On Writing and Healing *(1995), a*
candid collection of personal essays and stories dealing with such themes as
the pain of racism, the power of motherhood and friendship, reclaiming
women's rituals, and healing from abuse. Joanne Arnott has also written
Ma MacDonald *(1993), a book for children about home birth, following*
the classic nursery rhyme pattern. Her essays and poems have been fre-
quently anthologized and appeared in such journals as Open Letter, Vox
Feminarum, *and* sub-TERRAIN, *Vancouver's literary magazine of alter-*
native writing.

In the following essay, Joanne Arnott uses her own experience as work-
shop participant and facilitator to offer some advice on how to become an
ally in anti-racism struggle.

Speak Out, For Example

One day, I stopped by unexpected at a friend's place, knock knock. As she opened the door, she said with pretend irritation, "What do you want now?" When she saw it was me, she laughed. "Sorry. I thought it was my mutt…"

No dear woman, it is not your mutt. It is someone else's mutt at the front door.

At the time I was too surprised, and too unsafe, to do more than focus my attention carefully on whatever had brought me to her door in the first place. But the incident has stayed with me, the sort of sting that crystallizes much into its simplicity.

In 1989, I attended an Unlearning Racism workshop presented by Rikki Sherover-Marcuse, and subsequently have attended and led many such workshops. I have met a diversity of women and men with mixed/multiple heritages. I will take a few minutes, now, to talk about racism, but there is no way that I can speak for everyone. The format I will use is that of a Speak Out exercise, as taught by Rikki Sherover-Marcuse. It is used as a tool for educating people, and as a platform for people targeted for oppression to speak *and be heard.* I will address these three points:

1. What I want you to know abut me and my people.
2. What I never want to hear again.
3. What I expect of you as my allies.

Your job is just to listen. If you are also a mixed-race person, take some time to answer the questions for yourself. Remember to leave space for your feelings, because feelings and experience are essential and need to be channelled, embraced, and cherished. If you are not a mixed-race person, please repeat whatever you remember of what I said in response to points 1 and 3, and bear 2 in mind but remember, I really don't want to hear it again.

1. What I want you to know about me and my people:

ABOUT ME: I am a person of mixed Native and European ancestry, and I know lots about my European ancestry and almost nothing abut my Native heritage: this is one impact of racism. I was raised in a white community as a white working class person. When, as a child, I or my sisters or brothers attempted to talk about our relationship to or similarities with Native people, we were punished. Our parents seemed to believe in lies about our ancestry, and we were forced to believe, or pretend to believe, the same: this is one aspect of internalized racism. At the same time that this white-out policy was in effect, we were constantly being recognized by friends and strangers, by people not under the sway of the family's survivalist lies.

This combination of input created in me an attempt to sort a world of responses to a Métis person through an insecure identity of whiteness. Confusion, dissonance, incongruity, self-doubt, endless inadequacy, deep shame were the results. The process of healing has been a tearing down and tearing up of almost every constituent belief that I held about myself and my world, and a recentering in the truth of body, mind, of spirit, a reawakening of my deep self and a reconstruction of my social self, my being in the world, on this new/old/original foundation.

ABOUT MY PEOPLE: People with multiple ethnic heritages are an extremely diverse bunch of people. Our looks are diverse, our habits and heritages are diverse, our knowledge of ourselves, our ancestries, our traditions, our families, are diverse. To use the example of mixed Native and European heritage people, some of us are raised on reserve, in the bush, in small towns, on farms, in cities, and/or any combination of these places; as Indians, as Métis, as "breeds," as whites, Blacks, Asians; with great pride, with great shame, with full knowledge, in complete ignorance, with double and triple messages about who we are and about our place in the world. For many of us, the greatest source of racism, hurt and shame is our own families. For many of us, our families are the cradles of safety against racist abuse and rejection from the outside world.

Big Issues: passing, and the not-Black-enough, not-Indian enough hassles we put on ourselves, collect from other people. "Where are you from?" "Are you two related?" In terms of multigenerational denial, complicities, it is important for us to acknowledge the privileges of European people, the very real dangers to our physical survival as Indians, Blacks, Asians in the context of the Americas. The decisions of family members to deny who we are do not come easy, they are meant to save lives. It is one strategy. Many of us choose other strategies, or override the decisions of our predecessors to reclaim the fullness and complexity of who we are and the histories of our families and communities. To attempt to enforce silence is soul murder. To attempt to induce identifications that are, because of racism, too threatening, is to rip a seed from its pod and is pointless: the seed will either ripen in its own time, or it will moulder and die within its protective casing.

Further layers of complexity get laid in when we are raised by people not targeted for oppression in the same way we are, the situation of the black child of the white woman who affectionately called him "mutt" to her Métis girlfriend. Our worlds differ fundamentally, in how we are received and who we are received by, and there are basic truths and survival skills a person of colour must learn that white parents don't know about.

Possibly the most difficult issue for people of mixed heritage is that of belonging, and a part of that is safety: constantly testing the waters to see how I am seen, and what the perceiver's response to their perceptions might be. The wide world that is laid open for people with multiple heritages is a well of potential, centered in a

sometimes perilous terrain, The sliding identity that can be so difficult at first can become a very powerful tool for peacemakers.

2. What I never want to hear again:

"Mutt"   "Half-breed"   "Heinz 57"   "Wannabe"

I never want to face another door opened by a mother who calls
the child of her own body racist names.

3. What I expect of you as my allies:

Question: What is an ally?

*An ally can be a friend, family member, co-worker, complete
stranger; but none of these is automatically an ally. Ideally, an ally is
someone who is aware of their own issues of hurt and oppression, accumulated over the years, and is healing, and who is aware of the differences between us and who cherishes me, intervenes when they can to
interrupt attacks against me, and supports me in my struggles against
oppression and internalized oppression.*

*The possibility for every one of us to be allies against oppression is
always present. Mistakes are made, and as allies, we commit ourselves to
confronting rather than ignoring them, and doing the emotional and
other kinds of work needed to correct and clean up mistakes and misunderstandings.*

Notice the great pain carried by many, many, many mixed heritage people. Notice our strength, our great pride. Notice us, everywhere in the world.

Stop making assumptions about the heritage of other people,
thinking that if someone looks white, looks European, that they
want to hear your racist jokes in a buddy-buddy fashion. Or conversely, if someone looks Indian, that they are an automatic font of
deep wisdom via continuous ancient tradition.

As an ally you must never expect me to choose sides, because I
am all sides. You must never silence the parts of me that need to be
given voice, especially when the parts of me do not agree. I need the
fullness of that space to sort out the contradictions of my life experience, and to solidify a grounded and well-rounded sense of who I
am, my place, and what my work in the world might be, based on
that reality.

What I expect of my allies is not to divide up the world by race
and caste without acknowledging that every single boundary is

blurred, and that these blurrings occur not only out of a conqueror mentality, but also out of love and need, and further that these blurrings have a name: we are called human beings. What I expect of my allies is to expect full pride from me, and to foster it.

We all learn the same racist crap, and we all need to stop perpetrating it on ourselves, on one another, and on the young people. Participating in the diminishing of ourselves and of others is how we have learned to survive, and it takes a conscious effort, storming and weeping, and a courageous collaboration to turn things around. There are many things that each one of us can do. Actions large and small can be taken. Alone, together. Heal old wounds, demand the fullness of life. Listen carefully. Speak out.

TOPICS FOR DISCUSSION

1. Why is Arnott's essay written in the form of what she calls "a Speak Out exercise?" Who is her audience and what does she expect from her audience?

2. According to her, what different survival strategies do people of colour employ in order to cope with racism and internalized racism?

3. What would the process of "unlearning racism" imply for racially marginalized groups and for those who enjoy the white privilege?

Henry Martey Codjoe

*Henry Martey Codjoe was born in Ghana, West Africa, and in 1974
immigrated to Canada. He is an alumnus of the Norman Paterson School
of International Affairs, in the area of Development. He has lived in
Quebec, Ontario, and Alberta, before moving to the Unites States, where
he works as Professor of Social Science at Dalton State College in Georgia.
His research focuses on colonial education and underdevelopment in West
Africa. While working as a policy consultant for the Department of
Education in Alberta, he wrote an essay called "Why We Need Black
History Month—All Year Round," which has been widely reprinted. He
deplores the tragic situation of many Black and African children in a
North American school system that has continually perpetrated racist stereo-
types about African history and has deprived these children of any knowl-
edge about their ancestral heritage.*

The essay below comes from the book Talking About Identity:
Encounters in Race, Ethnicity, and Language, *edited by Carl E. James
and Adrienne Shadd (2001). Henry Martey Codjoe tackles the question of
"reverse racism"—whether Blacks and, by extension, other people of colour,
can be racist. The author interrogates and historicizes different meanings of
race and racism. In his argument, he adopts a constructionist perspective,
that is, a methodological approach which refuses to see such conceptual categories as race, gender, class, sexuality, or identity as "naturally given,"
viewing them instead as socially constructed and historically contingent.*

Can Blacks be Racist? Reflections on
Being "Too Black and African"

I am on dangerous terrain here. I am going to discuss a contentious subject: issues of race and racism in Canadian society, particularly as they affect Blacks/African Canadians. Using my own
personal experiences and complemented by research on race relations, I intend to probe the meanings of "race" and "racism" and

why they are such powerful social forces. I am particularly interested in the charge by some whites that Blacks are and can be racist.

Given their personal experiences and outlook, whites and Blacks have different interpretations of what it means to be racist. Indeed, Blacks and whites do not possess the same experiences because, as David Mura (1999: 97) explains it:

> For some people, the categories of race have caused a whole range of negative experiences. For other people the same categories have enabled them to escape these experiences. For some people the categories of race have excluded them from certain privileges. For others the same categories have availed them of certain privileges. For all people the categories of race have meant their ancestors experienced difficult histories.

Following this premise, I argue that Blacks may be *prejudiced* but cannot be racist, and that the notion of "Black racism" is a contradiction in terms.

Reconstructing my being from African to Black

More than once I have been called a "Black racist" for being "too Black and African" (see Codjoe 1994). How could this be? Well, until I came to Canada from my native Ghana, I had known all my life that I was African. It was not until I started living in North America that I found I was "Black" (Busia 1998: 274). My identity was *socially constructed* from African to Black. I was told, on many occasions, that I was different. I did not belong. My stay in Canada would be temporary. Canada is a "white man's country." Never mind that "exiles, migrants, immigrants and refugees have turned the [country] into [a] multicultural state" (Busia 1998: 279).

Many a time I was asked when I would go back to Africa, as if Africa was one country where all Black people lived. It didn't matter that I was a Canadian citizen and had lived in Canada for most of my adult life: many years more than many white immigrants. Yet I was not Canadian. I was Black, and Blacks don't belong in Canada. They belong to Africa, and go back they must. Canada is a white country, and to be Canadian means to be white. And so in this dichotomy of race, "Those who are not White are presumed to be recent arrivals and often told to go 'back where they came from'" (Rosenblum and Travis 2000: 16).

Consequently, it was not long before, as a student in the late 1970s and early 1980s, I was socialized into racialized thinking. The sheer power that race held in people's imaginations made me intensely conscious of race and racial difference. Like Randall Robinson, writing in his *Defending the Spirit: A Black Life in America*, I became "obsessively black." Race became "an overarching aspect of my identity." I also believed that Canada "has made me this way. Or, more accurately, White [Canadians] have made me this way" (Robinson 1999: xiii).

That being the case, I embraced my blackness and Africa. I discovered myself as an African like never before. I developed Black consciousness. I would not say I was militant, but I was no longer ashamed of being Black or African. I "emancipated myself from mental slavery," as Bob Marley would say. I almost dropped my name Henry: too European, I thought. I asked my friends to call me Martey, my African name. If the dominant society is going to define me as Black, then I will do the defining. I will establish the boundaries of my being. The dominant culture will not dispossess me of my being with every glance. They can call me Black, but I will tell you what kind of Black I am. My new identity could be viewed in "a context in which ethnic minorities are articulating the desire to have our voices heard, a desire to celebrate our own signs of difference and validate our stories" (Busia 1998: 273). It is ironic and somewhat embarrassing to admit to myself that I learned more about myself now as an African or a Black person in Canada than I had in my native Ghana.

But alas, my new-found identity was seen as racist. By embracing Africa and espousing Black pride and nationalism I became, for some people, a Black racist—a person who hated white people and Canada. By embracing my blackness, I was perceived to be rejecting everything white. How ungrateful after all that Canada had done for me! How racist of me!

Since then I have always been baffled when I hear the charge of racism levelled against Blacks. Can Blacks really be racist? Is there Black racism, like white racism? Are they the same things? What are we talking about here? It appears that some whites think Blacks are and can be racist. In fact, accusations of "Black racism" or what is now referred to as "reverse racism" have been with us for a long time. Black nationalists like Malcolm X were always accused of being "anti-white." In a 1964 Harvard Law School Forum, Malcolm X was asked the difference between white racism and Black racism—as if the two were synonymous. In more recent times, Beverly Daniel Tatum, an African American psychologist, professor, and author of *Why Are All the Black Kids Sitting Together in the Cafeteria?* (1997), says she is often asked during her workshops on racism whether "people of colour" can be racist.

What is this thing called "race"?

Truthfully, I had not been used to the intractability of race in North America until I came to Canada. As fellow Ghanaian A.P.A. Busia notes: "It has been a hard lesson, because in Ghana nobody notices. In a land where we are 'Black,' that blackness is not significant to a child's mind." Therefore, "When you are born in a land where everyone seems made in your likeness, you do not, as a group, have to learn strategies of self-affirmation and self-love to counter the opposing, culturally dominant force of mirrors in which you don't figure, have no reflection, or are given images of yourself which do in any way reflect the selves you see inside" (Busia 1998: 269-273).

So one can imagine how green I was about racial matters during my early years in Canada. I had no idea that race mattered so much, that whites and Blacks were living racially structured lives, and that there existed a racially hierarchical society in which people occupied structural or institutional positions by virtue of their "racial" belonging. It was quite a revelation. I learned very quickly about race. But what is this thing called "race" that has occupied us for so long? Why does race matter so much?

There is consensus among most social scientists today that "race" as we have come to know and use it in society is arbitrarily and socially defined (James 1999). The proposition that race is a "social and cultural construction" has almost become an academic cliché. All the same, an examination of Canadian history shows that what W.E.B. Du Bois once called the "color line" is indeed a social and cultural construction, created to differentiate racial groups and to show the superiority or dominance of one race over another. Indeed, as Rosenblum and Travis (2000: 16-17) note:

> The term *race* first appeared in the Romance languages of Europe in the Middle Ages to refer to breeding stock. A "race" of horses described common ancestry and a distinctive appearance or behavior. *Race* appears to have been first applied to New World peoples by the Spanish in the 16th century. Later it was adopted by the English, again in reference to people of the New World, and generally came to mean "people," "nation," or "variety." By the late 18th century, when scholars became more actively engaged in investigations, classifications, and definitions of human populations, the term "race" was elevated as the one major symbol and mode of human group differentiation employed extensively for non-European groups.... [Thus] the idea of race emerged among all the European colonial powers, although their conceptions of it varied. However,

only the British in North America and South Africa constructed a system of rigid, exclusive racial categories and a social order based on race, a "racialized social structure."

Pointing out, then, that "race continues to be one of the most salient and significant categories into which we place people in this society," James Jones, in his *Prejudice and Racism* (1997: 3) states, "We create these social categories, place people in them, and then treat members of the categories on the basis of the labels we have affixed to them."

How one is treated in these social categories depends on whether you belong to the "historically advantaged majorities" or the "historically disadvantaged minorities." It does not matter that these categories are "socially imagined and not biologically real categories." But because we continue to act as if these social categories are real and to associate people's colours with their "races," the concept of race has become real in its consequences. Thus, "whether or not 'black' people and 'white' people actually exist is not as important as the fact that human beings behave as if they do" (Allahar 1993: 39). So race becomes important because we make it important. Hence, "From the constructionist perspective, race exists because we have created it as a meaningful category of difference among people" (Rosenblum and Travis 2000: 18). It is a very powerful social force.

Indeed, few issues in our time have possessed such an overpowering impact upon the world as race. All over the world racial divisions, discrimination, and conflict have created problems for societies. In North America, race and its lingering effects of racism continue to be a grave source of advantage and disadvantage. Racism continues to operate under an ideology that justifies the dominance of one race over another (Mura 1999).

So, what do I mean by racism?

For the sake of my argument here, I will employ a number of definitions of racism. Specifically, I refer to racism as "the way that relations between [whites] and [Blacks] are organized such that Whiteness is perceived as normal and neutral while blackness stigmatizes groups and individuals as exceptional, problematic, exotic, or threatening" (Thompson 1997: 10). It presupposes a "belief in the inherent superiority of one race over all others and thereby the right to dominance" (Lorde 1992: 496).

Looking at the concept historically, Manning Marable (1992: 5) adds that racism is "a system of ignorance, exploitation, and power

used to oppress African Americans ... and other people on the basis
of ethnicity, cultures, mannerisms, and color." Rooted in European
global expansion that began in the late fifteenth century, it is the
"ideology that considers a group's unchangeable physical characteristics to be linked in a direct, causal way to the psychological or intellectual characteristics, and that on this basis distinguishes between
superior and inferior racial groups" (Feagin and Feagin 1996: 7).

This singling out of groups on the basis of real and alleged physical characteristics has been used over time to connote the more
common term *race*, and the approach has used colour and other
physical characteristics to signify who is "inferior" or "superior." In
other words, racism has meant:

> an ideology promoting an uncritical acceptance, and negative
> social definitions of a group often identified by physical fea-
> tures (e.g., skin color); and is premised on the belief in the cul-
> tural and biological superiority of a particular racial group over
> others. Insofar as racism is supported by a system of inequality
> and oppression constructed within societies, it is more than
> individual; it is structural and institutional. (James 1995: 49)

In this regard, and viewed in the U.S. context, "Racism can be
viewed as the socially organized set of attitudes, ideas, and practices
that deny African Americans and other people of color the dignity,
opportunities, freedoms, and rewards that this nation offers" (Feagin
and Vera 1995: 7).

From these definitions of racism we can deduce two significant
points: first, the belief of one group to be superior; and, second, the
group that believes itself to be superior has the power to carry out its
racist behaviour (Solorzano 1997). This it does, as David Wellman
points out in his *Portraits of White Racism*, on an "advantage based
on race." According to Wellman (1993: 4), "Regardless of its historically specific manifestations, racism today remains essentially what it
has always been: a defense of racial privilege." In this regard,
Frankenberg (1993b: 54) adds, "It is a position of structural advantage, associated with 'privileges' of the most basic kind, including,
for example, higher wages, reduced chances of being impoverished,
longer life, better access to healthcare, better treatment by the legal
system, and so on."

These points take the position that racism is about institutional
power and privilege. In this case, racism is not simply a matter of
bigotry or prejudice, and that is where the problem arises. I believe
that when whites say Blacks are racist, what they really mean is that
Blacks are *prejudiced*. They consider prejudice and racism to be one

and the same. I think there is a qualitative difference between the two, and they should not be confused or used interchangeably. What do I mean by prejudice here? I like the definition provided by Jones in his *Prejudice and Racism* (1997:10). He defines prejudice as "a positive or negative attitude, judgement, or feeling about a person that is generalized from attitudes or beliefs held about the group to which the person belongs." This definition of prejudice is qualitatively different from the other various definitions of racism. If "racism is a system of power as well as of beliefs and actions, [and] through which the power and resources of a given society are distributed unequally and unjustly" (Mura 1999: 102), then it is not the same as prejudice (Codjoe 1998).

Is there such a thing as Canadian racism? You bet there is

What is interesting about the discussion of race relations and racism in Canada is its denial. There is a folk wisdom in Canada that holds the view that "we do not have a Black problem." We love our Black people here. There is no racial hostility. It's those nasty Americans who hate their Black people. As George Elliott Clarke (1998: 100-1) notes, "The most significant difference between Canada and the U.S. is, finally, that America has a race problem. In Canada, the party line goes, there are no racists save those who watch too much American television. Whenever some blatantly racist event transpires, the official line is to deny it." Most Blacks are still puzzled about how Canada has been able to maintain a reputation for tolerance and harmony when it comes to race relations. Even the Economic Council of Canada, in "Economic and Social Impacts of Immigration" (1991), published just before its closure in June 1992, concluded, "There is no significant discrimination against immigrants in general or coloured immigrants in particular" (quoted in Reitz 1993: 32). However, as J.G. Reitz and R. Breton (1994: v) say in the Foreword to their book *The Illusion of Difference: Realities of Ethnicity in Canada and the United States*, "Canadians think of themselves as being more tolerant of racial minorities, more welcoming of newcomers, more respectful of cultural differences than their neighbours to the south." But, they note, this is more illusion than reality. As Stanley Barrett (1987: 307, 325) notes, "Racism in Canada has been institutionalized.... Racism in this country is as deeply rooted as that in the United States." Indeed, as Reitz and Breton contend, there may be only an illusion of difference between Canada and the United States when it comes to race relations. They point out:

The general cultural differences between Canada and the United States imply differences of tone in ethnic and race relations in the two countries. The Canadian style is more low-key than the American; moreover, Canadians have a conscious tradition of tolerance that Americans do not have. *In terms of their effects on the experiences of minority groups, however, these differences are more apparent than real.* (1994: vi; emphasis added)

Like most Blacks in Canada I have experienced my share of Canadian racism. I have been through—several times—the ugly rite of passage every Black person has to go through in North America: being called a "nigger." These epithets hurt, but the most insidious one is the one called "smiling racism" or "quiet racism" (Chigbo 1989); and they say Canada is well known for this mode of racism because "White Canada imagines itself to be congenial, hospitable, tolerant" (Clarke 1998: 101; see also Chigbo 1989). This racism is the covert type: "Persons making covert, racially biased decisions do not explicitly broadcast their intentions; instead, they veil them or provide reasons that society will find more palatable" (Scheurich and Young 1997: 5). I have heard many Blacks in Canada say they would prefer the American "no holds bared racism in your face" to Canada's "stab me behind my back racism." Whenever I think of my experiences of getting a job in Canada, I couldn't help but agree with the covert nature of Canadian racism.

When I left university to look for a job, I was armed with an undergraduate and two graduate degrees. I thought my job search would be easy. I was wrong. After failing in one province, I moved to another. It was still the same. I was so desperate that I took a job working in a restaurant. By the time I got my first interview for a position that befitted my educational qualifications, I had applied for and received rejection letters from more than two hundred positions. I kept every one of those letters. That period was the most difficult of all the years that I have lived in Canada. It was a traumatic experience, one that I will never forget.

My first job was a temporary position. I believed the supervisor who hired me just took pity on me. In those job interviews I did everything that needed to be done. I spent money on polished resumés. I printed them on expensive paper. Maybe I spoke too softly at the interviews. I began to speak louder and clearer. Maybe I didn't look the interviewer straight in the face. I gazed. Maybe my handshake was not strong enough. I squeezed hard. Maybe I wasn't dressed well enough. With some help, I bought an expensive suit.

Maybe I didn't ask enough questions. I bombarded my interviewers with questions. Nothing worked. Well, I couldn't help with my accent. That I could not change. What was it then? What was I not doing right? Nonetheless, I persisted.

My break came after two years of unemployment. I will never forget how I got that first full-time, permanent job. I had applied for the position the first time I saw it. It suited me well. It didn't ask for the ubiquitous "Canadian experience." It looked very good, I applied for it, and my application worked. I went for an interview. By that time I had been to so many job interviews that I had become a pro. I eased through the interview, so I thought. I felt good. A week or so later the rejection letter arrived. They had found a suitable candidate. A few days after, I saw the same job ad again. How could that be? Maybe it didn't work out with the acceptable candidate, I thought. I applied again. I am sure they recognized my resumé. I was called for an interview. The routine and questions were the same. The interviewers were the same. I felt confident. I had been down this road before. My handshake was unusually firm.

I anxiously awaited the good news this time. It did not come. Another rejection letter. *Tant pis.* Maybe next time. I continued to look. In a week or so, there it was again: the same job ad for which I had been rejected twice. I couldn't believe it. What was going on? So I applied again, though I debated that move this time. I was so desperate, almost two years without work, that I went for it. I thought this time I would not be called for an interview. They had seen enough of me. I was wrong. To my surprise, I was called again for an interview. It was the same supervisor of the unit and the same human resource personnel who met with me. The supervisor jokingly remarked about the number of times we had met.

The interview went fine. When I went home, I did something I had never done before. I wrote a letter to the supervisor. It went something like this:

> You have interviewed me several times for this job. Obviously, you deemed me qualified; otherwise you wouldn't be inviting me for interviews. The job calls for a graduate degree. I have two. You want a Canadian citizen or a landed immigrant. I have Canadian citizenship. True, I don't have experience, but the job says it's an entry one and does not specify much experience. What are you looking for exactly? What is it am I saying at the interview that does not convince you that I can do the job? I know I am qualified to do the job. I can do it. Just give me a chance to prove myself. You can always get rid of me if you think I am not up to it. I beg you to give me a chance to prove myself. That's all I'm asking for. Please.

I prayed and mailed the letter. God answered my prayers. I made it. My two-year search for a job was over. When I reported to work the first day, the supervisor told me that it was my letter that finally made him hire me. Apparently, he had agonized over it. There was no doubt in my mind that had I been white, I would have had the job the first or second time. Meanwhile, I knew all my white class-mates had landed jobs, even though I had better academic creden-tials. In fact, some were embarrassed to see me still looking for work. We all knew the reason, but couldn't say.

I know some readers might be skeptical of this story, but my case is not alone. I know many Africans and Black Canadians who have had a difficult time finding good work. These are people with excellent academic credentials, and if it had not been for the colour of their skin they would have quickly become gainfully employed. My own brother, armed with an M.B.A., could not find work; in the end he settled for a job as a dishwasher. Indeed, considerable research and reporting document the racism and discrimination that Black Canadians suffer from in gaining employment, and detail the experiences of the many educated Black and Asian immigrants who end up in lowly jobs (see, for example, Henry 1994; Malarek 1985; Chigbo 1989; Ip 1988; Canadian Press 1994; Canada 1985). The instances of racist hiring practices are endemic in Canadian society. The systematic and substantial barriers to equality in employment are overwhelming.

Ironically, I had to move to the United States, considered by Canadians to be more racist, to get a job as director of a research institute. I know it would have been hard, if not impossible, to get such a job in Canada. My brother, too, had to move to the United States to find a job more commensurate with his graduate business education, and he now works as a vice-president with a major bank in New York City. He tried many times to land a position with a Canadian bank but never did receive an interview. I know many Canadians of African origin who have also moved to the United States and found meaningful work, which is a shame. As Africans, some of us have worked very hard to integrate and become Canadian. Yet we were always racially defined as the "other." No matter how much we tried, it appears that the standards for full membership as a Canadian are still related to whiteness.

Canada's "smiling racism" was with me until the very day I left the country. The realtor who showed our house to prospective buyers quietly hinted that if I wanted my house to sell quickly, I would have to remove all traces of anything that indicated that Blacks had lived in the house: no family pictures, no African art or crafts, everything Black or African must go, and we must be out of the house before he showed the house to prospective buyers. He would call and let us know. No matter what we were doing, we must leave. One time we were late in getting out and we ended up hiding in our minivan in the garage. When he showed the garage, we ducked. It was a shameful and degrading experience. The house sold, but my wife and I never did meet the family that bought it. What this and other experiences taught me is best summed up by L. Steinhorn and B. Diggs-Brown (1999: 78): "What is so corrosive for Blacks is that there is no escaping these racial indignities. No matter how much you've accomplished, no matter how wealthy you may be, no matter how many people you employ, presumptions are made about you that are based solely on the colour of your skin."

You bet there is racism in Canada. Poll after poll has shown that Canadians are not really tolerant of people who are not white, and that, on the contrary, they are a "systematically racist people whose very institutions are exclusive" (Paris 1995).

So, is there such a think as Black racism?

Show me a white Canadian who has to go through what I and many African Canadians go through finding work, and I will tell you there is no such thing as Black racism. When Tatum (1997: 10) is asked in her workshops on race relations, "Can people of colour be racist?" she replies, "The answer depends on your definition of racism." She continues:

> If one defines racism as a racial prejudice, the answer is yes. People of color can and do have racial prejudices. However, if one defines racism as a system of advantage based on race, the answer is no. People of color are not racist because they do not systematically benefit from racism. And equally important, there is no systematic cultural and institutional support or sanction for the racial bigotry of people of color. In my view, reserving the term "racist" only for behaviours committed by whites in the context of a white-dominated society is a way of acknowledging the ever-present power differential afforded whites by the culture and institutions that make up the system of advantage and continue to reinforce notions of white superiority.

I also share the view expressed by Feagin and Vera (1995: x):

> What is often referred to as "black racism" consists of judgements made about Whites by some black leaders or commentators to the effect that "no White people can be trusted" or

"the White man is the devil." But these critical ideas or negative prejudices are not the equivalent of modern White racism. The latter involves not just individual thoughts but also widely socialized ideologies and omnipresent practices based on entrenched racialized beliefs. The prejudice and myths used to justify anti-black actions are not invented by individual perpetrators, nor are they based on personal experience. These patterns of highly racialized thought are embedded in the culture and institutions of a White-centered society.

Whites who say Blacks are racist tend to view or define racism in individual terms and to treat bias among Blacks as if it were fundamentally more fearsome than bias among whites. But this is a weak argument. It is a limited and narrow definition of racism. Seeing racism as a form of prejudice is not sufficient if we correctly conceptualize racism as "institutional and structural," that is, as "a network of traditions, legitimating standards, material and institutional arrangements, and ideological apparatuses that, together, serve to perpetuate hierarchical social relations based on race" (Thompson 1997: 9). This means that it is wrong to restrict our understanding of racism to an individualized arena, because that approach serves as a barrier to a broader and more comprehensive understanding of the phenomenon. Racism is more than a matter of individual prejudice and scattered episodes of discrimination (James 1995; Mura 1999; Feagin and Vera 1995).

Believe me, there is no such thing as Black racism

Deep inside, whites know that Blacks have a hard time, but will not acknowledge it. I am sure my white friends knew that the problems I had finding work had to do with race. Now, don't get me wrong. I have known whites who have also had a hard time finding work. But their experiences pale in comparison to what many African Canadians go through on a daily basis. Sometimes, when I relate experiences of discrimination to white colleagues, they find it hard to believe. I am sure that there are Blacks who make up or exaggerate their personal experiences with racism. But I know it did not take my white classmates two years to find work. Some found work even before they graduated.

Again, the racism most Blacks face is structural and institutional. The barriers that are erected when Africans look for work are prime examples. Let's take the issue of "Canadian experience." Many of us were born outside of Canada and so have no "Canadian experience" when we apply for work. In my case, I came to Canada when I was young. I had never worked before. But when it came time to look for work, I knew my accent would be a problem. In fact, I was told so by many. There was really nothing I could do about it. I have known some African friends who tried very hard to get rid of their African accents. Indeed, some tried so hard it would be difficult to tell they were African if you were speaking to them on the telephone. Yet, they tell me, when they show up for job interviews, employers are shocked to find they are Black, but not before they remark how well they speak English. It is always a no-win situation. According to Grace-Edward Galabuzi, a Ugandan immigrant and former co-ordinator of Toronto-based Alliance for Employment Equity, "Blacks suffer from discrimination in employment," but "Africans suffer more than most because of their accent." This structural barrier "is further compounded by the stereotypical image of Africans as primitive and incompetent." Consequently, according to Galabuzi, "The majority end up working at menial jobs because they are excluded from jobs commensurate with their qualifications" (quoted in Chigbo 1989: 438).

I know many whites would not trade places with Blacks. This reminds me of a *Nightline* program I watched several years ago. It was a segment on racial division in America. Whites who moments earlier had denied that racism was a problem finally conceded that being Black might be more difficult than being white. One man remarked, "I'd rather be white. It's easier. I admit that it's easier to be white. I admit that Blacks got a bad hand dealt to them." When the moderator asked how much compensation they would seek if they were to change from white to Black, one said, "I would take $50 million, then I could live anywhere. I wouldn't have to deal with any racism" (quoted in Berger 1999: 12).

That story goes to show "the value that White people place on their own skins. Indeed, to be White is to possess a gift whose value can be appreciated only after it is taken away " (quoted in Mura 1999: 125-26). Black comedian Chris Rock captured this in a monologue: "There ain't no White man in this room that will change places with me—and I'm rich! That's how good it is to be White. There's a one-legged busboy in here right now that's going: 'I don't want to change. I'm gonna ride this White thing out and see where it takes me'" (Harmon 2000). "Whiteness," as a research respondent told Frankenberg (1993b: 51), is "a privilege enjoyed but not acknowledged, a reality lived in but unknown."

So believe me when I say there is no such thing as Black racism. If we understand racism as structural, then it's difficult to say Blacks can be racist. At the same time, I would be foolish and dishonest to say that some Blacks do not harbour any hostilities towards whites. But to say that whites are as vulnerable to Black prejudice as Blacks are to white racism is stretching it. Those experiences cannot be the same. Race and racism are far more powerful in determining the life chances of Blacks than they are for whites. I can say that Black prejudice or so-called racism towards whites is not pervasive.

I don't believe that as Blacks we have the power and wherewithal to discriminate and oppress whites. Whites who never live through the daily inconvenience and degradation of being Black don't fully and perhaps never will understand how profoundly different the Black daily experience is from theirs. Notes Marian Wright Edelman in her book The *Measure of Our Success: A Letter to My Children and Yours*: "It is utterly exhausting being Black—physically, mentally, and emotionally.... There is no respite or escape from your badge of colour" (quoted in Feagin and Sikes 1995: 3). No white person in North America can say with honesty that they have suffered in such ways because of "black racism." Blacks are still far more likely than whites to identify race discrimination as a pervasive problem in North American society. The lengths to which many whites will go to avoid intimate contact with anything Black shows how Blacks have been stereotyped and demonized as a people.

The notion of "Black racism" is, therefore, a contradiction in terms. More than most groups in North America, Blacks bear the stigma of "the savage" and "continue to be seen as an inferior species, not only unsuited for equality but not even meriting a chance to show their worth. White immigrants only hours off the boat, while in some cases subjected to scorn, are allowed to assert their superiority to Blacks" (Hacker 1992: 14). This has always been the case.

Blacks don't make up the stories of oppression. They are real. They are not fantasies. But instead of being avoided, or ignored—instead of constantly running up against the brick wall of silence—racism must be acknowledged, confronted, and talked about. There must be understanding and respect for the diversity of Canadian society. There is so much we can all do together as Canadians to make this world a better place for all. To paraphrase Martin Luther King, Jr., we should all be judged by the content of our character and not by the colour of our skins. It may be a dream, but it is a dream worth fighting for.

WORKS CITED

Berger, M. 1999. *White Lies: Race and the Myths of Whiteness.* New York: Farrar, Straus, Giroux.

Busia, A.P.A. 1998. "Re-locations—Thinking Britain from Accra, New York, and the Map Room of the British Museum." In *Multicultural States: Rethinking Difference and Identity,* ed. D. Bennett. New York: Routledge.

Chigbo, O. 1989. "Land of 'Smiling Racism': Canada's Image as a Racially Tolerant Society Is a Myth," *West Africa,* March 20-26: 438.

Clarke, George Elliott. 1998, "White Like Canada," Transition, Issue 73, 7, 1:98–109.

Codjoe, H.M. 1994. "Black Nationalists Beware! You Could Be Called a Racist for Being 'Too Black and African.'" In *Talking about Difference: Encounters in Culture, Language and Identity,* ed. Carl E. James and Adrienne Shadd. Toronto: Between the Lines.

Feagin, J.R. and H. Vera. 1995. White Racism: The Basics. New York: Routledge.

Feagin, J.R. and M.P. Sikes. 1994. Living with Racism: The Black Middle-Class Experience. Boston: Beacon Press.

Frankenberg, Ruth. 1993. "Growing up White: Feminism, Racism and the Social Geography of Childhood." Feminist Review, 45: 51–84.

Hacker, A. 1992. *Two Nations: Black and White, Separate, Hostile, Unequal.* New York: Charles Scribner's Sons.

Harmon, A. 2000. "A Limited Partnership—How Race Is Lived in America."

James, Carl. E. 1995. "Reverse Racism": Students' Response to Equity Programs. *Journal of Professional Studies,* 3, 1.

_____. 1999. *Seeing Ourselves: Exploring Race, Ethnicity and Culture.* Toronto: Thompson Educational Publishing.

Jones, James. 1997. *Prejudice and Racism.* 2nd ed. New York: McGraw-Hill.

Lorde, Audre. 1992. "Age, Race, Class, and Sex: Women Redefining Difference," In Race, Class, and Gender: An Anthology, ed. M.L. Anderson and P. Hill Collins. Belmont, Cal.: Wadsworth Publishing.

Mura, David. 1999. "Explaining Racism to My Daughter," In *Racism Explained to My Daughter—With Response from W. Ayers, L.D. Delpit, D. Mura, and P. Williams,* ed. T.B. Jellon. New York: The New Press.

Paris, Edna. 1995. "Adapting to Canada and Racism." *The Globe and Mail,* March 4, 1995.

Reitz, J.G. and R. Breton. 1994. *The Illusion of Difference: Realities of Ethnicity in Canada and the United States.* Toronto: C.d. Howe Institute.

Robinson, Randall, 1999. *Defending the Spirit: A Black Life in America.* New York: Plume Books

Rosenblum, K.E. and T.C. Travis. 2000. "Constructing Categories of Difference." In *The Meaning of Difference: American constructions of Race, Sex and Gender, Social Class, and Sexual Orientation,* ed. K.E. Rosenblum and T.C. Travis. 2nd ed. Boston: McGraw-Hill.

Scheurich, J.J. and M.D. Young 1997. "Colouring Epistemologies: Are Our Research Epistomologies Racially Biased?" *Educational Research,* 26, 4: 4–15.

Solorzano, G.D. 1997. "Images and Words that Wound: Critical Race Theory, Racial Stereotyping, and Teaching Education." *Teacher Education Quarterly,* Summer: 5–19.

Thomson, A. 1997. "For: Anti-Racist Education." *Curriculum Inquiry,* 27, 1: 7–44.

Wellman, D.T. 1993. *Portraits of White Racism.* 2nd ed. Cambridge: Cambridge University Press.

TOPICS FOR DISCUSSION

1. Why does Codjoe call issues of race relations and racism in Canadian society "a contentious subject"? What definitions of racism does he use in his argument?

2. Based on the author's experiences, explain how an African is "socialized into racialized thinking" upon arriving in Canada.

3. Why does Codjoe view race as a "constructed" rather than "real" category?

4. What is the meaning of "smiling racism" in Canada? What examples of "smiling racism" are quoted in the essay?

5. According to the author, why is the notion of "Black racism" a contradiction in terms?

Vinita Srivastava

Vinita Srivastava lives in Toronto. She works as a radio artist, poet, writer, and social activist. She has published a children's book, A Giant Named Azalea *(1991), which makes visible the inadequacies of Canadian multiculturalism. The story addresses racial conflicts as seen from the perspective of Shanti, a young South Asian girl, whose friendship with another girl, Jackie, becomes threatened when Jackie's mother refuses to let them play together.*

The story "Grappling" deals with race and gender discrimination entrenched in the judicial system. More specifically, it shows the ordeal of a female victim of sexual assault who is forced to relive her trauma on the witness stand facing her attacker. Although the woman's race and ethnicity compound the gender bias evident during her cross-examination, she manages to triumph in the end.

Grappling

Vinita Srivastava slowly sank underground. As she sank, her eyes slipped to the sign denoting the subway station. Occupying her mind with only tangible visuals, she noncommittally noticed long winter coats and walking stereos on their way to work.

Subway signs look like tombstone markings.

Court today. Fourth bloody day.

Another sleepless night. (What would help—to spend it with you?)

Another sleepless night. Explanations don't expand from my tongue. I am alone on a busy street. So many kisses and extended arms. If I were more alone would I want them? I am a submarine. Armoured. Trapped in a smaller world. I am a caged animal, let out only to jump through fired hoops at the circus. Trained, fed and stalked.

There is a delay at the Doncaster subway. I should have walked. Vinita fixed her eyes on the large yellow and black poster in front of her. Join the fast track through courses at George Brown College. Join the fast track. Join the fast track. Join the fast track. George Brown College. Join the fast track. At least a five minute delay they announce. Mob mentality last time the subway went out. I wish everybody had decided to throw out temporality. Spirituality sit. Instead it looked like Chicken Little was right. (The sky was falling.) People running by—angry that you too are not in a rush. Storming off to life-saving-boardroom-shelters. Join the fast track. I'll be late. Join the fast track....

This courthouse was once beautiful. Now, holes in the stairs, uneven marble, and smokers everywhere. So what if I was two hours late yesterday? Not as if they needed me to testify until today. No need for them to put an APB on me. Vinita approached Mr. Looks-like-Michael-moustache.

"Where were you? We were supposed to start at seven o'clock this morning!"

Cop humour. Vinita smiled for him.

More people here today. Odd group. There's my bench. Empty. Mr. Moustache stands as usual. Strange how that worked. Those not remotely belonging to the judicial system sit, those who do, stand. Strange how it also splits up men and women. Pretty soon I'll be surrounded by suit legs, and pipes and cigarettes. Vinita takes a seat on the very hard bench outside courtroom number 126 in front of the "No Smoking, Maximum Fine $1000.00" sign.

Yes, officer, I'd like to report three lawyers breaking the law on the second floor of Old City Hall.

Yes, all smoking. Yes, all male, Yes, all arrogant.

What's wrong. WRONG. What's wrong?

Yes, I'd like to report something strange going on in my street. Another battle. Fist on fist. Scream. Inside I am growing, swelling, bursting, running through orange stomachs, hoping for a nice blue instead. The orange liquid concrete in my stomach and my shoulders slowly solidifies. I have been thrown into a small blue pool. All four corners are visible. Then, as the concrete sinks, not at all.

The two young men in the odd group outside the courtroom harmonize to occupy themselves.

I write the songs that make the whole world sing.

Wonder why everyone thinks they're here on drug charges? Vinita slowly swallowed the small group to her left. An old woman in a grey coat and slippers, three young women in pantsuits and high heels, and two long-haired young men in jeans. Together, a family. How can I file for divorce, Mama? the young woman asks.

Amazing Grace.

How Sweet the Sound.

What do you want a divorce for?

Steve. Vinita maintained her façade of reading her book as she waited to learn more.

Hush little baby don't say a word.

He's dead, you don't have to divorce a dead man. You're a widow.

Vinita smiled. Getting up to relieve the wooden bench, Vinita strained to see inside number 126.

Look! There.

The glass window on the door to the courtroom. Feels like I'm looking through Him's glasses. The egg-eyed sergeant arrived bearing coffee. The four police officers, and the custodian/witness enveloped the sergeant. Vinita remained fixed, unsure. The janitor was still upset that he went outside in the cold to smoke, while the lawyers stayed warm.

Have some coffee, Vinita, the sergeant prescribed. But not too much or you'll be in the bathroom all afternoon. At least that's what coffee does to me, the sergeant chuckled, looking up for approval. After the cream and sugar, the police officer lived on the Toronto's Daily Tabloid.

Police officers ogling sunshine girls. I can't hide my disapproval any more. It's too obvious. Chicken wings and beer and degrading woman jokes. Night out on the town. Damn.

Noticing Vinita's alienation from the group of men, the officers offered her the golden boy.

No thanks. (Small black-and-white versus full colour page.)

I don't read that OTHER paper. They're biased against us, one of the officers justified to Vinita. Oh. What about the other one? There ARE three. (Vinita clenched to casually continue.)

Look, the sergeant glared, that's not the immigration truck that comes in here every morning. It's a truck full of city criminals coming to court. And they think we're racist. Can't help if there are more black criminals in this city.

Living in this city we are told that we are wonderfully multicultural. But I know this society of multi-cultures as one culture of vultures circle above us looking for rotting meat.

Beat the rap man! A black youth shouts to the black un-uniformed police officer sitting next to the Mr. Moustache on the bench outside the courtroom.

You'll be next, Vini-TTa, a sergeant warns, make sure you're not chewing any gum or they'll make you stick it on the end of your nose! The sergeant shakes his head, marvelling at his own humour.

Vinita Sree-vis-ta-va, a court guard announces, struggling with the name, causing the courtroom waiters to look up at Vinita getting

up from her wooden bench. Vinita stretches into court number 126.
A black gown with red trimming envelopes the white judge. Eagle
face. Heard she's turned MAN. Mahogany everything. Kermit the
Frog green. White faces. Large old windows, beautiful, but ruined by
the heating radiators underneath them. A large viewing gallery.

All rise.

I thought they only did that in movies.

The defendant makes a show of trying to rise out of his wheelchair. Asshole. He didn't need a wheelchair four months ago.

Hold the Bible in your right hand and swear.

Shit. Funny. Just listen to the man. Hindu by birth, non-
religious by choice. My anger swells. I wonder if they have a copy of
the Koran, or the Bhagavadgita, or the Torah, or any other sacred
documents besides the Bible? Aren't they supposed to offer us a
choice?

Without too much apparent hesitation, Vinita picked up the
pocket Bible on her right.

Do you promise to tell the whole truth and nothing but the
truth?

NO!? How would they know if someone was lying? I thought
all witnesses got some sort of chair. Even if it is a hard wooden one.
But remain standing and uncomfortable please. Mr. Young
Moustache told me to be extra polite to Mr. Weasel. Defence hates
it when you answer their weasely questions politely.

Spell your full name please.

V-I-N-I-T-A. S as in Sam, R-I, V as in Victor, A-S . . .

Next?!

Recount. Srivas-T-A-V-A.

Miss Ser-Vis-Tah; is that the correct pronunciation? The
defence lawyer smiled as he looked directly at Vinita.

Uh no, but don't worry about it. Vinita looked down slightly.

The defence lawyer gave a large smile.

O! But we must.

All right, if the weasel insists (let's make him speak Hindi). The
correct pronunciation is Vinita Shrrevastahvah. Vinita pronounced
with extreme rapidity.

Miss Sree vaas ta va? The defence attorney politely asked. Knew
I'd get him. No victory.

No. Vinita smiled. Shrrevastahvah, Vinita calmly replied with
her grade two teacher-like voice. Slower, anglicized, articulated.

He still mispronounced it. Small victories. Pretty shallow.
Weasel. Trying to make friends. His smile looks phony.

Do NOT return that smile. My tiny battles are turned big by
new hatreds, useless victories. Why am I here?

Vinita, can you tell us what happened to you on the night of December 8, 1988 at approximately 9:04 pm?

Seems like they already know what happened. Why am I here? They will not make me cry.

In detail? Vinita looked up for support towards the crown attorney, who offered none. Felt like I was being followed as soon as I left the subway.

A woman talked into a Darth Vadar mask. Or maybe it's more like an airplane oxygen mask. It looks smelly. For the record. A very small moustached man sits directly to her right. He is holding a small paperback. Probably Plato. What's he doing here?

What time exactly did you arrive on the subway platform?

EXACTLYYYYY? Who knows EXACTLY what time it is ever? It did TOO happen.

How many seconds were you on the platform before you noticed another man?

One Mississippi, two Mississippi. I don't know. Shut up.

When you first looked up, how far away was he?

Think. Wish I could close my eyes. I am afraid, was afraid. Ten feet, ten yards? Ten metres?

You've indicated that the platform was empty when he first yelled. And to be fair to you, I have used your word "yell." Would you say that if other people were there on the platform they would have heard this "yell"?

Indicated. Said. Justice. Vantage points. I can't get another. I only know what I heard, I can't give you any information about someone else's vantage point. Vinita answered somewhat facetiously. The School of Philosophy, thank you Socrates for your arrogance.

Describe your attacker.

My memory shuts off. Look. I said look. Come. I said come with me. I start with me in my red jacket. No. Later, at home, I am wearing the green. He wears a charcoal grey coat just past or above his knees. Stubble. White. Charcoal hair. Thin hair. Behind his ears. Mid-fifties. Hands holding knife.

Forget. Forget. NO. I said forget.

Describe his voice.

It was gruff. Vinita replied, after a pause, directly to the defence lawyer, avoiding her peripheral view of the man in the wheelchair to her left.

What was the tone and how deep was his voice?

Tone. Timbre. Weasel. I am fed up, and I don't care. He RAN four months ago. What's he doing in a wheelchair?

Do you sing? He was an alto, and definitely not a baritone.

Vinita smiled into a giggle.

Weasel. Not so serious any more. I still have concrete shoulders.
Back room watchers didn't think court was like this.

It is aggravatingly unclear.

Hands with knives and nicotine stains. Now, hands that turn
the wheelchair. WHEELCHAIR.

I am an angry animal waiting to get out. I want to make him
RUN now like he did before. RUN. Instead I jump through fire. I
am trained. I am fed. I am stalked.

How big was his knife?

Confusion. The weasel smiles, noting the confusion on my face.
Well, was it uh, six inches, twelve inches, one, ... or ... ah ... two
... inches thick? Surely you must have some idea? Vinita attempts to
demonstrate with her two hands. But for the record, it must be said.

I am a locomotive labouring along. He must look so nice to
those others, an elderly harmless man, with slicked hair, in a blue
suit, in a wheelchair.

How was he holding the knife? Like this ... like this ... or
maybe like this? The weasel moves his hands in yet another position.

Is there anything else you can tell me about his hands?

Think. Was it really like this? High. Yes. His hands are high in
his chest.

You mean you didn't notice all the nicotine stains, the brown
spots, all over his hands?

Silence, the court feels silent. You fool. Maybe his knife wasn't
so big. Did I really see his hands? The crown attorney looks like
she's given up.

The knife, not the hands. The hands do not matter. I saw the
knife.

I wonder if years from now people will say to the weasel;
Remember when you put that guy in that wheelchair? That was the
most brilliant move of your defence career.

I fall backward in time to the beginning.

I am not yet eleven years old. I remember my mother, my busy,
caring, wonderful mother. We are shopping together. Stainless steel
pans. Plastic boxes. Books and Toys. Mittens. Every aisle that I go to
so does the man behind me. I am scared.

WHAT IS HE DOING?

Suddenly aching to find my mother or my sister who I do find
in the Books and Toys. So does the man behind me.

Determined to find my mother I grab my sister and, calm and
terrified, find shelter in the stainless steel with my unsuspecting
mum.

I leap back to the present and realize that the face of the man in
the wheelchair looks like the face of the man in the store.

I want to get rid of this man. Play judge. Why is killing someone a dream? I think about my drugstore psychology.

Yesterday a man on the bus stared and stared. The woman across from me looked up to him, looked down again.

HOLD your head up. I silently scream.

She is reduced to ashamed embarrassment. He followed her off the bus—I wanted to come between them—but he was quick. I wanted to trip him.

I walk out of courtroom number 126. Determined. I am too angry to cry. Hold. I said hold your head up.

The sergeant comes to shake my hand.

I leave the courthouse. People walk around me and through me. Just like the cold wind that travels into my body. The cold air enters my body and then becomes warm air, and I am aware of the warmth that my body radiates.

Then I spot the weasel.

I'm sorry I was so rough on you in there. But it's a job and somebody had to do it.

I say nothing to him. But I am filled with pride. Look, just look. He knows I have power.

I can see through to him. And he is shocked by my strength.

Like the stars grappling desperately for a space to be seen through the clouds, I burst into the space around me. Grappling. I am a resilient, reticent, glowing star.

My dance is quiet. Glorious. And I am power.

TOPICS FOR DISCUSSION

1. What stylistic devices are used so as to capture emotional changes in the narrator? Explain the shifts in the use of pronouns from third-person ("Vanita") to first-person ("I").

2. Find examples of situations or references in the text that reveal the narrator's gender consciousness and her perception of sexism in her environment.

3. How are law enforcement and the legal system depicted in the story? What gender and race biases are shown to exist in this context?

4. Explain the meaning of "grappling" in the title of the story.

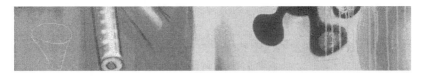

LANGUAGE/
CULTURE/
DISPLACEMENT

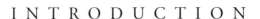

INTRODUCTION

One of the most difficult problems of multiculturalism is the privileged status of bilingualism and marginalization of languages other than English and French. While for most Canadians fluency in one of the official languages is a necessity, different writers in this unit ponder different aspects of linguistic enrichment or linguistic dispossession that may be caused by the influence of the dominant language. In the context of globalization and Canada's postcolonial situation, the processes of hybridization (or mixing) of languages and creation of different language diasporas seem to be inevitable. As a result, we see both the emergence of several varieties of English that are assigned a lesser status by mainstream speakers, and the presence and flourishing of diverse cultures in their traditional heritage languages.

What often fails to be addressed in the debates about multiculturalism and language policies is the tragedy of disappearing Native languages. Unlike Basil Johnston, whose essay is included in this unit, the writer Emma LaRocque views the relationship of Native cultures to English less in terms of oppressor language, but as a language that today has a potential to unify Native peoples. However, the fate of Native cultures and languages in Canada illustrates yet another danger, in addition to extinction, namely, the danger of appropriation. According to the Native arts critic Loretta Todd, cultural appropriation occurs "when someone else speaks for, tells, defines, describes, represents, uses, or recruits the images, stories, experiences, dreams of others for their own. Approrition occurs also when someone else becomes the expert on your experience, and they are deemed more knowledgeable about who you are than yourself." Fighting for their right to speak in their own voice, Native writers explain that Native stories, when "retold" from another culture's perspective, lose their traditional functions. Native storytelling is inspired by such characteristics of Native cultures as dependence on oral traditions, recognition of the spiritual as central to daily life, the view of the individual as grounded in the community, and the view of art as related to political values. It reminds us of the complexities involved in the relationship between languages and cultures that are not always accessible through translation.

Christl Verduyn

*Born in Amsterdam, Christl Verduyn is of Dutch extraction. She teaches
Canadian literature, Canadian studies, and women's studies at Wilfrid
Laurier University in Waterloo, Ontario. Her academic interests revolve
around multiculturalism, women's life writing, and ethnic and Québécois
literatures. She writes both in English and in French. She has authored and
edited many scholarly publications, including* Margaret Laurence: An
Appreciation *(1988),* Dear Marian, Dear Hugh: The MacLennan-
Engel Correspondence *(1995),* Lifelines: Marian Engel's Writings
(1995), for which she received the Gabrielle Roy Book Prize, and Marian
Engel's Notebooks *(1999). She is editor of* Literary Pluralities *(1998), a
volume of essays on Canadian multicultural writing, and* Aritha Van
Herk: Essays on Her Works *(2001). "Entranced" comes from her collection of poems* Silt *(Guernica 2002).*

Entranced

les extrêmes se touchent
my father says
curving over
his work
words born
died
carved in stone

chisel and hammer
he shapes words
foreign to him

for me words
a new world

fingers lingering
I trace letter
by letter

let her
learn them
as I make them
says the father
to the mother

and I enter language
as my father
engraves

a beginning
this engraving

I am enthralled
wholly
entranced

TOPICS FOR DISCUSSION

1. Christl Verduyn's poem can be read as an extended metaphor, where an ordinary situation acquires a deeper symbolic meaning. What specific childhood memory does the speaker recall? Why has the moment captured in the poem become meaningful to her?

2. What ideas can be implied by slipping from "words" to "worlds" and by using the image of "entering"?

3. What does the poem suggest about the differences between the father and the daughter?

Eva Hoffman

*Eva Hoffman was born in 1945 in Cracow, Poland, to a family of
Holocaust survivors; they left for Canada when she was fourteen years old.
After a few years in Vancouver, she went to study in the United States,
where she completed her Ph.D. in English at Harvard University. She has
been an editor of* The New York Times Book Review *and now lives in
London, England. She has published* Lost in Translation *(1989), from
which the following excerpt has been taken;* Exit into History: A Journey
Through the New Eastern Europe *(1993), a travelogue of her visit to
post-communist countries; and* Shtetl: The Life and Death of a Small
Town and the World of Polish Jews *(1997), a study of the history of
Bransk, a small town that functions as a microcosm of Polish-Jewish relations.* Lost in Translation *is an autobiographical text in which she analyzes
her immigrant experience in terms of a linguistic and psychological make-
over that accompanies her transition from one culture to another. She
describes the frustrating ironies of learning a second language and the
attendant loss of identity; she also explores how fluency in a language sets
up a class structure.*

from Lost in Translation

Every day I learn new words, new expressions. I pick them up
from school exercises, from conversations, from the books I take out
of Vancouver's well-lit, cheerful public library. There are some turns
of phrase to which I develop strange allergies. "You're welcome," for
example, strikes me as a gaucherie, and I can hardly bring myself to
say it—I suppose because it implies that there's something to be
thanked for, which in Polish would be impolite. The very places
where the language is at its most conventional, where it should be
most taken for granted, are the places where I feel the prick of
artifice.

Then there are words to which I take an equally irrational
liking, for their sound, or just because I'm pleased to have deduced

their meaning. Mainly they're words I learn from books, like "enigmatic" or "insolent"—words that have only a literary value, that exist only as signs on the page.

But mostly, the problem is that the signifier has become severed from the signified. The words I learn now don't stand for things in the same unquestioned way they did in my native tongue. "River" in Polish was a vital sound, energized with the essence of riverhood, of my rivers, of my being immersed in rivers. "River" in English is cold—a word without an aura. It has no accumulated associations for me, and it does not give off the radiating haze of connotation. It does not evoke.

The process, alas, works in reverse as well. When I see a river now, it is not shaped, assimilated by the word that accommodates it to the psyche—a word that makes a body of water a river rather than an uncontained element. The river before me remains a thing, absolutely other, absolutely unbending to the grasp of my mind.

When my friend Penny tells me that she's envious, or happy, or disappointed, I try laboriously to translate not from English to Polish but from the word back to its source, to the feeling from which it springs. Already, in that moment of strain, spontaneity of response is lost. And anyway, the translation doesn't work. I don't know how Penny feels when she talks about envy. The word hangs in a Platonic stratosphere, a vague prototype of all envy, so large, so all-encompassing that it might crush me—as might disappointment or happiness.

I am becoming a living avatar of structuralist wisdom; I cannot help knowing that words are just themselves. But it's a terrible knowledge, without any of the consolations that wisdom usually brings. It does not mean that I'm free to play with words at my wont; anyway, words in their naked state are surely among the least satisfactory play objects. No, this radical disjoining between word and thing is a desiccating alchemy, draining the world not only of significance but of its colors, striations, nuances—its very existence. It is the loss of a living connection.

The worst losses come at night. As I lie down in a strange bed in a strange house—my mother is a sort of housekeeper here, to the aging Jewish man who has taken us in return for her services—I wait for that spontaneous flow of inner language which used to be my night-time talk with myself, my way of informing the ego where the id had been. Nothing comes. Polish, in a short time, has atrophied, shriveled from sheer uselessness. Its words don't apply to my new experiences; they're not coeval with any of the objects, or faces, or the very air I breathe in the daytime. In English, words have not penetrated to those layers of my psyche from which a private conversation could proceed. This interval before sleep used to be the time when my mind became both receptive and alert, when images and words rose up to consciousness, reiterating what had happened during the day, adding the day's experiences to those already stored there, spinning out the thread of my personal story.

Now, this picture-and-word show is gone; the thread has been snapped. I have no interior language, and without it, interior images—those images through which we assimilate the external world, through which we take it in, love it, make it our own—become blurred too. My mother and I met a Canadian family who live down the block today. They were working in their garden and engaged us in a conversation of the "Nice weather we're having, isn't it?" variety, which culminated in their inviting us into their house. They sat stiffly on their couch, smiled in the long pauses between the conversation, and seemed at a loss for what to ask. Now my mind gropes for some description of them, but nothing fits. They're a different species from anyone I've met in Poland, and Polish words slip off them without sticking. English words don't hook on to anything. I try, deliberately, to come up with a few. Are these people pleasant or dull? Kindly or silly? The words float in an uncertain space. They come up from a part of my brain in which labels may be manufactured but which has no connection to my instincts, quick reactions, knowledge. Even the simplest adjectives sow confusion in my mind; English kindliness has a whole system of morality behind it, a system that makes "kindness" an entirely positive virtue. Polish kindness has the tiniest element of irony. Besides, I'm beginning to feel the tug of prohibition, in English, against uncharitable words. In Polish, you can call someone an idiot without particularly harsh feelings and with the zest of a strong judgment. Yes, in Polish these people might tend toward "silly" and "dull"—but I force myself toward "kindly" and "pleasant." The cultural unconscious is beginning to exercise its subliminal influence.

The verbal blur covers these people's faces, their gestures with a sort of fog. I can't translate them into my mind's eye. The small event, instead of being added to the mosaic of consciousness and memory, falls through some black hole, and I fall with it. What has happened to me in this new world? I don't know. I don't see what I've seen, don't comprehend what's in front of me. I'm not filled with language anymore, and I have only a memory of fullness to anguish me with the knowledge that, in this dark and empty state, I don't really exist.

For my birthday, Penny gives me a diary, complete with a little lock and key to keep what I write from the eyes of all intruders. It is that little lock—the visible symbol of the privacy in which the diary is meant to exist—that creates my dilemma. If I am indeed to write something entirely for myself, in what language do I write? Several times, I open the diary and close it again. I can't decide. Writing in Polish at this point would be a little like resorting to Latin or ancient Greek—an eccentric thing to do in a diary, in which you're supposed to set down your most immediate experiences and unpremeditated thoughts in the most unmediated language. Polish is becoming a dead language, the language of the untranslatable past. But writing for nobody's eyes in English? That's like doing a school exercise, or performing in front of yourself, a slightly perverse act of self-voyeurism.

Because I have to choose something, I finally choose English. If I'm to write about the present, I have to write in the language of the present, even if it's not the language of the self. As a result, the diary becomes surely one of the more impersonal exercises of that sort produced by an adolescent girl. These are no sentimental effusions of rejected love, eruptions of familial anger, or consoling broodings about death. English is not the language of such emotions. Instead, I set down my reflections on the ugliness of wrestling; on the elegance of Mozart, and on how Dostoyevsky puts me in mind of El Greco. I write down Thoughts. I Write.

There is a certain pathos to this naïve snobbery, for the diary is an earnest attempt to create a part of my persona that I imagine I would have grown into in Polish. In the solitude of this most private act, I write, in my public language, in order to update what might have been my other self. The diary is about me and not about me at all. But on one level, it allows me to make the first jump. I learn English through writing, and, in turn, writing gives me a written self. Refracted through the double distance of English and writing, this self—my English self—becomes oddly objective; more than anything, it perceives. It exists more easily in the abstract sphere of thoughts and observations than in the world. For a while, this impersonal self, this cultural negative capability, becomes the truest thing about me. When I write, I have a real existence that is proper to the activity of writing—an existence that takes place midway between me and the sphere of artifice, art, pure language. This language is beginning to invent another me. However, I discover something odd. It seems that when I write (or, for that matter, think) in English, I am unable to use the word "I." I do not go as far as the schizophrenic "she"—but I am driven, as by a compulsion, to the double, the Siamese-twin "you."

My voice is doing funny things. It does not seem to emerge from the same parts of my body as before. It comes out from somewhere in my throat, tight, thin, and mat—a voice without the modulations, dips, and rises that it had before, when it went from my stomach all the way through my head. There is, of course, the constraint and the self-consciousness of an accent that I hear but cannot control. Some of my high school peers accuse me of putting it on in order to appear more "interesting." In fact, I'd do anything to get rid of it, and when I'm alone, I practice sounds for which my speech organs have no intuitions, such as "th" (I do this by putting my tongue between my teeth) and "a," which is longer and more open in Polish (by shaping my mouth into a sort of arrested grin). It is simple words like "cat" or "tap" that give me the most trouble, because they have no context of other syllables, and so people often misunderstand them. Whenever I can, I do awkward little swerves to avoid them, or pause and try to say them very clearly. Still, when people—like salesladies—hear me speak without being prepared to listen carefully, they often don't understand me the first time around. "Girls' shoes," I say, and the "girls'" comes out as a sort of scramble. "Girls' shoes," I repeat, willing the syllable to form itself properly, and the saleslady usually smiles nicely, and sends my mother and me to the right part of the store. I say "Thank you" with a sweet smile, feeling as if I'm both claiming an unfair special privilege and being unfairly patronized.

It's as important to me to speak well as to play a piece of music without mistakes. Hearing English distorted grates on me like chalk screeching on a blackboard, like all things botched and badly done, like all forms of gracelessness. The odd thing is that I know what is correct, fluent, good, long before I can execute it. The English spoken by our Polish acquaintances strikes me as jagged and thick, and I know that I shouldn't imitate it. I'm turned off by the intonations I hear on the TV sitcoms—by the expectation of laughter, like a dog's tail wagging in supplication, built into the actors' pauses, and by the curtailed, cutoff rhythms. I like the way Penny speaks, with an easy flow and a pleasure in giving words a fleshly fullness; I like what I hear in some movies; and once the Old Vic comes to Vancouver to perform *Macbeth*, and though I can hardly understand the particular words, I am riveted by the tones of sureness and command that mold the actors' speech into such majestic periods.

Sociolinguists might say that I receive these language messages as class signals, that I associate the sounds of correctness with the social status of the speaker. In part, this is undoubtedly true. The class-linked notion that I transfer wholesale from Poland is that belonging to a "better" class of people is absolutely dependent on speaking a "better" language. And in my situation especially, I know that language will be a crucial instrument, that I can overcome the stigma of my marginality, the weight of presumption against me, only if the reassuringly right sounds come out of my mouth.

Yes, speech is a class signifier. But I think that in hearing these varieties of speech around me, I'm sensitized to something else as well—something that is a matter of aesthetics, and even of psychological health. Apparently, skilled chefs can tell whether a dish from some foreign cuisine is well cooked even if they have never tasted it and don't know the genre of cooking it belongs to. There seem to be some deep-structure qualities—consistency, proportions of ingredients, smoothness of blending—that indicate culinary achievement to these educated eaters' taste buds. So each language has its own distinctive music, and even if one doesn't know its separate components, one can pretty quickly recognize the propriety of the patterns in which the components are put together, their harmonies and discords. Perhaps the crucial element that strikes the ear in listening to living speech is the degree of the speaker's self-assurance and control.

As I listen to people speaking that foreign tongue, English, I can hear when they stumble or repeat the same phrases too many times, when their sentences trail off aimlessly—or, on the contrary, when their phrases have vigor and roundness, when they have the space and the breath to give a flourish at the end of a sentence, or make just the right pause before coming to a dramatic point. I can tell, in other words, the degree of their ease or disease, the extent of authority that shapes the rhythms of their speech. That authority—in whatever dialect, in whatever variant of the mainstream language—seems to me to be something we all desire. It's not that we all want to speak the King's English, but whether we speak Appalachian or Harlem English, or Cockney, or Jamaican Creole, we want to be at home in our tongue. We want to be able to give voice accurately and fully to ourselves and our sense of the world. John Fowles, in one of his stories in *The Ebony Tower*, has a young man cruelly violate an elderly writer and his manuscripts because the legacy of language has not been passed on to the youthful vandal properly. This seems to me an entirely credible premise. Linguistic dispossession is a sufficient motive for violence, for it is close to the dispossession of one's self. Blind rage, helpless rage is rage that has no words—rage that overwhelms one with darkness. And if one is perpetually without words, if one exists in the entropy of inarticulateness, that condition itself is bound to be an enraging frustration. In my New York apartment, I listen almost nightly to fights that erupt like brushfire on the street below—and in their escalating fury of repetitious phrases ("Don't do this to me, man, you fucking bastard, I'll fucking kill you"), I hear not the pleasures of macho toughness but an infuriated beating against wordlessness, against the incapacity to make oneself understood, seen.

Anger can be borne—it can even be satisfying—if it can gather into words and explode in a storm, or a rapier-sharp attack. But without this means of ventilation, it only turns back inward, building and swirling like a head of steam—building to an impotent, murderous rage. If all therapy is speaking therapy—a talking cure—then perhaps all neurosis is a speech dis-ease.

TOPICS FOR DISCUSSION

1. How does Hoffman describe the situation of a person transplanted from one linguistic universe to another? What is the connection between language and "self"?

2. How does a beginner experience a new language? What does it mean that "the signifier has become severed from the signified"?

3. What frustrations and paradoxes are involved in learning a new language? Why does Hoffman feel that any translation from one language to another is inadequate?

4. How does social context determine the use of language? How do "class signals" affect her perception of accent? When can "self-assurance and control" in the use of language be achieved?

5. What does "linguistic dispossession" mean to Hoffman? How does she react to the initial loss of her mother tongue? Why does she have trouble deciding which language to use in her private diary?

Genni Gunn

Genni Gunn was born in Italy and came to Canada when she was eleven. She has published six books: two novels—Tracing Iris *and* Thrice Upon a Time; *a short story collection,* On the Road; *a prose/poetry collection,* Mating in Captivity; *and two collections of poetry by Dacia Maraini, translated from the Italian,* Devour Me Too *and* Traveling in the Gait of a Fox. *Her prose, poetry, and translations have appeared and been anthologized in journals in Canada and the U.S. including* Story, Best Canadian Stories, *and* The Journey Prize Anthology.

The Middle Ground

They came to live in Vancouver after her husband died: Rosalba and her small son, Claudio—her son who, in spite of her husband's persistent teachings, grew more Canadian each year. When he was born, Giulio had made her promise to speak only Italian to the boy—a rule she insisted upon even now that he was almost six. But the boy grew more Canadian each year. He would sit on her lap and listen attentively to stories (in Italian, always in Italian) about her parents. "*Il nonno e la nonna,*" Rosalba had taught him to say. But he had no grandparents here, no olive trees and no watermelons to hug. Claudio told her the other children laughed when he told them these stories. The boy had never been to Italy. His imagined homeland was no different to him than Canada had been to Rosalba before she came. It was not his fault that he could not remember the taste of prickly-pears, persimmons and fresh fruit.

In Vancouver, Rosalba bought persimmons in a little Chinese store on Commercial Drive. But they had been picked too soon and she could not find the right words to describe their real taste.

She'd been in Canada almost ten years, had come at nineteen to live in Victoria where Giulio taught Italian Studies at the University. But Rosalba had always loved Vancouver, its mountains and ocean so close together she could almost smell the Adriatic Sea: Trieste leaning lazy against low-slung mountains, rooftops baked ruddy in the hot summers. From the viewpoint up near the Conservatory in Queen Elizabeth Park, she could almost imagine herself sitting on the stone wall of the old castle that overlooked Trieste. Only the cobblestones were missing and the long steep hills and curved narrow roads leading to the university. In Vancouver, a different beauty: the clumps of evergreens, cedar-shake roofs and coloured houses. Then the downtown high-rises jutting into the sky, dwarfed by the backdrop of mountains.

She came to Vancouver to teach Italian at a school set in Little Italy and filled with a mixture of first and second-generation Italian teenagers. It had been the natural thing for her to do, now that Giulio was gone. Many of the students came from small villages in southern Italy and spoke only dialects. Most had never learned proper Italian grammar. Strange that she should be the one to recreate with patience a language and a culture for strangers' children—she, who could not keep her own son from becoming Canadian.

The changes had been subtle. Like the night he'd asked her to read him a story in English, although she always read to him from *Il Tesoro*. She had been raised on it herself. The thick red volume with gold-embossed printing on the cover, the fairy-tales and jokes and pictures—all part of her childhood. She could almost recite each word by heart. She'd said "no," of course, and read him his favourite story. But the next day, seized with unbearable guilt, she'd gone to a book store and bought *Peter Pan*, in English.

And another evening, when he'd asked if they could order pizza with pineapple on top, she'd said, "absolutely not, that's not real pizza," and had made him one at home, the way her mother had taught her. But later, she'd opened a can of pineapple chunks and let him put them on top of his. She was trying to keep him Italian, but the boy grew more Canadian each year.

In the ten-block radius encircling Commercial Drive, a new Italy had been established long before she came. Here, families lived the traditional roles of their homeland. Some women were still clad in dark dresses that reached to below their knees, their elbows covered with shawls and cardigans. It made Rosalba think of Goya's *Disasters of War*. All that black—black skirts, black hair, black eyes. Only the shop windows on Commercial Drive twinkled with vibrant colours. Mannequins sporting the newest fashions from Rome smiled into the street, eyes vacant, smooth blond bobs and turned-up noses. Rosalba wished they didn't look so *American*. She'd always said *America* when she was in Italy, even though she'd been speaking of Canada. From across the ocean, there had been only one continent, no differentiation between countries. She supposed it was the same for Italy. Canadians thought of Italians as one people—all born of the same fat little dark-haired Italian Mother Earth. But she had only to think of her youth, of the many provinces and dialects, of the animosity between North and South, water and mountains.

She had chosen Vancouver, when her husband died, because of Commercial Drive, because of the mountains and the ocean. When the insurance money came, she went house-hunting with Claudio. At first, they looked in the Italian district. Rosalba tip-toed politely from house to house. "The bathroom counters are all marble. My husband had it sent direct from Italy, you know." Windows shuttered, floors glistening, Madonnas mounted on corner altars in the hall. "And that couch belonged to my grandmother. But we're going back. I'll sell it, if you're interested." Plaster busts of Roman Emperors; outdoors, lions guarding a driveway and at the back, a clothesline to the hydro pole. "These dryers make clothes yellow." And the neighbours peering from doorsteps. "And where are you from, Signora?" All so *Italian*. After the fifth house, Rosalba hurried Claudio into the car seat and drove back to their rented apartment. Inside, she took a deep breath and leaned back on the couch. She had panicked back there, among icons, and idols; she felt she might be absorbed into their darkness, their familiarity. She waited a few days, then contacted a real-estate firm. She asked the school secretary to call for her. "It's my accent," she explained apologetically. "They think I'm stupid."

The real-estate lady showed her houses on the West Side, tall beautiful wooden houses made of bleached grey cedar and nicked with skylights that captured the dawn. She loved these monolithic structures, the white inner walls and the echo of her heels on the hardwood floors. Although she longed to live in one of these houses, she settled finally on a sturdy, squat bungalow with precise rectangular windows with nine panes in each. She bought it because of its cream stucco exterior that reminded her of the white stone of her parents' house. She bought it because it seemed more *Italian*, and this was her concession for not buying one within the Italian district.

She enrolled Claudio in first grade at the elementary school just two blocks away from their new home and made arrangements to have a babysitter take him there in the mornings and pick him up at the end of the day. She had to leave much earlier than he did, to drive across town and be settled into the classroom before her students arrived.

"Now don't you let anyone call you anything but *Claudio*," she said on the first morning, squeezing him to her and wishing she could go with him. "Repeat it slowly if they say it wrong." Rosalba hated the way people here pronounced her name "Rozelba" or "Ruzolba," as if there were no such thing as a soft *r* or *s*. Often, she tried to break it down phonetically: "Ross-al-ba," or "Row-sal-ba, like rosary," she'd say. But they forgot too soon.

At her school, she noticed Peppi Armano immediately. He had a physical disability and always entered her ninth grade class after all the other students were seated. He mumbled an apology although his eyes—black moons in round white saucers—were defiant.

He walked slowly, painfully, his small hands grasping the combination locks on the lockers that lined the hallways. Her classroom was upstairs, and she grew accustomed to the shuffling of feet after the bell had rung. At times, she watched Peppi make his way up or down the stairs, one foot at a time on each step. She wanted to help him, to take his free hand, the one which was not so tightly clasped to the banister, and walk down with him, but she was afraid to show her concern because Peppi kept his head down and stared only at his feet. At the end of the first week, he stayed after class and stood in front of her desk until she prompted him, "Is there something I can do?"

He blushed and for a moment let go of her desk with both hands, trying to stand up straight as he spoke. "About my being late," he said in a muffled, quiet voice, "I have to wait until the others have gone. It's easier when I can hold on to the lockers. My legs ... ," he stopped and leaned against the desk and Rosalba felt tears sting her eyes.

"I understand," she said. But she didn't and later, asked the Principal about it.

"Friedreich's ataxia," the Principal told her. "His parents want to buy him a wheelchair, but he won't hear of it. He's a very stubborn boy. We've talked to him on many occasions."

After that, it seemed her ears were attuned to the sound of Peppi's small feet as they dragged through the halls. She could hear lock after lock swinging on its gate after he'd passed. She imagined she could count the lockers by his steps, by his hands which clung to the round black dials. She asked the Principal if she could have a room on the bottom floor. But he said it was impossible to reroute the school for Peppi. There were too many classes, too many students, too many timetables. "We have to do what's best for the majority," he said. And Rosalba lay in bed at night and tried to think of ways to help one small boy.

She noticed that Peppi remained reserved and always a little apart from the rest of the students. On one occasion, when she organized an after-school trip to the Italian Cultural Centre to see an Italian film, Peppi did not come. She waited for him until one of the students told her that his brother had taken him home at the usual time.

Rosalba went to see Mrs. Crombie, the school counsellor, to ask about Peppi's family.

"As far as we can tell," Mrs. Crombie said, "the parents are overprotective. The boy has no friends—in fact, goes nowhere without either one of his parents or his brother. If only he'd agree to use a wheelchair." She paused. "Has he talked to you about it?"

Rosalba shook her head.

"Poor kid. Last year, we tried talking to the parents ... but you know how it is with these families. They believe they're doing what's best for him." She tapped her pen on her desk for a moment, then looked up at Rosalba. "Why don't you talk to them? They might listen to you, if you spoke in their language."

Their language. Rosalba noticed the choice of words. Mrs. Crombie had not said, *your language. Their language*, as if *they* were somehow different from her. She said, "It's *my* language too."

And Mrs. Crombie smiled. "Yes, but you're different."

Strange the concept of foreigners. And how cultures could be massed under one umbrella. Yet individuals were considered separate. She wanted to shout, "I'm Italian." But she shook her head instead and said nothing. When she was still in Italy and the tourist season began, she had thought of all Americans in the same way. She had never considered each person as separate and distinct, but rather had seen Americans as a collective of brash, loud, forward people, with bermuda shorts and cameras. And when she'd had occasion to meet one, she too had thought that one person was different. The prejudice, then, came out of ignorance, out of the stereotypes they all accepted.

"What is a Wop?" Claudio asked.

Rosalba said, "Schoolchildren often give names to things they don't understand. You are *Italian.*"

"I don't want to be Italian," Claudio said, "because Italians are Wops. And I don't want to be a Wop."

The first few weeks of school passed quickly. She was busy with marking papers, remembering names, preparing a five-minute skit in Italian to be performed for the school. I must do something about Peppi, Rosalba thought, just as soon as I'm more settled. She became aware that Claudio had started to speak English to her at home. At first, he began with a sentence here and there that she asked him to repeat in Italian, as if she couldn't understand.

Two months into the school year, Claudio announced, "I'm not going to speak Italian at home any more."

Rosalba pleaded with him (in Italian), "You'll forget the language," she said. Then, "If your father were alive, he'd be heartbroken."

But Claudio was obstinate. "I don't want to," he said. "What's the use of it, anyway? Nobody in my school speaks Italian."

And Rosalba went to bed feeling guilty and thought about what Giulio would have done in this case. Giulio would have enrolled the boy in a school in the Italian district, where he would be with other Italian children. Each day, he grew more Canadian. And she was afraid to draw him back, to make him live a life he'd never known. She noticed that her students at school were distressed, secretive, trying to cope with the mixture of cultures—their survival dependent on the separation rather than the integration of the two. Was it fair, she thought, to force them to abide by rules that made no sense here, rules which had been implemented for a different culture in a different time?

What startled her the most was that the majority of the Italians she'd met adhered to strict oppressive customs to which she had not been exposed even in Italy. They had brought with them a culture several decades old. Things changed, times changed even in Italy, but these people insisted on remaining the same. "If you stand still, you go backward." She'd read that somewhere, and now the words appeared to make much more sense.

Rosalba asked Peppi to come and see her after school.

"I'll have to phone my brother and tell him what time to pick me up."

"I'll call him," Rosalba said, "and tell him not to come."

He looked at her doubtfully. "Oh, he'll come anyway."

Peppi arrived at 4:00 p.m., after the school halls had thinned out. He stood at her desk and when she told him to sit down, he reluctantly did so. She thought that if he could have managed it, he would have run out of the room, so much did he resemble a trapped animal.

She stared at the papers on her desk and tried to find opening words. "Peppi," she finally began. "I had a talk with Mrs. Crombie."

"It's about the wheelchair, isn't it? Why does everyone talk behind my back?"

"No one is talking behind your back. We're all very concerned about you. Your parents—"

"I'm tired of their concern." His voice rose in pitch. "They always decide everything for me. Nobody asks me what I want."

She stared at him for a moment, then asked softly, "What do *you* want, then?"

"I want to—be myself," he said. "I want to do things myself. They treat me like I can't even think."

"Maybe they're trying to do what's best for you." She paused. "If you can think for yourself, then surely you must realize that a wheel-chair would help you tremendously."

"I can manage just fine on my own."

She said nothing, waiting, noting the tremor in his words.

"And besides, if I get the stupid wheelchair, they'll never let me out of their sight. I don't want it!"

"You know," Rosalba said after a moment. "It might not be at all how you think. With a wheelchair, you'd be able to get around on your own a lot easier. For instance, you wouldn't need anyone to take you to or from school."

"Oh sure. As if they'd let me go alone." He sat, quiet, staring at his hands. "I'm not even allowed to go to a movie by myself. Not unless Papa drives me. It's *embarrassing*. Being watched all the time. If it wasn't for the law here, I bet I wouldn't even be allowed to go to school; they'd keep me at home always."

"Do you want me to talk to them?" she asked.

He shrugged. "I don't think it would do any good."

A few days later, Rosalba called Peppi's parents and asked them to come to the school to speak to her. She distinctly said she wanted to see them both.

They came a little past six. She'd asked the babysitter to stay late, even though Claudio had insisted that he was old enough to be left alone for a few hours. Mr. Armano was short and round and Rosalba could see that the boy's beauty came from his mother. She was dressed much older than her years. She could not have been much more than thirty, yet she carried herself like an old woman. Her hair was smoothed back into a bun at the nape of her neck, tight and shiny, making her eyes—Peppi's eyes—appear even larger and rounder than they were. Mrs. Armano kept wringing her hands. "Is something wrong?" Mr. Armano said in English as soon as he walked into the room. "Peppi did something bad? We teach him in the house. We give him the manners—"

"No," Rosalba interrupted, and spoke in Italian. "He's done nothing wrong. He's a very good student."

The Armanos looked at her, puzzled. "Then why did you want us to come if there's nothing wrong?"

Rosalba made them sit in two of the desks of the classroom. She explained to them that Peppi was growing up, that he needed to spend time with people his own age. She asked them why Peppi had not come to see the film with the class.

Mrs. Armano clenched and unclenched her hands on her lap. "He's sick," she said.

"He has a *physical* disability," Rosalba said more sharply than she'd meant to, "but this doesn't mean he can't do a lot of things other boys his age do."

Mrs. Armano looked away. "But he might hurt himself—"

"Mrs. Armano, it's part of growing up. You know that. You've raised another boy."

"Yes, but Peppi is different," she said solemnly.

"Perhaps you're trying to keep him different," Rosalba concluded.

And that night, after she tucked Claudio into bed, she thought about the Armanos, about the fine line between protectiveness and suffocation, about Peppi's symbolic stand against it. She heard Claudio's voice a few days earlier:

"Mamma, don't hold my hand when we're out."

"But why not?"

"I'm too old and Jimmy says only babies hold their mother's hand."

She had told him about her family—her brothers and sisters—and how they still held hands even as adults. But he'd slipped his fingers out of hers as she talked and hooked them into the opening of his pocket. Claudio becoming more Canadian—was she, too, trying to keep him different?

She acted as mediator between Peppi and his parents, spoke to them twice more over the next month, and was finally able to convince them to agree to a compromise: they would allow Peppi to come to school alone if he used the wheelchair. It was only a small concession, but for Peppi, the first triumph of a new independence.

She watched him anxiously that first day, his hands caressing the chrome of the large new wheels. He smiled shyly at her at the end of the day, when he left her classroom with the other teens.

She sat at her desk, long after they'd all gone, and thought about Claudio and herself. She too was trying to do what was best for him. She thought of Giulio, his smile there in Trieste. He'd preserved laughter and bittersweet memories like pressed flowers of intense moments with his family and friends. He had not been rigid. He had embraced the new way of life and enriched it with the old.

Rosalba remained in her classroom, thinking, until the janitor asked her to leave so he could lock up the school.

When she arrived home, she saw Claudio sitting at his little table, drawing a picture for her. "I missed you," he said in Italian and buried his face in her skirt. "I missed you too, Claudio," she answered in English. Then she took him onto her lap and told him stories of Italy.

TOPICS FOR DISCUSSION

1. Why does Rosalba's nostalgia for her Italian past seem meaningless to her son Claudio? Why does she want to keep him from being Canadian? What are the "subtle changes" that Claudio undergoes in becoming more Canadian?

2. What conflicts over the use of the mother tongue may arise in immigrant families? What difficulties in maintaining the mother tongue are highlighted by the story?

3. Why does Rosalba doubt the validity of imposing rules "implemented for a different culture in a different time"? Why does she panic "among icons and idols"? Why do immigrant cultures often become fossilized?

4. How does the part of the plot involving Peppi's oppression by his parents contribute to the unity of the story? What does Rosalba learn from this experience that helps her settle her own problems with Claudio?

5. Genni Gunn, alongside other authors such as Isabel Vincent or Ann Jew, shows different patterns of cross-cultural interactions. Discuss examples of separation (ghettoization), assimilation, and integration (Gunn's "middle ground") as models of immigrant behaviour found in their stories.

Garry Engkent

Garry Engkent was born in 1948, in Sun Wui county of the Chinese province Guangdong, and came to Canada in the 1950s. He has completed a Ph.D. in English at the University of Toronto and has taught at a number of Canadian universities and community colleges. He is currently working on a novel. With his wife Lucia, he has also written several textbooks and readers for teaching English. "Why My Mother Doesn't Speak English" was first published in the anthology of Chinese-Canadian writing Many-Mouthed Birds *in 1991. The narrator's mother has lived in Canada for decades but has never learned English for a variety of reasons. The isolation of having one language forces her to depend on others, first her husband and, after his death, her son. Introducing this story to students in one of his textbooks, Garry Engkent calls it "autobiographical fiction [that] is based on the author's life, but...is not meant to be an accurate account of what actually happened." The narrator of the story is unnamed.*

Why My Mother Can't Speak English

My mother is seventy years old. Widowed for five years now, she lives alone in her own house except for the occasions when I come home to tidy her household affairs. She has been in *gum san*, the golden mountain, for the past thirty years. She clings to the old-country ways so much so that today she astonishes me with this announcement:

"I want to get my citizenship," she says as she slaps down the *Dai Pao*, "before they come and take away my house."

"Nobody's going to do that. This is Canada."

"So everyone says," she retorts, "but did you read what the *Dai Pao* said? Ah, you can't read Chinese. The government is cutting back on old-age pensions. Anybody who hasn't got citizenship will lose everything. Or worse."

"The *Dai Pao* can't even typeset accurately," I tell her. Sometimes I worry about the information Mother receives from that biweekly community newspaper. "Don't worry—the Ministry of Immigration won't send you back to China."

"Little you know," she snaps back. "I am old, helpless, and without citizenship. Reasons enough. Now, get me citizenship. Hurry!"

"Mother, getting citizenship papers is not like going to the bank to cash in your pension cheque. First, you have to—"

"Excuses, my son, excuses. When your father was alive—"

"Oh, Mother, not again! You throw that at me every—"

"—made excuses, too." Her jaw tightens. "If you can't do this little thing for your own mother, well, I will just have to go and beg your cousin to ..."

Every time I try to explain about the ways of the *fan gwei*, she thinks I do not want to help her.

"I'll do it, I'll do it, okay? Just give me some time."

"That's easy for you," Mother snorts. "You're not seventy years old. You're not going to lose your pension. You're not going to lose your house. Now, how much *lai-shi* will this take?"

After all these years in *gum san* she cannot understand that you don't give government officials *lai-shi*, the traditional Chinese money gift to persons who do things for you.

"That won't be necessary," I tell her. "And you needn't go to my cousin."

Mother picks up the *Dai Pao* again and says: "Why should I beg at the door of a village cousin when I have a son who is a university graduate?"

I wish my father were alive. Then he would be doing this. But he is not here, and as a dutiful son, I am responsible for the welfare of my widowed mother. So I take her to Citizenship Court.

There are several people from the Chinese community waiting there. Mother knows a few of the Chinese women and she chats with them. My cousin is there, too.

"I thought your mother already got her citizenship," he says to me. "Didn't your father—"

"No, he didn't."

He shakes his head sadly. "Still, better now than never. That's why I'm getting these people through."

"So they've been reading the *Dai Pao*."

He gives me a quizzical look, so I explain to him, and he laughs.

"You are the new generation," he says. "You didn't live long enough in *hon san*, the sweet land, to understand the fears of the old. You can't expect the elderly to renounce all attachments to China for the ways of the *fan gwei*, white devils. How old is she, seventy now? Much harder."

"She woke me up this morning at six, and Citizenship Court doesn't open until ten."

The doors of the court finally open, and Mother motions me to hurry. We wait in line for a while.

The clerk distributes applications and tells me the requirements. Mother wants to know what the clerk is saying, so half the time I translate for her.

The clerk suggests that we see one of the liaison officers.

"Your mother has been living in Canada for the past thirty years and she still can't speak English?"

"It happens," I tell the liaison officer.

"I find it hard to believe that—not one word?"

"Well, she understands some restaurant English," I tell her. "You know, French fries, pork chops, soup, and so on. And she can say a few words."

"But will she be able to understand the judge's questions? The interview with the judge, as you know, is an important part of the citizenship procedure. Can she read the booklet? What does she know about Canada?"

"So you don't think my mother has a chance?"

"The requirements are that the candidate must be able to speak either French or English, the two official languages of Canada. The candidate must be able to pass an oral interview with the citizenship judge, and then he or she must be able to recite the oath of allegiance—"

"My mother needs to speak English," I conclude for her.

"Look, I don't mean to be rude, but why didn't your mother learn English when she first came over?"

I have not been translating this conversation, and Mother, annoyed and agitated, asks me what is going on. I tell her there is a slight problem.

"What problem?" Mother opens her purse, and I see her taking a small red envelope—*lai-shi*—I quickly cover her hand.

"What's going on?" the liaison officer demands.

"Nothing," I say hurriedly. "Just a cultural misunderstanding. I assure you."

My mother rattles off some indignant words, and I snap back in Chinese: "Put that away! The woman won't understand, and we'll be in a lot of trouble."

The officer looks confused, and I realize that an explanation is needed.

"My mother was about to give you a money gift as a token of appreciation for what you are doing for us. I was afraid you might misconstrue it as a bribe. We have no intention of doing that."

"I'm relieved to hear it."

We conclude the interview, and I take Mother home. Still clutching the application, Mother scowls at me.

"I didn't get my citizenship papers. Now I will lose my old-age pension. The government will ship me back to China. My old bones will lie there while your father's will be here. What will happen to me?"

How can I teach her to speak the language when she is too old to learn, too old to want to learn? She resists anything that is *fan gwei*. She does everything the Chinese way. Mother spends much time staring blankly at the four walls of her house. She does not cry. She sighs and shakes her head. Sometimes she goes about the house touching her favourite things.

"This is all your dead father's fault," she says quietly. She turns to the photograph of my father on the mantel. Daily, she burns incense, pours fresh cups of fragrant tea, and spreads dishes of his favourite fruits in front of the framed picture as is the custom. In memory of his passing, she treks two miles to the cemetery to place flowers by his headstone, to burn ceremonial paper money, and to talk to him. Regularly, rain or shine, or even snow, she does these things. Such love, such devotion, now such vehemence. Mother curses my father, her husband, in his grave.

When my mother and I emigrated from China, she was forty years old, and I, five. My father was already a well-established restaurant owner. He put me in school and Mother in the restaurant kitchen, washing dishes and cooking strange foods like hot dogs, hamburgers, and French fries. She worked seven days a week from six in the morning until eleven at night. This lasted for twenty-five years, almost to the day of my father's death.

The years were hard on her. The black-and-white photographs show a robust woman; now I see a withered, frail, white-haired old woman, angry, frustrated with the years, and scared of losing what little material wealth she has to show for the toil in *gum san*.

"I begged him," Mother says. "But he would either ignore my pleas or say: 'What do you need to know English for? You're better off here in the kitchen. Here you can talk to the others in our own tongue. English is far too complicated for you. How old are you now? Too old to learn a new language. Let the young speak *fan gwei*. All you need is to understand the orders from the waitresses.

Anyway, if you need to know something, the men will translate for you. I am here; I can do your talking for you.'"

As a conscientious boss of the young male immigrants, my father would force them out of the kitchen and into the dining room. "The kitchen is no place for you to learn English. All you do is speak Chinese in here. To survive in *gum san*, you have to speak English, and the only way you can do that is to wait on tables and force yourselves to speak English with the customers. How can you get your families over here if you can't talk to the immigration officers in English?"

A few of the husbands who had the good fortune to bring their wives over to Canada hired a retired school teacher to teach a bit of English to their wives. Father discouraged Mother from going to those once-a-week sessions.

"That old woman will get rich doing nothing. What have these women learned? *Fan gwei* ways—make-up, lipstick, smelly perfumes, fancy clothes—like whores. Once she gets through with them, they won't be Chinese women any more—and they certainly won't be white either."

Some of the husbands heeded the words of the boss, for he was older than they, and he had been in the white devils' land longer. These wives stayed home and tended the children, or they worked in the restaurant kitchen, washing dishes and cooking *fan gwei* foods, and talking in Chinese about the land and the life they had been forced to leave behind.

"He was afraid that I would leave him. I depended on him for everything. I could not go anywhere by myself. He drove me to work and he drove me home. He only taught me how to print my name so that I could sign anything he wanted me to, bank cheques, legal documents …"

Perhaps I am not Chinese enough any more to understand why my mother would want to take in the sorrow, the pain, and the anguish, and then to recount them every so often.

Once, I was presumptuous enough to ask her why she would want to remember in such detail. She said that the memories didn't hurt any more. I did not tell her that her reminiscences cut me to the quick. Her only solace now is to be listened to.

My father wanted more sons, but she was too old to give him more. One son was not enough security he needed for old age. "You smell of stale perfume," she would say to him after he had driven the waitresses home. Or, to me, she would say: "A second mother will not treat you so well, you know," and, "Would you like another mother at home?" Even at that tender age, I knew that in China a husband could take a second wife. I told her that I didn't need another mother, and she would nod her head.

When my father died five years ago, she cried and cried. "Don't leave me in this world. Let me die with you."

Grief-stricken, she would not eat for days. She was so weak from hunger that I feared she wouldn't be able to attend the funeral. At his grave side, she chanted over and over a dirge, commending his spirit to the next world and begging the goddess of mercy to be kind to him. By custom, she set his picture on the mantel and burned incense in front of it daily. And we would go to the cemetery often. There she would arrange fresh flowers and talk to him in the gentlest way.

Often she would warn me: "The world of the golden mountain is so strange, *fan gwei* improprieties, and customs. The white devils will have you abandon your own aged mother to some old-age home to rot away and die unmourned. If you are here long enough, they will turn your head until you don't know who you are— Chinese."

My mother would convert the months and the days into the Chinese lunar calendar. She would tell me about the seasons and the harvests and festivals in China. We did not celebrate any *fan gwei* holidays.

My mother sits here at the table, fingering the booklet from the Citizenship Court. For thirty-some years, my mother did not learn the English language, not because she was not smart enough, not because she was too old to learn, and not because my father forbade her, but because she feared that learning English would change her Chinese soul. She only learned enough English to survive in the restaurant kitchen.

Now, Mother wants *gum san* citizenship.

"Is there no hope that I will be given it?" she asks.

"There's always a chance," I tell her. "I'll hand in the application."

"I should have given that person the *lai-shi*," Mother says obstinately.

"Maybe I should teach you some English," I retort. "You have about six months before the oral interview."

"I am seventy years old," she says. "*Lai-shi* is definitely much easier."

My brief glimpse into Mother's heart is over, and it has taken so long to come about. I do not know whether I understand my aged mother any better now. Despite my mother's constant instruction, there is too much *fan gwei* in me.

The booklet from the Citizenship Court lies, unmoved, on the table, gathering dust for weeks. She has not mentioned citizenship again with the urgency of that particular time. Once in a while, she would say: "They have forgotten me. I told you they don't want old Chinese women as citizens."

Finally, her interview date is set. I try to teach her some ready-made phrases, but she forgets them.

"You should not sigh so much. It is bad for your health," Mother observes.

On the day of her examination, I accompany her into the judge's chamber. I am more nervous than my mother.

Staring at the judge, my mother remarks: "*Noi yren.*" The judge shows interest in what my mother says, and I translate it: "She says you're a woman."

The judge smiles. "Yes. Is that strange?"

"If she is going to examine me," Mother tells me, "I might as well start packing for China. Sell my house. Dig up your father's bones, and I'll take them back with me."

Without knowing what my mother said, the judge reassures her. "This is just a formality. Really. We know that you obviously want to be part of our Canadian society. Why else would you go through all this trouble? We want to welcome you as a new citizen, no matter what race, nationality, religion, or age. And we want you to be proud—as a new Canadian."

Six weeks have passed since the interview with the judge. Mother receives a registered letter telling her to come in three weeks' time to take part in the oath of allegiance ceremony.

With patient help from the same judge, my mother recites the oath and becomes a Canadian citizen after thirty years in *gum san*.

"How does it feel to be a Canadian?" I ask.

"In China, this is the eighth month, the season of harvest." Then she adds: "The *Dai Pao* says that the old-age pension cheques will be increased by nine dollars next month."

As we walk home on this bright autumn morning, my mother clutches her piece of paper. Citizenship. She says she will go up to the cemetery and talk to my father this afternoon. She has something to tell him.

TOPICS FOR DISCUSSION

1. Whom does Engkent have in mind as his readers? What is his purpose in using Chinese words and expressions in the story written in English?

2. Characterize the narrator's attitude to his mother. How does their relationship change in the course of the story?

3. How do the mother's old attitudes continue to colour her experience and expectations in Canada? What are the reasons why she has not learned English? Why did his father discourage her from doing so?

4. Comment on the narrator's statement that he is "not Chinese enough any more" to understand both his father's double standards for men and women and his mother's stubborn refusal to learn English.

Basil H. Johnston

*Basil H. Johnston, born in 1929 on the Parry Island Reserve, is an Ojibwa
writer, ethnologist, and educator. He was educated at Loyola College in
Montreal and the Ontario College of Education. He is the recipient of the
Order of Ontario and an honorary doctorate from the University of
Toronto. He has published fiction, autobiography, translations, humour,
poems, essays, reviews, and children's books; he has also worked for film and
television. His scholarly and writing interests focus on Ojibwa language,
history, and culture. His titles include* Moose Meat and Wild Rice
(1978), Ojibwa Heritage *(1976),* Ojibwa Ceremonies *(1978),* How
Birds Got Their Colours *(1978),* Tales the Elders Told *(1981),* Indian
School Days *(1988),* Tales of the Anishinaubaek *(1993),* The
Manitous: The Spiritual World of the Ojibwa *(1995),* The Bear-Walker
and Other Stories *(1995),* The Star Man and Other Tales *(1997), and*
Crazy Dave *(1999). Before his retirement, he worked in the department of
ethnology of the Royal Ontario Museum in Toronto. Johnston is predominantly concerned with the preservation of the language and culture of his
people who refer to themselves as Anishinaubae, or "the good beings."*

One Generation From Extinction

Within the past few years Gregor Keeshig, Henry Johnston,
Resime Akiwenzie, Norman McLeod, and Belva Pitwaniquot died.
They all spoke their tribal language, Anishinaubae (Ojibwa). When
these elders passed away, so did a portion of their tribal language
come to an end as a tree disintegrates by degrees and in stages until
it is no more; and, though infants were born to replenish the loss of
life, not any one of them will learn the language of their grandfa-
thers or grandmothers to keep it alive and to pass it on to their
descendants. Thus language dies.

In some communities there are no more Gregor Keeshigs,
Henry Johnstons, Resime Akiwenzies, Norman McLeods, Belva

Pitwaniquots; those remaining have no more affinity to their ancestral language that they do to Swahili or Sanskrit; in other communities the languages may not survive beyond a generation. Some tribal languages are at the edge of extinction, not expected to survive for more than a few years. There remain but three aboriginal languages out of the original fifty-three found in Canada that may survive several more generations.

There is cause to lament but it is the native peoples who have the most cause to lament the passing of their languages. They lose not only the ability to express the simplest of daily sentiments and needs but they can no longer understand the ideas, concepts, insights, attitudes, rituals, ceremonies, institutions brought into being by their ancestors; and, having lost the power to understand, cannot sustain, enrich, or pass on their heritage. No longer will they think Indian or feel Indian. And though they may wear 'Indian' jewellery and take part in pow-wows, they can never capture that kinship with and reverence for the sun and the moon, the sky and the water, or feel the lifebeat of Mother Earth or sense the change in her moods; no longer are the wolf, the bear, and the caribou elder brothers but beasts, resources to be killed and sold. They will have lost their identity which no amount of reading can ever restore. Only language and literature can restore the 'Indian-ness'.

Now if Canadians of West European or other origin have less cause than 'Indians' to lament the passing of tribal languages and cultures it is because they may not realize that there is more to tribal languages than 'ugh' or 'how' or 'kimu sabi.' At most and at best Euro-Canadians might have read or heard about Raven and Nanabush and Thunderbird and other 'tricksters'; some may have even studied 'Culture Myths', 'Hero Tales', 'Transformation Tales', or 'Nature Myths and Beast Fables', but these accounts were never regarded as bearing any more sense than 'Little Red Riding Hood' or 'The Three Little Pigs'. Neither language nor literature were ever considered in their natural kinship, which is the only way in which language ought to be considered were its range, depth, force, and beauty to be appreciated.

Perhaps our Canadian compatriots of West European origin have more cause to lament the passing of an Indian language than they realize or care to admit. Scholars mourn that there is no one who can speak the Huron language and thus assist scholars in their pursuit of further knowledge about the tribe; scholars mourn that had the Beothuk language survived, so much more would be known about the Beothuk peoples. In mourning the extinction of the language, scholars are implicitly declaring that the knowledge derived from a study of snowshoes, shards, arrowheads, old pipes, shrunken heads and old bones, hunting, fishing, transportation, food preparation, ornamentation, and sometimes ritual is limited. And so it is; material culture can yield only so much.

Language is crucial. If scholars are to increase their knowledge and if they are to add depth and width to their studies, they must study a native language and literature. It is not enough to know linguistics or to know a few words or even some phrases or to have access to the Jesuit *Relations,* Chippewa *Exercises,* Ojibwa *Texts,* or a *Dictionary of the Otchipwe Language.* Without a knowledge of the language scholars can never take for granted the accuracy of an interpretation of translation of a passage, let alone a single word; nor can they presume that their articles, tracts, treatises, essays bear the kind of accuracy that scholarship and integrity demand. They would continue to labour under the impression that the word 'manitou' means spirit and that it has no other meaning. Superstitious nonsense, according to the white man. They do not know that the word bears other meanings even more fundamental than 'spirit', such as, and/or pertaining to the deities; of a substance, character, nature, essence, quiddity beyond comprehension and therefore beyond explanation, a mystery; supernatural; potency, potential. What a difference such knowledge might have made in the studies conducted by Ruth Landes or Thomas B. Leekley, and others on the Anishinaubae tribe. Perhaps, instead of regarding 'Indians' as superstitious for positing 'spirits' in trees or in other inanimate or insensate objects, they might have credited them with insight for having perceived a vital substance or essence that imparted life, form, growth, healing, and strength in all things, beings, and places. They might have understood that the expression 'manitouwan' meant that an object possessed or was infused with an element or a feature that was beyond human ken; they might have understood that 'w'manitouwih' meant that he or she was endowed with extraordinary talents, and that it did not mean that he or she was a spirit.

Language is essential. If scholars and writers are to know how 'Indians' perceive and regard certain ideas they must study an 'Indian' language. When an 'Anishinaubae' says that someone is telling the truth, he says 'w'daeb-awae'. But the expression is not just a mere confirmation of a speaker's veracity. It is at the same time a philosophical proposition that, in saying, a speaker casts his words and his voice only as far as his vocabulary and his perception will enable him. In doing so the tribe was denying that there was absolute truth; that the best a speaker could achieve and a listener expect was the highest degree of accuracy. Somehow that one expression 'w'daeb-awae' set the limits of a single statement as well as setting limits on all speech.

There was a special regard almost akin to reverence for speech and for the truth. Perhaps it was because words bear the tone of the speaker and may therefore be regarded as belonging to that person; perhaps it is because words have but a fleeting momentary existence in sound and are gone except in memory; perhaps it is because words have not ceased to exist but survive in echo and continue on in infinity; perhaps it is because words are medicine that can heal or injure; perhaps it is because words possess an element of the man-itou that enables them to conjure images and ideas out of nothing, and are the means by which the autissokanuk (muses) inspired men and women. It was not for nothing that the older generation did not solicit the autissokanuk to assist in the genesis of stories or in the composition of changes in seasons other than winter.

To instil respect for language the old counselled youth, 'Don't talk too much' (Kegon zaum-doongaen), for they saw a kinship between language and truth. The expression is not without its face-tious aspect but in its broader application is was intended to convey to youth the other notions implicit in the expression 'Don't talk to much', for the injunction also meant "Don't talk too often ... Don't talk too long ... Don't talk about those maters that you now nothing about.' Were a person to restrict his discourse, and measure his speech, and govern his talk by what he knew, he would earn the trust and respect of his (her) listeners. Of that man or woman they would say 'w'daeb-awae.' Better still, people would want to hear the speaker again and by so doing bestow upon the speaker the oppor-tunity to speak, for ultimately it is the people who confer the right of speech by their audience.

Language was a precious heritage; literature was no less precious. So precious did the tribe regard language and speech that it held those who abused language and speech and truth in contempt and ridicule and withheld from them their trust and confidence. To the tribe the man or woman who rambled on and on, or who let his tongue range over every subject or warp the truth was said to talk in circles in a manner no different from that of a mongrel who, not knowing the source of alarm, barks in circles (w'geewi-animoh). Ever since words and sounds were reduced to written symbols and have been stripped of their mystery and magic, the regard and reverence for them have diminished in tribal life.

As rich and full of meaning as may be individual words and expression, they embody only a small portion of the entire stock and potential of tribal knowledge, wisdom, and intellectual attainment, the greater part is deposited in myths, legends, stories, and in the lyrics of changes that make up the tribe's literature. Therein will be found the essence and the substance of tribal ideas, concepts, insights, attitudes, values beliefs, theories, notions, sentiments, and accounts of their institutions and rituals and ceremonies. Without language scholars, writers and teachers will have no access to the depth and width of tribal knowledge and understanding, but must continue to labour as they have done these many years under the impression that 'Indian' stories are nothing more than fairy tales or folklore, fit only for juvenile minds. For scholars and academics Nanabush, Raven, Glooscap, Weesaukeechauk, and other mythological figures will ever remain 'tricksters', culture heroes, deities whose misadventures were dreamed into being only for the amusement of children. Primitive and pagan and illiterate to boot, 'Indians' could not possibly address or articulate abstract ideas or themes; neither their minds nor their languages could possibly express any idea more complex than taboos, superstitions, and bodily needs.

But were ethnologists, anthropologists, linguists, teachers of native children and writers and native literature – yes, even archaeologists – to learn a native language, perhaps they might learn that Nanabush and Raven are not simply 'tricksters' but the caricatured representations of human nature and character in their many facets; perhaps they might give thought to the meaning and sense to be found in Weesaukeetchauk, The Bitter Soul. There is no other way except through language for scholars to learn or to validate their studies, their theories, their theses about the values, ideals or institutions or any other aspect of tribal life; there is no other way by which knowledge of native life can find increase. Not good enough is to say in hushed tones after a reverential description of a totem pole or the lacing of a snowshoe, 'My, weren't they clever.'

Just consider the fate of 'Indian' stories written by those who knew nothing of the language and never did hear any of the stories in their entirety or in their original version but derived everything that they knew of their subject from second, third, and even fourth diluted sources. Is it any wonder then that the stories in *Indian Legends of Canada* by E.E. Clark or in *Manabozho* by T.B. Leekley are so bland and devoid of sense. Had the authors known the stories in their 'Indian' sense and flavour, perhaps they might have infused their versions with more wit and substance. Had the authors known that the creation story as the Anishinaubae understood it to mean was intended to represent in the most dramatic way possible the process of individual development from the smallest portion of talent to be retrieved from the depths of one's being and then given growth by breath of life. Thus a man and woman are to develop themselves, create their own worlds, and shape their being and give meaning to life. Had the authors known this meaning of the Creation Story, perhaps they might have written their accounts in terms more in keeping with the sense and thrust of the story. But not knowing the language nor having heard the story in its original text or state, the authors could not, despite their intentions, impart to their accounts the due weight and perspective the story deserved. The stories were demeaned.

With language dead and literature demeaned, 'Indian' institutions are beyond understanding and restoration. Let us turn back the calendar two and a half centuries, to that period when the 'Indian' languages were spoken in every home, when native literature inspired thought, and when native 'Indian' institutions governed native 'Indian' life. It was there that a native institution caught the imagination of the newcomers to this continent. The men and women who founded a new nation to be known as the United States of America took as their model for their constitution and government the principles of government and administration embodied in The Great Tree of Peace of the Five Nations Confederacy. The institution of The Great Tree of Peace was not then too primitive nor too alien for study or emulation to the founders of the United States. In more recent years even the architects of the United Nations regarded the 'Indian institution of The Great Tree of Peace not as primitive organization beneath their dignity and intellect, but rather as an institution of merit. There exist still 'Indian' institutions that may well serve and benefit this society and this nation, not as dramatically as did The Great Tree of Peace the United States of America, but bestow some good as yet undreamed or unimagined. Just how much good such institutions may confer upon this or some future generation will not be known unless the 'Indian' languages survive.

And what is it that has undermined the vitality of some of the 'Indian' languages and deprived this generation and this society of the promise and the benefit of the wisdom and the knowledge embodied in tribal literature?

In the case of the Beothuk and their language, the means used were simple and direct: it was the blade, the bludgeon, and the bullet that were plied in the destruction of the Beothuk in their sleep, at their table, and in their quiet passage from home to place of work, until the tribe was no more. The speakers were annihilated; no more was the Beothuk language spoken; whatever their wisdom or whatever their institutions, the whole of the Beothuk heritage was destroyed.

In other instances, instead of bullets, bludgeons, and bayonets, other means were used to put an end to the speaking of an 'Indian' language. A kick with a police riding boot administered by a 175-pound man upon the person of an eight-year-old boy for uttering the language of a savage left its pain for days and its bruise upon the spirit for life. A boy once kicked was not likely to risk a second or a third. A slap in the face or a punch to the back of the head delivered even by a small man upon the person of a small boy left its sting and a humiliation not soon forgotten. And if a boot or a fist were not administered, then a lash or a yardstick was plied until the 'Indian' language was beaten out. To boot and fist and lash was added ridicule. Both speaker and his language were assailed. 'What's the use of that language? It isn't polite to speak another language in the presence of other people. Learn English! That's the only way you're going to get ahead. How can you learn two languages at the same time? No wonder kids can't learn anything else. It's a primitive language; hasn't the vocabulary to express abstract ideas, poor. Say "ugh". Say something in your language! ... How can you get your tongue around those sounds?' On and on the comments were made, disparaging, until in too many the language was shamed into silence and disuse.

And how may the federal government assist in the restoration of the native languages to their former vigour and vitality and enable them to fulfil their promise?

The Government of Canada must finance the establishment of either provincial or regional language institutes to be affiliated with a museum or a university or a provincial native educational organization. The function of the 'institute', to be headed by a native person who speaks, reads, and writes a native language, will be to foster research into language and to encourage the publication of lexicons, dictionaries, grammars, courses, guides, outlines, myths, stories, legends, genealogies, histories, religion rituals, ceremonies, chants, prayers, and general articles; to tape stories, myths, legends, grammars, teaching guides and outlines and to build a collection of written and oral literature and to make same accessible to scholars, teachers, and native institutions; and to duplicate and distribute written and oral literature to the native communities and learning institutions. The native languages deserve to be enshrined in this country's heritage as much as do snowshoes, shards, and arrowheads. Nay! More.

But unless the writings, the essays, stories, plays, the papers of scholars, academics, lexicographers, grammarians, etymologists, playwrights, poets, novelists, composers, philosophers are published and distributed, they can never nurture growth in language or literature. Taking into account the market represented by each tribe, no commercial publisher would risk publication of an 'Indian' book. Hence, only the federal government has the means to sponsor publication of an 'Indian text', either through a commercial publisher or through the Queen's Printer. The publication of an 'Indian' book may not be a commercially profitable enterprise, but it would add to the nation's intellectual and literary heritage.

TOPICS FOR DISCUSSION

1. What evidence of the passing of Native languages does Basil Johnston present in his essay? How do languages become extinct?

2. How does he explain the value of language as oral transmission as opposed to writing?

3. According to the author, why does the loss of language lead to the demeaning of the entire culture? What other consequences does he discuss?

4. How can Native peoples and other Canadians benefit from the restoration of Native languages?

Nuzhat Amin

Nuzhat Amin was born in Pakistan and came to Canada in 1975. She has a Ph.D. in Education from OISE/University of Toronto. Her focus is on linguistic imperialism of the English language. For her doctoral research, she interviewed minority teachers of ESL (English as a Second Language) and found out that they question the dominant view that immigrants get empowered through acquisition of "Canadian" English. Nuzhat Amin has written about marginalization and has promoted equitable participation of immigrant women of colour who are highly skilled professionals. Canada recruits foreign-trained immigrants from the professional classes in the former British and American colonies. But a lot of those women who were university professors in their homelands become ESL teachers in Canada. Nuzhat Amin has been teaching women's studies at the University of Toronto and is co-editor of Canadian Woman Studies: An Introductory Reader *(1999). She also writes fiction and was the First Place Winner of the* Varsity *Short Story Contest for her story "Doe Lake Palace." The essay "South Englishes, North Englishes" was first published in 1997. Note that the expression "native speaker" in the context of ESL refers to those for whom English is a mother tongue. It is precisely native speaker versus non-native speaker models of English that Nuzhat Amin questions below.*

South Englishes, North Englishes

"That Indian accent...you'll have to get rid of it if you want to get anywhere in this field... You know, you have to learn to talk like a Canadian...."

This was in 1975 when I first came to Canada, at my first job—as an editorial assistant in a television station. I get upset even now—22 years later—when I think of the boss advising me how to make it as a journalist in Canada. Get rid of that accent....

I was an experienced journalist when I left Pakistan in 1973. I had worked for a number of years as an assistant editor in an

English-language daily newspaper in Karachi. Then I spent two years training in print, radio, and TV journalism in Germany before I emigrated to Canada.

I have spoken English all my life. In school. At college. In my social life. At work. Even at home, most of the time. Growing up in a middle-class urban family in postcolonial Pakistan, English ruled our lives. It was equated with intelligence, knowledge, culture, and was also a way of getting ahead. Predictably, I went on to get two Master's degrees, in English literature and English language.

And here was this man telling me to go to accent reduction classes. No one told my colleagues from England to learn to talk Canadian-style.

The "you-have-an-accent" accusation has been a motif of my life in Canada. This construction has disempowered me in my careers as a journalist and an English-language teacher. My purpose in this space is to show how the English language is implicated in the continuing domination of the people of the South/the Third World by the people of the North/the First World. My focus here is women from the South, more specifically from former British colonies such as Bangladesh, India, Pakistan, and Sri Lanka among others, who "choose" to emigrate to the English-speaking countries of the North.[1] I suggest that this was/is not so much a matter of choice, but that, in fact, women like myself were/are "destined by the social/economic structure" to play a particular role in the international division of labour. The women I describe in this article grew up speaking English in their home countries.

ENGLISH IN POSTCOLONIAL PAKISTAN

Was it a mere accident that British schools in the Indian subcontinent instilled in their students shame of their own language and culture? According to Kazi, it was *no* accident; the goals of the British education policy were to get political control and to produce a cost-effective administrative bureaucracy. In the early days of colonialism, the British sought the help of British missionaries to control the indigenous educational institutions in order to exert their own political control. But later, with the growing unrest against British officers in India, and in the face of payments of heavy salaries to a bureaucracy of Englishmen, the British decided to create "an indigenous class of a privileged few for bureaucratic jobs" (Kazi 32).

To describe the British rationale for introducing English in India, Kazi quotes Macaulay's 1835 Minute to the British Parliament:

> In India, English is the language spoken by the ruling class. It is spoken by the higher class of natives at the seats of government.... We must do our best to form a class who may be interpreters between us and the millions whom we govern.... A class of persons, Indian in blood and colour, but English in taste, in opinions, in morals, and in intellect. (33)

Kazi comments that a crucial part of this education policy was that the British, through English education, did *not* introduce the knowledge of economics, technology, science and politics, but instead introduced English literature, philosophy and metaphysics in an "imitative fashion." As a result, he continues, "students were able to recite King Alfred or an Oxford text, but they learned nothing of their own background and were sometimes even unable to translate English passages into their own vernacular languages" (33).

The main objective of the colonial educators in the Indian subcontinent was, as Macaulay put it, "to have a class of persons, Indian in blood and colour, but English in taste, in opinions, in morals, and in intellect." In this objective they succeeded. My behaviour, decisions, and perception of experiences were, and to a lesser extent still are, influenced by my Eurocentric upbringing in a newly decolonized society. This was a society where the older generation had internalized the colonizer's values, and made sure that the younger generation learnt the all-important lesson: white is best. I grew up thinking of Pakistanis, much as in writer Naipaul's characterization of the colonized, as those condemned only to use the telephone, never to invent it, and that only the English—and by association white people—could invent, could write, could govern (see Said 209).

My Catholic convent school reinforced this message. British schools in the Indian subcontinent further fragmented their students by taking away their language. Himani Bannerji observes that the vernacular—Bengali—was such a low priority in her high school in the then East Pakistan (now Bangladesh) that they did not even have a Bengali teacher. When she decided to "take it as a subject" for the U.K.-based Senior Cambridge exam, special arrangements had to be made. At my school we did have a daily Urdu class, but very little was expected of us, so much so that when I finished school I was unable to write a letter to my mother in Urdu, although I could construct a letter in stilted French. As Bannerji puts it, the legacy of colonialism in modern India, as in pre-independence India, was that "the way to advancement lay through proficiency in English and collaboration with Colonial State and Western capital" (38).

ENGLISH IN CANADA

What happens to women from the South, including the South Asians whose education I have described, when they emigrate to the North? Amina Jamal concluded after living in Canada for three years that her decision to emigrate to Canada was not a neutral one; that she was a product of Macaulay's scheme for creating a class of Indians who would play a particular role in the international division of labour and certainly in their home countries.

In Canada, as in other English-speaking countries of the North, emphasis on "proper," "real," "native-speaker" English works in concert with racism and sexism to further disempower women immigrants from the South, who are, by definition, women of colour. Roxana Ng, whose focus is women immigrants, draws attention to the unequal access to power by members of society, be they women or people from "visible minority" groups. Immigrants from visible minority groups are disadvantaged in a competitive labour market in which Canadian—or English-speaking—training and work experience are major determinants for entry into different occupational classifications:

> Many visible minority immigrants, even those in professional and highly skilled technical occupations in the home countries have to take lower positions because of the lack of recognition by Canadian government and employers of their qualifications and credentials. (Ng 29)

Ng also suggests that immigrants from developing countries face discrimination in education. Quoting a Saskatchewan-based study, she charges that there's a "racist bias" in Canada's accreditation process; only four of the 95 immigrant women interviewed—those whose degrees were from British or American universities—were given recognition of upper level education.

The dominant group's negative perception of women of colour, says Ng, is seen in the way the term "immigrant women" is generally used.[2] It embodies "class, ethnic, and racial biases" as it is equated with the stereotype of "visible minority" women, who either do not speak English or speak it with an accent other than British or

American, and women who have low-paid, low-status jobs (21). I would qualify Ng's observation. Although there is indeed a hierarchy among accents, all accents associated with white countries or the North have a higher status than accents associated with non-white countries or the South. As John Edwards points out, views of language often correspond to views of the social status of language users. "In this sense," he adds, "the language, dialect, or accent employed provides a simple label which evokes a social stereotype which goes far beyond language itself" (79). He observes that even dictionary definitions of accent help to sustain the view that non-standard accents are a deviant from the norm; and cites the Oxford English Dictionary (OED):

> a mode of utterance which consists mainly in a prevailing quality of tone, or in a peculiar alteration of pitch, but may include mispronunciation of vowels or consonants, misplacing of stress, and misinflection of a sentence. (OED, qtd. In Edwards 79)

Edwards comments that the OED definition of accent does not match with the "value-free judgment of linguists," and that the OED definition "reflect[s] many popular conceptions of what an accent is, and who has one." He concludes: "It is still not difficult to find people who deny that they speak with any accent at all" (79). Mari Matsuda makes a similar point.

> Everyone has an accent ... but when an employer refuses to hire a person "with an accent," they are referring to a hidden norm of non-accent.... People in power are perceived as speaking normal, unaccented English. Any speak that is different from that constructed norm is called an accent. (1361)

Thus women from the South, whose accents are obviously different from the particular accent that people in power in Canada or the United States have, are denied employment on the basis of having an accent. "You have a heavy accent and people don't understand what you're saying" is a refrain familiar to women from the South like myself who are denied employment on this basis. You have an accent, South women are told by people who seem to believe that they themselves are accent-less, a linguistic feat which is not possible.

This accusation is also used to deny voice to South women. Referring to the power wielded by people who are in a position to decide what is not an acceptable accent, June Jordan talks of her experiences of being discriminated against for having an accent that is different from the constructed norm. A white woman telephoned her to ask her to appear on her television program: "She felt free to tell me that if I sounded 'Black' then she would not 'hire' me" (40). I, too, am constantly asked questions about my "accent" by colleagues who appear to think—much as Matsuda points out—that they either do not have an accent or have the right accent.

Another source of disempowerment for South women is the preference given to native speakers of English, and the assumption that only white people are native speakers, and, therefore, that only white people know "good" English. I consider myself to be a native speaker of English on the grounds that English is the language I know best, but my colleagues—teachers of English and English as a second language (ESL), linguists, and applied linguists—often position me as a non-native speaker, I would say, because I am non-white and I have a Pakistani accent. When I say that I am a native speaker, there is a look of bewilderment and disbelief on their faces. The following is one such conversation with a colleague who is well-known in the field of English-language teaching. She was asking my views on being an ESL teacher from the point of view of being a "non-native" speaker. I interrupted, "I am a native speaker."

Silence, Then. "Were you born in Canada?"

"No," I replied.

"Where were you born?"

"In Pakistan."

My interrogator breathed a sigh of relief and said without words, "So I was right. You're *not* a native speaker." She then asked. "What is your first language?"

My reply, "If you mean which language do I know best, it is English, not Urdu." I said this because there is debate as to what "first language" means. Some linguists (for example, Ferguson; Kachru) have pointed out that the terms "first language," "mother tongue," and "native speaker" do not make sense in the context of English being a world language. My colleague dropped the subject, but that does not mean that she changed her assumptions about who is a native speaker. I do not think that I am being considered by this colleague or any other for membership to the Inner Circle of Native Speakers of English.

So whenever "native speaker" expertise is required, for example, for English-language teaching, journalism, and advertising, women from the South are discriminated against on the basis that they are not native speakers. It appears that just as people in power decide who has an accent, they also decide who is a native speaker, and who, therefore, has ownership of English.

CONCLUSION

We have seen how the English language is implicated in the domination of women from the South, how women from former British colonies who emigrate to the English-speaking countries of the North are further disempowered—ironically, through the language to which they feel they have as much ownership as people in the North. I have suggested that these women immigrants were "groomed" by the social structure, the economic structure, and the internalization of colonization to be estranged from the countries of their birth and that the English-speaking countries of the North as their real home—an illusion these women believe until they try to make their home in their new countries of estrangement.

[1]India became independent from British colonization in 1947. Pakistan was formed as an independent country from the predominantly Muslim areas of India in 1947.
[2]It is common knowledge that white women who emigrate to Canada from the United States or England are not perceived as "immigrants"; conversely, Black women whose families have lived in Canada for generations are often asked, "Where are you from?"

WORKS CITED

Bannerji, H. "The Sound Barrier: Translating Ourselves in Language and Experience." *Language in Her Eye.* Ed. L. Scheier. Toronto: Coach House Press, 1990.

Edwards, J.R. *Language and Disadvantage.* London: Edward Arnold, 1979.

Ferguson, C. Foreword. *The Other Tongue: English Across Cultures.* Ed. B. Kachru. Urbana: University of Illinois Press, 1982, rpt. 1992.

Kachru, B.J., ed. *The Other Tongue: English Across Cultures.* Urbana: University of Ilinois Press, 1992.

Kazi, A.A. *Ethnicity and Education in Nation-Building: The Case of Pakistan.* Lanham: UP of America, 1987.

Jamal, A. "Identity, Community, and the Postcolonial Experience of Migrancy." OISE/UT: Unpublished paper, 1995.

Jordan, J., "White English, Black English: The Politics of Translation." *Moving Towards Home.* London: Virago, 1989.

Matsuda, M. "Voices of America: Accent, Anti-discrimination, Law, and a Jurisprudence for the Last Reconstruction." *The Yale Law Journal* 100 (1991): 1329–1407.

Ng, R. "Racism, Sexism, and Visible Minority Immigrant Women in Canada." *Zeitscrift der Gesellschaft fuer Kanada-Studien* 10.2 (1990): 21–34.

Said, E.W. "Representing the Colonized: Anthropology's Interlocutors." *Critical Inquiry* 15.1 (1989): 205–225.

TOPICS FOR DISCUSSION

1. Compare the British education policy applied to Canada's Native peoples to that in the former British colonies in the South. How can the differences be explained? See texts by Pauline Johnson, Pat Deiter-McArthur, Basil H. Johnston, or Carol Geddes.

2. How does Nuzhat Amin show the continuing legacy of colonialism in modern India, Bangladesh, or Pakistan?

3. Why is "having an accent" a source of disempowerment for immigrant women from the South? What does the phrase "ownership of English" mean? Compare the problem with "accent" as experienced by Eva Hoffman and Nuzhat Amin.

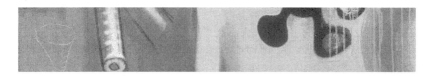

EDUCATION/
DIFFERENCE/
POWER

INTRODUCTION

Schools can be viewed as microcosms of society in that they reflect social relations of power and stratifications. Historically, schools have been instruments of assimilation into the dominant "norm"—be it a national, cultural, linguistic, social, educational, gender, or beauty norm. Institutions such as schools perpetuate these norms through peer pressure and demands of conformity.

Often in the past, and sometimes still today, Canadian schools, rooted in white, Western European cultural assumptions, could be seen as places of institutional racism. The system of residential schools, run by the missionaries and later by government, was based on such cultural assumptions. Too often the values of Native and immigrant cultures have been denigrated, repressed, and lost. Although today the political climate is more accepting of differences, most schools still teach conformity to the liberal, multicultural ideal that "we are all different but essentially the same, that is, human." Teachers and students are afraid to talk about differences of power among diverse groups, and they do not go beyond diversity understood as diversity of food and culture. However, as the stories included in this unit show, norms can be challenged by individuals or resisted by entire populations.

Rita Joe

Rita Joe is a Mi'kmaq, born in 1932 in Whycocomagh, Nova Scotia. As a child, she was brought up by foster families. She lives on the Eskasoni Reserve in Cape Breton. She has raised eight children of her own, and adopted two more. Her work often reflects the time she spent in a residential school. She says that she writes always with children in mind, so that others may come to understand the right of her people to education and dignity. She first won honours for her work at the Nova Scotia Writers' Federation Competition in 1974. Her collections of poetry include Poems of Rita Joe *(1978),* Song of Eskasoni: More Poems of Rita Joe *(1988), and* Inu and Indians We're Called *(1991). In 1996, Rita Joe published her autobiography,* Song of Rita Joe: Autobiography of a Mi'kmaq Poet. *With Lesley Choyce, she has edited* The Mi'kmaq Anthology *of fiction, poetry, and autobiographical writing. For her activism on behalf of Native children's education, Rita Joe received the Order of Canada in 1990. She was also awarded an honorary doctorate from Mount St. Vincent University. Commenting on the poem "Who Are You?" in her autobiography, she explains: "This experience of belonging to an alien nation made a permanent impression on me. Even today, I use the method of peaceful confrontation to fight it."*

Who Are You?

Wen net ki´l?	Who are you?
Pipanimit nuji-kina´muet ta´n jipalk.	Question from a teacher feared.
Netakei, aqq i´-naqawey;	Blushing, I stammered
Koqoey?	What?
Ktikik nuji-kina´masultite´wk	Other students tittered
kimelmultijik.	I sat down forlorn, dejected,
Na epa´si, taqawajitutm,	And made a vow
Aqq elui´tmasi	That day
Na na´kwek.	
Espi-kjijiteketes,	To be great in all learnings,
Ma´jipajita´siw.	No more uncertain.
Espitutmukewey kina´matnewey-	My pride lives in my education,
iktuk eyk,	And I will relate wonders
Aqq kinua´tuates pa´qalaiwaqann	to my people.
ni´n nikmaq.	

TOPICS FOR DISCUSSION

1. What do you think is the significance of Rita Joe's decision to write this poem in two languages?

2. What does the speaker's flashback to her school days reveal about the experiences of a Native child in a non-Native school?

Carol Geddes

*Carol Geddes is from the Tlingit Nation in the Yukon. She left the Yukon
as a teenager and graduated with a B.A. from Carleton University. She
obtained a graduate degree in Communications from Concordia University
and has worked in the film industry. In 1981, Geddes directed her first
documentary,* Places for Our People, *focusing on the Montreal Native
Friendship Centre. For the National Film Board's Studio D, she made*
Doctor, Lawyer, Indian Chief *(1984), portraying five Native women who
share their success stories. Her most recent NFB films include* Picturing the
People: George Johnston, Tlingit Photographer *(1997), a historical documentary about a man who made a unique photographic record of his
people during a time of change, and* Half a World Apart and a Lifetime
Away *(1996), about the First Nations leader Ovid Mercredi, who after a
summer of violence and standoffs on Native reserves travels to India to
explore the non-violent political teachings of Mahatma Ghandi. Geddes
has also worked as a producer. Her documentaries have garnered her many
national and international awards. In addition to film, she uses anima-
tion, drama, magazine writing, and education to describe the problems
that Aboriginal people face in both Native and white societies. Geddes is
known as a community activist, serving on the board of Women's Television
Network, the NFB Aboriginal Selection Committee, Yukon Heritage
Resources Board, and the Yukon Arts Centre Board. In partnership with
the Aboriginal Peoples Television Network (APTN), she offers a screen-
writing workshop for Aboriginal storytellers at the Banff Centre. "Growing
Up Native" was first published in* Homemaker's Magazine *in 1990.
Geddes describes the Teslin Tlingit people's way of life as it has been transformed by contact with a European wage-based economy and especially by
education in residential schools. Only when she attends university as an
adult does she reverse the poor self-image inflicted upon her as a Native
child by her Christian missionary teachers.*

Growing Up Native

I remember it was cold. We were walking through a swamp near
our home in the Yukon bush. Maybe it was fall and moose-hunting

season. I don't know. I think I was about four years old at the time. The muskeg was too springy to walk on, so people were taking turns carrying me—passing me from one set of arms to another. The details about where we were are vague, but the memory of those arms and the feeling of acceptance I had is one of the most vivid memories of my childhood. It didn't matter who was carrying me—there was security in every pair of arms. That response to children is typical of the native community. It's the first thing I think of when I cast my mind back to the Yukon bush, where I was born and lived with my family.

I was six years old when we moved out of the bush, first to Teslin, where I had a hint of the problems native people face, then to Whitehorse, where there was unimaginable racism. Eventually I moved to Ottawa and Montreal, where I further discovered that to grow up native in Canada is to feel the sting of humiliation and the boot of discrimination. But it is also to experience the enviable security of an extended family and to learn appreciate the richness of the heritage and traditions of a culture most North Americans have never been lucky enough to know. As a film-maker, I have tried to explore these contradictions, and our triumph over them, for the half-million aboriginals who are part of the tide of swelling independence of the First Nations today.

But I'm getting ahead of myself. If I'm to tell the story of what it's like to grow up native in northern Canada, I have to go back to the bush where I was born, because there's more to my story than the hurtful stereotyping that depicts Indian people as drunken welfare cases. Our area was known as 12-mile (it was 12 miles from another tiny village). There were about 40 people living there—including 25 kids, eight of them my brothers and sisters—in a sort of family compound. Each family had its own timber plank house for sleeping, and there was one large common kitchen area with gravel on the ground and a tent frame over it. Everybody would go there and cook meals together. In summer, my grandmother always had a smudge fire going to smoke fish and tan moose hides. I can remember the cosy warmth of the fire, the smell of good food, and always having someone to talk to. We kids had built-in playmates and would spend hours running in the bush, picking berries, building rafts on the lake and playing in abandoned mink cages.

One of the people in my village tells a story about the day the old lifestyle began to change. He had been away hunting in the bush for about a month. On his way back, he heard a strange sound coming from far away. He ran up to the crest of a hill, looked over the top of it and saw a bulldozer. He had never seen or heard of such a thing before and he couldn't imagine what it was. We didn't have magazines or newspapers in our village, and the people didn't know that the Alaska Highway was being built as a defence against a presumed Japanese invasion during the Second World War. That was the beginning of the end of the Teslin Tlingit people's way of life. From that moment on, nothing turned back to the way it was. Although there were employment opportunities for my father and uncles, who were young men at the time, the speed and force with which the Alaska Highway was rammed through the wilderness caused tremendous upheaval for Yukon native people.

It wasn't as though we'd never experienced change before. The Tlingit Nation, which I belong to, arrived in the Yukon from the Alaskan coast around the turn of the century. They were the middlemen and women between the Russian traders and the Yukon inland Indians. The Tlingit gained power and prestige by trading European products such as metal goods and cloth for the rich and varied furs so much in fashion in Europe. The Tlingit controlled Yukon trading because they controlled the trading routes through the high mountain passes. When trading ceased to be an effective means of survival, my grandparents began raising wild mink in cages. Mink prices were really high before and during the war, but afterwards the prices went plunging down. So, although the mink pens were still there when I was a little girl, my father mainly worked on highway construction and hunted in the bush. The Yukon was then, and still is in some ways, in a transitional period—from living off the land to getting into a European wage-based economy.

As a young child, I didn't see the full extent of the upheaval. I remember a lot of togetherness, a lot of happiness while we lived in the bush. There's a very strong sense of family in the native community, and a fondness for children, especially young children. Even today, it's like a special form of entertainment if someone brings a baby to visit. That sense of family is the one thing that has survived all the incredible difficulties native people have had. Throughout a time of tremendous problems, the extended family system has somehow lasted, providing a strong circle for people to survive in. When parents were struggling with alcoholism or had to go away to find work, when one of the many epidemics swept through the community, or when a marriage broke up and one parent left, aunts, uncles and grandparents would try to fill those roles. It's been very important to me in terms of emotional support to be able to rely on my extended family. There are still times when such support keeps me going.

Life was much simpler when we lived in the bush. Although we were poor and wore the same clothes all year, we were warm enough and had plenty to eat. But even as a youngster, I began to be aware of some of the problems we would face later on. Travelling missionaries would come and impose themselves on us, for example. They'd sit at our campfire and read the Bible to us and lecture us about how we had to live a Christian life. I remember being very frightened by stories we heard about parents sending their kids away to live with white people who didn't have any children. We thought those people were mean and that if we were bad, we'd be sent away, too. Of course, that was when social workers were scooping up native children and adopting them out to white families in the south. The consequences were usually disastrous for the children who were taken away—alienation, alcoholism and suicide, among other things. I knew some of those kids. The survivors are still struggling to recover.

The residential schools were another source of misery for the kids. Although I didn't have to go, my brothers and sisters were there. They told stories about having their hair cut off in case they were carrying head lice, and of being forced to do hard chores without enough food to eat. They were told that the Indian culture was evil, that Indian people were bad, that their only hope was to be Christian. They had to stand up and say things like "I've found the Lord," when a teacher told them to speak. Sexual abuse was rampant in the residential school system.

By the time we moved to Whitehorse, I was excited about the idea of living in what I thought of as a big town. I'd had a taste of the outside world from books at school in Teslin (a town of 250 people), and I was tremendously curious about what life was like. I was hungry for experiences such as going to the circus. In fact, for a while, I was obsessed with stories and pictures about the circus, but then when I was 12 and saw my first one, I was put off by the condition and treatment of the animals.

Going to school in Whitehorse was a shock. The clash of native and white values was confusing and frightening. Let me tell you a story. The older boys in our community were already accomplished hunters and fishermen, but since they had to trap beaver in the spring and hunt moose in the fall, and go out trapping in the winter as well, they missed a lot of school. We were all in one classroom and some of my very large teenage cousins had to sit squeezed into little desks. These guys couldn't read very well. We girls had been in school all along, so, of course, we were better readers. One day the teacher was trying to get one of the older boys to read. She was typical of the teachers at that time, insensitive and ignorant of cultural complexities. In an increasingly loud voice, she kept commanding him to "Read it, read it." He couldn't. He sat there completely still, but I could see that he was breaking into a sweat. The teacher then said, "Look, she can read it," and she pointed to me, indicating that I should stand up and read. For a young child to try to show up an older boy is wrong and totally contrary to native cultural values, so I refused. She told me to stand up and I did. My hands were trembling as I held my reader. She yelled at me to read and when I didn't she smashed her pointing stick on the desk to frighten me. In terror, I wet my pants. As I stood there fighting my tears of shame, she said I was disgusting and sent me home. I had to walk a long distance through the bush by myself to get home. I remember feeling this tremendous confusion, on top of my humiliation. We were always told the white teachers knew best, and so we had to do whatever they said at school. And yet I had a really strong sense of receiving mixed messages about what I was supposed to do in the community and what I was supposed to do at school.

Pretty soon I hated school. Moving to a predominantly white high school was even worse. We weren't allowed to join anything the white kids started. We were the butt of jokes because of our second-hand clothes and moose meat sandwiches. We were constantly being rejected. The prevailing attitude was that Indians were stupid. When it was time to make course choices in class—between typing and science, for example—they didn't even ask the native kids, they just put us all in typing. You get a really bad image of yourself in a situation like that. I bought into it. I thought we were awful. The whole experience was terribly undermining. Once, my grandmother gave me a pretty little pencil box. I walked into the classroom one day to find the word "squaw" carved on it. That night I burned it in the wood stove. I joined the tough crowd and by the time I was 15 years old, I was more likely to be leaning against the school smoking a cigarette than trying to join in. I was burned out from trying to join the system. The principal told my father there was no point in sending me back to school so, with a Grade 9 education, I started to work at a series of menial jobs.

Seven years later something happened to me that would change my life forever. I had moved to Ottawa with a man and was working as a waitress in a restaurant. One day, a friend invited me to her place for coffee. While I was there, she told me she was going to university in the fall and showed me her reading list. I'll never forget the minutes that followed. I was feeling vaguely envious of her and, once again, inferior. I remember taking the paper in my hand, seeing the books on it and realizing, Oh, my God, I've read these books! It hit me like a thunderclap. I was stunned that books I had read were being read in university. University was for white kids, not native kids. We were too stupid, we didn't have the kind of mind it took to do those things. My eyes moved down the list, and my heart started beating faster and faster as I suddenly realized I could go to university, too!

My partner at the time was a loving supportive man who helped me in every way. I applied to the university immediately as a mature student but when I had to write Grade 9 on the application, I was sure they'd turn me down. They didn't. I graduated five years later, earning a bachelor of arts in English and philosophy (with distinction)....

Today, there's a glimmer of hope that more of us native people will overcome the obstacles that have tripped us up ever since we began sharing this land. Some say our cultures are going through a renaissance. Maybe that's true. Certainly there's a renewed interest in native dancing, acting and singing, and in other cultural traditions. Even indigenous forms of government are becoming strong again. But we can't forget that the majority of native people live in urban areas and continue to suffer from alcohol and drug abuse and the plagues of a people who have lost their culture and have become lost themselves. And the welfare system is the insidious glue that holds together the machine of oppression of native people.

Too many non-native people have refused to try to understand the issues behind our land claims. They make complacent pronouncements such as "Go back to your bows and arrows and fish with spears if you want aboriginal rights. If not, give it up and assimilate into white Canadian culture." I don't agree with that. We need our culture, but there's no reason why we can't preserve it and have an automatic washing machine and a holiday in Mexico, as well.

The time has come for native people to make our own decisions. We need to have self-government. I have no illusions that it will be smooth sailing—there will be trial and error and further struggle. And if that means crawling before we can stand up and walk, so be it. We'll have to learn through experience.

While we're learning, we have a lot to teach and give to the world—a holistic philosophy, a way of living with the earth, not disposing of it. It is critical that we all learn from the elders that an individual is not more important than a forest; we know that we're here to live on and with the earth, not to subdue it.

The wheels are in motion for a revival, for change in the way native people are taking their place in Canada. I can see that we're equipped, we have the tools to do the work. We have an enormous number of smart, talented, moral Indian people. It's thrilling to be a part of this movement.

Someday, when I'm an elder, I'll tell the children the stories: about the bush, about the hard times, about the renaissance, and especially about the importance of knowing your place in your nation.

TOPICS   FOR   DISCUSSION

1. According to Geddes, what contradictions are involved in growing up Native in Canada? Why does she think that exploring these contradictions is necessary and fruitful?

2. What impact has contact with Europeans had upon the way of life of Yukon Native people? What different means of survival have people in the North been trying to adopt?

3. What conditions existed in the schools at Whitehorse? What methods did the white teachers use to humiliate Native students? Compare the role of missionary schools in Pauline Johnson's story "As It Was In the Beginning."

4. What was the turning point for Geddes in reclaiming her sense of self-worth?

5. Contact between Europeans and Native people is usually seen as a one-way process, with the dominant culture imposing its norms. How does Geddes visualize the possibility of influences running in the opposite direction? What traditional Native values could enrich the lives of other Canadians? Other examples can be found in Emma LaRocque's essay on poverty.

Mehri Yalfani

Mehri Yalfani was born in Hamadan, Iran. After high school, she moved to Teheran to pursue her education. She graduated in 1963 with a degree in electrical engineering. She began to write in high school. Her first short story collection, Happy Days, *was published in 1966, and her novel,* Before the Fall, *in 1980. In 1987, she immigrated to Canada. Her short story collection,* Birthday Party, *was published in 1991 in the United States, and her novel,* Someone Is Coming, *in 1994 in Sweden. In 1995, she published a haunting collection of stories and poems, called* Parastoo. *The stories in her most recent collection,* Two Sisters *(2000), look at women's relationships as mothers, sisters, and wives in post-revolutionary Iran, and later as immigrants and exiles in Canada. Mehri Yalfani writes in Farsi, her mother tongue, and has translated some of her work into English. In Canada, there is a vast body of ethnic literature produced in languages other than English and French. Like many other writers producing this multilingual literature, Mehri Yalfani forces us to rethink the category of national literature that has recently been extended to include multicultural writing in English and French. Her case raises an interesting question: Is Mehri Yalfani an Iranian Canadian writer or an Iranian writer living in Canada?*

Newcomer

The class had already started when Susan came in. She found a seat in the last row and sat down. The teacher said something but Susan did not understand. She just smiled. Susan had come up the stairs fast and her heart was beating in her chest like a drum. The teacher was talking to the students. She could not understand. She had been coming to this ESL class for two months. The words still had a strange sound to her. She had learned "hello," "good-bye," "yes" and "no." She had no problem in using the first two. She knew where to use them. But she always had problems with "yes" and "no." She misused them; answering questions sometimes she would say "yes," and after seeing the reaction of the other person, she would say "no."

The teacher was talking about the past tense. Susan sometimes understood the meaning of the sentences. The teacher wrote, "I had a house." The sentence stuck in her mind. She had a house too. She had a past too. She lost her concentration and dreamily went back to her own house.

The teacher wrote, "My house was big." Susan's reading was better than her listening. Her house was big too. Masoud has built a one-floor building on the big land they had inherited from her father. The building was surrounded by high trees. Looking through the window, she could see them. There was the white poplar and the fruit trees. They were full of blossoms in the spring, and in the summer they embraced the house like it was a baby.

The teacher wrote, "I loved my house." Susan thought about her house, about the big livingroom with windows on two sides, about the Tabriz rug that was like a painting, full of pictures of flowers and animals. She thought about the big ceramic bowl inherited from her grandfather and when Nima broke it with a ball, she had punished Nima and he had cried. The souvenir of her grandfather was damaged.

Susan thought about Nima. Nima was eighteen when the revolution started in Iran, and ... The teacher noticed her, and asked, "What happened!" Then she asked a question, a long sentence. Susan did not understand, but she tried to smile. She tried to stop the tears. She wiped out Nima's memory along with that of her house and the ceramic bowl. The teacher and students were looking at her. A girl from India had sat in front of her. She had braided hair and a tanned face. She wore a sari under her pink coat. Her sari was from green jura and Susan remembered Indian movies. The girl turned back and stared at Susan. Susan just smiled. Her smile was the only communication she had.

The teacher left Susan alone. Susan looked at the blackboard. The teacher had covered it with words that Susan more or less knew. A Chinese or Vietnamese man who sat at the front desk raised his hand and asked something. Susan couldn't recognize his nationality. To her, Asian people all looked like each other and they had the same accent. The teacher repeated his question. Susan understood the teacher better than she did the other students. Susan didn't hear some of this man's question and what she did hear was incomprehensible to her. She just understood a few words and guessed the meaning. Apparently he had said something about his country. Susan thought he had said, "My country was big." Susan told herself, "My country was big too." If she had had guts, she would have said this sentence out loud. But she was afraid. She was unable to say it. Instead she silently dreamt about her country, about the winding roads, about the mountains, about the cities she had visited, about the trip they had taken to the Shiraz. She had driven half of the way and Masoud the other half. Nima, Kahveh and Mozhgan had sat in the back seat. They sometimes sang, sometimes slept, sometimes they argued over something. She stared at the roads, the trees, the valleys and the newly harvested land. How much she loved travelling around the country.

Valentina raised her hand. Valentina was from South America. She was the only person whose name Susan had learned. Valentina reminded her of her sister, Simin. It was three months since Susan had left Iran and they had not heard anything of her. She did not know if Rozbeh was back from the war front line. She had received a letter from her brother Saeed, but he had not mentioned anything about Rozbeh. When Susan told Masoud, "I don't know why he has not written about Rozbeh," Masoud replied, "He must have forgotten. You know your brother and how absentminded he is. What do you expect from him?" Valentina was still talking to the teacher. Susan heard. She tried to pay attention. She dismissed Simin from her mind and just listened to Valentina.

Valentina was talking with difficulty. The words would not come to her mouth. She seemed to need more time to find a word. She lost the words in her mind and was looking for replacements. Susan thought, "She is like me. I also have to think a lot before I say something. I even forget the few words I know, or else I misuse them." Valentina was talking about revolution. Susan knew this word very well, but was unable to pronounce it. It was a difficult word, and her tongue wouldn't twist it in her mouth. Susan thought, "I wish that all people would talk the same language." She wanted to understand all that Valentina said. She wished that she could talk about the revolution. She wished she could understand the revolution. She wanted to know why there was a revolution in her country and why the revolution took her son away from her? And why the revolution forced her to sell her inherited home and why her family had to risk death to pass through the mountains, to flee from her country?

The teacher was talking to Valentina. Valentina had to spend a lot of time on every sentence. The teacher was very patient. Susan couldn't understand what they were saying. She had a lot of questions in her mind.

On the other side of the classroom, a young man whom Susan did not know got into the conversation. Then a third person joined in. It was clear that the revolution was an interesting subject. The whole class was talking about it. Susan was the only person who was quiet.

The teacher asked her something. Susan thought that the teacher was asking for her idea. She went red. She did not know what to say. What if she said "yes" and it did not make sense? So it was better to say "no." When the teacher heard "no," she smiled. The whole class laughed. Susan went even redder. She felt the sweat break out on her forehead. Then she smiled at the teacher. But she felt a bitter sorrow. She wished that she could talk about the revolution, about the day when three guards had come to her home. They had rummaged through the entire house. They had looked through her photo album and made fun of the pictures. She wanted to tell everyone about the days when they would not let them water the flowers and all the flowers had died in the June sunshine; about the days the whole family was in jail, even twelve-year-old Mozhgan. Two weeks later when they were released, Nima was not with them any more. Nima had been executed two nights after being arrested.

Susan wished she could talk, but she felt a piece of wood in her mouth instead of her tongue. She had incredible grief in her heart. She turned her eyes away from the blackboard and looked at the floor to hide her tears. All the class was talking. The words were vague sounds playing with her thoughts and memories. And she could not understand anything. She was quiet.

The class was finished. But the real silence was within her. She looked at the papers the teacher had handed her. She knew the letters but most of the words had no meaning for her. A pain of humiliation grasped her heart. She thought, "I must learn. I have to learn. I cannot stay silent...."

TOPICS FOR DISCUSSION

1. How do the past traumas interfere with Susan's life in the present? What factors in the present contribute to Susan's isolation from her new environment?

2. Why does Susan feel humiliated at the end of the class? Does anyone around her, including the teacher, seem to understand her silence?

3. Compare Mehri Yalfani's story to Helga Mills' article. What different approaches do they choose to write about the problems faced by refugee women? How effective is each writer's method?

Isabel Vincent

*Isabel Vincent is an award-winning investigative journalist and author
whose work has most recently appeared in the* New Yorker, Marie Claire,
The National Post, Saturday Night, *and South Africa's* Femina. *She has
also contributed to the Spanish- and Portuguese-language editions of* Marie
Claire. *A former chief of the Latin America Bureau for* The Globe and
Mail, *based in Rio de Janeiro, she has received numerous citations for her
work in the region. For her coverage of the cocaine trade in Rio de Janeiro's
shantytowns, she was a finalist for a National Newspaper Award (the
Canadian equivalent of the Pulitzer) in 1994. For her reporting on terrorism in Peru, she received an Inter-American Press Association Citation in
1993. Her book,* See No Evil: The Strange Case of Christine Lamont and
David Spencer *(1995), an exposé of Latin American terrorist groups, won
her Canada's prestigious Southam Fellowship and the Association of
Journalists' Award for excellence in investigative journalism. Her second book,*
Hitler's Silent Partners: Swiss Banks, Nazi Gold and the Pursuit of Justice
*(1997), details how the Nazis used Swiss banks to launder stolen gold. It
won the Yad Vashem Award for Holocaust History. In her most recent book,*
Avon Calling, *Isabel Vincent tackles globalization, describing the marketing
of Avon cosmetics in the remote regions of the Amazon rainforest in Brazil.
Isabel Vincent lives in Toronto and is fluent in Spanish, French, Portuguese,
and Quechua (modern Inca). This selection was originally published in* The
Globe and Mail *in December 1990. Isabel Vincent points to her school experience as one of the factors that have contributed to her gradual estrangement
from her own roots. The assimilation of her Portuguese parents into the
Canadian mainstream is incomplete, but Vincent, a second-generation
immigrant, has removed herself from her ethnic community in Toronto and
"Canadianized" herself so thoroughly that she is turned down for a newspaper job because, ironically, she is perceived as too "Anglo-Saxon."*

Finding a Nationality That Fits

We started to become Canadian the day my mother got her
first pair of pants.

They were gray-green gabardine with a high waist, and came wrapped in tissue paper in an Eaton's box. My mother reluctantly modelled them for my brother and me, all the while declaring that she couldn't imagine ever feeling comfortable with the stretchy cloth hugging her hips. Portuguese women didn't wear pants, only the *canadianas* dared wear anything so revealing. But in the same breath she'd rationalize that she spent too much money not to wear them, and besides they'd probably be warm in the winter.

That was in 1975, a few years after my family had made the big break and moved from the poor immigrant enclave of Kensington Market to the more upscale neighborhood of North York, where pockets of European immigration were just beginning to emerge. We were pioneers in a way. My father had been among the first wave of Portuguese immigrants to Canada in the early fifties, working a bleak stretch of railroad near Port Arthur—now Thunder Bay, Ont.—to earn enough money for my mother's passage across the Atlantic. My mother arrived sea-sick in Halifax in 1955, and took a slow train to Toronto, where she joined my father in a roach-infested flat on Nassau Avenue in the Market.

My mother still speaks of those early *sacrifícios*: living in a cold climate with cockroaches and mutely shopping for groceries, pointing out items to a local shopkeeper because she couldn't speak English. Her language skills were so tenuous that she once interpreted a greeting from an Orthodox Jew who lived in the neighborhood as an offer to buy my brother.

In those days, Toronto police used to disperse small crowds of Portuguese men who lingered too long outside cafes. Despite a burgeoning group of immigrants, there were few Portuguese speakers, even in the market.

But by 1975, the market became a Saturday-morning diversion for us, a place to shop for salted cod and fresh vegetables. To the hearty Portuguese immigrants who still worked in the factories and construction yards, and rented windowless basements in the market, we were on our way up. After all, there were very few Portuguese families north of Eglinton Avenue. Although we lived in a mostly Jewish and Italian neighborhood, we were finally becoming Canadian. Or so I thought.

I learned English in my first year of school. Multiculturalism was just beginning and hyphenated Canadians were beginning to flourish. I played with Italian-Canadians, Lithuanian-Canadians and Chinese-Canadians, but at that time nobody—especially suburban 7-year-olds—seemed able to pronounce "Portuguese-Canadian," so I told people I was Greek; it was easier to say. My brother went even further, changing his name to something faintly Anglo-Saxon, so his teachers and classmates wouldn't get tongue-tied around those sloshy Portuguese vowels and embarrass him. It seemed a very practical idea at the time, and I reluctantly followed suit.

But we still had problems, and didn't seem to belong. We never quite fit into the emerging Portuguese community, growing up around the parish of St. Mary's Church and the Toronto branch of the popular Benfica soccer club on Queen Street West. We were strangely aloof with our compatriots, most of whom had emigrated from the Azores, and whose guttural form of Portuguese we had difficulty understanding. My brother and I balked at heritage-language classes and remained passive spectators at the annual religious processions.

But if we had trouble dealing with our peers in downtown Toronto, in North York we were not much better off. My mother and aunts spoke disparagingly of the *canadianas*, Canadian women who (they were sure) knew nothing about how to keep a clean house or cook a decent meal. My mother taught me to cook and sew, and she and my aunts teased my brother, saying someday he'd marry a *canadiana* and would end up doing all his own housework.

For all her predictions, my mother was delighted to find out that she had been wrong. My brother, a physician, did marry a Canadian, but he doesn't do much of the housework. These days, my mother's biggest problem is pronouncing the name of her new grandson, Matthew Loughlin MacLean Vincent.

As I grew older I developed a nostalgia for my Lusitanian past, and tried desperately to reintegrate into the community. But I soon grew to hate the hypocrisy of some of my compatriots, most of whom were immigrants who chose to spend several years working in Canada, only to retire to the Portuguese country-side and build their palatial retreats with the fat pensions they collected from the Canadian government. Like my father, who learned English quickly and severed ties with his homeland, I became a staunch Canadian. I could sing *The Maple Leaf Forever* before I was 10, and spent my childhood years in French immersion. I became so good at masking my heritage that a few years ago when I applied for a job at a Toronto newspaper I was turned down because I was perceived as being too Anglo-Saxon.

"If you were ethnic, I'm sure they would have hired you on the spot," the wife of the paper's managing editor told me a year later.

But for most of my life being Portuguese seemed to me a liability. And then my mother bought that important first pair of pants. For a while it seemed that my life had changed. I was proud of my mother: she was becoming like all of the other mothers in the neighborhood.

But my excitement was short-lived. A few days later, she decided they just wouldn't do. She carefully wrapped them back up in the tissue paper, placed them in the cardboard Eaton's box, and returned them to the store.

TOPICS FOR DISCUSSION

1. The motif of her mother's first pair of pants functions as a framing device here. How does it symbolize the major differences between the author and her mother?

2. What range of responses to her new country does Vincent register among different generations of Portuguese immigrants? How is class mobility linked to assimilation?

3. Vincent doesn't feel quite Canadian, but she also feels estranged from the Portuguese community. Why? What methods have Vincent and her brother used to "Canadianize" themselves?

4. In her school years and later in her career, the author has perceived her ethnicity as an obstacle, an asset, or both. Does she ever resolve the ambiguity of her feelings about her ethnic heritage and sense of belonging?

5. The title of this essay may suggest that nationality can be fitted and changed at will, like an article of clothing. How true is this statement with regard to Vincent, her family, white immigrants in general, and those who are perceived as "visible minorities"?

Himani Bannerji

*Himani Bannerji was born in Bangladesh in 1942 and educated in
Calcutta. She came to Canada in 1969. She teaches Sociology at York
University, Toronto. Her research interests include women and development, colonial and postcolonial societies, feminist theory, anti-racist theory,
and immigrant women in Canada. She has published* The Writing on the
Wall: Essays on Culture and Politics *(1993),* Thinking Through: Essays
on Feminism, Marxism, and Anti-Racism *(1995), and* The Dark Side
of the Nation: Essays on Multiculturalism, Nationalism and Gender
(1999). She has also edited Returning the Gaze: Essays on Racism,
Feminism and Politics *(1993). Through her essays, she has established
herself as one of the leading figures in cultural and anti-racist criticism in
Canada. In addition to her scholarly achievements, Himani Bannerji is a
poet and fiction writer, with two volumes of poetry,* A Separate Sky *(1982)
and* Doing Time *(1986), as well as a novel for children,* Coloured
Pictures *(1992). The story below demonstrates that Canadian schools,
despite their increasingly multicultural makeup, sometimes fail to include
the experiences of all children. It captures the young protagonist in a
moment of coming into an awareness of racial identity when she begins to
see herself as "different."*

The Other Family

When the little girl came home it was already getting dark. The
winter twilight had transformed the sheer blue sky of the day into
the colour of steel, on which were etched a few stars, the bare winter
trees and the dark wedges of the house tops. A few windows cast a
faint glow on the snow outside. The mother stood at her window
and watched the little hooded figure walking toward the house. The
child looked like a shadow, her blue coat blended into the shadows
of the evening. This child, her own, how small and insubstantial she

seemed, and how alone, walking home through a pavement covered with ice and snow! It felt unreal. So different was this childhood from her own, so far away from the sun, the trees and the peopled streets of her own country! What did I do, she thought, I took her away from her own people and her own language, and now here she comes walking alone, through an alien street in a country named Canada.

As she contemplated the solitary, moving figure, her own solitude rushed over her like a tide. She had drifted away from a world that she had lived in and understood, and now she stood here at the same distance from her home as from the homes which she glimpsed while walking past the sparkling clean windows of the sandblasted houses. And now the door bell rang, and here was her daughter scraping the snow off her boots on the door mat.

Dinner time was a good time. A time of warmth, of putting hot, steaming food on to the table. A time to chat about the important things of the day, a time to show each other what they had acquired. Sometimes, however her mother would be absent-minded, worried perhaps about work, unsettled perhaps by letters that had arrived from home, scraping her feelings into a state of rawness. This was such an evening. She had served herself and her child, started a conversation about their two cats and fallen into a silence after a few minutes.

"You aren't listening to me, Mother."

The complaining voice got through to her, and she looked at the indignant face demanding attention from the other side of the table. She gathered herself together.

"So what did he do, when you gave him dried food?"

"Oh, I don't quite remember, I think he scratched the ground near his bowl and left."

The child laughed.

"That was smart of him! So why don't we buy tinned food for them?"

"Maybe we should," she said, and tried to change the topic.

"So what did you do in your school today?"

"Oh, we drew pictures like we do every day. We never study anything—not like you said you did in your school. We drew a family, our family. Want to see it?"

"Sure, and let's go to the living room, OK? This is messy." Scraping of the chairs and lighting of the lamps in the other room. They both made a rush for the most comfortable chair, both reached it at the same time and made a compromise.

"How about you sit in my lap? No? OK, sit next to me then and we will squeeze in somehow."

There was a remarkable resemblance between the two faces, except that the face of the child had a greater intensity, given by the wide open eyes. She was fine boned, and had black hair framing her face. Right now she was struggling with the contents of her satchel, apparently trying to feel her way to the painting.

"Here it is," she said, producing a piece of paper. "Here's the family!"

The mother looked at the picture for a long time. She was very still. Her face had set into an expression of anger and sadness. She was trying very hard not to cry. She didn't want to frighten the child, and yet what she saw made her feel distant from her daughter, as though she was looking at her through the reverse end of a telescope. She couldn't speak at all. The little girl too sat very still, a little recoiled from the body of her mother, as though expecting a blew. Her hands were clinched into fists, but finally it was she who broke the silence.

"What happened?" she said. "Don't you like it?"

"Listen," said the mother, "this is not your family. I, you and your father are dark-skinned, dark-haired. I don't have a blond wig hidden in my closet, my eyes are black, not blue, and your father's beard is black, not red, and you, do you have white skin, a button nose with freckles, blue eyes and blond hair tied into a pony tail? You said you drew our family. This is not it, is it?

The child was now feeling distinctly cornered. At first she was startled and frightened by her mother's response, but now she was prepared to be defiant. She had the greatest authority behind her, and she now summoned it to her help.

"I drew it from a book," she said, "all our books have this same picture of the family. You can go and see it for yourself. And everyone else drew it too. You can ask our teacher tomorrow. She liked it, so there!"

The little girl was clutching at her last straw.

"But you? Where are you in this picture?" demanded her mother, but now thoroughly aroused. "Where are we? Is this the family you would like to have? Don't you want us anymore? You want to be a *mem-sahib,* a white girl?"

But even as she lashed out these questions the mother regretted them. She could see that she made no sense to the child. She could feel the unfairness of it all. She was sorry that she was putting such a heavy burden on such young shoulders.

"First I bring her here," she thought, "and then I try to make her feel guilty for wanting to be the same as the others." But something had taken hold of her this evening. Panic at the thought of losing her child, despair and guilt galvanized her into speech she regretted, and she looked with anger at her only child, who it seemed wanted to be white, who had rejected her dark mother. Someday this child would be ashamed of her, she thought, someday would move out into the world of those others. Someday they would be enemies. Confusing thoughts ran through her head like images of an uncontrollable television screen, in the chaos of which she heard her ultimate justification flung at her by her daughter – they wanted me to draw the family, didn't they? "They" wanted "her" to draw "the family." The way her daughter pronounced the words "they" or "the family" indicated that she knew what she was talking about. The simple pronoun "they" definitely stood for authority, for that uncontrollable yet organized world immediately outside, of which the school was the ultimate expression. It surrounded their own private space. "They" had power, "they" could crush little people like her anytime "they" wanted to, and in "their" world that was the picture of the family. Whether her mother liked it or not, whether she looked like the little girl in it or not, made not one jot of difference. That was, yes, was the right picture. As these thoughts passed through her mind, her anger ebbed away. Abandoning her fury and distance, the mother bowed her head at the image of this family and burst into sobs.

"What will happen to you?" she said. "What did I do to you?"

She cried a great deal and said many incoherent things. The little girl was patient, quietly absorbing her mother's change of mood. She had a thoughtful look on her face, and bit her nails from time to time. She did not protest any more, but nor did she cry. After a while her mother took her to bed and tucked her in, and sat in the kitchen with the fearful vision of her daughter always outside of the window of the blond family, never the center of her own life, always rejecting herself, and her life transformed into a gigantic peep show. She wept very bitterly because she had caused this destruction, and because she had hated her child in her own fear of rejection, and because she had sowed guilt into her mind.

When her mother went to bed and closed the door, the child, who has been waiting for long, left the bed. She crossed the corridor on her tiptoes, past the row of shoes, the silent gathering of the overcoats and the mirror with the wavy surface, and went into the washroom. Behind the door was another mirror, of full length, and clear. Deliberately and slowly the child took off the top of her pyjamas and surveyed herself with grave scrutiny. She saw the brownness of her skin, the wide, staring, dark eyes, the black hair now tousled from the pillows, the scar on her nose and the brownish pink of her mouth. She stood a while lost in this act of contemplation, until the sound of soft padded feet neared the door, and a whiskered face peeped in. She stooped and picked up the cat and walked back to her own room.

It was snowing again, and little elves with bright coloured coats and snow in their boots had reappeared in the classroom. When finally the coats were hung under pegs with names and boots neatly stowed away, the little girl approached her teacher. She had her painting from the day before in her hand.

"I have brought it back," she said.

"Why?" asked her teacher, "don't you like it any more?"

The little girl was looking around very intently.

"It's not finished yet," she said. "The books I looked at didn't have something. Can I finish it now?"

"Go ahead," said the teacher, moving on to get the colours from the cupboard.

The little girl was looking at the classroom. It was full of children of all colours, of all kinds of shapes of noses and of different colours of hair. She sat on the floor, placed the incomplete picture on a big piece of newspaper and started to paint. She worked long at it – and with great concentration. Finally it was finished. She went back to her teacher.

"It's finished now," she said. "I drew the rest."

The teacher reached out for the picture and spread it neatly on a desk. There they were, the blond family arranged in a semicircle with a dip in the middle, but next to them, arranged alike, stood another group – a man, a woman, and a child, but they were dark-skinned, dark-haired, the woman wore clothes from her own country, and the little girl in the middle had a scar on her nose.

"Do you like it?"

"Who are they?" asked the teacher, though she should have known. But the little girl didn't mind answering this question one bit.

"It's the other family," she said.

TOPICS FOR DISCUSSION

1. What anxieties does the mother experience comparing her daughter's life to her own? Why does she fear for their future?

2. What is the mother's reaction when her daughter shows her a picture of a family she drew at school that day?

3. How does the incident with the picture change the daughter's self-perception? Whom does she mean by "the other family"?

David Arnason

*David Arnason is a poet, novelist, satirist, playwright, critic, screenwriter,
and editor. He was born in 1940 in Gimli, Manitoba, the oldest Icelandic
community in Canada. He has an M.A. from the University of Manitoba
and a Ph.D. from the University of New Brunswick. He teaches English
and creative writing at the University of Manitoba. His academic interests
include Canadian literature, semiotics, deconstruction, and discourse
analysis. He has also taught Canadian literature in Tasmania, Germany,
and France. Arnason founded the* Journal of Canadian Fiction *and was
one of the founders of Turnstone Press. He has published two collections of
poetry,* Marsh Burning *(1980) and* Skrag *(1987); five collections of stories,* Fifty Stories and a Piece of Advice *(1982),* The Circus Performers'
Bar *(1984),* The Happiest Man in the World *(1989),* If Pigs Could
Fly… *(1995), and* The Dragon and the Dry Goods Princess *(1997);
and a novel,* The Pagan Wall *(1992). Recently, the journal* Prairie Fire
*devoted an entire issue to David Arnason (Spring 2001, volume 22,1).
Arnason's interest in his ethnic roots is reflected in* The New Icelanders: A
North American Community, *which he edited, and in the film documentary* Tied by Blood: A Journey into Genealogy, *for which he co-authored
and narrated the script.*

*Arnason's name is associated with postmodern fiction in Canada. He
writes humorous and formally innovative stories that examine gender and
other stereotypes with an ironic eye. He often uses parody. Arnason calls the
stories from* The Dragon and the Dry Goods Princess, *from which
"Return of the Frogs" has been taken, "fractured prairie tales"—a pun on
"fairy tales."*

Return of the Frogs

Once, in a slightly better time than our own, a farmer lived with
his wife and daughter on a farm just outside Portage la Prairie. His
daughter was neither very beautiful nor very good, but she was the
only daughter he had and he loved her dearly. Her name was
Virginia, but she had rechristened herself Gina.

Gina was fifteen and she planned to be an NHL goalie when she grew up. She was already the top goalie in the midget B league in the Southwest Manitoba Amateur Hockey League, and only six months ago, in an exhibition game against Fargo, North Dakota, she'd had a shutout.

One day she was throwing her baseball against the side of the barn when it bounced crazily and fell into an old well. She looked into the well, but instead of seeing her ball, she saw a frog.

"Hey you!" she shouted to the frog who was swimming around in the water. "How about getting my ball out of the well?"

The frog made a noise that sounded like "chuggarumm."

"No, I'm serious," she said. "If you get my ball out of that well, you can eat off my plate and sleep in my bed and everything. And if you're really good, I'll give you a kiss and turn you into a fairy prince. Then we can get married and live happily ever after."

The frog didn't reply, but he dived down into the well and disappeared. Gina waited a few minutes, but no frog appeared so she walked back to the house. The school bus would be by in a few minutes anyway.

"You're not going to school dressed like that," her mother told her. "Put on something decent, and make it snappy. The bus will be here in a minute."

"What's wrong with what I'm wearing?" Gina asked.

"You'll be mistaken for the janitor," her mother replied. "And if I'm not mistaken, there's manure on the cuffs of those jeans. Now change."

"Sheesh."

"And don't swear. It's not becoming in a lady."

"I didn't swear. I just said sheesh. And I'm not a lady. The only ladies in this place are members of the Ladies Aid, and you can't join until you're ninety."

"You are getting entirely too big for your britches, young lady. I swear, I don't know what I'm going to do with you."

"You shouldn't swear," Gina told her, skipping out of the room. "It isn't nice."

She missed the bus of course. She put on a miniskirt, and her mother wouldn't let her wear that either. Finally she dressed in a pair of slacks and a sweater than made her look like a bag of potatoes, but her mother thought she looked nice.

"She's missed the bus again, Roy," her mother said. "I don't know how she's going to survive in the world by herself. Can you give her a lift to school?"

"Sure," her dad said. "I got to go to town to get a carburetor kit for the John Deere anyway. C'mon, Princess."

Gina's dad let her drive the half-ton all the way to the edge of the town. Then he dropped her off at the new high school. The bell had rung, but most of the kids were still outside. "Be good," her dad said. "Don't take any wooden nickels."

"You're a sweetheart, Roy," Gina said, and she blew him a kiss. She'd started calling him Roy a couple of months ago, but not when her mother was around. He seemed to like it, but it enraged her mother. She'd once called her Margaret instead of Mom and been grounded for a week.

School had just started a couple of weeks ago, and nothing was settled yet. Last year, her best friend had been Trish, but now Trish was best friends with Cristal, and Gina didn't think it was fair. The town kids could play together all summer, but she had to help on the farm, so when she got back to school every fall things were all changed.

Math class was the last class of the day, and Miss Miller, who taught it, was Gina's favourite teacher. She caught Gina after class and asked if she could have a few words with her.

"As long as I catch my bus," Gina said. "I missed it this morning, and if I miss it again I'm in deep doo-doo."

"It'll just take a minute. Look, Gina, we're having try-out for cheerleaders on Wednesday. If you want to come out, I'll give you a ride home afterward. You're really athletic, and I think you'd have a really good chance. Both Trish and Cristal are trying out."

"No," Gina said. "No thanks. I'd sooner be the one who gets cheered."

"Are you going out for hockey again?"

"You bet."

"Look, Gina," her teacher said. "I'm all for liberation and equal opportunities. You know that. But are you sure that playing hockey is a realistic choice? It keeps you kind of isolated from the rest of the kids."

"That's their problem," Gina said. "I've got to catch a bus. So long."

When Gina got home, her baseball was drying out on the front steps.

"I scooped it out for you with the fish net," her dad said. "It should be okay as soon as it dries out."

"Thanks, Roy. You didn't happen to see a frog, did you?"

"As a matter of fact, I did. Great big bugger. He must have fallen in. I scooped him out too and let him go."

"He's actually an enchanted prince," Gina told her father. "I told him that if I got my ball back he could eat off my plate and sleep in my bed. I suppose he'll be around later."

"Don't you go kissing any frogs," her dad said. "Not when you're fifteen. I've got enough problems around here. Finish university, then you can kiss all the frogs you want."

"I'm not going to university," she reminded him. "I'm going to be an NHL goalie."

"Right," he said. "I forgot. Anyway, I've got cows to milk, Princess. You go on in and study. And try not to fight with your mom."

"Are you sure she's my mom? Mightn't she actually be a wicked stepmother?"

"She's your mom, all right. Forty-eight hours of labour and she still hasn't forgotten it. Be good, please?"

"Right on, Roy. You go round up the herd, and I'll deal with Dale Evans."

Gina's mother was in the kitchen making jelly. The kitchen was full of steam and her mother's glasses were covered with steam from the boiling jelly.

"Anything I can get you?" Gina asked. "Eye of newt or tail of frog? Finger of birth-strangled dog?"

"If you're going to quote Shakespeare," her mother said, "try to get it right." Her mother had been an English teacher in some distant, unthinkable past, and she seemed to have memorized every poem in the English language. At the moment, she look exasperated.

"Whatever," Gina answered, and she brooded for a minute on a fly that was circling the butter dish. "I was talking to Miss Miller today," she went on. "She wants me to go out for cheerleaders."

"And?" said her mother, leaving the question hanging there.

"I think maybe I will."

"I don't think you'd like it much," her mother said. "You're not the type."

"What is that supposed to mean?" Gina asked. "Not the pretty type? Not the sexy type?"

"Not the cheerleader type," her mother said. "And you know precisely what I mean."

"Too cranky, too bad-tempered, too hard to get along with?"

"Precisely."

And Gina did not go out for cheerleaders, because she suspected that her mother was right. She did go out for the juvenile hockey team. There was a new coach this year, a guy named Semchuk, who had played in the AHL and had been called up for one game with the Red Wings but had been thrown out of the game in the first period for fighting. He was good-looking in a barnyard sort of way, but very bad tempered. He didn't even want Gina to try out, because he said he was looking for the league title and he didn't want to wreck the team's chances. Still, he let her come to the first couple of practices and even grudgingly admitted that she was pretty good for a girl. But when he posted the roster her name was not on it. Instead, Danny Reimer was the first goalie, and the back-up was Bill Klassen, who couldn't even skate.

Gina was weeping in a back stall in the barn when her father found her.

"Hey, Princess," he said. "NHL goalies don't cry."

"It's not fair," Gina told him. "I'm better than anybody else that tried out. I'm the only chance we've got to win the league title. But I'm not going to get a chance." And she starts to cry again.

"Hold on. Hold on," her father said. "It's not the end of the world."

"Yes it is," Gina said. "It is the end of the world. It's the end of my world. It's the end of everything I ever wanted."

But the world didn't end. Gina went out for cheerleaders and, as Miss Miller had predicted, she made it. And, as her mother had predicted, she hated every minute of it. She hated the other girls, and they hated her because she was the only one who got every drill perfect. And she hated the uniform. And she detested football because it was a stupid game.

"There's a frog in the basement," her mother told her. "A huge horrible green frog. Can you get rid of it?"

"Right," Gina said. "Exactly what I need."

"What are you doing here?" Gina asked the frog when she found it behind the dryer in the basement. "You didn't come through. No free wishes for this girl."

The frog made a croaking noise, possibly "chugarumm," and he jumped into the corner where her baseball and glove were lying.

"Oh," Gina said. "The ball. But you didn't get it. Roy did. He had to rescue you as well."

The frog didn't say anything. He just puffed out his cheeks.

"All right," Gina told it. "A bargain's a bargain." And she took the frog up to her room and put it in a cage that had been empty since her hamster, Jeffrey, had died a couple of years ago. Then she went around the house catching flies for it. There weren't very many, but she found some dead ones between the windows in her room and gave them to him. That night, just as she was going to bed, she picked up the frog. He was sort of dried out, and not slimy at all. She held him up to the light.

"Now if I give you a kiss," she said, "you have to promise to turn into a prince." The frog blinked its big eyes. "Here goes," and she planted a big, noisy kiss on the top of his head. Nothing happened.

"Right," Gina said. "A dud. A misfire. A blank cartridge. With my luck you'll turn out to have some disgusting disease and I'll catch it and die."

The next day the frog was gone. Vanished. No amount of searching could find him. But there was a new guy in school, and all the girls were buzzing about him. His name was Jean-Claude Grenwill, and his father was the new dentist in town. Within a week, he was the first-string quarterback, and the team, which hadn't won a game until then, finally had need for cheerleaders.

Gina went out for a Coke with Trish and Cristal and tried as hard as she could not to get into a fight with either of them. They reported the rumour that Jean-Claude had a girlfriend back in Montreal who was an actress and that none of the local girls was going to have a chance.

And yet, only a couple of weeks later, Jean-Claude hung around after the football practice watching the cheerleaders do their drills. Gina was intensely conscious of her body and her little uniform. She wished she could put on her goalie uniform, complete with mask. After the drills, Jean-Claude came up to her.

"You're really good," he told her. "You're a terrific athlete."

"This is my last practice," she said. "I'm turning in my uniform. No more cheerleading for me."

"That's too bad," Jean-Claude said. "This team needs all the cheering it can get."

"I don't want to cheer," Gina said. "I want to play." It seemed important to her that she make him understand that she wasn't really a cheerleader.

"You want to play football?"

"No. Hockey. I'm a goalie. I'm the best goalie in the whole goddam province and they won't let me play." And she burst into tears.

"Whoa, wait," he said. "What's this all about?"

And so she told him everything. She told him how rotten and corrupt the world was, and how unfair everything was, and she ended by telling him that if he wanted to watch her boobs bounce in a skimpy uniform, he could forget about that too. And, as a post-script, she mentioned that she hated him.

"Hang on," he said. "I've got an idea." And he told her about a special hockey school that was being held in Montreal at Christmas, just for goalies. And he told her that it was being run by the most famous NHL goalie who had ever lived, a name that took her breath away.

"Great," she said. "It will only cost a billion dollars, and they won't let me in because I'm a girl."

But she talked to Roy, and Roy talked to Margaret, and in the end it turned out that they had some money they had been saving for a trip to Hawaii, but they had decided not to go to Hawaii after all. There was enough money to send her to Montreal, and so she went. The famous goalie made her work harder than she had ever worked in her life, and he made her forget all the tricks she had ever learned and just concentrate on stopping the puck.

Then Danny Reimer got sick over Christmas and Bill Klassen broke his leg skiing, so the coach phoned her and asked if she'd fill in for a game. She did, and she got a shutout, and Jean-Claude sat behind the goal and cheered like crazy.

After the game Jean-Claude walked her over to the Mitchell's place where her parents were waiting for her to drive her back to the farm. Just before they got to the door, they stopped, and Jean-Claude kissed her, a long, lovely kiss.

Gina stepped back. "Please don't be offended," she told him, "but you look an awful lot like a frog I used to know."

TOPICS FOR DISCUSSION

1. The story shows gender stereotyping as part of school life and sports. What forms does Gina's rebellion against popular gender norms take?

2. How does Arnason use humour to subvert the reader's conventional expectations?

3. What elements suggest that the story may be looked at as a parody of the fairy tale? How does the use of parody affect the story's message?

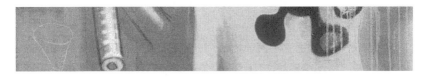

GENDER/
FAMILIES/
RELATIONSHIPS

I N T R O D U C T I O N

Today's science looks at gender and sexuality not as fixed, biologically determined aspects of human identity, but rather as socially
constructed categories of difference. Gender and sexuality are
reflected both in personal identity and in social interactions—what
kinds of gender and erotic possibilities are available to individuals in
a particular society at any given time in history. The social dimension

of gender is expressed in the French philosopher Simone de Beauvoir's statement that "one is not born a woman, but rather becomes, a woman," which might equally well apply to men's situation. From their early days, boys and girls are socialized into gender roles and types of behaviour associated with current notions of femininity and masculinity. Since these norms and notions are historically and geographically varied, we have traditional categories of male and female, but also transsexual and transgender individuals. Similarly, a wider recognition that the heterosexual norm is not the only way of expressing human desire allows gay, lesbian, and bisexual people to be more outspoken about their identity.

Gender and sexual revolution, in addition to other social, economic, and technological changes, has transformed the traditional patterns of family life in Canada. As a result of women's growing participation in the labour force, lower fertility rates, greater social acceptance of single-parent families and common-law unions, increase in divorce and separation rates, and widespread social diversity, we have a greater flexibility and diversity also in family forms and structures. The model of the male breadwinner, nuclear family is statistically disappearing. Instead, we have extended families in many immigrant communities, two-breadwinner families, one-parent families, merged families, or same-sex partner families.

In this unit, but also in other places in the book, we hear voices of different types of relationships, revealing the generation gaps and conflicts existing within families as well the deep love and childhood memories cherished for life. At its most tragic, the family can be a site of abuse, dysfunction, and neglect of children, where many things have been left "unsaid" or kept secret for years and where a failure of communication can lead to isolation, despair, and death.

Bernice Lever

Born in 1936 in British Columbia, Bernice Lever is a poet, prose writer, editor, and educator. She studied English and creative writing with Irving Layton at York University, Toronto, and between 1972 and 1987, she edited Waves, *a literary magazine. Since 1967 until her recent retirement to BC, she coordinated the Richvale Writers' Club in Richmond Hill, Ontario. She is former Vice-President of the League of Canadian Poets, as well as a member of the Canadian Authors Association and the Canadian Poetry Association. She has given poetry readings from coast to coast. For many years she taught English and creative writing at Seneca College. She has three children and two grandchildren. Her publications include five collections of poems,* Excuses, for All Occasions *(1979),* Yet, Woman I Am *(1979),* Sometimes the Distance *(1986),* The Waiting Room *(1993), and* Things Unsaid *(1996). She also edited* Singing: An Anthology of Women's Writing from Canadian Prisons *(1980). She is currently working on three more books:* Seven Stages of Relationships, Lies for All Occasions, *and* My Cocoon Is Broken, *a book of healing chants with art therapy. Bernice Lever has also written an innovative text-book for teaching English grammar through colour-coding, called* The Colour of Words *(1989).*

Things Unsaid

A family stays together
    waiting for what may get said
the unspoken, dreaded rebukes,
the secret revelation from dying beds,
the verbal burdens passed on
    from generation to generation.

How much shall we tell –
     what can these offspring withstand?

Boredom sets in after the shock of hearing
     this!   that!   is that all?
No need to stay once ALL is known.

Afraid to lose children, already
     beyond the age
               to be set loose,
parents do not complain.

Children afraid to lose
     those free handouts
     so preferred to earnings,
do not criticize parents.

Grandparents who know the games
     that silent smiles can play,
do not name the deeds
     nor misdeeds done
               nor uncover lies of love
silently accepting anything
     a relative says or does.

Keys of knowledge can turn rusty with disuse
as our door never creaks to new vistas
     nor swings open to our own challenges

as we get locked in
          our family's history rut.

T O P I C S   F O R   D I S C U S S I O N

1. Why is the speaker's vision of family relationships so dark?
   What attitudes does she identify among different relatives?

2. What is the effect of "things unsaid" on the family?

3. Explain the final metaphor of getting "locked in." What connotations are brought into the poem by the word "rut"?

Mordecai Richler

*Mordecai Richler was born in 1931, in a Jewish neighbourhood of
Montreal, and died in 2001. He is one of Canada's most celebrated writers.
In addition to being a novelist, he was also an essayist, journalist,
humourist, author of children's books, travel writer, anthologist, and
award-winning screenwriter. His grandfather immigrated to Canada from
Galicia in 1904 and worked as a street peddler. Richler spent several years
travelling and living in Europe, notably in London, England, from 1957
to 1972. In 1968-69 he was writer-in-residence at Concordia University.
He has published eleven novels, the best of which are* The Apprenticeship
of Duddy Kravitz *(1959),* Cocksure *(1968),* St. Urbain's Horseman
(1971), Joshua Then and Now *(1980),* Solomon Gursky Was Here
(1989), and Barney's Version *(1998). Richler won numerous awards for
his writing, including two Governor General's Awards for* Cocksure *and*
St. Urbain's Horseman, *as well as children's book awards for his* Jacob
Two-Two *books. His essays often provoked controversy; his opinion on
Quebec's nationalist language policies and his anti-orthodox stance antago-
nized both Quebec separatists and the Montreal Jewish community. Critic
Robert Fulford recognizes Mordecai Richler's role in the process of transfor-
mation in English-speaking Canada from monoculturalism to multicultur-
alism: "When [Richler] was first writing and identifying himself strongly as
a Jew, that was really unusual." In the 1950s and early 1960s, before multiculturalism became a popular trend, Richler focused on local, mostly
Jewish, communities. The essay reprinted here comes from* Home Sweet
Home: My Canadian Album *(1984). In this memoir of his father,
Richler talks about the differences that separated them and admits that his
perception of his father remains full of "unresolved mysteries."*

My Father's Life

After the funeral, I was given my father's *talis,* his prayer shawl,
and (oh my god) a file containing all the letters I had written to him
while I was living abroad, as well as carbon copies he had kept of the
letters he had sent me.

December, 18, 1959: "Dear Son, Last week I won a big Kosher Turkey, by bowling, when I made the high triple for the week. How I did it I do not know, I guess I was lucky for once, or was it that the others were too sure of themselves, being much better at the game than I am."

February 28, 1963: "This month has been a cold one, making it difficult, almost impossible to work outside. Yes! it's been tough. Have you found a title for your last novel? What can you do with a title like this? 'UNTIL *DEBT* DO US PART'?"

His letter of February 28, 1963, like so many other written that year, begins. "Thanks for the cheque." For by that time we have come full circle. In the beginning it was my father who had sent checks to me. Included in the file I inherited were canceled checks, circa 1945, for $28 monthly child support, following the annulment of my parents' marriage. A bill dated January 15, 1948, for a Royal portable, my first typewriter; a birthday gift. Another bill, from Bond Clothes, dated August 21, 1950, on the eve of my departure for Europe, for "1 Sta. Wag. Coat, $46.49."

My own early letters to my father, horrendously embarrassing for me to read now, usually begin with appeals for money. No, *demands*. There is also a telegram I'd rather forget. March 11, 1951. IMPERATIVE CHECK SENT PRONTO MADRID C O COOKS WAGON LITS ALCALA NR 23 MADRID. BROKE. MORDECAI.

Imperative, indeed.

I was also left a foot-long chisel, his chisel, which I now keep on a shelf of honor in my workroom. Written with a certain flourish in orange chalk on the oak shaft is my father's inscription:

> Used by M.I. Richler
> Richler Artificial Stone Works
> 1922
> De La Roche Street
> *NO* SUCCESS.

My father was twenty years old then, younger than my eldest son is now. He was the firstborn of fourteen children. Surely that year, as every year of his life, on Passover, he sat in his finery at a dining-room table and recited, "We were once the slaves of Pharaoh in Egypt, but the Lord our God brought us forth form there with a mighty hand and an outstretched arm." But, come 1922, out there in the muck of his father's freezing backyard on De La Roche Street in Montreal—yet to absorb the news of his liberation, my father was still trying to make bricks with insufficient straw.

Moses Isaac Richler.

Insufficient straw, *NO* SUCCESS, was the story of his life. Neither of his marriages really worked. There were searing quarrels with my older brother. As a boy, I made life difficult for him. I had no respect. Later, officious strangers would rebuke him in the synagogue for the novels I had written. Heaping calumny on the Jews, they said. If there was such a thing as a reverse Midas touch, he had it. Not one of my father's penny mining stocks ever went into orbit. He lost regularly at gin rummy. As younger, more intrepid brothers and cousins began to prosper, he assured my mother, "The bigger they come, the harder they fall."

My mother, her eyes charged with scorn, laughed in his face, "You're the eldest and what are you?"

Nothing.

After his marriage to my mother blew apart, he moved into a rented room. Stunned, humiliated. St. Urbain's cuckold. He bought a natty straw hat. A sports jacket. He began to use aftershave lotion. It was then I discovered that he had a bottle of rye whiskey stashed in the glove compartment of his Chevy. My father. Rye whiskey. "What's that for?" I asked, astonished.

"For the femmes," he replied, wiggling his eyebrows at me. "It makes them want it."

I remember him as a short man, squat, with a shiny bald head and big floppy ears. Richler ears. My ears. Seated at the kitchen table at night in his Penman's long winter underwear, wetting his finger before turning a page of the *New York Daily Mirror*, reading Walter Winchell first. Winchell, who knew what's what. He also devoured *Popular Mechanics, Doc Savage,* and *Black Mask.* And, for educational purposes, *Reader's Digest.* My mother, on the other hand, read Keats and Shelley. *King's Row. The Good Earth.* My father's pranks did not enchant her. A metal ink spot on her new chenille bedspread. A felt mouse to surprise her in the larder. A knish secretly filled with absorbent cotton. Neither did his jokes appeal to her. "Hey, do you know why we eat hard-boiled eggs dipped in salt water just before the Passover meal?"

"No, Daddy. Why?"

"To remind us that when the Jews crossed the Red Sea they certainly got their balls soaked."

Saturday mornings my brother and I accompanied him to the Young Israel synagogue on Park Avenue near St. Viateur. As I was the youngest, under bar-mitzvah age, and therefore still allowed to carry on the Sabbath, I was the one who held the prayer shawls in a little purple velvet bag. My father, who couldn't stomach the rabbi's windy speeches, would slip into the back room to gossip with the other men before the rabbi set sail. "In Japan," my father once said, "there is a custom, time-honored, that before he begins, a speaker's hands are filled with ice cubes. He can shoot his mouth off for as long as he can hold the ice cubes in his hands. I wouldn't mind if the rabbi had to do that."

He was stout, he was fleshy. But in the wedding photographs that I never saw until after his death the young man who was to become my father is as skinny as I once was, his startled brown eyes unsmiling behind horn-rimmed glasses. Harold Lloyd. Allowed a quick no-promises peek at the world and what is had to offer, but clearly not entitled to a place at the table.

My father never saw Paris. Never read Yeats. Never stayed out with the boys drinking too much. Never flew to New York on a whim. Nor turned over in bed and slept in, rather than report to work. Never knew a reckless love. What did he hope for? What did he want? Beyond peace and quiet, which he seldom achieved, I have no idea. So far as I know he never took a risk or was disobedient. At his angriest, I once heard him silence one of his cousins, a cousin bragging about his burgeoning real estate investments, saying, "You know how much land a man needs? Six feet. And one day that's all you'll have. Ha, ha!"

Anticipating Bunker Hunt, my father began to hoard American silver in his rented room. A blue steamer trunk filling with neatly stacked piles of silver dollars, quarters, dimes. But decades before their worth began to soar, he had to redeem them at face value. "I'm getting hitched again," he told me, blushing. He began to speculate in postage stamps. When he died at the age of sixty-five I also found out that he had bought a city backlot somewhere for $1,200 during the Forties. In 1967, however—riding a bloated market, every fool raking it in—the estimated value of my father's property had shrunk to $900. All things considered, that called for a real touch of class.

I was charged with appetite, my father had none. I dreamed of winning prizes, he never competed. But, like me, my father was a writer. A keeper of records. His diary, wherein he catalogued injuries and insults, betrayals, family quarrels, bad debts, was written in a code of his own invention. His brothers and sisters used to tease him about it. "Boy, are we ever afraid! Look, I'm shaking!" But as cancer began to consume him, they took notice, fluttering about, concerned. "What about Moishe's diary?"

I wanted it. Oh, how I wanted it. I felt the diary was my proper inheritance. I hoped it would tell me things about him that he had always been too reticent to reveal. But his widow, an obdurate lady, refused to let me into the locked room in their apartment where he kept his personal papers. All she would allow was, "I'm returning your mother's love letters to her. The ones he found that time. You know, from the refugee."

That would have been during the early Forties, when my mother began to rent to refugees, putting them up in our spare bedroom. The refugees, German and Austrian Jews, had been interned as enemy aliens in England shortly after war was declared in 1939. A year later they were transported to Canada on a ship along with the first German and Italian prisoners of war. On arrival at the dock in Quebec city, the army major who turned them over to their Canadian guards said, "You have some German officers here, very good fellows, and some Italians, they'll be no trouble. And over there," he added, indicating the refugees, "the scum of Europe."

The refugees were interned in camps, but in 1941 they began to be released one by one. My father, who had never had anybody to condescend to in his life, was expecting real *greeners* with sidecurls. Timorous innocents out of the *shtetl* who would look to him as a master of magic. Canadian magic. Instead, they patronized him. A mere junk dealer, a dolt. The refugees turned out to speak better English than any of us did, as well as German and French. After all they had been through over there, they were still fond of quoting a German son of a bitch called Goethe. "Imagine that," my father said. They also sang opera arias in the bathtub. They didn't guffaw over the antics of Fibber McGee 'n' Molly on the radio; neither were they interested in the strippers who shook their nookies right at you from the stage of the Gayety Theatre, nor in learning how to play gin rummy for a quarter of a cent a point. My mother was enthralled.

My father was afraid of his father. He was afraid of my unhappy mother, who arranged to have their marriage annulled when I was thirteen and my brother eighteen. He was also afraid of his second wife. Alas, he was even afraid of me when I was a boy. I rode streetcars on the Sabbath. I ate bacon. But nobody was ever afraid of Moses Isaac Richler. He was far too gentle.

The Richler family was, and remains, resolutely Orthodox, followers of the Lubavitchre rabbi. So when my mother threatened divorce, an all but unheard-of scandal in those days, a flock of grim rabbis in flapping black gabardine coats descended on our coldwater flat on St. Urbain Street to plead with her. But my mother, dissatisfied for years with her arranged marriage, in love at last, was adamant. She had had enough. The rabbis sighed when my father, snapping his suspenders, rocking on his heels—*speaking out*—stated his most deeply felt marital grievance. When he awakened from his Saturday afternoon nap there was no tea. "Me, I like a cup of hot tea with lemon when I wake up."

In the end, there was no divorce. Instead, there was an annulment. I should explain that in the Province of Quebec at that time each divorce called for parliamentary approval. A long, costly process. A lawyer, a family friend, found a loophole. He pleaded for an annulment. My mother, he told the court, had married without her father's consent when she had still been a minor. He won. Technically speaking, I used to brag at college, I'm a bastard.

Weekdays my father awakened every morning at six, put on his phylacteries, said his morning prayers, and drove his truck through the wintry dark to the family scrapyard near the waterfront. He worked there for my fierce, hot-tempered grandfather and a pompous younger brother. Uncle Solly, who had been to high school, had been made a partner in the yard, but not my father, the firstborn. He was a mere employee, working for a salary, which fed my mother's wrath. Younger brothers, determined to escape an overbearing father, had slipped free to form their own business, but my father was too timid to join them. "When times are bad they'll be back. Remember the Depression. Oh, boy!"

"Tell me about it," I pleaded.

But my father never talked to me about anything. Not his own boyhood. His feelings or his dreams. He never even mentioned sex to me until I was nineteen years old, bound for Paris to try to become a writer. Clutching my Royal portable, wearing my Sta. Wag. coat. "You know what safes are. If you have to do it—*and I know you*—use 'em. Don't get married over there. They'd do anything for a pair of nylon stockings or a Canadian passport."

Hot damn, I hoped he was right. But my father thought I was crazy to sail for Europe. A graveyard for the Jews. A continent where everything was broken or old. Even so, he lent me his blue steamer trunk and sent me $50 a month support. When I went broke two years later, he mailed me my boat fare without reproach. I told him that the novel I had written over there was called *The Acrobats* and he immediately suggested that I begin the title of my second novel with a B, the third with a C, and so on, which would make a nifty trademark for me. Writing, he felt, might not be such a nutty idea after all. He had read in *Life* that this guy Mickey Spillane, a mere *goy*, was making a fortune. Insulted, I explained hotly that I wasn't that kind of writer. I was a serious man.

"So?"

"I only write out of my obsessions."

"Ah, ha," he said, sighing, warming to me for once, recognizing another generation of family failure.

Even when I was a boy his admonitions were few. "Don't embarrass me. Don't get into trouble."

I embarrassed him. I got into trouble.

In the early Forties, my father's father rented a house directly across the street from us on St. Urbain, ten of his fourteen children still single and rooted at home. The youngest, my Uncle Yankel, was only three years older than I was and at the time we were close friends. But no matter what after-school mischief we were up to, we were obliged to join my grandfather at sunset in the poky little Gallicianer *shul* around the corner for the evening prayers, a ritual I didn't care for. One evening, absorbed in a chemistry experiment in our "lab" in my grandfather's basement, we failed to appear. On his return from *shul*, my grandfather descended on us, seething, his face bleeding red. One by one he smashed our test tubes and our retorts and even our cherished water distiller against the stone wall. Yankel begged forgiveness, but not me. A few days later I contrived to get into a scrap with Yankel, leaping at him, blackening his eye. Oh boy, did that ever feel good. But Yankel squealed on me. My grandfather summoned me into his study, pulled his belt free of his trousers, and thrashed me.

Vengeance was mine.

I caught my grandfather giving short weight on his scrapyard scales to a drunken Irish peddler. My grandfather, Jehovah's enforcer. Scornful, triumphant, I ran to my father and told him his father was no better than a cheat and a hypocrite.

"What do you know?" my father demanded.

"Nothing."

"They're anti-Semites, every one of them."

My grandfather moved to Jeanne Mance Street, only a few blocks away, and on Sunday afternoons he welcomed all the family there. Children, grandchildren. Come Hanukkah, the most intimidating of my aunts was posted in the hall, seated behind a bridge table piled high with Parcheesi games one year, Snakes and Ladders another. As each grandchild filed past the table he was issued a game. "Happy Hanukkah."

My grandfather was best with the babies, rubbing his spade beard into their cheeks until they squealed. Bouncing them on his lap. But I was twelve years old now and I had taken to strutting down St. Urbain without a hat, and riding streetcars on the Sabbath. The next time my father and I started out for the house on

Jeanne Mance on a Sunday afternoon, he pleaded with me not to disgrace him yet again, to behave myself for once, and then he thrust a *yarmulke* at me. "You can't go in there bareheaded. Put it on."

"It's against my principles. I'm an atheist."

"What are you talking about?"

"Charles Darwin," I said, having just read a feature article on him in *Coronet*, "or haven't you ever heard of him?"

'You put on that *yarmulke*," he said, "or I cut your allowance right now."

"O.K., O.K."

"And Jewish children are not descended from monkeys, in case you think you know everything."

"When I have children of my own I'll be better to them."

I had said that, testing. Sneaking a sidelong glance at my father. The thing is I had been born with an undescended testicle and my brother, catching me naked in the bathroom, had burst out laughing and assured me that I would never be able to have children or even screw. "With only one ball," he said, "you'll never be able to shoot jism."

My father didn't rise to the bait. He had worries of his own. My mother. The refugee in the spare bedroom. His father. "When you step in the door," he said, "the *zeyda* will ask you which portion of the Torah they read in *shul* yesterday." He told me the name of the chapter. "Got it?"

"I'm not afraid of him."

My grandfather, his eyes hot, was lying in wait for me in the living room. Before a court composed of just about the entire family, he denounced me as a violator of the Sabbath. A *shabus goy*. Yankel smirked. My grandfather grabbed me by the ear, beat me about the face, and literally threw me out of the house. I lingered across the street, waiting for my father to seek me out, but when he finally appeared, having endured a bruising lecture of his own, all he said was, "You deserved what you got."

"Some father you are."

Which was when I earned another belt on the cheek.

"I want you to go back in there like a man and apologize to the *zeyda*."

"Like hell."

I never spoke to my grandfather again.

But when he died, less than a year after the annulment of my parents' marriage, my mother insisted it was only proper that I attend his funeral. I arrived at the house on Jeanne Mance to find the coffin set out in the living room, uncles and aunts gathered round. My Uncle Solly drove me into a corner. "So here you are," he said.

"So?"

"You hastened his death; you never even spoke to him even though he was sick all those months."

"I didn't bring on his death."

"Well, smart guy, you're the one who is mentioned first in his will."

"Oh."

"You are not a good Jew and you are not to touch his coffin. It says that in his will. Don't you dare touch his coffin."

I turned to my father. Help me, help me. But he retreated, wiggling his eyebrows.

So many things about my father's nature still exasperate or mystify me.

All those years he was being crushed by his own father, nagged by my mother, teased (albeit affectionately) by his increasingly affluent brothers and cousins, was he seething inside, plotting a vengeance in his diary? Or was he really so sweet-natured as not to give a damn? Finally, there is a possibility I'd rather not ponder. Was he not sweet-natured at all, but a coward? Like me. Who would travel miles to avoid a quarrel. Who tends to remember slights—recording them in my mind's eye—transmogrifying them—finally publishing them in a code more accessible than my father's. Making them the stuff of fiction.

Riddles within riddles.

My father came to Montreal as an infant, his father fleeing Galicia. Pogroms. Rampaging Cossacks. But, striptease shows aside, the only theater my father relished, an annual outing for the two of us, was the appearance of the Don Cossack Choir at the St. Denis Theatre. My father would stamp his feet to their lusty marching and drinking songs; his eyes would light up to see those behemoths, his own father's tormentors, prance and tumble on stage. Moses Isaac Richler, who never marched, nor drank, nor pranced.

Obviously, he didn't enjoy his family. My mother, my brother, me. Sundays he would usually escape our cold-water flat early and alone and start out for the first-run downtown cinemas, beginning with the Princess, which opened earliest, continuing from there to the Capitol or the Palace, and maybe moving on to the Loew's, returning to us bleary-eyed, but satiated, after dark. Astonishingly, he kept a sharp eye out for little production errors. Discovering them filled him with joy. Once, for instance, he told us, "Listen to this, Clark Gable is sitting there in his newspaper office and he tells

Claudette Colbert he will be finished typing his story in an hour. But when she comes back and we are supposed to believe an hour has passed, *the hands on the clock on the wall haven't moved. Not an inch.*" Another time it was, "Franchot Tone is in this tank in the desert, you're not going to believe this, and he says 'O.K., men, let's go. Attack!" And they attack. But if you look closely inside the tank just before they push off, the fuel gauge is indicating EMPTY. No gas. Get it?"

The Best Years of Our Lives overwhelmed him.

"There's a scene in there where Fredric March burps. He's hung over, he drinks an Alka-Seltzer or something, and he lets out a good one. Right there on screen. Imagine."

My mother was fond of reminding me that the night I was born, my father had not waited at the hospital to find out how she was, or whether it was a boy or a girl, but had gone to the movies instead. What was playing, I wondered.

My father didn't dream of Italy, where the lemon trees bloomed. He never went for a walk in the country or read a novel, unless he had to, because it was one of mine and he might be blamed for it. Bliss for him was the Gayety Theatre on a Saturday night. My father and a couple of younger brothers, still bachelors, seated front row center. On stage, Peaches, Anne Curie, or the legendary Lili St. Cyr. My father, rapt, his throat dry, watching the unattainable Lili simulating intercourse with a swan as the stage lights throbbed, then trudging home through the snow to sit alone at the kitchen table, drinking hot milk with matzohs before going to sleep.

We endured some rough passages together. Shortly after the marriage annulment, I fought with my father. Fists flew. We didn't speak for two years. Then, when we came together again, meeting once a week, it wasn't to talk, but to play gin rummy for a quarter of a cent a point. My father, I began to suspect, wasn't reticent. He didn't understand life. He had nothing to say to anybody.

In 1954, some time after my return to Europe, where I was to remain rooted for almost two decades, I married a *shiksa* in London. My father wrote me an indignant letter. Once more, we were estranged. But no sooner did the marriage end in divorce than he pounced: "You see, mixed marriages never work."

"But, Daddy, your first marriage didn't work either and Maw was a rabbi's daughter."

"What do you know?"

"Nothing," I replied, hugging him.

When I married again, this time for good, but to another *shiksa*, he was not overcome with delight, yet neither did he complain. For after all the wasting years, we had finally become friends. My father became my son. Once, he had sent money to me in Paris. Now, as the scrapyard foundered, I mailed monthly checks to him in Montreal. On visits home, I took him to restaurants. I bought him treats. If he took me to a gathering of the Richler clan on a Sunday afternoon, he would bring along a corked bottle of 7-Up for me, filled with scotch whisky. "There'll be nothing for you to drink there, and I know you."

"Hey, Daddy, that's really very thoughtful."

During the Sixties, on a flying trip to Montreal, my publishers put me up at the Ritz-Carlton Hotel, and I asked my father to meet me for a drink there.

"You know," he said, joining me at the table, "I'm sixty-two years old and I've never been here before. Inside, I mean. So this is the Ritz."

"It's just a bar," I said, embarrassed.

"What should I order?"

"Whatever you want, Daddy."

"A rye and ginger ale. Would that be all right here?"

"Certainly."

What I'm left with are unresolved mysteries. A sense of regret. Anecdotes for burnishing.

My wife, a proud lady, showing him our firstborn son, his week-old howling grandchild, saying, "Don't you think he looks like Mordecai?"

"Babies are babies," he responded, seemingly indifferent.

Some years later my father coming to our house, pressing chocolate bars on the kids. "Who do you like better," he asked them, "your father or your mother?"

In the mid-Sixties, I flew my father to London. He came with his wife. Instead of slipping away with him to the Windmill Theatre or Raymond's Revue Bar, another strip joint, like a fool I acquired theater tickets. We took the two of them to *Beyond the Fringe*. "What did you think?" I asked as we left the theater.

"There was no chorus line," he said.

Following his last operation for cancer, I flew to Montreal, promising to take him on a trip as soon as he was out of bed. The Catskills. Grossinger's. With a stopover in New York to take in some shows. Back in London, each time I phoned, his doctor advised me to wait a bit longer. I waited. He died. The next time I flew to Montreal it was to bury him.

TOPICS FOR DISCUSSION

1. Why does Richler begin this portrait of his father by quoting excerpts from his father's letters? Why does he say at the end that "my father became my son"?

2. How has Richler portrayed himself as a young man? How does he express his ambivalent feelings about his father?

3. What was the relationship of Richler's father with his own tyrannical father? With his own family of wife and children? Why were Richler's parents unhappily married?

4. What similarities and contrasts between Richler and his father are developed in the text? To what degree does the author identify with his father?

5. How far does this essay illuminate different attitudes among different generations of the Montreal Jews? What do we learn about successive waves of Jewish immigrants to Canada? Contrast the motives for leaving Europe by Jews in earlier migrations and by refugee Jews during World War II.

Alistair MacLeod

*Alistair MacLeod was born in North Battleford, Saskatchewan, in 1936,
but at the age of ten moved with his family to a farm in Cape Breton. He
attended St. Francis Xavier University, University of New Brunswick, and
the University of Notre Dame, where he received his Ph.D. in English in
1968. He teaches English and creative writing at the University of
Windsor, Ontario. He spends every summer in Cape Breton, where he
writes in a cliff-top cabin. Although his literary output is relatively small
and includes only four books, he enjoys great critical acclaim for the extraordinary stylistic qualities of his prose. He has published two collections of
short stories,* The Lost Salt Gift of Blood *(1976) and* As Birds Bring
Forth the Sun and Other Stories *(1986). In 1999, he published his first
novel,* No Great Mischief, *which presents several generations of a family of
Scottish immigrants. It has been nominated for most of Canada's major literary awards and won the Trillium Prize. The novel is currently being
translated into many languages. MacLeod's most recent book is* Island
*(2000), which gathers into one volume all of his previously published sto-
ries, adding one new. His writing often depicts the harsh landscape of Cape
Breton and ethnic diversity of eastern Canada. Like many of his narratives,
the story "To Every Thing There Is a Season" emphasizes the power of the
past to affect the present.*

To Every Thing There Is a Season

I am speaking here of a time when I was eleven and lived with my
family on our small farm on the west coast of Cape Breton. My family
had been there for a long, long time and so it seemed had I. And
much of that time seems like the proverbial yesterday. Yet when I
speak on this Christmas 1977, I am not sure how much I speak with
the voice of what I have since become. And I am not sure how many
liberties I may be taking with the boy I think I was. For Christmas is a
time of both past and present and often the two are imperfectly
blended. As we step into its nowness we often look behind.

We have been waiting now, it seems, forever. Actually, it has been most intense since Halloween when the first snow fell upon us as we moved like muffled mummers upon darkened country roads. The large flakes were soft and new then and almost generous and the earth to which they fell was still warm and as yet unfrozen. They fell in silence into the puddles and into the sea where they disappeared at the moment of contact. They disappeared, too, upon touching the headed redness of our necks and hands or the faces of those who did not wear masks. We carried our pillowcases from house to house, knocking on doors to become silhouettes in the light thrown out from kitchens (white pillowcases held out by whitened forms). The snow fell between us and the doors and was transformed in shimmering golden beams. When we turned to leave, it fell upon our footprints and as the night wore on obliterated them and all the records of our movements. In the morning everything was soft and still and November had come upon us.

My brother Kenneth, who is two and a half, is unsure of his last Christmas. It is Halloween that looms largest in his memory as an exceptional time of being up late in magic darkness and falling snow. "Who are you going to dress up as at Christmas?" he asks. "I think I'll be a snowman." All of us laugh at that and tell him Santa Claus will find him if he is good and that he need not dress up at all. We go about our appointed tasks waiting for it to happen.

I am troubled myself about the nature of Santa Claus and I am trying to hang on to him in any way that I can. It is true that at my age I no longer *really* believe in him yet I have hoped in all his possibilities as fiercely as I can; much in the same way, I think, that the drowning man waves desperately to the lights of the passing ship on the high sea's darkness. For without him, as without the man's ship, it seems our fragile lives would be so much more desperate.

My mother has been fairly tolerant of my attempted perpetuation. Perhaps because she has encountered it before. Once I overheard her speaking about my sister Anne to one of her neighbours. "I thought Anne would *believe* forever," she said. "I practically had to tell her." I have somehow always wished I had not heard her say that as I seek sanctuary and reinforcement even in ignorance I know I dare not trust.

Kenneth, however, believes with unadulterated fervour, and so do Bruce and Barry who are six-year-old twins. Beyond me there is Anne who is thirteen and Mary who is fifteen, both of whom seem to be leaving childhood at an alarming rate. My mother has told us that she was already married when she was seventeen, which is only two years older than Mary is now. That too seems strange to contemplate and perhaps childhood is shorter for some than it is for others. I think of this sometimes in the evenings when we have finished our chores and the supper dishes have been cleared away and we are supposed to be doing our homework. I glance sideways at my mother, who is always knotting or mending, and at my father, who mostly sits by the stove coughing quietly with his handkerchief at his mouth. He has "not been well" for over two years and has difficulty breathing whenever he moves at more than the slowest pace. He is most sympathetic of all concerning my extended hopes and says we should hang on to the good things in our lives as long as we are able. As I look at him out of the corner of my eye, it does not seem that he has many of them left. He is old, we think, at forty-two.

Yet Christmas, in spite of all the doubts of our different ages, is a fine and splendid time, and now as we pass the mid-point of December our expectations are heightened by the increasing coldness that has settled down upon us. The ocean is flat and calm and along the coast, in the scooped-out coves, has turned to an icy slush. The brook that flows past our house is almost totally frozen and there is only a small channel of rushing water that flows openly at its very centre. When we let the cattle out to drink, we chop holes with the axe at the brook's edge so that they can drink without venturing onto the ice.

The sheep move in and out of their lean-to shelter restlessly stamping their feet or huddling together in tightly packed groups. A conspiracy of wool against the cold. The hens perch high on their roosts with their feathers fluffed out about them, hardly feeling it worthwhile to descent to the floor for their few scant kernels of grain. The pig, who has little time before his butchering, squeals his displeasure to the cold and with his snout tosses his wooden trough high in the icy air. The splendid young horse paws the planking of his stall and gnaws the wooden cribwork of his manger.

We have put a protective barricade of spruce boughs about our kitchen door and banked our house with additional boughs and billows of eel grass. Still, the pail of water we leave standing in the porch is solid in the morning and has to be broken with the hammer. The clothes my mother hangs on the line are frozen almost instantly and sway and creak from their suspending clothespins like sections of dismantled robots: the stiff-legged rasping trousers and the shirts and sweaters with unyielding arms outstretched. In the morning we race from our frigid upstairs bedrooms to finish dressing around the kitchen stove.

We would extend our coldness half a continent away to the Great Lakes of Ontario so that it might hasten the Christmas coming of my oldest brother, Neil. He is nineteen and employed on the "lake boats," the long flat carriers of grain and iron ore whose season ends the day after December 10, depending on the ice conditions. We wish it to be cold, cold on the Great Lakes of Ontario, so that he may come home to us as soon as possible. Already his cartons have arrived. They come from different places: Cobourg, Toronto, St. Catharines, Welland, Windsor, Sarnia, Sault Ste. Marie. Places that we, with the exception of my father, have never been. We locate them excitedly on the map, tracing their outlines with eager fingers. The cartons bear the lettering of Canada Steamship Lines, and are bound with rope knotted intricately in the fashion of sailors. My mother says they contain his "clothes" and we are not allowed to open them.

For us it is impossible to know the time or manner of his coming. If the lakes freeze early, he may come by train because it is cheaper. If the lakes stay open until December 20, he will have to fly because his time will be more precious than money. He will hitchhike the last hundred or hundred and fifty kilometres from either station or airport. On our part, we can do nothing but listen with straining ears to radio reports of distant ice formations. His coming seems to depend on so many factors which are out there far beyond us and over which we lack control.

The days go by in fevered slowness until finally on the morning of December 23 the strange car rolls into our yard. My mother touches her hand to her lips and whispers "Thank God." My father gets up unsteadily from his chair to look through the window. Their longed-for son and our golden older brother is here at last. He is here with his reddish hair and beard and we can hear his hearty laugh. He will be happy and strong and confident for us all.

There are three other young men with him who look much the same as he. They too are from the boats and are trying to get home to Newfoundland. They must still drive a hundred and sixty kilometres to reach the ferry at North Sydney. The car seems very old. They purchased it in Thorold for two hundred dollars because they were too late to make any reservations, and they have driven steadily since they began. In northern New Brunswick their windshield wipers failed but instead of stopping they tied lengths of cord to the wipers' arms and passed them through the front window vents. Since that time, in whatever precipitation, one of them has pulled the cords back and forth to make the wipers function. This information falls tiredly but excitedly from their lips and we greedily gather it in. My father pours them drinks of rum and my mother takes out her mincemeat and the fruitcakes she has been carefully hoarding.

We lean on the furniture or look from the safety of sheltered door-ways. We would like to hug our brother but are too shy with strangers present. In the kitchen's warmth, the young men begin to nod and doze, their heads dropping suddenly to their chests. They nudge each other with their feet in an attempt to keep awake. They will not stay and rest because they have come so far and tomorrow is Christmas Eve and stretches of mountains and water still lie between them and those they love. After they leave we pounce upon our brother physically and verbally. He laughs and shouts and lifts us over his head and swings us in his muscular arms. Yet in spite of his happiness he seems surprised at the appearance of his father whom he has not seen since March. My father merely smiles at him while my mother bites her lip.

Now that he is here there is a great flurry of activity. We have left everything we could until the time he might be with us. Eagerly I show him the fir tree on the hill which I have been watching for months and marvel at how easily he fells it and carries it down the hill. We fall over one another in the excitement of decoration.

He promises that on Christmas Eve he will take us to church in the sleigh behind the splendid horse that until his coming we are all afraid to handle. And on the afternoon of Christmas Eve he shoes the horse, lifting each hoof and rasping it fine and hammering the cherry-red horseshoes into shape upon the anvil. Later he drops them hissingly into the steaming tub of water. My father sits beside him on an overturned pail and tells him what to do. Sometimes we argue with our father, but our brother does everything he says.

That night, bundled in hay and voluminous coats, and with heated stones at our feet, we start upon our journey. Our parents and Kenneth remain at home but all the rest of us go. Before we leave we feed the cattle and sheep and even the pig all that they can possibly eat so that they will be content on Christmas Eve. Our parents wave to us from the doorway. We go six kilometres across the mountain road. It is a primitive logging trail and there will be no cars or other vehicles upon it. At first the horse is wild with excite-ment and lack of exercise and my brother has to stand at the front of the sleigh and lean backwards on the reins. Later he settles down to a trot and still later to a walk as the mountain rises before him. We sing all the Christmas songs we know and watch for rabbits and foxes scudding across the open patches of snow and listen to the drumming of partridge wings. We are never cold.

When we descend to the country church we tie the horse in a grove of trees where he will be sheltered and not frightened by the many cars. We put a blanket over him and give him oats. At the church door the neighbours shake hands with my older brother. "Hello, Neil," they say. "How is your father?"

"Oh," he says, just "Oh."

The church is very beautiful at night with its festooned branches and glowing candles and the booming, joyous sounds that come from the choir loft. We go through the service as if we are mesmerized.

On the way home, although the stones have cooled, we remain happy and warm. We listen to the creak of the leather harness and the hiss of runners on the snow and begin to think of the potentiality of presents. When we are about a kilometre from home the horse senses his destination and breaks into a trot and then into a confident lope. My brother lets him go and we move across the winter landscape like figures freed from a Christmas card. The snow from the horse's hooves falls about our heads like the whiteness of the stars.

After we have stabled the horse we talk with our parents and eat the meal our mother has prepared. And then I am sleepy and it is time for the younger children to be in bed. But tonight my father says to me, "We would like you to stay up with us a while," and so I stay quietly with the older members of my family.

When all is silent upstairs Neil brings in the cartons that contain his "clothes" and begins to open them. He unties the intricate knots quickly, their whorls falling away before his agile fingers. The boxes are filled with gifts neatly wrapped and bearing tags. The ones for my younger brothers say "from Santa Claus" but mine are not among them anymore, as I know with certainty they will never be again. Yet I am not so much surprised as touched by a pang of loss at being here on the adult side of the world. It is as if I have suddenly moved into another room and heard a door click lastingly behind me. I am jabbed by my own small wound.

But then I look at those before me. I look at my parents drawn together before the Christmas tree. My mother has her hand upon my father's shoulder and he is holding his ever present handkerchief. I look at my sisters who have crossed this threshold ahead of me and now each day journey farther from the lives they knew as girls. I look at my magic older brother who has come to us this Christmas from half a continent away, bringing everything he has and is. All of them are captured in the tableau of their care.

"Every man moves on," says my father quietly, and I think he speaks of Santa Claus, "but there is no need to grieve. He leaves good things behind."

T O P I C S   F O R   D I S C U S S I O N

1. How does the narrator capture the sensibility of the eleven-year-old boy?

2. Why are Christmas memories important to the narrator? Interpret the father's words at the end of the story.

3. What kind of family portrait has been preserved in the narrator's childhood memories? Are there any "things unsaid" in this family?

Frank G. Paci

Frank G. Paci was born in Pesaro, Italy, in 1948 and came to Canada with his parents in 1952. He studied English and education at the University of Toronto, where he was encouraged to write by Margaret Laurence. In 1980 he received an M.A. in English from Carleton University. He taught English for several years in Sault Ste. Marie and Toronto. In 1988-89 he was writer-in-residence at York University. He has published eight novels, The Italians *(1978),* Black Madonna *(1982),* The Father *(1984),* Black Blood *(1991),* Under the Bridge *(1992),* Sex and Character *(1993), and* The Rooming-House *(1996). The last three form a narrative sequence that he plans to continue. His most recent novel,* Icelands *(1999), deals with the triumphs and pitfalls of hockey. His works are characterized by realism and a thematic consistency in exploring the lives of Italian immigrant families in Northern Ontario, especially the impact of immigration upon their self-image. He is one of the most important Italian Canadian writers working in English. The excerpt below comes from* The Father. *The father in the story is determined to pass on the Italian family tradition of bread making. However, the mother uses the son's disability to prevent him from getting into apprenticeship.*

Mancuso's and Sons

I n the kitchen his father spoke to him like a grownup as he was having his coffee.

"I started to work when I was nine years old," he said in Italian. "My father owned the only bakery in the town in the Abruzzi. We only made large loaves of rough bread that weighed 4 kilos. Large loaves taste better because they take longer to bake, and therefore more flavour and aroma are in the oven. Then, after I got my papers as a master baker, I made my special kind of bread. The people in the town called it *Orestepane*. Bread named after me, you understand. When my father had to stop working because of arthritis I was the only baker there. If I didn't bake bread no bread was sold. But then, in the army in Rome, the officers made me make lighter pasty bread I didn't like. We called it black bread because of the black shirts. Then, when I was a prisoner of war in North Africa, I almost went crazy because I didn't have anything to do most of the time. Many soldiers went crazy, Stefano. It was a bad time. Our nails didn't grow and our hair fell out because we didn't have any vitamins. Friends of mine died of starvation and pneumonia and jaundice—much worse than your hand."

Stefano sipped his cocoa and listened intently. He had never heard his father speak so long, except for the time they went fishing at Echo Bay. Stefano didn't ask any questions. He was content just to listen. "How can the fish bite a worm that talks so much," he recalled his father saying.

His father wore a white short-sleeved shirt and white pants. They were immaculately clean and looked soft from repeated washings. Every third day Maddelena washed a batch of his whites. They hung like cut-outs on the line: shirt, pants, shirt, pants.

His father's black hair glistened with brilliantine. He had a handsome face, with smooth pale skin and a cleft on his chin. Stefano had heard his mother say jokingly that the only reason she married him was that he looked like Valentino and her father. He had never seen Valentino, but his grandfather, whose picture was in his parents' bedroom, did look a little like his father. Oreste, though, had gentle and kind eyes. Stefano had rarely seen him angry. Even when he had to discipline them Stefano could tell his heart wasn't in it. Maddelena had to goad him into using his belt. When he hit, though, it hurt.

Oreste was his most cheerful in the mornings when he was in the bakery whistling or singing while baking bread with Amelio. "Bread can't grow," he'd say, "under the hands of a sad man." Then he'd go on delivery in the Ford station-wagon. Besides fishing, he liked to play cards with his friends at the Marconi Hall, just a couple of houses up the street.

"People are funny here," Oreste would say, shaking his head. "They don't like their work at the steel plant. In Italia life is more important, you understand. To work is to live."

When they finished their breakfast they went through the side door of the kitchen and into the storage-room of the bakery. Oreste had told him the bakery had been built just after the First World War. The previous owner had been old Giuseppe, the Marchegian. Stefano was too young to remember much of him, except that he used to give him pieces of bread. His dad worked in the bakery alongside the old man until Giuseppe had to retire. There was no-one in his family to take over the business, so it had passed into

Oreste's hands. Afterwards, for almost a year, the old man couldn't stay away from the bakery. Oreste would let him come and help out. Giuseppe passed on all his methods and treated Oreste like a son. When the old man died his father closed the bakery for three days. He hung a black wreath on the door and stayed at the Marconi for a long time.

At the front of *Mancuso's and Sons* was the shop where Maddelena sold the bread. The loaves were piled just behind the large plate-glass window and behind the counter. They made an assortment of crusty breads in various sizes. Above the counter was a sign with the varieties sold and the prices. His father's specialty was a large loaf with a shiny brown crust and a long cut on the top.

Behind the storage-room it was like a cave. There was a large hearth oven made of bricks on one side and a long counter on the other. Except for a small mixing-machine everything was done by hand.

Oreste explained a few details about the nature of dough and how it had been left to rise during the night. In a few minutes Amelio DiLabio came through the back and they were ready to start. Amelio was a short squat Calabrian who was the only other person working with his father. As soon as Amelio saw him his face lit up.

"*Bravo*, Stefano! You learn the business now, hey?"

Stefano smiled and stood to the side. Oreste took out a white paper cap from his back pocket and put it on. Stefano saw his father turn his face away for a moment, as if he had something in his eye. Then he made the sign of the cross.

Amelio was beaming. "*Vieni qui*, Stefano. I show you how to light the oven."

After he lit the oven he said, "The oven is the most important part of the bakery, Stefano. This is an old oven made of bricks, see. The stone inside is important for the taste. We make our bread just like the Romans did thousands of years ago."

Stefano listened in awe.

Oreste said, "People were making bread before they could write."

Afterwards they dumped a large pan of dough onto the counter and started to make bread. Amelio cut chunks of dough and weighed them on a flat scale while Oreste shaped them into loaves. They worked fast without talking, conscious of his presence. Then Amelio started to whistle. He had such a sharp clear whistle that Stefano took notice of him more closely.

In no time it was very warm in the small room. The clean yeasty smell of the dough was strong and made Stefano a little giddy. He looked at the sliced dough with the small bubbles at the side. Something made him reach out to touch it.

Amelio laughed heartily. "Good, hey. Just like the body of a woman. You'll know soon."

He had close-cropped brown hair and a ruddy face, with broken veins all over—and reminded Stefano of a cartoon character.

"Your father and I," Amelio went on, his face, lighting up like a Christmas tree, "we bake bread for a long time. The best bread in the West End.... in the country. And this dough—" he brought the end of his cupped fingers to his lips and kissed them with an exaggerated show of emotion—"I say it to you right now, is better than any woman."

Oreste laughed. "Better than any woman you know, that's for sure."

Throwing his head back like an opera singer, Amelio suddenly broke into song. "*Oy Marie, Oy Marie ...*"

"Stefano," his father called out to him. "Come up here beside me."

Stefano watched closely as his father kneaded the hunks of dough. His hands worked fast at the beginning—punching down the roughness, poking and rolling the unformed chunk and sprinkling flour over it. But as the loaf began to take final shape he slowed down and took greater care. Stefano noticed the long tapering fingers of his father's hands. Whitened with flour they moved with slow, deft movements, as if caressing the dough. At the end he dipped a small brush in a jar that contained a yellowish liquid and brushed the top of each loaf.

"This is my secret method," his father said proudly. "It is responsible for the special crust of *Mancuso's and Sons.*" He paused as he took a knife and cut a long slash on top of each loaf. "Crust is the soul of the bread, figlio mio. Never forget. In this country they don't believe in crust."

"Daddy, what's in the jar?"

Oreste looked attentively at him and smiled. But he didn't answer.

Carefully he placed each loaf on a tray. Every so often Amelio put the loaves into the oven on a flat wooden board with a long handle shaped like a paddle. In a while there was a delicious smell in the room.

"See how it's done, Stefano," Oreste said. "You have to touch it a certain way. With the heel of your palms. Then the fingers. Add a little flour. Don't let it get too pasty. But just right. There, see. There's nothing better to eat in the world than bread. But good bread, not the stuff they make over here. Like those soft mushy rolls and the hamburger buns and the sliced paste they call sandwich bread. *Mannaggia America,* they don't know bread at all in this country!"

Stefano was surprised by his father's outburst. Amelio laughed good-naturedly, but Oreste gave him a long look and cursed a few times in Italian.

Finally his father put a hunk of dough in place and said, "Try it yourself, Stefano. Put some flour on your hands first."

All activity stopped. It didn't take him long to realize why. Since his accident his mother had fussed over him so much he hadn't been allowed to do much of anything. Certainly not to play games with the other kids. Or to work in the bakery.

With his left hand he cautiously started to knead the dough. His ears burned with embarrassment. He could feel their eyes on him. It made him so self-conscious of his deficiency he wanted to run and hide. Only the persistence of some inner voice kept him rooted to the spot. The dough was tougher than he thought. He couldn't put much pressure on it with one hand alone. Awkwardly he brought his deformed hand up to the counter and used it to keep the roll in place.

"*Bravo,* Stefano!" his father cried out.

Stefano turned and saw the fierce look of joy on his father's face.

"*Bravo!*" Oreste cried out again, shaking his fist in the air.

Stefano returned the look. His heart was bursting with happiness.

Soon he was shaping the tough dough into something resembling a loaf of bread. Amelio started to sing again and his father whistled as he went about his business. Without any further need of instruction Stefano continued making loaves. When he had four done he stepped back and surveyed his work.

"Ready for the oven?" Amelio called out.

Stefano didn't know what to say.

"Brush them first," his father instructed.

Stefano dipped the brush and coated his loaves with his father's secret formula. It had an eggy smell.

"Here," Amelio came up to him. "This is what we did in the old country with our very first loaf." He rolled two long sticks of dough.

"Which one is your first?" he asked Stefano.

Stefano indicated the smallest of the four loaves. Amelio very carefully made an S and an M on top with the sticks of dough.

"Now you'll know," his father said, taking a towel and mopping his forehead. "We keep the first loaf to remind us of the care we put into it. So that every one after will have the same care."

They were standing in silence when his mother appeared on the scene. She was in her blue robe. Her long red hair was uncombed.

Stefano looked at her in triumph. He was about to show her the loaf he had made when he noticed the way she was regarding Oreste. Amelio stepped back and looked after the oven. Oreste looked at the floor.

His mother came up to him and took his hand. She didn't even notice what he had done. She was looking all along at Oreste, not at him.

"I told you, didn't I?" his mother said in an angry tone.

Oreste looked up bewildered.

"Aw, Maddelena, what harm will it do?" he said.

"He's too delicate, I told you."

"When I was nine—"

"Oh, shut up, when you were nine!" she lashed out at him.

Stefano had to hold himself back from crying. She was holding his good hand so firmly that she was crunching the knuckles.

Oreste shook his head and gave Stefano a pitiful look.

"He has to learn sometime," he said with annoyance.

"Learn what?" she snapped.

"To work with his hands."

"*Ma, stai zitto, ignorante!*" she yelled at him. "Can't you see?"

Stefano's ears burned with embarrassment. No-one looked at him. He put his deformed hand behind his back.

He could feel his mother trembling with rage. He tried to break free of her hold, but she only held him tighter, hurting his hand. Oreste kept silent, staring at the floor like a student who had done something wrong at school.

"Daddy," Stefano pleaded, as if his father needed a little coaxing.

But Oreste wouldn't look up to face him. Stefano couldn't understand why he didn't just speak out and tell her to go back in the kitchen where she belonged. They had work to do.

"Daddy," he called out again.

He was afraid to say anything more in case the fish wouldn't bite.

But before anything else could happen his mother whisked him out of the bakery and into his bedroom. His clothes were removed and his hands washed of flour. He was put back to bed. Somehow he was too numb to cry.

When he came home from school that day he found a loaf of baked bread in his room. It had a shiny crust with his initials on the top. He kept it hidden for seven days until his mother found it and threw it away because it had hardened into stone.

TOPICS FOR DISCUSSION

1. Oreste relates his life experiences to the theme of baking bread as passing the legacy of the father on to the son. What in the family's present situation accounts for a disruption of this tradition?

2. Characterize the father and son relationship in the story. How does the son's disability affect his parents' attitudes to him? Compare Stefano's situation to that of Peppi in Genni Gunn's story "The Middle Ground."

3. What traditional view of gender roles does the Italian family in the story represent? Compare attitudes to gender in Katherine Vlassie's "A Bit of Magic" and Isabel Vincent's "Finding a Personality That Fits."

Austin Clarke

Austin Clarke was born in Barbados in 1934 and came to Canada in 1955, to study economics and political science at Trinity College, University of Toronto. He interrupted his study to devote himself to writing. Since 1964, he has published 10 novels and 5 collections of stories, dealing with experiences in the African diaspora in the United States, Britain, Canada, and the West Indies. His first novels, The Survivors of the Crossing *(1964) and* Amongst Thistles and Thorns *(1965), helped him to secure teaching positions at a number of American universities, including Yale. Before his return to Toronto in 1977, he had held several diplomatic jobs for the government of Barbados, for example, serving as Cultural Attache in Washington, D.C. His novels,* The Meeting Point *(1967),* Storm of Fortune *(1971), and* The Bigger Light *(1975), form a trilogy about Caribbean immigrants in Toronto. Called "the grand-daddy of African-Canadian literature," Clarke was the first African Canadian writer to enjoy great popularity and critical reputation. In 1999, he won the W.O. Mitchell Prize, awarded annually to a Canadian writer who has produced an outstanding body of work and served as a mentor for other writers. Earlier, his memoir,* Growing Up Stupid under the Union Jack *(1980), received the Casa de las Amercas prize for addressing the legacy of colonialism and racism. The novel* The Question *(1999) was nominated for the Governor General's Award, while another novel,* The Origin of Waves *(1997), won the Rogers Communications Writers' Development Trust Prize for Fiction. Clarke has also written* Pigtails 'N' Breadfruit: A Culinary Memoir *(1999), celebrating food as defining home and culture for the Africans in Barbados. His next novel, is* The Polished Hoe, *will be published in 2002.*

Commenting on the political aspects of his writing, Clarke comments in an interview: "A good writer knows when he is submerging the politics in a piece for the art. The bad artist, until he becomes better, cannot understand how politics is connected in art and how one has got to restrain oneself if one is putting across a political situation" (1980).

The story "A Wedding in Toronto" comes from Clarke's first short story collection, When He Was Free and He Used to Wear Silks *(1971), exploring black-white relations and different situations in the lives of West Indian immigrants in Toronto.*

A Wedding in Toronto

"**A** police coming in a man's house, and at a wedding reception to boot! and breaking up a party? Merely because some old can't-sleep bitch next door or down-below can't find a man or something? What kind o' place, what sort o' country is this? It never happened in Barbados and it never could. Imagine a police in Barbados coming into a man's house, during a party, and a wedding party at that, to tell that man he is making too much noise! Man, that policeman's arse would be so stiff with lashes he would never do that again! A police coming into a man's apartment, and breaking up a wedding reception because some old bitch who can't sleep, complained?" Boysie never got over the shock of seeing the policeman at the door, standing like a monument to something, with an untranslatable expression on his face, with one hand resting perhaps absent-mindedly on the holster of his gun, and the other raised and caught in the slow-motion paralysis of knocking on the apartment door again. It was a loud, firm knock of authority. The wedding guests were, at that time, in the middle of speeches; and Boysie, who was the master of ceremonies, had been saying some amusing things about marriage. It was at the point when he was saying, *Ecce homo*, over and over again (using his best stentorian, oratorical Barbadian dialect), exhorting them, as: "La-dies and gentlemen! ladies and gentlemen too! greetings and salutation, because on this most auspicious of evenings, on the aurora of long and felicitous matrimony, I say to you, to you, ladies and gentlemen, I say, *ecce homo*, behold the man! *ecce homo*, here I stand!" (Freeness, dressed to kill in a three-piece suit; Matthew Woods, spic and span; Estelle, beautiful as a virgin, as a star; and many other West Indians crammed into the happy apartment, screamed for joy when Boysie began this speech, his fifth for the afternoon's festivities. Each wedding guest, including Agatha the bride, and Henry the bridegroom, had made a speech. Some had made two speeches. Boysie had made his first about an hour after the wedding party returned to the apartment. It was five o'clock then. Now, after many toasts and speeches and eats and drinks, Boysie was captivating his audience again. The time was midnight. The guests liked it, and they bawled and told Boysie they liked it. Henry, sober and married; Agatha turning red, and flushed, and happy, and drunk as Dots, Boysie's wife, held her head back and exposed the silver cavities filled with silver, and said "I could have another wedding reception like this tomorrow! One like this every month!") "I say to you, ladies and gentlemen, I say, *ecce homo*, behold the man! *ecce homo*, here I stand! Here I stand, ladies and gentlemen, with a glass of drink in my hand, wherewithal for to mitigate the aridity of my thirst. And as I have arisen from my esteemed seat this fifth time, and as I have quoth to you, *bon swarr* my dear Agaffa, goodevening Henry, you lucky old Bajan bastard!" And it was here, in the roar of acceptance by each person in the room when they held their glasses up, and Boysie's glass was held right there, at the correct angle, that the knock brutalized the apartment. Its suddenness made them notice it. But they had no suspicions. Boysie said, with his glass still raised, "Perhaps, ladies and gentlemen, it is some poor suppliant wanting warmth of this nocturnal congregation." And he moved away towards the door, his drink still in his hand, to invite the person inside to partake of the hospitality. Bernice went over to Agatha to fix the veil on her dress and therefore, fortunately, blocked her view of the police officer at the door standing with his hand on his holster. Boysie didn't lose his aplomb. The police officer was very polite to him. "Break it up soon, buddy. It's past midnight. The neighbours're complaining about the noise."

Boysie was going to offer the officer a drink, but he changed his mind.

"Don't let me get another report that you're making noise, eh? Break it up soon, buddy."

Boysie did not move from the door until the officer of the law walked back to the elevator; and he did not move until he saw him get into it; and Dots, who had put a record on the machine the moment she heard the officer's voice, was now standing beside Boysie, like a real wife, supportingly.

"And the poor girl's enjoying herself so much! And on her wedding day? Jesus Christ, these people is savages, man. They're damn uncivilized! You mean to tell me, on the girl's wedding day?" Boysie put his arm round Dots' new, shiny, almost bare shoulder, and he squeezed her a little bit, and said, "We going party till that son-of-a-bitch come back!" Boysie left her, and went to Bernice and whispered in her ear, "The po-lice!" Bernice suddenly got tense. "But only me and Dots, and now you, know 'bout it. So keep it dark. Keep it dark." Bernice relaxed because of this confidence. "We got to go on. How the hell could we ask the people to leave? How would Agaffa feel? How would Henry feel, on his wedding night to boot?"

So Boysie and Dots and Bernice made certain not to let Agatha and Henry feel the tension that had begun to creep into the party. It was impossible to recapture the gaiety and the enjoyment that was in the room before the policeman knocked on the door. Dots would have had the guests leave immediately after one more respectable drink; she would have insisted upon it, because she had just moved into the apartment building and she wanted to live quietly, and also because Agatha and Henry had to go on their honeymoon, to Niagara Falls. But Boysie said no, "This is a wedding. Not any old man party with beatniks." And he left Dots standing there arguing the wisdom of his suggestion with Bernice, and he went to the record player, and looked through the pile of calypso records. (This record player had arrived from Eaton's department store two hours before the wedding reception began, delivered on a hire-purchase, the monthly payments of which were fifty-five dollars and twenty-five cents and which Dots did not know how she would meet; but the sound was high and loud and high-fidelity and stereophonic too, and the beauty and the loudness of the sound allayed their fears of having the machine repossessed. "Man, let we play the thing for today then, and enjoy it, and then see what happen, man!" And Boysie agreed to that, although before Dots said so, he had already agreed in his mind to keep the record player.) Boysie now selected a calypso by the Mighty Sparrow, *Shanty Town People*, in which Sparrow was complaining of having to move out of his comfortable apartment, in Trinidad, because people from the slums had encroached on his location on the hill. The music raged, as the spirits in the guests and in the drinks raged. Estelle was beautiful in her wedding-party dress. She was thinking of how very close she herself had come to marriage. And more than once, during the hectic afternoon and night, she wondered where the hell her man, Sam Burrmann, was at this happy time. But she soon put him out of her mind; and she devoted all her body and energy to Matthew Woods, who shook his body in time in dance as if he was in some mad trance. *Sunday morning, they fighting, they drinking, they beating pan ... send for the police, still the bacchanal won't cease.* It was a royal time. It was an ironic time to have a calypso reproduce the exact conditions of a party at which the police had come. And judging by the hour hand, it was Sunday morning too! But no one cared for Toronto, or the police, or the neighbours: this was a wedding, and as Dots said, "A person can only get married one time. Even if he divorce and marry a second time, the second time don't seem to be like the first time! So the first time is the time!" Boysie was dancing with her. Brigitte, a German immigrant working as a domestic, had held on to Freeness the whole day, probably by design; probably by the suggestion of Boysie (whose woman she was; Boysie who now in the castle of skin and pride, in his briar patch of host and wedding-giver, had no time for outside-women); and Bernice was dancing with a man who nobody knew, who nobody invited, but who was treated with the same courtesy and hospitality as the bridegroom, or as if he was the bride's father. Agatha's father hadn't arrived yet. Agatha's mother hadn't arrived yet. Agatha's friends, Agatha's many friends from the university, and her lawyer-friend (all of whom had been sent invitations—that was Boysie's personal gift to the couple) hadn't arrived yet. It had been a sorrowful sight at the church, when it was found out that no one was sitting on the bride's side as witness and evidence. Dots quickly saw the situation developing, and quickly saw the embarrassment it would cause Agatha when she arrived sweet and young, virginal and white in her long dress, to glance over the wide expanse of the desert of her friends. And Dots ushered and re-ushered half of the church over to Agatha's side. When the organ roared and snorted through the Wedding March, everybody was laughing, even Agatha. Reverend Markham was happy. It was his first inter-racial wedding ceremony. The choir was in good voice, loud when it was supposed to be loud, soft when the organist breathed with the organ and whispered that the choir should be like a piano, pianissimo. But when they were in the office signing away their lives and their promises to one another, Dots stood like a mother-hen on the top steps of the church, directing the people (those who didn't have cars) to cars and warning the photographer who had arrived late, "Look here! don't take the whole day, hear? We have things waiting at the wedding reception." And after that she whispered in Bernice's ears, "It's a shame, a great burning shame that that bastard, Agatha's father, thinks he is too great and too proud to come and witness his own daughter on her wedding day. A person does only have one wedding day in her life and that bastard didn't even come. He did not come."

"And the mother ain't turned up yet, neither."

"Bernice, gal, you are seeing and witnessing the ways o' white people. They would kill their own flesh-and-blood just to prove a blasted point."

"It is sad, though."

Estelle had overheard, and she said, "They love one another, though. Henry and Agatha. And they won't be living at the parents."

"Still's a blasted shame!"

And now, at the reception, nobody apparently tired after so many hours of eating and drinking and dancing with the problems of *Shanty Town People* being reproduced for them by the visit of the policeman and by the record itself, these West Indians and two white women, Brigitte and Agatha ("She's a Wessindian now, gal! We adopt Agatha now that her own people and her parents let her down. Godblummuh, we is one people who don't reject nobody through colour prejudice.") ... *I tired and I disgust ... big Sunday evening, they cussing, they fighting, they gambling, they beating pan and bup-bup!-iron bolt, won't cease ...* There were fifty-one persons (with the un-invited man) in the apartment now, at one-thirty Sunday morning. Boysie has his arms in the air and is dancing as if his body has been seized by some voodoo, or St. Vitus dance mood; Dots has thrown one brocaded expensive slipper somewhere in a corner, and she is jumping up. The record, a favourite with everybody in the room, is put on again. It is put on three times, four times, five times, six times; and Boysie says on the seventh time, "Man, play that thing one more time, do, man!" And it is put on the eighth time ... *and big Sunday morning, they cussing they fighting they gambling; they beating pan and bup-bup!-iron bolt and stone pelting, send for the police, still the bacchanal won't cease, so they violent so they fast, they better go back to their mansion on the Labasse ...* A smudge of fatigue and sweat walked imperceptibly from under Estelle's hairy armpits. Bernice noticed it; and she took Estelle into Dots' bedroom and rubbed some of Dots' under-arm deodorant, "Ban," on the story-telling odour. Estelle smiles, and dashes back out to dance. Agatha, with the first signs of marriedhood and possessiveness, sits and watches Henry dance with a very thin, tight, tense and at the same time, sexy black woman, holding him like a leech in heat; and Agatha continues to watch as if she is comparing her body with the black woman's body in the bedroom of her mind; she watches the woman's hips as they do things with the rhythm of the calypso which she herself, legal and wedded to Henry for better and for worse, knows she cannot do, cannot ever learn to do in this way. Some men are in the kitchen, eating, as they have been doing since five o'clock. ("Boysie!" one of them said, about six o'clock, "we intend to eat every fucking thing in your apartment, boy! So, relax.") There is a big argument going on about cricket. None of these men has seen a cricket Test match in five years, not since they left their homes in the islands. But they are now arguing about Sir Frank Worrell, and the cover drive he made off Alec Bedser at Lords in 1950, many many years ago. One man says, "Be-Christ, them English-people think they could play cricket! Be-Jesuschrist, they can't play no cricket in truth! They *playing* they great. But godblummuh! when Sir Frank leaned into that out-swinger from Bedser, and Sir Frank make a little thing, *so!* be-Christ, it went to the fucking boundary like lightning for four! Right offa Worrell wrist!" And another man smiled, took a sip of his whiskey and said, "And all o' wunnuh in here know that Worrell have more wrist-work in his strokes than Boysie in there have stones in his underwears!" And like a contagion, everybody in the kitchen bawled and poured himself another, larger drink. The record is changed. Sparrow is talking about his boyhood. The men dropped their glasses and ran for the women sitting around the room. They reached out their hands and lifted the dripping, shining, shiningly-dressed, rouged-and-perfume-smelling tired ladies off their chairs. Boysie is dancing with Dots, as if they are lovers: close. His brilliantined head, which had sweated for hours, four hours under his stocking-top, is sleeked down and shining; and Dots' hairdo, done amidst pain and time, talk and gossip in Azan's Beauty world the previous Thursday, when the shop was noisy and filled with domestics and talk about "I hear Enid sleeping with a Jew-man. You hear so, too?", and the waiting was long for those without an appointment, and for those with an appointment, "The girl we meet one day in the subway, that girl wearing the mini, the midi maxi whatever the hell you calls it! Anyhow, she I talking about. She gone and get sheself in trouble. *Pregnunt!*" Dots had listened and had held her peace; and then someone said, Dots had never seen this woman in the parlour before, "This rich-rich Jewish girl I hear is marrieding some Bajan man or other, and somebody tell me his name is Henry-something, or the other, but Christ! to imagine that I been here so blasted long and nobody, not even a Jew-man hasn't asked me a question. I must be getting old, and looking it, too!" And then they all laughed. Except Dots. *Now, I am a rebel, I seeking my revenge any kind o' way, I'm a devil. I don't laugh, I don't smile I don't play ...* Boysie is not smiling. He doesn't smile when he is dancing. He is holding Dots so close that he can feel something stiffening in his trousers legs: but she is his wife and he her husband ... *Anytime we meet, man-to-man, it's blood and sand!* (Estelle thinks back to the time not long ago when Bernice and Dots, Boysie and Henry visited her in the small room she lived in on Bedford Road, when they found her hungry and depressed, delirious with fever and thoughts about Sam Burrmann a Jewish lawyer who left her after she told him she was pregnant for him; and she thinks about it now, dancing with the man nobody invited, the man who told her he is some kind of agent selling some product which Estelle does not understand, thinking of this man dancing with her so close, touching the child in her womb put there by another man. And she thinks of Bernice. "What a life, what a hard life these West Indians live in this place!" And she thinks of what her life might be. There is a man standing beside her, watching her face, but not caring for her thoughts because he wants her to have one thought on her mind, tonight after the reception. He is the man nobody invited. He is standing in front of her now like a threat, like a challenge. ("Henry married, Boysie married, every-other bitch in here have a husband ... I wonder if ...") The man wants to dance with this "prettiest lady in this place." The compliment is sincere, and Estelle makes herself prettier by doing something to her face and her lips, saliva on them now, and she stands up just as Sparrow says, *They treat me like a savage, of me they take advantage; when I young and growing up in town, all o' them bad-johns used to knock me down* ... A tear is crawling like perspiration down Estelle's face. The man does not notice. He has his mind on other parts of her body.)

It was then that the second knocking was heard on the apartment door. Boysie went to the door. The same policeman, plus another one, were standing there. "I told ya," the first policeman said. There was no anger in his voice. He seemed rather peeved that someone had called to report noise in the apartment; he seemed as if he had been taken away form something he was doing, something he enjoyed doing; as a man who had been roused from a poker game would look; as if he had been disturbed from the pants of some woman, somewhere down in the jungle of apartments nearby. Boysie knew what to do.

The guests began leaving right away. Everybody except those who were staying for the night, those who lived there: Boysie and Dots, Bernice and Estelle. Henry looked at the policemen and said things in his heart which if they were audible would have given him a beating and then a long jail term. Agatha began to cry. She was still wearing her wedding gown; Henry was in his formal morning suit; he and she still in the clothes that began their new life together. The policemen waited until every one of the guests left. As Agatha walked beside Henry along the long corridor, as if she was still walking that interminable aisle up the mile to face the altar and the cross and the Maker stretched out on a cross and Reverend Markham, women with curlers in their hair peeped through open doors; and just as the policemen passed them and went down into the half-awake apartment building, in the elevator going out, one of the white ladies, in a torn pink nightgown which showed the black-ness between her thighs vaguely, hissed, "Bitch! Trash!" and slammed her apartment door. The others, among the onlooking guard of honour and dishonour, shook their heads and did not slam their doors: but nobody knew what they were saying in their hearts behind their closed doors. In the confusion, in all the disappoint-ment and crying (Dots and Bernice and Estelle remained sitting on the large new couch, crying for Agatha's sake; and Agatha herself had left in tears, and had touched each of their cheeks with the tears of her kisses as she tried to smile goodbye), the record player was still commenting: *They treat me like a savage ... they treat me like a savage ... they treat me like a savage ... they treat me like a savage ... they treat me like a savage ...* and before Estelle got up to take it off, she thought again of the strange man who nobody invited who had asked her to dance just at that point; and it seemed very long ago that her happiness happened. Now, Boysie was walking back along the quiet corridor, alone.

TOPICS FOR DISCUSSION

1. What racial tensions surrounding the Caribbean community does Clarke's story reveal? Describe the portrait of the Caribbean community emerging from the story.

2. Consider different reactions to the wedding of Agatha and Henry by the party guests, the police officer, Agatha's family and friends, and the apartment neighbours.

3. Discuss the ironic effect created by Clarke's use of the calypso as a commentary on the situation that has occurred in the story.

Anne Jew

Anne Jew graduated with a degree in English from the University of British Columbia. She writes both fiction and film scripts. Her works have been published in Poem Canada *and* Room of One's Own. *Her monthly film and video column, "The Bijoux," appears in* Discorder *magazine. She is presently collaborating with the National Film Board on a script for an educational short about racism, as well as on a screenplay about female vampires. She is also working on her first novel. The story reprinted here comes from the anthology* Many-Mouthed Birds: Contemporary Writing by Chinese Canadians *(1991). Anne Jew describes a generational conflict in an immigrant family clashing over the issue of interracial dating. Three generations of the Chinese family demonstrate different stages of detachment from their traditional culture. Although ethnicity plays an important role, the young narrator and her rebellion against her family's values resonates with all readers in this coming-of-age story.*

Everyone Talked Loudly in Chinatown

Lately I have been walking home from school in the sunshine with Todd. It's October and the leaves have turned, though the temperature hasn't changed since the end of August. My father says the reason for this is there were two Junes in the Chinese calendar this year. I wonder if that makes this year thirteen months long or if one month is left out to fit it into the regular calendar. But I don't ask. He would launch into a long, boring explanation of the history of the Chinese calendar and say it was superior to the Western calendar. If it was anyone else, I would probably ask.

Todd is very good looking. All the girls at school think so, and it makes me feel good when they turn to look at us walk down the hall together. Sometimes on our walk home we stop at the park to sit on the swings and talk. Actually Todd talks a lot and I listen. He usually describes his daily visit to the vice principal, the cars he wants, and the bands he likes. There is a Led Zeppelin logo drawn onto the back of his jean jacket in black felt pen which kind of bothers me.

"Have you ever really listened to their lyrics? They just make so much sense." It's his favourite band.

I try hard to stay interested in what he says and ask him questions, but mostly I end up nodding my head and saying, "Uh huh, uh huh." He doesn't seem to mind my quietness though. His eyes are clear blue, almost like glass, and it's hard to describe the feeling I get when he looks at me. My whole body feels like it's melting to the ground, and I'm always surprised to see that it hasn't.

Today Todd walks me to the beginning of my block as usual and then crosses the street to go on. My mother would start to ask questions if she saw us together.

As I enter the house, I pass my grandmother's room to go upstairs. She is lying in there dying. I throw my bag into my room and head into the kitchen. I take out a bag of chips from the cupboard and pour a glass of orange juice and join my brother in the living room where he is watching a rerun of "The Brady Bunch." It's the one where Jan refuses to wear her glasses and smashes into the family portrait with her bike. After a while I forget about the Bradys and start to daydream about Todd.

The next thing I know, my mother is waking me up to feed my grandmother, whose hands shake all the time so she can't do it herself. My brother and I take turns every night.

I stand by the window in the kitchen waiting for my mother to put the food onto the dinner tray. I draw hearts encircling Todd's initials and mine on the steamed glass.

"Hey, what are you doing?" she asks. I quickly wipe away the evidence.

"Nothing."

Her dinner is basically the same every night—soup, rice with water, steamed vegetables, salted fish and a thermos of tea. When I go into the room, she is sleeping with the quilt drawn up to her chin, which is usually how I find her now. Before, my mother would move her to an armchair by the window where she could watch people walk by or she would watch the new television set my father bought for her. Her favourite shows were "The Roadrunner" and "The Beverly Hillbillies," both which I couldn't stand. She would point and laugh and mumble something in Chinese. She didn't understand them, but I think she liked their movements. Now she stays in bed, too weak to get up.

She looks really old. I think she's almost eighty-four, but no one knows for sure. They didn't have birth certificates in China then, and she had to lie about her age when she came over to Canada. Her skin is bunched up like fabric and it just kind of hangs from her cheekbones. But it feels thin and soft. I touched it once when she was asleep. Her hair is grey and white and oily. It's combed back, making her forehead look like a shiny grapefruit. The lobes of her ears have been stretched by the weight of gold earrings I have never seen her take off. She is hardly moving. She almost looks as if she were dead already.

"Grandmother, it's time to eat rice."

She briefly opens her eyes and then closes them again.

"Grandmother, it's time to eat rice," I repeat a little louder.

She opens her eyes again, and I bring the tray closer for her to see. She starts to sit up, and I put down the tray to help her. After I prop her up onto some pillows, I tuck a paper napkin into the neck of her pyjamas and begin to feed her. I really hate doing it and I always want it to be over as soon as possible. Luckily she has been eating less and less. I have been begging my mother to do it instead, but so far she hasn't given in.

"You're not the one who has to bathe her and change the sheets. Don't be so bad. You are the only one she has treated well. She is going to die soon anyway."

My mother can't wait for my grandmother to die. She is always telling my brother and me how she was treated like a slave by Grandmother when she first married my father.

"Why didn't you stand up for yourself?" I ask.

"Oh, you don't know what it was like then."

We start with the soup. The spoon makes a clanging noise as it knocks against her teeth, sending a shiver through me. She still has all of them, which is amazing since my mother already has false front teeth. She doesn't chew the food very much though. It stays in her mouth a while, and then she makes a great effort to swallow. I try to show her how to chew by making exaggerated movements with my mouth, but she just ignores me. She finishes the soup, and we start on the rice in water. Some of it dribbles out of her mouth, so I have to scrape it off her chin and spoon it back in like I'm feeding a baby. I feel disgusted and guilty and I don't know why. I also feel guilty for not spending more time with her and for not wanting to spend more time with her. Todd would die if he knew I had to do this.

She is a grown-up who has always taken care of me, but now I have to take care of her. It bothers me. She used to be different.

When I was little, she would take me to Chinatown every weekend. We would go to a small pastry shop at the corner of Pender and Gore. I would have a Coke and a coconut bun while she had tea with the owners. I had to call them Uncle and Auntie although they weren't related to us. They spoke to each other about the people they knew: who was dying, who was dead, whose daughter-in-law was lazy. They drew out their words into sighs and shook their heads at the misfortunes of others. Sometimes they would comment on me, looking at me as if I couldn't see or hear them.

"Look at that high nose. She doesn't look Chinese."

"She is such a shy cute girl."

I usually watched the customers, the bell tinkling above the door as they came and went. Most were short, chubby women with unmade faces and hair. They always looked tired and reminded me of my mother. They carried plastic shopping bags with different shop logos on them in Chinese characters, and their children would run around them as they tried to order. They would scream out their orders and at their children at the same time.

There were also old stooping men with brown spots on their faces and the odd gold front tooth, and old women with straight grey hair pinned back over their ears. The old people were always buried under layers of clothing no matter what season it was.

Each time we left, the owners would give me a box of barbecued pork buns to take home.

"Lin, thank Uncle and Auntie."

"Thank you Uncle and Auntie."

"What a cute girl."

My grandmother was very popular in Chinatown. While we shopped we would be stopped every few feet by her acquaintances. Everyone talked loudly and waved their arms. I couldn't understand why they had to be so loud. It seemed uncivilized. She also took me to visit her friends and I would occupy myself with extra game pieces while they played mah-jong.

But as I started to grow up, I stopped going to Chinatown with her, where it was too loud, and then I stopped spending time with her altogether. I started to play with friends who weren't loud and who weren't Chinese. This upset my mother. She was suspicious of all other cultures. My best friend for a long time was a German girl who lived up the block. Everything was neat and orderly at her house, and her mother was a quiet, pleasant woman who offered me green apples from their tree. My mother only bought red ones in Chinatown.

Grandmother eats the rest of the rice and some vegetables and then motions me to stop. I wipe her mouth and chin and help her to lie down again. She closes her eyes, and I turn out the light and climb the stairs to my own dinner.

On our walk home from school the next day, Todd asks me to see a movie with him. I lie to my parents and tell them I am going with my girlfriend Sandra. She swears not to say anything to anyone. Todd pays for the movie and popcorn, and we sit in the back row of the theatre. He puts one arm around me, balances the bucket of popcorn on his knee, holds his drink between his legs, and eats and drinks with his other hand. I am impressed. I usually gorge myself on popcorn, but I feel compelled to eat one kernel at a time.

Halfway through *The Great Santini* and after we've finished the popcorn, Todd offers me a Certs. Then after a while he turns to me and kisses me on the lips. He opens his mouth on mine, and not knowing what to do, I open my mouth. I feel his tongue moving around in my mouth, so I move my tongue around in his. He still tastes faintly of popcorn under the flavour of the Certs. Just as I'm becoming used to the new sensation, he stops and kisses me on the lips and turns back to the movie. I can feel saliva clinging to the edges of my mouth, and not wanting to wipe it away with my hand, I press my face into his shoulder, hoping his shirt will absorb the moisture. It works.

As we leave the theatre, Todd takes hold of my hand. I am quickly beginning to fall in love.

"Now that was a great movie. That Robert Duvall guy is one harsh dude. What'd you think? Did you like it?"

"Yeah, I thought it was quite good."

"Yeah, it was great."

My hand feels good in his, but his strides are twice as long as mine, so our mismatched rhythms make us bounce along instead of walk. By now I am truly in love and I let him take me all the way home. Only the living room light is on, so we sit in the darkness of the carport in the back. Todd kisses me again and we move our tongues around. I am lost in the kissing until a car's headlights shine at us as it pulls into the driveway.

"Oh my God! It's my mother!"

I grab Todd's arm, and we run to the front of the house.

"Go! Hurry up!" He quickly kisses me and runs up the block. I stand around debating whether to go inside or escape to Sandra's house. I finally decide to go in. My mother and father are standing in the living room.

"How can you be so fearless! Going out with a white boy!" screams my mother.

My father walks up to me, his eyes wide with anger, and slaps me on the face. Automatically, I slap him back. He is stunned and I take the opportunity to run into my room. I expect him to come charging after me, but I am left alone for the rest of the night. It is only when the last light is turned out that I start to cry.

When I wake up hours later, my eyelashes are clumped together with dried tears. I didn't draw the curtains, so the moon shines into my room. Everything looks calm and quiet covered in moonlight. It comforts me. Todd, my father—it seemed to happen so long ago.

Only the hum of the fridge can be heard as I creep out into the hallway. I slowly climb down the stairs to my grandmother's bedroom. I imagine the sound of movement as I enter, but I stop and there is nothing. It is dark, so I feel my way over to the window and draw the curtains back a little. She is so still in the moonlight. I go to her and touch her face. It is soft, but cool. The shadows make it look almost ghostly. I take her hand, bony and fragile, and find she has no pulse. I drop it instantly and stand back to look at her. She is dead, I think. I stare at her face expecting it to move, but somehow it looks peaceful. I take her hand again, kneel beside the bed, and rest my head against her. Soon I am asleep.

TOPICS FOR DISCUSSION

1. How is Lin's teenage rebellion against her parents manifested in the story? How is it complicated by her gender and ethnic background?

2. What is the grandmother's role in the story? How does it change over time? Why does Lin go to her grandmother's room after a fight with her parents?

3. Discuss different gender roles assumed by male and female characters in the story (the daughter, mother, father, grandmother, and the daughter's boyfriend). Compare the treatment of gender issues here with those in another Chinese Canadian story, Garry Engkent's "Why My Mother Can't Speak English." What distance between parent and child is created by cultural and generational differences in their attitudes to gender?

Linda Svendsen

*A fiction writer and screenwriter, Linda Svendsen was born in Vancouver
in 1954. After graduating from the University of British Columbia, she
moved to New York City, where she completed her Masters of Fine Arts at
Columbia University. In 1989, she returned to Canada and currently
teaches creative writing at the University of British Columbia.* She edited
Words We Call Home: Celebrating Creative Writing at UBC *(1990).
She published* Marine Life *(1992), a collection of eight interlocking stories,
which was nominated for the* LA Times *First Novel Award. In 2000,*
Marine Life *was made into a movie, directed by Anne Wheeler and star-
ring Cybil Sheppard. Linda Svendsen's screenplays include the CBC movie*
The Diviners, *based on Margaret Laurence's novel, and* At the End of the
Day: The Sue Rodriguez Story, *which was the winner of the 1999 Top
Ten Award from the Writers Guild. Her writing, focused on the lives of
girls and women, can be compared to Alice Munro's. Svendsen examines the
problems of dysfunctional families, where the need to be loved exists among
alcoholism, divorce, emotional trauma, and abuse. In "White Shoulders,"
the narrator, Adele, offers a glimpse of the apparently successful marriage of
her sister, Irene, and a Belgian man, Peter. Irene's blindness and Adele's self-
imposed passivity when faced with a suspicion of incest between Peter and
his daughter Jill, lead to a tragedy.*

White Shoulders

My oldest sister's name is Irene de Haan and she has never hurt
anybody. She lives with cancer, in remission, and she has stayed
married to the same undemonstrative Belgian Canadian, a brake
specialist, going on thirty years. In the family's crumbling domestic
empire, Irene and Peter's union has been, quietly, and despite
tragedy, what our mother calls the lone success.

Back in the late summer of 1984, before Irene was admitted
into hospital for removal of her left breast, I flew home from New
York to Vancouver to be with her. We hadn't seen each other for

four years, and since I didn't start teaching ESL night classes until mid-September, I was free, at loose ends, unlike the rest of her family. Over the past months, Peter had used up vacation and personal days shuttling her to numerous tests, but finally had to get back to work. He still had a mortgage. Their only child, Jill, who'd just turned seventeen, was entering her last year of high school. Until junior high, she'd been one of those naturally well-rounded kids – taking classes in the high dive, water ballet, drawing and drama, and boy-hunting in the mall on Saturdays with a posse of dizzy friends. Then, Irene said, overnight she became unathletic, withdrawn and bookish: an academic drone. At any rate, for Jill and Peter's sake, Irene didn't intend to allow her illness to interfere with their life. She wanted everything to proceed as normally as possible As who wouldn't.

In a way, and this will sound callous, the timing had worked out. Earlier that summer, my ex-husband had been offered a temporary teaching position across the country, and after a long dinner at our old Szechuan dive, I'd agreed to temporarily revise our custody arrangement. With his newfound bounty, Bill would rent a California townhouse for nine months and royally support the kids. "Dine and Disney," he said.

I'd blessed this, but then missed them. I found myself dead asleep in the middle of the day in Jane's lower bunk, or tuning in late afternoons to my six-year-old son's, and Bill's, obsession, *People's Court.* My arms ached when I saw other women holding sticky hands, pulling frenzied children along behind them in the August dog days. So I flew west. To be a mother again, I'd jokingly told Irene over the phone. To serve that very need.

Peter was late meeting me at the airport. We gave each other a minimal hug, and then he shouldered my bags and walked ahead out into the rain. The Datsun was double-parked, hazards flashing, with a homemade sign taped on the rear window that said STUD. DRIVER. "Jill," he said, loading the trunk. "Irene's been teaching her so she can pick up the groceries. Help out for a change." I got in, he turned on easy-listening, and we headed north towards the grey mountains.

Irene had been in love with him since I was a child; he'd been orphaned in Belgium during World War II, which moved both Irene and our mother. He'd also reminded us of Emile, the Frenchman in *South Pacific,* because he was greying, autocratic and seemed misunderstood. But the European charm had gradually worn thin; over the years, I'd been startled by Peter's racism and petty tyranny. I'd often wished that the young Irene had been fondled off her two feet by a breadwinner more tender, more local. Nobody else in the family agreed and Mum had even hinted that I'd become bitter since the demise of my own marriage.

"So how is she?" I finally asked Peter.

"She's got a cold," he said, "worrying herself sick. And other than that, it's hard to say." His tone was markedly guarded. He said prospects were poor; the lump was large and she had the fast-growing, speedy sort of cancer. "But she thinks the Paki quack will get it when he cuts," he said.

I sat with that. "And how's Jill?"

"Grouchy," he said. "Bitchy." This gave me pause, and it seemed to have the same effect on him.

We pulled into the garage of the brick house they'd lived in since Jill's birth, and he waved me on while he handled the luggage. The house seemed smaller now, tucked under tall Douglas firs and fringed with baskets of acutely pink geraniums and baby's breath. The back door was open, so I walked in; the master bedroom door was ajar, but I knocked first. She wasn't there. Jill called, "Aunt Adele?" and I headed back down the hall to the guest room, and stuck my head in.

A wan version of my sister rested on a water bed in the dark. When I plunked down I made a tiny wave. Irene almost smiled. She was thin as a fine chain; in my embrace, her flesh barely did the favour of keeping her bones company. Her blondish hair was quite short, and she looked ordinary, like a middle-aged matron who probably worked at a bank and kept a no-fail punch recipe filed away. I had to hold her, barely, close again. Behind us, the closet was full of her conservative garments – flannel, floral – and I understood that this was her room now. She slept here alone. She didn't frolic with Peter anymore, have sex.

"Don't cling," Irene said slowly, but with her old warmth. "Don't get melodramatic. I'm not dying. It's just a cold."

"Aunt Adele," Jill said.

I turned around; I'd forgotten my niece was even there, and she was sitting right on the bed, wedged against a bolster. We kissed hello with loud smooch effects – our ritual – and while she kept a hand on Irene's shoulder, she stuttered answers to my questions about school and her summer. Irene kept an eye on a mute TV – the U.S. Open – although she didn't have much interest in tennis; I sensed, really, that she didn't have any extra energy available for banter. This was conversation, not rudeness.

Jill looked different. In fact, the change in her appearance and demeanour exceeded the ordinary drama of puberty; she seemed to be another girl – shy, unsure and unable to look me in the eye. She wore silver wire glasses, no makeup, jeans with an oversize kelly-green sweatshirt and many extra pounds. Her soft straw-coloured hair was pulled back with a swan barrette, the swan's eyes downcast. When she passed Irene a glass of water and a pill, Irene managed a swallow, then passed it back, and Jill drank, too. To me, it seemed she took great care, twisting the glass in her hand, to sip from the very spot her mother's lips had touched.

Peter came in, sat down on Jill's side of the bed and stretched both arms around to raise the back of his shirt. He bared red, hairless skin, and said, "Scratch."

"But I'm watching tennis," Jill said softly.

"But you're my daughter," he said. "And I have an itch."

Peter looked at Irene and she gave Jill a sharp nudge. "Do you poor dad," she said. "You don't even have to get up."

"But aren't I watching something?" Jill said. She glanced around, searching for an ally.

"*Vrouw*," Peter spoke up. "This girl, she doesn't do anything except mope, eat, mope, eat."

Jill's shoulders sagged slightly, as if all air had suddenly abandoned her body, and then she slowly got up. "I'll see you after, Aunt Adele," she whispered, and I said, "Yes, sure," and then she walked out.

Irene looked dismally at Peter; he made a perverse sort of face – skewing his lips south. Then she reached over and started to scratch his bare back. It was an effort. "Be patient with her, Peter," she said. "She's worried about the surgery."

"She's worried you won't be around to wait on her," Peter said, then instructed, "Go a little higher." Irene's fingers crept obediently up. "Tell Adele what Jill said."

Irene shook her head. "I don't remember."

Peter turned to me. "When Irene told her about the cancer, she said, 'Don't die on me, Mum, or I'll kill you.' And she said this so serious. Can you imagine?" Peter laughed uninhibitedly, and then Irene joined in, too, although her quiet accompaniment was forced. There wasn't any recollected pleasure in her eyes at all; rather, it seemed as if she didn't want Peter to laugh alone, to appear as odd as he did. "Don't die or I'll kill you," Peter said.

Irene had always been private about her marriage. If there were disagreements with Peter and there had been – I'd once dropped in unannounced and witnessed a string of Christmas lights whip against the fireplace and shatter – they were never rebroadcast to the rest of the family; if she was ever discouraged or lonely, she didn't confide in anyone, unless she kept a journal or spoke to her own God. She had never said a word against the man.

The night before Irene's surgery, after many earnest wishes and ugly flowers had been delivered, she asked me to stay late with her at Lion's Gate Hospital. The room had emptied. Peter had absconded with Jill – and she'd gone reluctantly, asking to stay until I left – and our mother, who'd been so nervous and sad that an intern had fed her Valium from his pocket. "Why is this happening to her?" Mum said to him. "To my only happy child."

Irene, leashed to an IV, raised herself to the edge of the bed and looked out at the parking lot and that kind Pacific twilight. "That Jill," Irene said. She allowed her head to fall, arms crossed in front of her. "She should lift a finger for her father."

"Well," I said, watching my step, aware that she needed peace, "Peter's not exactly the most easygoing."

"No," she said weakly.

We sat for long time, Irene in her white gown, me beside her in my orange-and-avocado track suit, until I began to think I'd been too tough on Peter and had distressed her. Then she spoke. "Sometimes I wish I'd learned more Dutch," she said neutrally. "When I met Peter, we married not speaking the same language, really. And that made a difference."

She didn't expect a comment – she raised her head and stared out the half-open window – but I was too shocked to respond anyway. I'd never heard her remotely suggest that her and Peter's marriage had been less that a living storybook. "You don't like him, do you?" she said. "You don't care for his Belgian manner."

I didn't answer; it didn't need to be said aloud. I fumed away. "I'm probably not the woman who can best judge these things," I said.

Out in the hall, a female patient talked on the phone. Irene and I both listened. "I left it in the top drawer," she said wearily. "No. The bedroom." There was a pause. "The desk in the hall, try that." Another pause. "Then ask Susan where she put it, because I'm tired of this and I need it." I turned as she hung the phone up and saw her check to see if money had tumbled back. The hospital was quiet again. Irene did not move, but she was shaking; I found it difficult to watch this and reached out and took her hand.

"What is it?" I said. "Irene."

She told me she was scared. Nor for herself, but for Peter. That when she had first explained to him about the cancer, he hadn't spoken to her for three weeks. Or touched her. Or kissed her. He'd slept in the guestroom, until she'd offered to move there. And he'd been after Jill to butter his toast, change the sheets, iron his pants. Irene had speculated about this, she said, until she'd realized he was acting this way because of what had happened to him when he was little. In Belgium. Bruges, the war. He had only confided in her once. He'd said all the women he'd ever loved had left him. His mother killed, his sister. "And now me," Irene said. "The big C which leads to the big D. If I move on, I leave two children. And I've told Jill they have to stick together."

I got off the bed. "But, Irene," I said, "she's not on earth to please her father. Who can be unreasonable. In my opinion."

By this time, a medical team was touring the room. The junior member paused by Irene, and said, "Give me your vein."

"In a minute," she said to him, "please," and he left. There were dark areas, the colour of new bruises, under her eyes. "I want you to promise me something."

"Yes."

"If I die," she said, "and I'm not going to, but if I do, I don't want Jill to live with you in New York. Because that's what she wants to do. I want her to stay with Peter. Even if she runs to you, send her back."

"I can't promise that," I said. "Because you're not going to go anywhere."

She looked at me. Pale, fragile. She was my oldest sister, who'd always been zealous about the silver lining in that cloud; and now it seemed she might be dying, in her forties – too soon – and she needed to believe I could relieve her of this burden. So I nodded, *Yes.*

When I got back, by cab, to Irene and Peter's that night, the house was dark. I groped up the back steps, ascending through a hovering scent of honeysuckle, stepped inside and turned on the kitchen light. The TV was going – some ultra-loud camera commercial – in the living room. Nobody was watching. "Jill?" I said. "Peter?"

I wandered down the long hall, snapping on switches: Irene's sickroom, the upstairs bathroom, the master bedroom, Peter's domain. I did a double-take; he was there. Naked, lying on top of the bed. His still hand holding his penis – as if to keep it warm and safe – the head shining. The blades of the ceiling fan cut in slow circles above him. His eyes were vague and didn't turn my way; he was staring up. "Oh, sorry," I whispered, "God, sorry," and flicked the light off again.

I headed back to the living room and sat, for a few seconds. When I'd collected myself, I went to find Jill. She wasn't in her downstairs room, which seemed typically adolescent in its decor – Boy George poster, socks multiplying in a corner – until I spotted a quote from Rilke, in careful purple handwriting, taped to her long mirror: "Beauty is only the first touch of terror we can still bear."

I finally spotted the light under the basement bathroom door.

"Jill," I said. "It's me."

"I'm in the bathroom," she said.

"I know," I said. "I want to talk."

She unlocked the door and let me in. She looked tense and peculiar; it looked as if she'd just thrown water on her face. She was still dressed in her clothes from the hospital – and from the day before, the kelly-green sweat job – and she'd obviously been sitting on the edge of the tub, writing. There was Papermate, a pad of yellow legal paper,. The top sheet was covered with verses of tiny backward-slanting words. There was also last night's pot of Kraft Dinner on the sink.

"You're all locked in," I said.

She didn't comment, and when the silence stretched on too long I said, "Homework?" and pointed to the legal pad.

"No," she said. Then gave me a look and said, "Poem."

"Oh," I said, and I was surprised. "Do you ever show them? Or it?"

"No," she said. "They're not very good." She sat back on the tub. "But maybe I'd show you, Aunt Adele."

"Good," I said. "Not that I'm a judge." I told her Irene was tucked in and that she was in a better, more positive frame of mind. More like herself. This seemed to relax Jill so much, I marched the lie a step further. "Once your mum is out of the woods," I said, "your father may lighten up."

"That day will never come," she said.

"Never say never," I said. I gave her a hug – she was so much bigger than my daughter, but I embraced her the same way I had Jane since she was born: a hand and a held kiss on the top of the head.

She hugged me back. "Maybe I'll come live with you Auntie A."

"Maybe," I said, mindful of Irene's wishes. "You and everybody," and saw the disappointment on her streaked face. So I added, "Everything will be all right. Wait and see. She'll be all right."

And Irene was. They claimed they'd got it, and ten days later she came home, earlier than expected. When Peter, Jill and I were gathered around her in the sickroom, Irene started cracking jokes about her future prosthetic fitting. "How about the Dolly Parton, hon?" she said to Peter. "Then I'd be a handful."

I was surprised to see Peter envelop her in his arms; I hadn't ever seen him offer an affectionate gesture. He told her he didn't care what size boob she bought, because breasts were for the hungry babies – not so much for the husband. "I have these," he said. "These are mine. These big white shoulders." And he rested his head against her shoulder and looked placidly at Jill; he was heavy but Irene used her other arm to bolster herself, hold him up, and she closed her eyes in what seemed to be joy. Jill came and sat by me.

Irene took it easy the next few days; I stuck by, as did Jill, when she ventured in after school. I was shocked that there weren't more calls, or cards, or visitors except for Mum, and I realized my sister's life was actually very narrow, or extremely focused: family came first. Even Jill didn't seem to have any friends at all; the phone never rang for her.

Then Irene started to push herself – she prepared a complicated deep-fried Belgian dish; in the afternoon, she sat with Jill, in the Datsun, while Jill practised parallel parking in front of the house and lobbied for a mother-daughter trip to lovely downtown Brooklyn for Christmas. And then, after a long nap and little dinner, Irene insisted on attending the open house at Jill's school.

We were sitting listening to the band rehearse, a *Flashdance* medley, when I became aware of Irene's body heat – she was on my right – and asked if she might not want to head home. She was burning up. "Let me get through this," she said. Then Jill, on my other side, suddenly said in a small tight voice, "Mum." She was staring at her mother's blouse, where a bright stitch of scarlet had shown up. Irene had bled through her dressing. Irene looked down. "Oh," she said. "Peter."

On the tear to the hospital, Peter said he'd sue Irene's stupid "Paki bugger" doctor. He also said he should take his stupid wife to court for loss of sex. He should get a divorce for no-nookie. For supporting a one-tit wonder. And on and on.

Irene wasn't in any shape to respond; I doubt she would have anyway.

Beside me in the back seat, Jill turned to stare out the window; she was white, sitting on her hands.

I found my voice. "I don't think we need to hear this right now, Peter," I said.

"Oh, Adele," Irene said warningly. Disappointed.

He pulled over, smoothly, into a bus zone. Some of the people waiting for the bus weren't pleased. Peter turned and faced me, his fingers punctuating. "This is my wife, my daughter, my Datsun." He paused. "I can say what the hell I want. And you're welcome to walk." He reached over and opened my door.

The two women at the bus shelter hurried away, correctly sensing an incident.

"I'm going with Aunt – " Jill was barely audible.

"No," said Irene. "You stay here."

I sat there paralyzed. I wanted to get out, but didn't want to leave Irene and Jill alone with him; Irene was very ill, Jill seemed defenseless. "Look," I said to Peter, "forget I said anything. Let's just get Irene there, okay?"

He pulled the door shut, then turned front, checked me in the rearview one last time – cold, intimidating – and headed off again. Jill was crying silently. The insides of her glasses were smeared; I shifted over beside her and she linked her arm through mine tight, tight. Up front, Irene did not move.

They said it was an infection which had spread to the chest wall, requiring antibiotics and hospital admission. They were also going to perform more tests.

Peter took off with Jill, saying that they both had to get up in the morning.

Before I left Irene, she spoke to me privately, in a curtained cubicle in Emergency, and asked if I could stay at our mother's for the last few days of my visit; Irene didn't want to hurt me, but she thought it would be better, for all concerned, if I cleared out.

And then she went on; her fever was high, but she was lucid and fighting hard to stay that way. Could I keep quiet about this to our mother? And stop gushing about the East to Jill, going on about the Statue of Liberty and the view of the water from the window in the crown? And worry a little more about my own lost children and less about her daughter? And try to be more understanding of her husband, who sometimes wasn't able to exercise control over his emotions? Irene said Peter needed more love, more time; more of her, God willing. After that, she couldn't speak. And, frankly, neither could I.

I gave in to everything she asked. Jill and Peter dropped in together during the evening to see her, I visited Irene, with Mum, during the day when Peter was at work. Our conversations were banal and strained – they didn't seem to do either of us much good. After I left her one afternoon, I didn't know where I was going and ended up at my father's grave. I just sat there, on top of it, on the lap of the stone.

The day before my New York flight, I borrowed my mother's car to pick up a prescription for her at the mall.

I was window-shopping on my way back to the parking lot when I saw somebody resembling my niece sitting on a bench outside a sporting goods store. At first, the girl seemed too dishevelled, to dirty-looking, actually, to be Jill, but as I approached, it became clear it was her. She wasn't doing anything. She sat there, draped in her mother's London Fog raincoat, her hands resting on her thickish thighs, clicking a barrette open, closed, open, closed. It was ten in the morning; she should have been at school. In English. For a moment, it crossed my mind that she might be on drugs; this was a relief; it would explain everything. But I didn't think she was. I was going to go over and simply say, *Yo, Jill, let's do tea*, and then I remembered my sister's frightening talk with me at the hospital and thought, *Fuck it. Butt out, Adele*, and walked the long way around. I turned my back.

One sultry Saturday morning, in late September – after I'd been back in Brooklyn for a few weeks – I was up on the roof preparing the first lessons for classes when the super brought a handful of mail up. He'd been delivering it personally to tenants since the box had been ripped out of the entrance wall. It was the usual stuff and a thin white business envelope from Canada. From Jill. I opened it: *Dearlingest* (sic) *Aunt Adele, These are my only copies. Love, your only niece, Jill. P.S. I'm going to get a job and come see you at Easter.*

There were two. The poems were carefully written, each neat on their single page, with the script leaning left, as if blown by a stiff breeze. "Black Milk" was about three deaths: before her beloved husband leaves for war, a nursing mother shares a bottle of old wine with him, saved from their wedding day, and unknowingly poisons her child and then herself. Dying, she rocks her dying child in her arms, but her last conscious thought is for her husband at the front. Jill had misspelled wedding; she'd put *weeding*.

"Belgium" described a young girl ice skating across a frozen lake – Jill had been to Belgium with her parents two times – fleeing an unnamed pursuer. During each quick, desperate glide, the ice melts beneath her until, at the end, she in underwater: "In the deep cold / Face to face / Look, he comes now / My father / My Maker." The girl wakes up; it was a bad dream. And them her earthly father appears in her bed and, "He makes night / Come again / All night," by covering her eyes with his large, heavy hand.

I read these, and read them again, and I wept. I looked out, past the steeples and the tar roofs, where I thought I saw the heat rising, toward the green of Prospect Park, and held the poems on my lap, flat under my two hands. I didn't know what to do; I didn't know what to do right away; I thought I should wait until I knew clearly what to say and whom to say it to.

In late October, Mum phoned, crying, and said that Irene's cancer had not been caught by the mastectomy. Stray cells had been detected in other areas of her body. Chemotherapy was advised. Irene had switched doctors; she was seeing a naturopath. She was paying big money for an American miracle gum, among other things.

Mum also said that Jill had disappeared for thirty-two hours. Irene clamed that Jill had been upset because of a grade – a C in Phys. Ed. Mum didn't believe it was really that; she thought Irene's condition was disturbing Jill, but hadn't said that to Irene.

She didn't volunteer any information about the other member of Irene's family and I did not ask.

In November, Bill came east for a visit and brought the children, as scheduled; he also brought a woman named Cheryl Oak. The day before Thanksgiving, the two of them were invited to a dinner party, and I took Graham and Jane, taller and both painfully shy, with me to Central Park. It was a crisp, windy night. We watched the gi-normous balloons being blown up for the Macy's parade and bought roasted chestnuts, not to eat, but to warm the palms of our hands. I walked them back to their hotel and delivered them to the quiet, intelligent person who would probably become their step-mother, and be good to them, as she'd obviously been for Bill. Later, back in Brooklyn, I was still awake – wondering how another woman had succeeded with my husband and, now, my own little ones – when Irene phoned at three a.m. She told me Jill was dead. "There's been an accident," she said.

A few days later, my mother and stepfather picked me up at the Vancouver airport on a warm, cloudy morning. On the way to the funeral, they tried to tell me, between them – between breakdowns – what had happened. She had died of hypothermia; the impact of hitting the water had most likely rendered her unconscious. She probably hadn't been aware of drowning, but she'd done that, too. She'd driven the Datsun to Stanley Park – she'd told Irene she was going to the library – left the key in the ignition, walked not quite to the middle of the bridge and hoisted herself over the railing. There was one eyewitness: a guy who worked in a video store. He'd kept saying, "It was like a movie. I saw this little dumpling girl just throw herself off."

The chapel was half-empty, and the director mumbled that that was unusual when a teenager passed on. Irene had not known, and neither had Mum, where to reach Joyce, our middle sister, who was missing as usual; Ray, our older brother, gave a short eulogy. He stated that he didn't believe in any God, but Irene did, and he was glad for that this day. He also guessed that when any child takes her own life, the whole family must wonder why, and probably do that forever. The face of my sister was not to be borne. Then we all sang "The Water Is Wide," which Jill had once performed in an elementary school talent show. She'd won Honourable Mention.

After the congregation dispersed, Peter remained on his knees, his head in his hands, while Irene approached the casket. Jill wore a pale pink dress and her other glasses, and her hair was pinned back, as usual, with a barrette this time, a dove. Irene bent and kissed her on the mouth, on the forehead, then tugged at Jill's lace collar, adjusting it just so. It was the eternal mother's gesture, that finishing touch, before your daughter sails out the door on her big date.

I drank to excess at the reception; we all did, and needed to. Irene and I did not exchange a word; we just held each other for a long minute. From a distance, and that distance was necessary, I heard Peter talking about Belgium and memories of his childhood. On his fifth birthday, his sister, Kristin, had sent him a pencil from Paris, a new one, unsharpened, and he had used it until the lead was gone and it was so short he could barely hold it between his fingers. On the morning his mother was shot, in cold blood, he'd been dressing in the dark. The last thing she had said, to the Germans, was, "Don't hurt my little boy." This was when Mum and I saw Irene go to him and take his hand. She led him down the hall to his bedroom and close the door behind them. "Thank God," Mum said. "Thank God, they have each other. Thank God, she has him."

And for that moment, I forgot about the despair that had prompted Jill to do what she did, and my own responsibility and silence, because I was alive and full of needs, sickness and dreams myself. I thought, *No, I will never tell my sister what I suspect, because life is short and very hard,* and I thought, *Yes, a bad marriage is better than none,* and I thought, *Adele, let the sun go down on your anger, because it will not bring her back,* and I turned to my mother. "Yes," I said. "Thank God."

TOPICS FOR DISCUSSION

1. What troubling signals did Adele receive about the situation in her sister Irene's family? Why did she ignore these signals? What are the consequences of her silence?

2. The narrator seems to subscribe to a tragic view of family relationships. How does the behaviour of different members of her

family illustrate the opposite pull of love for others and the need to satisfy one's own individual needs?

3. Explain the ironies of the title and in the ending of the story.

4. We live in a culture that repeatedly sacrifices its children through violence, abuse, and other dysfunction that they witness and/or experience. Does the story suggest any ways that the cycle can be broken?

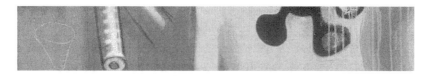

WORK/
POVERTY/
CHOICES

INTRODUCTION

What counts as work? The boundaries of our definitions have been pushed to include unpaid work done mostly by women whose labour in the home remains largely invisible. Work has always been not only a means of earning livelihood, but also a source of dignity for most people. However, our society still has to cope with the unequal distribution of work and income. Despite different initiatives to close the gap, groups such as women, immigrants, Native people, people of colour, or people with disabilities report difficulties finding jobs commensurate with their qualifications, getting promotions, or being paid adequately (for example, women, on average, still earn 80 cents to every dollar made by men). Especially, new immigrants often encounter the problem of lack of "Canadian experience"—an excuse for not hiring and an effective form of gatekeeping.

We often hear that anyone can succeed, that everyone has a choice, and that it is up to the individual to decide what he or she will do with their lives. However, for many people their choices are limited. Many people in Canada live in poverty as a result of joblessness, lack of opportunity, or being tied to poorly paid jobs. Poverty creates class stratifications from which it is sometimes hard to escape and limits children's chances.

This unit shows how people often excluded from the system—women, immigrants, people of colour, and Native people—persevere in their struggle for equitable treatment and find ways to challenge and subvert the dominant definitions of belonging and success. We can also look at the writers of diverse backgrounds, showcased in this book, as themselves representing models of perseverance and embodiments of success stories.

Chinese Wall Writings

*The inscriptions below, hidden beneath layers of paint and whitewash,
were discovered in November 1977, during the demolition of the
Immigration Building in Victoria, B.C. Some messages were carved on the
cell walls with a sharp point; other messages were written with pen and
ink. Dr. David Chuenyan Lai, at that time a geographer at the University
of Victoria, managed to read the inscriptions and translate them into
English. They were written in traditional verse form or in running prose.
Here they appear in free translation taken from Lai's article "A 'Prison' for
Chinese Immigrants, "The* Asianadian, *Vol. 2, No. 4.*

*The Immigration Building was built in 1908, and over the years it
served a number of purposes. At one time it included cells in which Chinese
immigrants were confined until their transit papers could be processed. The
"wall writing" attests to the loneliness, humiliation, pride, ambition, and
confusion of the immigrants. Each Chinese dreamed that Canada would
be, for him, the Gim Shan (Gold Mountain) where he could seek—and
find—his fortune. In these cells each man could only dream.*

Chinese Wall Writings

Notice

Fellow countrymen, read the following notice quickly:
Having amassed several hundred dollars,
I left my native home for a foreign land.
To my surprise, I was kept inside a prison cell!
Alas, there is nowhere for me to go from here,
I can see neither the world outside nor my dear parents.
When I think of them, tears begin to stream down.
To whom can I confide my mournful sorrow,
But to etch in a few lines on this wall.

*— Anonymous, from Beiyang, Xinhui County,
Guangdong Province*

A Mr. Lee from Taishan County, Guangdong Province, carved a poem on a wall on 4 September 1911:

Sitting alone in the Customs office,
My heart aches.
Had I not been poor,
I would not have travelled far away from my home.
I went abroad upon my brother's advice.
The black devil here is ruthless,
He forces the Chinese to sweep and clean the floor.
Two meals a day are provided
But I wonder when I will be homeward bound.

An anonymous person wrote the following:

Deserting my parents, wife and children, I come to the Gold Mountain because I am poor. I remember their words that they have tried by various means to raise a thousand and some odd dollars for my passage. I have now safely arrived but unexpectedly the people here wanted to examine my eyes, forced me to strip to the waist and to take off my pants to lay bare my body. I have much been abused and insulted because China is weak and I am poor. I always think of my parents. My dear fellow countrymen, we should return home and help build our mother country strong and rich.

The sorrow and anger of the imprisoned immigrants were vividly expressed in their poems. The following one was written in 1919:

I have always yearned to reach for the Gold Mountain.
But instead, it is hell, full of hardship.
I was detained in a prison and tears rolled down my cheeks.
My wife at home is longing for my letter
Who can foretell when I will be able to return home?

Another poem reads as follows:

I am in prison because I covet riches.
Driven by poverty I sailed over here on the choppy sea.
If only I did not need to labour for money,
I would already have returned home to China.

TOPICS FOR DISCUSSION

1. What specific details about the abuse and insult experienced by Chinese immigrants at the hands of immigration officers are revealed by these personal testimonials?

2. What motive is most often cited for leaving China? What regrets and longings do the immigrants voice in their inscriptions?

3. On the basis of "Chinese Wall Writings" and Joy Kogawa's *Itsuka,* compare the role that the Canadian government had played in both encouraging immigration and disenfranchising immigration from Asia.

Katherine Vlassie

Katherine Vlassie was born in 1935 in Winnipeg, a second-generation Greek Canadian. After raising her children, she turned to writing in 1980 and enrolled in a creative writing course. She lives in Toronto. Her first published book is a collection of stories linked by the same characters, Children of Byzantium *(1987), from which "A Bit of Magic" has been taken. The stories have been inspired by the letters Vlassie's father sent to her mother from Canada in 1915. Vlassie admits that there are certain similarities between her mother and Eleni, the protagonist of the book. Asked about the importance of her Greek background to the story, Vlassie replies: "I would like the book to stand on its own—as the story of a woman, because that's really what I was writing about. I was writing about a woman who lives in silence, and what it does to her. I guess in my mind I play down the ethnic connection, and play up the role of the church, the patriarchal world, being a stranger in a strange land, both the male world and a different country—not necessarily that it is a Greek story." The story, however, shows multiple subversions not only of expected gender roles in a traditional family, but also of the mainstream orientalizing gaze turned towards some immigrants. Eleni, through her exaggerated performances of "otherness" as Madame Zolta, uses to her own advantage her clients' stereotypes of exotic difference they expect to find in "Eastern" women.*

A Bit of Magic

"I told Alekos I could look for a job," Matina said. "You can imagine how he reacted to that."

Eleni lay down her sewing. "Even if he allowed it," she said thoughtfully, "what would you do?"

"I don't know!" Matina sank back on the couch, bit at the edge of a fingernail. "Maybe Anna has the answer in those cups of hers."

She turned to her sister-in-law who was coming into the living room with a tray of Turkish coffee.

Eleni pushed aside a pile of English magazines and children's books to make room on the coffee table.

"I offered to help out," Anna said. She set down the tray and handed around the coffee. "Pavlo refused to discuss it."

"He's right," Eleni said. "You have small children to worry about."

Matina put down her coffee. "Whereas you and I, *Elenáki*, with ours at school all day, have plenty of time." She twisted a strand of hair around her finger. "There must be something we're good for," she said, "something we can do. Even without Anna's education."

"Costa says things will get better soon," Eleni said.

"How long have they all been saying that!" Matina cried.

At the beginning, the depression had been just a word to explain why they couldn't have the little extras they'd become used to over the years, but lately it had started to touch them in places they understood. Darning underwear and socks that were almost threadbare, layering newspaper inside shoes that were worn thin at the soles, frequent meals of *fasoláda*, the bean soup they all knew from earlier years in Greece, were daily reminders of the poverty they'd thought was behind them.

"Alekos complains every day about the rich customers at the store, with their maids and big cars, who won't pay their bills," Matina said. "When I ask him why he keeps selling to them, he says they owe so much he has to or they'll never pay up."

"I don't understand," Eleni said. She put down her coffee, picked up her sewing again.

"Do you think I do? We fight about it all the time. That and everything else."

Matina couldn't sit still, fidgeting with her coffee cup, turning it round and round in her fingers, watching Eleni calmly darning one of her son's undershirts for the dozenth time, Anna quietly sipping her coffee. Their complacency exasperated her. She was angry with Alekos much of the time as well, the way he'd criticize her whenever she tried to talk to him about money or the possibility of her taking a job; what would she do, he'd say sarcastically, except to go out and clean houses; or else he'd turn pompous and announce that he would never allow his wife to work.

"Turn over your cup," Anna said to Matina. "I'll have time to read at least one before Mike wakes up."

"All right. All right." She finished up the coffee, put the cup upside down on the saucer, turned it three times, made a wish, shook the cup to make sure the grounds were well drained, and handed it over.

Anna placed the cup on the palm of one hand and rotated it slowly with the fingers of the other, all the while staring down at the blackened shapes formed by the coffee. For all her scoffing, Matina couldn't help but get caught up in the aura of mystery created by her sister-in-law as she gazed solemnly into the turning cup. It was all nonsense, of course. Matina knew exactly what was coming next. Anna would stop the turning and point dramatically at the cup, as if, all at once, it was magically made clear to her and she could actually gaze beyond the coffee and into the future.

"Enough theatrics," Matina said. "Get on with it."

"Wait," Anna said sharply. "I have to be sure."

Matina let out a sigh, waited as long as she could. "Do you see a job or money in there?" she asked finally.

Anna pointed. "There, at the side. Do you see the bird? It's almost at the rim."

"All I see," Matina said staring in at the tiny cup, "is the big clump of grounds at the bottom. Doesn't that mean worry?"

"Yes, but see how the worry disappears? The bird is taking it away."

"Tell me more nice things," Matina said, settling in.

"I tell you only what the cup says."

Anna found letters and good omens, prophesied much activity, and said Matina's wish would come true. "I see you all dressed up," she said at one point. "A masquerade."

"Oh, good, a party."

Anna shook her head very slowly. "You'll be the only one in costume."

Mike's cries broke into their mood. Anna put down the cup, smiled normally once again, and went to get her son.

Matina was too restless to go straight home after she and Eleni left Anna's. She went walking instead, down one residential street and up another until she was practically lost. She realized where she was when she reached a cluster of small shops. In the days when they'd had their car, they'd sometimes driven through the area. She paused to admire an exquisite white crepe evening gown at Belle's French Fashions and an enormous bouquet of deep red roses that filled the window of McClary's Flower Shop, but walked quickly by the display of imported foods at Smith and Son. A group of ladies in fur capes and feather hats walking out of Morgan's Restaurant and Tea Room across the street caught her attention. When they disappeared, laughing, around the corner, she crossed over. She was curious to see inside, but heavy curtains covered the windows. A sign by the door read: *Tea-Cup Reading by Madame Rosa: Monday, Wednesday, Friday: 2-4.*

All the way home, Matina thought about what she'd stumbled across, and told herself that if she were superstitious she'd take it as an omen. Still, she hardly slept that night, and the next morning, as soon as Alekos had gone to work and Irini to school, she left for Eleni's. On the way, she stopped at the grocery store and bought a small packet of tea.

"English tea," she explained to Eleni.

"How do you make it?"

"Like *camomíli*, I imagine."

Eleni put a heaping spoonful of the tea into a saucepan, added cold water and put it on the stove. When it came to a boil, she turned the heat down, added some honey, and let the mixture simmer.

"Don't use that," Matina said as Eleni took the strainer out of the cutlery drawer.

"What's gotten into you?" Eleni asked.

"Make sure lots of leaves get into the cups," Matina said. Eleni poured as instructed and they watched the leaves settle at the bottom of each cup. "Are you going to tell me what you're up to?" Eleni asked as they waited for the tea to cool down enough to drink.

"We're going to tell fortunes," Matina said.

"We need coffee grounds for that."

"The *englézi* read tea leaves. They even have shops where you can go to drink tea and then have a Madame somebody or other tell your fortune." She looked impatiently at Eleni. "You've seen them in passing."

"You didn't go inside one!"

"Oh, don't look so worried."

"I am worried. You've been acting very strangely lately. I wouldn't put it past you to go into one of those places just to make Alekos angry." They both knew how their husbands felt about women going into restaurants or tea rooms unaccompanied—it was something only *xénes*, foreigners, did.

"Drink," Matina said, handing her the cup.

"Fine. We won't talk about it. I'd just like to know what you're up to." Eleni sipped the tea, made a face, and pushed her cup away. "The *englézi* have no taste," she said.

"Don't be fussy." Matina drank and winced. They tried adding more honey but in the end had to throw out the bitter stuff in order to get at the leaves.

They clumped together in Matina's cup, but spread themselves around in Eleni's. "There, you see, they make different patterns," Matina cried happily. "Let's find letters and trips and birds and things now."

"You've gone crazy, Matina," Eleni said finally.

"No, listen, I have a wonderful idea, and you're going to help me." It seemed reasonable, she explained to Eleni, that if telling fortunes was as easy as Anna seemed to make it, and if the *englézi* offered tea cup reading in their stores, why not dress up in costume, read tea cups in a restaurant, and get paid for it?

"You intend to turn yourself into a *gyftisa*, a gypsy, and go out among strangers!" Eleni cried. "What will Alekos say?"

"You don't think I'd tell him!"

For every sensible argument Eleni could think of against the wild scheme, Matina had an answer: no one would ever find out; the children needed new clothes; Christmas was coming; but most important of all, they needed the money.

Eleni gave up trying to talk sense to Matina, peered at the leaves stuck to the bottom of her cup and handed it over. "All right, Madame *Gyftisa*, what do you see?"

Matina laughed and hugged Eleni. "I see a secret admirer, a mysterious stranger, sudden wealth, good luck in the form of, ah, let's see now, what is it, ah, it's getting clearer, yes, that's it … the letter M!" She paused dramatically, looked up. "The letter M," she went on most solemnly, "will be important to you. A person whose name begins with that initial will bring you great wealth." She put down the cup. "How's that?"

"How will you say all those things in English?"

"I'll be the mysterious lady from the mysterious east, like in the moving pictures. They all speak funny English, too."

"You'll need a special outfit then, mysterious lady."

"That's where you come in, *Elenáki*." Matina smiled sweetly. "You're so good at sewing."

After a week of practising her fortune-telling on Anna and standing still for Eleni who sewed and fitted the costume for the mysterious lady of the east, Madame Zolta was ready to make her appearance.

"What does it mean?" Eleni asked.

"Zolta? I don't know. Nothing. It sounds oriental. Better than Madame Rosa. Very dull."

"You won't be dull in that outfit." Eleni surveyed her handi-work. Bits and pieces of materials from worn-out dresses and panels from curtains that had strangely lost some of their fulness had been

worked into an ensemble that resembled nothing less than the most
spectacular Hollywood Arabian Nights outfit.

Matina twirled around Eleni's living room bedecked in a pair of
emerald-green Turkish-like balloon pants and a jewel-encrusted black
velvet vest with flouncing red sleeves. A long scarf of black chiffon
turbaned her head then draped around the lower part of her face.

"We need to make up the eyes," Eleni said, scanning her creation. "And we forgot shoes."

They rummaged in closets and trunks until Eleni found a pair
of purple Chinese slippers embroidered with black and silver thread.

"Perfect," Matina cried.

They made up the eyes, lining them heavily in black, then Eleni
held out the dark red velvet cloak that had once been Matina's hall
curtains, and Matina stepped inside.

Once Madame Zolta was outfitted to their satisfaction, Matina
decided an all-black turbaned outfit would be perfect for Madame's
servant.

"Oh no! Not me!"

"*Elenáki?*"

"Don't *Elenáki* me. I said I'd help with the sewing, that's all!"

"No one will recognize us."

"I can't go into a strange place full of foreigners."

"We'll be together. I'll do the talking."

"What if Costa finds out?"

"How could he find out? Our own mothers wouldn't recognize
us in such outfits!"

Eleni crossed herself. "May the Virgin forgive me."

Matina jumped up and kissed her.

Madame Zolta, swathed in her red velvet cloak and heavily veiled,
walked into Morgan's Restaurant and Tea Room the following
Thursday afternoon at two o'clock sharp. She was accompanied by
her maid, cloaked and turbaned in black. The maid carried a small
black satchel.

Madame asked to speak to Mr. Morgan. He seemed a bit taken
aback when he saw the pair, but he sat them down at a table in the
rear of the dimly-lit restaurant.

"I already got a dame who tells fortunes," he said.

Matina shrugged out of her cloak the way she'd been practicing
and lowered her eyelids. "I am coming two days only," she said in
her best Greta Garbo voice. "Tuesday, Thursday."

Morgan pulled a cigar out of his inside coat pocket and twirled
it in his fingers. "Tea cup reading every day," he said thoughtfully.

Matina held her breath. Eleni stared at the table top. He snipped off the end of the cigar, put it to his lips, licked it around then took it out again.

"Yeah, well, I guess it wouldn't hurt. Tell ya what, ladies, we'll give it a try. Two cents a cup." Matina nodded. Eleni sat as though frozen. "What's your names?"

"Madame Zolta," Matina answered grandly, then gestured toward Eleni. "My maid-servant."

"I only pay for one."

"My servant attends me."

"Sure, okay ladies; whatever you like." He shoved his cigar back in his pocket. "You can start today," he said and left them at the table.

Matina nudged Eleni, who was clasping the satchel. "Take out the cloths," she whispered. Eleni opened the bag and took out a piece of green embroidered material fringed in black. She spread it over the table top. Then she took out a small square of pale rose silk and covered the table lamp with that. She closed the satchel, put it at her feet, and the two women waited in silence.

In a matter of minutes, Morgan was back at their side. "What the ... what's this?"

"I will tell the fortunes now," Madame Zolta said, "I have prepared."

"Not here lady. You gotta go table to table. And get rid of those." He pointed at the pieces of material covering his lamp and his table.

"Madame Zolta cannot be without special cloths," Matina said, "carried in special bag by maid-servant." She tried to assume the look she'd seen on Anna's face whenever she was getting into the mood to read cups.

Morgan walked away muttering. They saw him go and speak to the three waitresses clustered at the front, shrug and settle himself behind the counter.

Matina waited nervously, fingering the fringes of the tablecloth, afraid someone would recognize her, worried that she'd get confused during a reading. Eleni sat in silence. The two women watched for customers, but all they saw coming in from the autumn cold were *zevgarákia*, couples, who slid into the dark, high-backed booths lining the side walls of the restaurant. The round centre tables with petal-like lamps seemed to be reserved for the few ladies who came in.

The afternoon was almost over before two elderly ladies, one in a green jersey and matching hat, the other in a mauve print with a black hat, walked up to Madame Zolta's table, overturned teacups in hand. Eleni jumped up and took her place behind Matina as they had practiced, and Matina gave each what she hoped was a good afternoon's worth of heavily-accented fortunes.

With their four pennies between them, they trudged home later that afternoon.

"It'll be better next time, you'll see," Matina said.

"I was so nervous. I'm glad the place is dark."

"Don't worry. We don't know any of those people. They're mostly rich ladies anyway."

"What about the *zevgarákia*?"

"They're too busy with each other to notice us."

The following Tuesday, the sign outside the Tea Room included a note about Madame Zolta, and that day the two women went home with a pair of nickels between them.

"You see, it's working!" Matina cried.

Eleni was still nervous.

In only a few weeks ladies were lining up awaiting their turns to have the fascinating Madame Zolta look into their futures. Soon Morgan began advertising her as *Clairevoyante Extraordinaire*. He suggested she begin reading daily.

"Madame Rosa?" Matina asked.

"There's plenty for two," Morgan said, fingering his unlit cigar.

"We will share?" Matina asked. Morgan nodded. "Not the two cents," she added.

"Don't worry lady. You'll get your full cut."

"Madame Rosa, she go to tables?"

"Yeah."

"I go to tables." Matina was feeling more comfortable now as Madame Zolta; each day it became easier to make up pretty stories for the well-dressed ladies who sat across from her in the soft lights of the Tea Room.

On the way home, she explained Morgan's offer to Eleni, who'd only understood a few of his English words. "You don't have to come and play servant any more," Matina said.

"I don't mind," she said, but she did mind and they both knew it. Matina was her dearest friend, and the extra money made a difference, but as much as she tried she couldn't stop worrying about Costa, certain that he'd come home one night with an accusation she would be unable to deny.

"I know you hate it, *Elenáki*." Matina linked their arms. "It's all right."

"I don't want to leave you alone."

"Servant must obey," Matina said in her Madame Zolta voice, and refused to discuss it further.

By the time winter set in, Madame Zolta had been at Morgan's Restaurant and Tea room long enough so that all the children, Matina's, Eleni's and Anna's, had new woollen vests, underwear and socks. Their husbands didn't notice; nor did they realize that fresh yarn rather than old was being knit into sweaters, mitts and scarves. It was amazing, they were told, how one little soup bone could make such a meaty soup.

Husbands, Matina claimed, were easily fooled. It was a Sunday evening and they were in Anna's kitchen finishing up the dinner dishes. Eleni wondered if it might not be a good idea to tell them the truth.

"You can't mean that," Matina said. She stopped wiping a glass and stared at Eleni.

"They might find it amusing, you turning yourself into a gypsy and telling fortunes," Eleni said. "They know how you like to dress up."

Often, at parties, Matina would disappear, only to come back outfitted in some outlandish costume and start to perform. Sometimes she'd dance, other times she'd mimic what she'd seen in the moving pictures. Alekos was one of the first to laugh at her antics.

"You talk as though it's the same thing!" Matina snapped. "You know they have no sense of humour when it comes to their wives doing anything other than being their wives."

"She's right," Anna said.

"Not Pavlo," Eleni said. "He's always been so, I don't know, modern, I think."

"He is when we're alone, at home, and with the children. But Pavlo won't go against his brother."

"And we all know how stubborn my dear Alekos is."

"That's why I admire you, Matina," Anna said.

"You admire me?" Matina sank onto a chair. "You, with all your schooling?"

Anna threw her washcloth into the sink. "You're the one who had the courage to go out and do something that had to be done," she said. "You're never afraid, Matina. That's a wonderful trait."

In all the years they'd known her, Anna had never spoken so passionately. Eleni was silent as she put the dishes away in the cupboard. Even Matina, rarely at a loss for words, didn't know what to say. Her only refuge was her role. "I'm not afraid to make a fool of myself," she said with a laugh, "if that's something to be proud of."

Money was slowly piling up at home, well-hidden among the linens where no one but Matina probed. Every time she'd add a few coins or bills to her collection she'd think about how good the holidays would be this year. She'd find a way to explain the extra money to Alekos. The few dollars she made were nothing compared to the huge bills he had to contend with, but she found comfort in the fact that she was helping in some small way by not having to ask for everyday things. It was even getting easier with him now; he was still preoccupied with business, but there were fewer fights.

In the meantime, it gave her pleasure to appear at the Tea Room in her Arabian Nights costume, being sought out by well-dressed ladies. Her early fears of stumbling over her English, or of making the same speech more than once to the *englézes*, who all looked alike, never happened. In time it even became easier for her to vary the stories. It was as though, from the time she'd begun donning her strange apparel, her imagination had been given free rein, and tales of mysterious strangers, of adoring lovers and jealous dark-haired women, were easily woven out of the patterns she saw in the cups.

It amazed Matina, who hated the cold and went out in winter only when it was absolutely necessary, that so many ladies would brave the blustery weather merely to have their fortunes told. The couples who favoured the darkened booths didn't seem daunted by the cold either. Each time she glanced over at them, huddling together, oblivious to everything but each other, a wave of nostalgia for the early days with Alekos overcame her, but she quickly dismissed the past and returned to the important business of spinning tales.

On one especially bitter and windy day not one lady was waiting for Madame Zolta when she walked in, something that hadn't happened since the first few times. Matina sat at her back table telling herself it had finally turned cold enough to keep even her most loyal customers away, while arguing back that they may well have tired of her and her silly stories, until she realized that what was really bothering her was that she didn't want to stop appearing as Madame Zolta. It was no longer just the money they sorely needed that drew her to the Tea Room, or even the excitement of being someone else for a few hours every day, it was being admired and sought out by these *englézes* who, with all their riches, still needed someone like her to weave a bit of magic into their lives.

To get her mind off these confusing thoughts, she concentrated on the couples. They were mostly young, but an older man with a youngish girlfriend caught her eye. The man had his back to her and a hat covered his head, but she could tell he was old from the way he hunched his back. The girl was pretty in a modern sort of way with her short, sleek hairdo, and a hat perched on the side of her head. She held a cigarette casually between enamelled finger nails. Matina wondered about the man's wife; he surely had a wife; she was probably at home tending to the children, if she wasn't in another Tea Room hearing about a mythical secret admirer.

A few ladies mercifully appeared, shaking the snow off their fur collars as they came in, and soon the room was filled with the aroma of brewing tea. Matina quickly dismissed both her fears of being forgotten and the casual love-affairs around her, concentrating instead on her paying clients. She flowed from table to table collecting her tickets, offering dreams of romance to warm up the day.

She was at a table with three ladies, tea cup in hand, when laughter intruded from behind. She turned at the infectious sound. It was the modern girl with the older man. He stood up then and turned, and for a moment, for a brief moment, even in her shock, she saw clearly how youthful the girl's laughter made him.

Then in an instant he was an old man again, an ugly old man, and she wanted to rush up and strike out at his gloating, leering, disgusting face, and tear at the girl, at her grinning young face, and at his, his stupid, stubborn, hateful old man's face, that was hers, hers for over thirty years, since they were children, lovers, poor together and happy, that pitiful aging man, no different from other aging men, yet she'd thought he was, more fool she, aging woman spinning dreams for other foolish women.

Matina never went back to the Tea Room. She burned the costume and refused to talk about any of it with Anna or Eleni. At Christmas the house was filled with the fragrance of roasting birds and honey-soaked delicacies, and at New Year's St. Basil left many presents for the children. When Alekos asked how she managed it all, she told him she'd been saving up and went on to talk of other things.

TOPICS FOR DISCUSSION

1. What forms does the husbands' control over their wives' lives take in Vlassie's story? How does it compare to male domination in Garry Engkent's story? Do women in both stories find ways to undermine this control?

2. What survival skills do women demonstrate in the face of economic hardships and poverty? What is the importance of female bonding?

3. What does Matina's tea-cup reading mean to her? How is she empowered through it? How does it affect her relationship with her husband?

4. What is "a bit of magic" that Matina brings into her own and other people's lives?

Maxine Tynes

*Born in 1949, Maxine Tynes has lived, studied, and worked all her life in
Dartmouth, Nova Scotia. She is a seventh-generation descendant of the
Black United Empire Loyalists, who after the American Revolution, in
1783, arrived in large numbers in Nova Scotia, where they had been
promised land in exchange for supporting the British. A graduate of
Dalhousie University, Maxine Tynes is currently on its Board of Governors,
the first Africadian to hold this post. She teaches high school and is a
former freelance broadcaster with CBC Radio. She has co-written and performed a docudrama based on the death of the South African freedom
fighter Stephen Biko. Her poems have appeared in numerous journals and
anthologies. Her first book,* Borrowed Beauty *(1988), won the Milton
Acorn People's Poetry Award. Her other collections of poetry include*
Woman Talking Woman *(1990),* Save the World for Me *(1991), and*
The Door of My Heart *(1993). In 1990, the Maxine Tynes Room
opened at the Dartmouth Public Library. In 1992, she received an honorary doctorate from Mount Saint Vincent University. She has also been
involved as an activist for the rights of the disabled. Here is how she
describes her commitment: "To be seen, heard, recognized, validated,
included, empowered—is the theme of my life. This imperative that I feel
and that I exercise is not limited to the disabled agenda. As a feminist; as
an African Canadian; as someone who comes from a grassroots, working
class Maritime background, this is the imperative that has fuelled my life."
Her short story "In Service" was broadcast on CBC in 1991, and in 1993
it was adapted for screen. It brings one aspect of Nova Scotian African
Canadian women's experience vividly to life.*

In Service

In Service. I grew up hearing those words. As a little girl in my
mother's kitchen, I would hear those words. In Service.

"She went In Service."

With little-girl ears where they shouldn't be, bent to lady-talk. That scary, hushed, exciting lady-talk between my mother and women who came to see her. Tea and talk. Lady-talk.

In Service. Mama and Miss Riley. Mama and Aunt Lil. Mama and Helen. Helen. The one grown-up person we were allowed to say the name of without a Miss or Aunt in front. Helen. I love to say her name and feel her velvet hats. Tams. She always chewed Juicy Fruit gum.

It was always the same. Talk of dark and mysterious women-things, softly spoken. Lips would burble tea in cups. Eyes would roll slowly or point sharply when certain things were said, names were named. Sometimes talk of Mama's In Service memories; of her grandmother, a ten year old girl being sent from the country, from Preston, to be In Service. Talk of Aunt Lil, and, sometimes with her. Laughing Aunt Lil, with hair like fleeting movie star dreams. Aunt Lil who always included laughing in her lady-talk. And Miss Riley, who never did.

These conversations always seemed to carry their own colours. This one – scary, smoky black, light misty grey. Lady-talk. "Children should be seen and not heard." "Keep in a child's place." I was afraid of those hard, red sentences Mama always had ready during lady-talk. I had to go where they couldn't see me. But in a small house, the scary grey black mist of lady-talk can always find you.

In Service. Sterling silver, glowing the dark-and-sunlight words to me. Like the lone brass button always at the bottom of Mama's button box, when I would sneak the polish to it, to bring back the shine. The Mysteries of In Service were all confused and glowing with parade dreams and uniforms marching by in a flash of things shiny and formal.

"Yes, girl, she went In Service when she was ten."

"It was right after I went In Service that Uncle Willy died."

"She was In Service for years."

"She died In Service."

My little-girl mind imagined shiny, wonderful things, not clearly defined. Not knees sore from years on hardwood floors. Not hands cracked, dry and painful, calloused and scrubworn. Not early morning walking miles into town to start the day off right with morning labours for some family. Not always going to and coming from the back door. Not "speak when you're spoken to," see and don't see, hear and don't hear, in case you anger them and they let you go. Not eating their leftovers in the kitchen alone. Not one dollar a day for back-breaking floors, walls, dishes, furniture, windows, washing, ironing, sweat-soaked labour. In Service.

"She died in service." That describes Helen. I was allowed to say her name. Velvet tams and Juicy Fruit gum every night in Mama's kitchen. When I was little, I was allowed to stand by her and feel her tams. When I got older, she'd be there every night, watching me cry into cold dishwater.

And still the tams were there. The ruby, the emerald green, the midnight velvet blue of them glowed richly against the grey-black, soft and wooly head. Sometimes she would reach up, too, to finger that soft glow; almost as if to make sure that lovely part of her was still there. Helen's hands against such splendid velvet were like wounds; flags of the world of drudgery that were her days.

Helen was someone's girl, this never married Black lady, already in middle age by the time I was old enough to know her. Somebody's girl. Not in the romantic notion of being somebody's girl (friend). Helen was some white lady's girl; some white family's girl. She came to our house every night as if it was a target; an end point to her day; to sit in our kitchen with a cup of tea; to read the paper. She never took her coat off.

The lady-talk would start. Mama and Helen. It was always about Helen's lady – the woman she worked for. "My family." "My Missus."

Helen "lived In Service," which added to the mystique of it all. My little-girl mind imagined something with a faint glow. Not a room off the back. Not living away from your family. In a house, a bed that was never yours.

Through my window, I could see "Helen's house" not far from my own. On Sunday walks with one or other of my older sisters, seeing "Helen's house" was to see a dream, or at least a story-book page. "Helen's house," huge and golden yellow, with a fence and a yard that held what, in later, grown-up years, I would know as a gazebo. But then, surely, that wonderful little in-the-yard house was where she lived, behind cool, dark green lattice. Helen's house. So different from my own, so squat and brown and hen-like. My house; teeming with the dozen of us. My house, that Helen fled to each night; to maybe, for a little while, be a little of what my mother was, and did and had. Mama, with hands on her own dishes; on her own child.

Helen had eyes that were always friendly. I would see them peek behind her tam, even as she sat, and sipped her tea, and waited for it all to happen every night. Waited in the wake of the dark and tiny storm of activity that hummed along after Mama; a whirl-wind of shooing the creeping horde of us; of moving through clouds of flour from baking; of ironing, of putting up late supper for Daddy; of watching and listening for Daddy; and finally settling down to braid my hair and have tea and lady-talk.

Sometimes Helen would bring a shopping bag full of clothes with her to show Mama. Clothes – castoff, not new – that her lady had given her. Clothes and hats. Velvet tams. Helen. Mama and Helen and lady-talk.

What did a little Black girl know, touching a velvet tam over hooded and frightened eyes? Helen. Perhaps she knew and feared the loneliness of her own life, circled round and round her like an echo; loneliness circled round and worn close, fitting her like the coats and tams from her shopping bag. Perhaps the secret mystery and the fear should hide deep in her eyes from me; from my little-girl eyes watching Helen bring the secret of In Service each night. This work, this life, this loneliness all too real for her. A dark and female mystery still for me.

Helen. Driven like a magnet to somebody else's kitchen; somebody else's child. Helen. With care-worn hands, handing me the future luxury of dreams, and thoughts, and "I remember Helen," and the awful mystery of In Service unravelled now from the whispers of lady-talk, found now in the voice of those words.

Looking back, I know she was saving me. They all were. Helen. Mama. Miss Riley. Aunt Lil. My sisters. Known and unknown Black women. Armies of Black women in that sea of domestic service. With unlikely and unowned addresses. Waiting for buses on prestigious street corners. Carrying back bits and remnants of that other world of In Service in shopping bags; and wearing the rest in coats and velvet tams.

TOPICS FOR DISCUSSION

1. Tynes's story is a brief vignette offering an insight into the lives of "armies of Black women in [the] sea of domestic service." Discuss how, despite its short length, it manages to produce a powerful effect of oppression based on race, class, and gender.

2. Explain the ironies resulting from Tynes's use of the point-of-view of a little girl. Compare the use of "innocent-eye" narrator in Alistair MacLeod's story in Unit Five. Are there any similarities in the way they employ sensory memory?

3. Why does the narrator say in her tribute to Black women who went "In Service" that they were all "saving" her?

Yeshim Ternar

Yeshim Ternar, a Montreal writer, was born in 1956 in Istanbul, Turkey. From 1975 to 1979, she lived in the United States; in 1980, she came to Canada. She has a Ph.D. in cultural anthropology from McGill University in Montreal. She currently works as a consultant offering training work-shops on cross-cultural communication. Her fiction has appeared in Canadian, American, and European magazines and in several anthologies: Telling Differences *(1989),* Other Solitudes *(1990), and* Fire Beneath the Cauldron *(1991). She has published two collections of short stories,* Orphaned by Halley's Comet *(1991) and* True Romance with a Sailor *(1996). She is the author of* The Book & the Veil: Escape from an Istanbul Harem *(1994), a combination of essay and fiction, which goes back to the times of her great-grandmother and the world of harems in the declining Ottoman Empire. Her radio play, "Looking for Leonard Cohen" was broadcast by CBC in 1992. Her latest book, a novel called* Rembrandt's Model *(1999), moves between different settings and histor-ical times, including seventeenth-century Amsterdam, twentieth-century Montreal, and Istanbul. Her story "Ajax Là-Bas" shows an ambitious and intelligent young Turkish woman who pays her way through college by doing house cleaning. It addresses the problem of immigrants who often have to work below their qualifications, especially at the start of their life in Canada.*

Ajax Là-Bas

Saliha Samson sits on one of the empty washing machines in the basement and lights a cigarette. There are three loads of wash in the machines. The wash cycle takes 35 minutes; the drying cycle another 25. The French couple who employ her are very nice people. They leave for work early in the morning, as soon as she arrives at 8:30. They trust her with everything. They know she is a conscientious worker, that she doesn't slack off like some of the other cleaning women.

Madame Rivest tells Saliha to eat whatever she wants from the refrigerator. She always leaves some change in the ceramic vase on the telephone table just in case Saliha needs to get extra detergent, cigarettes, or whatever. Madame Rivest knows she likes to snack on strawberry and blueberry yoghurt, so she always makes sure there is some in the refrigerator for her. This morning she has told her she hasn't done her weekly shopping yet, so she is leaving some money for Saliha especially to buy fruit yoghurt.

Now that's a nice gesture! I wish everyone were like that, thinks Saliha as she takes a deep puff from her cigarette. The Rivests live a long ways off from where she lives. She has to take the 80 bus from Park Extension, then the metro at Place des Arts to Berri, and then change metros at Berri to go to Longueuil; afterwards she has to take yet another bus to come here. But the trip is worth it because some of the people she works for close to home treat her so badly that she'd rather lose an hour on the way and work for Madame and Monsieur Rivest. That's a lot easier than working for the two old spinsters on upper Querbes.

Saliha notices the unbalanced load signal flash on one of the washers, and gets off the machine she is sitting on to straighten things out. As she untangles the heavy blue cotton velour bedspread from the black rotor blades of the washing machine, she thinks it was lucky she decided to take this cigarette break in the basement because if she had gone straight upstairs to continue her vacuuming, she would have lost an extra 25 minutes by having to wait for this load after all the others were completed. That would have thrown her schedule off perhaps by an hour because she would have had to take the elevator up and down twice more and delay other tasks in the meantime. That's how cleaning jobs are. You have to plan what you're going to do and how, and in what order. Otherwise.... Well, the machine starts churning again and she jumps back on the machine she was sitting on before to finish her cigarette.

She has her period again. It's crazy, she thinks. Madame Rivest calls her every two weeks. And every other time she has to work for Madame Rivest, she gets her period. It's either the first day or the second day of her period when she has to make that long trip to come here. I've never had any luck with periods, thinks Saliha as she massages her back with her left hand. Saliha's dream is to be able to lie in bed the whole day when she gets her period. But it never works that way.

The first time she had her period when she was eleven, she was in Istanbul then, she ran up to her mom to announce it. Her mother slapped her. 'Why did you do that?' Saliha asked. 'So that you won't lose your wits.' Saliha went to her room and cried less for the mess of blood than for the fact that she was getting too old to play hopscotch. That was fifteen years ago. Saliha cannot remember when she stopped playing hopscotch, but it was at least a year after she got her first period.

Some things in life are like that. First they come to you like big worries, and you spend days and nights worrying about them, but they have the life span and personality of a soap bubble. They grow and grow like a wart in one's heart and just when you're sure they are big and strong and will never go away, they pop out of your life not even leaving a rind, not even a speck of dust, but the dry flake of a single detergent grain.

Canadians are funny, thinks Saliha. They have detergents and lotions and soaps for everything. Everything has its own cleanser here. And every cleanser has its own name. Like Mr Clean. But Mr Clean is also M. Net. Wisk! What a strange way to call your laundry detergent. And Ajax. Particularly Ajax. George, the Greek *dépanneur* at Park Ex, told her Ajax was a Greek hero. Old heroes live on as detergents in Canada. Saliha smiles at her own joke. She thinks she should write this to her mom.

The wash is done in one of the machines. She opens a dryer and transfers the load there. Just as she starts the dryer, the other two machines go off. So she puts these loads in the dryers too, and feeds quarters to the machines. It's time to go up and vacuum the Rivests' bedroom, she decides.

She goes up on the elevator, happy that no one else is on it. She hates to be seen in her work clothes. She is wearing a pink cotton jumper, a navy blue shirt with the sleeves rolled up underneath that, and knee socks and her red moccasins. She had tied a Turkish scarf on her head with a knot in the back to keep her hair away from her face. Madame Rivest says she looks like a school girl like that. But Saliha feels uneasy in her work clothes. After all, it is hard to resign herself to being a cleaning woman on the sly in Canada.

As she is vacuuming the Rivests' bedroom, she remembers her friend Frederiki's warning. Frederiki told her to be careful most when she is vacuuming because when you have the vacuum on full blast, you can't hear if someone is approaching from the back. Frederiki said she knows a couple of cases of rape that happened when the cleaning woman was vacuuming and the old geezer tip-toed and caught the cleaning woman and forced her on the bed... Saliha shivers at the thought. She drops the vacuum cleaner and goes to check if she locked both locks on the door. Not that M. Rivest would do anything like that. He has two married daughters, but you never know who might have keys to the apartment.

On her way back from the door, walking through the living room, Saliha checks the time on the mantel clock that she guesses comes from Spain. The clock is set in a gold and black lacework metal fan that reminds one of the Spanish flamenco dancers. The Rivests appear to be well-travelled people. Scattered about the apartment there are several photographs of Madame and M. Rivest, in silver-rimmed frames, from various countries. The one on the side table next to the loveseat in the living room looks like it was taken in Spain. Madame Rivest, looking several years younger, is smiling in front of a white-washed Mediterranean-type house with red gardenias blooming in clay pots along the window sill. She is slightly tanned. It is a sunny photograph, making Madame Rivest whose face carries many wrinkles from cold Canadian winters look out of place in the country where Saliha assumes the true residents greet the sunshine with less suspicion and distress.

Nevertheless, Madame Rivest smiles in that photograph as all middle-aged tourists do on well-deserved holidays. A straw handbag hangs from her left shoulder, and in her right hand, she holds something like a camera lens cover.

Saliha notes that the dryers must have completed their cycle, so she goes back to the bedroom and quickly finishes off the corners of the room with the special attachment Madame Rivest has taught her to use.

She takes along the yellow plastic laundry basket to carry the wash. She gets unlucky going down. A young housewife and her son step into the elevator on the second floor and ride with her to the main floor. Saliha tries to act oblivious to the woman's presence, but she winks surreptitiously at the little boy. The boy responds with a blank face.

Saliha is relieved when they get out. In the basement she quickly piles all the wash together in the laundry basket and after turning the drums around and feeling around the ridges for a stray sock or handkerchief, she goes up to the Rivests' apartment to sort the clothes. She is folding the towels and the sheets neatly and mechanically when she looks up at the ceiling of the Rivests' bedroom for an instant and starts remembering.

She is back in fourth grade at her elementary school on the Asian side of Istanbul. It was late September, several weeks into the fall term when the school principal had given the all-important Monday morning speech to the whole elementary school population: rows of fidgety kids lined up in twos behind overweight maternal teachers.

They had all finished pledging allegiance to the Turkish nation and Turkish morality. In unison, they had proclaimed the following verses with pride:

'I am Turkish, I am honest, I am industrious. My motto is: to love my inferiors, to respect my superiors, to love my country and my people more than my own life. May my existence be a gift to the existence of the Turkish people.'

It was after the whole schoolyard had fallen silent that the old principal had cleared his throat, adjusted his glasses with a nervous push of the index finger of his right hand, and straightened the arms of his worn navy blue jacket by pulling at the sleeves. He had then solemnly said, more like a poet than the disciplinarian that the Ministry of Education demanded him to be:

'My dear children, today I would like to tell you about your counterparts in America. Little boys and girls your age in America are very different from you in some very important respects. For one, they are often more industrious, and they are better behaved. I felt it was my duty to remind you of this after the very grave accidents your wild running about in the schoolyard during recesses last week has caused. Several of your friends are not at school today because they gashed their heads or sprained their ankles from all the savage games they have been playing. The weather has been very nice. The school year has just begun. Your teachers and I understand that you are all happy to join your friends after the summer holidays, but school is not a place where you come to play unruly games of tag and hide-and-seek. School is a place where you come to learn about the vital skills that you will need for all your lives and where you receive the benefits of civilization. Your counterparts in America understand what school is all about. At recess, they don't run around like you, but make use of their time to practise the knowledge that they learn in the classroom. For example, when they go out into the school-yard—and let me remind you that not all of them are blessed with a schoolyard such as ours—they examine their surroundings. Look at all the leaves on the ground about you. You have perhaps not noticed them during all your frenzied horseplay. An American child, however, would pick up a leaf, examine it, do research to identify it, and record his observations in his notebook. An American child would do the same for an ant, a worm, or a spider instead of madly crushing it. If you, as young Turks, the adults of the future, learn to do the same, you will help to build a better nation and honour this country that our great Ataturk had offered to you as your most cherished gift.'

With this, the principal ended his speech. Saliha felt she was one of the few who had heard the true message of the principal's words. She looked about and saw, for the first time, the mounds of leaves in the schoolyard and the shady corners teeming with insects. After that day, every dry copper-coloured leaf, every quiet ant bespoke of her new task to pay attention to the world.

Saliha went on to finish her primary school education with distinctions despite some uncomfortable failures in the science class of her fifth year. Then she went to teacher's college to become a primary school teacher. After teaching in remote Anatolian villages where she gained the awe and respect of the peasants, she came to Canada to join her brother who is an auto mechanic in Montreal. She is presently enrolled at Plato College on Park Avenue to learn English and French.

Saliha folds all the towels and linen neatly. She separates Madame Rivest's lingerie from M. Rivest's underwear and pairs up his socks. She puts away all of the clean laundry on the appropriate shelves in the closet and the dresser. She does not neglect to arrange what was already there before she puts away the newly washed clothes.

Everything looks fresh and clean! Only some light dusting remains to be done. Then she will clean the bathroom. First she'll throw away the dirty water in the pail from mopping the floors, then she'll rinse out the cleaning rags and put away all the cleaning materials. Afterwards she'll take her shower and scrub the bathtub clean.

But before she finishes up the remaining tasks, Saliha decides to take a cigarette break on the blue floral patterned armchair in the living room. She makes some fresh coffee in the kitchen, brings her cup over to the living room and lights a cigarette. She unties her scarf and lets her wavy black hair down. As she sips her coffee in between puffs, Saliha goes over her cleaning appointments for the next two weeks. To remember the exact dates, she visualizes the Chrysler calendar in her kitchen with pictures of different kimono-clad Japanese geishas for each month.

She has to clean for the two spinster sisters on Thursday. She certainly doesn't look forward to that one. They are very messy people. They are also very careful with their money.

Contrary to the Rivests, they always follow her around and check how much detergent and soap she uses. They never offer her much at lunchtime. Not that she would eat what they eat. They always eat some strange food that she is unaccustomed to, things like blood sausage and sauerkraut; topping it off with stale Mae West cakes they buy at Steinberg or Provigo. Saliha prefers to keep to herself when she works there.

On Friday afternoon, she will clean for the old Czech at Côte des Neiges. He is a kind and quiet man who doesn't demand much from Saliha. He is glad to have a woman clean up once every few weeks. When she is there, Saliha cooks a couple of light dishes for him. He is always grateful for that and gives her an extra two dollars.

Saliha hopes that Eleni will call her on the weekend to confirm a cleaning job next week. Eleni lives close to where Saliha lives in Park Extension. But the best part of working for Eleni is that at the end of the work day when she is done at her hairdressing salon downstairs, Eleni comes upstairs to have coffee with Saliha and trims her hair and manicures her nails as a gesture of appreciation. Eleni's house is large and demands all of Saliha's energy but the extra reward makes the effort worth it. Eleni expects the cleaning to be done well, but always offers refreshments like Kool-aid and Tang. Last time Saliha worked there, Eleni gave her some of her daughter's old clothes. Saliha hopes she might receive a reasonable sweater next time because she badly needs something a little fashionable for the end of the term party at Plato College.

Sipping the last of her coffee, Saliha rises from the armchair and looks around the living room to plan her dusting strategy. She will do just the outside panels of the display cabinet this time, leaving the silver goblets and British china for the next time. Then she will dust the buffet and the little figurines on top of it, taking care to dust off the folds of the Chinese jade Buddha. She decides not to waste too much time polishing the wood this time as all the wooden surfaces are still sparkling from the last time she did them. The Rivests don't seem to have invited anyone over for dinner in the meantime because the guest sets remain as she last arranged them.

Saliha has just finished drying her hair and changing into her street clothes after her shower when Madame Rivest comes back from work. She greets Saliha in French, glances around the house and shows her approval with many 'Ooh's and 'Wonderful's, stretching her words to make Saliha understand her heart-felt appreciation. Then she says in French that she will call Saliha again next week to confirm their next cleaning date. As she says this, Madame Rivest gestures as if she were dialing and holding on to the receiver of an imaginary telephone.

Of course Saliha can understand everything Madame Rivest is saying without the added gestures, but Madame Rivest is being so kind and helpful that Saliha decides not to use a couple of appropriate French phrases she has recently learned at Plato College.

Madame Rivest goes into her bedroom and comes back out with a sealed white envelope containing Saliha's thirty-five dollars. The Rivests are the only people that put Saliha's earnings in an envelope. They are considerate people.

As Saliha takes the envelope, she says, 'Merci beaucoup, Madame Rivest.' Stepping out the door, she switches the plastic bag containing her work clothes from her right hand to her left hand

and extends her right hand to Madame Rivest and says, 'Bonjour, Madame Rivest,' and smiles. These are the first real words she has uttered since she woke up that morning.

In the elevator, going down, Saliha is alone. She checks the contents of the envelope and smiles with satisfaction. Before the elevator reaches the ground floor, Saliha has time to reflect on her day. She has earned enough for the week's food and cigarettes. Last week, she paid the last instalment for her tuition at Plato College. She is tired but life is under control. Her only regret is that she hasn't answered Madame Rivest in longer sentences. But she chases away her regrets with a light shrug and admits the reality.

We come here to speak like them, she thinks; but it will be a long time before they let us practise.

T O P I C S   F O R   D I S C U S S I O N

1. How are we to interpret Saliha's joke that "old heroes live on as detergents in Canada"? Does this statement in any sense illuminate her own and some other immigrants' situation in Canada?

2. What is Madame Rivest's attitude to Saliha? Why does Saliha decide not to reveal her newly acquired fluency in French to Madame Rivest?

3. Comment on the last sentence of the story: "We come here to speak like them...but it will be a long time before they let us practise."

4. Compare the situation of overqualified immigrants struggling to find adequate jobs in a new country, as presented in the short stories written by Yeshim Ternar and Salwa Mohareb Said.

Denny Hunte

Denny Hunte was born in the Caribbean and immigrated to Toronto with his family in 1967. He graduated with a degree in Social Work and has been active in the community, serving as a youth worker and a social service worker. Currently, he is employed by the City of Toronto in the Community Services Department. The story below was originally published in the collection Experiencing Difference *(2000), edited by York University professor Carl. E. James. During a brief visit of a welfare worker to the apartment of a single mother who has a child from an interracial relationship, we are confronted with several problems resulting from racism and poverty.*

The Home Visit

Rusty nails and broken staples protrude from the wooden door of the Queen Street East address. I knock four times with my pen.

"Who is it?" a female voice asks.

The westbound Queen streetcar moves toward Parliament Street. Traffic lights flash red. Streetcar wheels screech.

"I am Mr. Maynard, from Social Services."

"Who is it?" the voice repeats.

A few seconds later, the loud pounding of feet echoes behind the door. The lock on the door clicks, the knob turns and the door opens to the full extension of the safety chain. A puff of smoke explodes in my face. I cough. Through the thinning smoke, a White woman in her early twenties with light brown, shoulder-length hair and a small, round face peeks from the other side of the door.

"What do you want?" she says.

I look at her, I look at the number on the apartment door and I look at the top left corner of the home visit request sheet in my hand:

Applicant: Ms. Nancy Davies
Age: 19
Status: Single parent

"Are you Ms. Davies?"

She stares. I pull a calling card from my jacket pocket and hand it to her.

"I am here to complete Ms. Davies' application for social assistance. Does she live here?"

The young woman stares at the calling card, glances at me and then rereads the card.

"Ms. Davies phoned the office yesterday and requested a home visit. She gave this as her address."

Without speaking or making eye contact, she studies my face. Her gaze descends to my chest, my stomach, my legs, my shoes and returns to my face. My cotton toque is pulled down over my forehead and ears. Our eyes lock as I step back from the door.

"You're the welfare worker?" she asks loudly.

I nod. "Yes, I am."

"You got something with your picture on it?"

I take off my toque, revealing my locks, squeeze the toque under my armpit, reach into my pants pocket, pull out my wallet and show her my employee ID card. She stares at my photo, taken ten years ago when I had closely cropped hair, smiles and releases the chain latch.

"Come on in."

I stare at her. "Are you Ms. Davies?"

"Oh! Yes. I am Nancy Davies." She smiles. "Please call me Nancy. Everybody calls me Nancy."

I nod.

"I didn't expect a worker to be here this early."

I glance at my watch: 8:35 am. At the last staff meeting, the area manager reminded us to start home visits within regular working hours; 8:30 am to 4:30 pm. If a job-related incident occurred outside normal hours, the department would not be liable.

Ms. Davies walks up the flight of wooden stairs, and I walk behind her. The stairs squeak. She is wearing a long blue housecoat and one pink slipper. Midway up the stairs, she glances over her shoulder.

"To be honest, I didn't expect you to be.... I expected ... you know ... I expected someone else." She smiles. "You don't look like a welfare worker."

"Thank you. I think I'll take that as a compliment. But what does a welfare worker look like?"

Ms. Davies stops and turns. Holding onto the wooden railing, she stares at the ceiling, takes a drag of her cigarette, holds her breath for a second and then exhales.

"Well. You know. Somebody who is like ..."

"Like what?" I ask. "Taller? Female? Older?"

She smiles. "You remind me of someone," she says.

"Is that so?"

At the top of the stairs, Ms. Davies slips her left foot into the other pink slipper.

"This is the apartment."

Ms. Davies ushers me inside. She throws the cigarette butt in the kitchen sink and points to a small table and four chairs. She nods toward a partially closed door across the room.

"Do you have to see Shaun? He is asleep in the bedroom. He has a bad cold."

"No, not really."

Nancy Davies and Shaun, her two-year-old son, live with Nancy's mom. Dance music from WBLK pulses from the bedroom.

"He kept me up all night. My mother leaves for work early in the morning. She says if I am going to stay with her, I'll have to pay half the rent, buy my own food and live by her rules."

Nancy walks into the kitchen, dampens a used jay-cloth, returns to the living room and wipes the plastic table cover and mats.

"Excuse the dirty dishes. Mom is a neat freak. She gets upset if I leave dirty dishes in the sink overnight. I have to wash them before she gets home from work."

Crumbs fall from the table into her cupped hand and onto the unswept wood floor. Ms. Davies tosses the jay-cloth towards the sink where it settles in an unwashed, yellow plastic dish filled with soapy water. Water beads on the plastic table mat. I place the application forms on my thighs and start the interview.

"Can I see a verifiable ID, please?"

Ms. Davies reaches into a glass fruit tray filled with colourful plastic fruit and pulls out a small leather wallet. She puts the wallet in the centre of the table, opens it and hands me her Canadian birth certificate.

"And do you have your son's birth certificate, Ms. Davies?"

She places her hand over her mouth and glances at me.

"Is something wrong?"

"Not really. But it sounds so strange when you call me Ms. Davies. Like I said, everyone calls me Nancy."

I nod.

Nancy lifts the fruit tray and removes a plastic birth certificate.

"And how have you managed financially until now?"

"I was living with friends for the past six months. I just moved back home less than a week ago."

"Do you have any assets?"

Nancy shakes her head. Silver earrings cut in the shape of Africa hang from both ears.

"Do you have any income?"

She knits her brow. I smile.

"Do you expect any income in the future? How have you survived financially until now?"

Nancy sighs as she exhales. She glances into the kitchen, looks out the living room window and taps on the table top with her long, polished nails.

"Are you on your mother's lease? How much rent do you pay your mother? And what is your mom's name?"

"Why do you need to know about her? She is not applying for welfare. She doesn't even know that I phoned the office."

"I need to record your living situation."

"Her name is Erma Davies."

I hear a key in the apartment door lock.

"Nancy!" a woman calls from the hallway.

Nancy raises her hands to her mouth.

"That is my mom," she says. "She is gonna be mad at me."

A woman stands inside the apartment door and glares at us. Nancy looks at me and I look at the woman.

"I told you not to bring anyone in my house," the woman says.

Erma Davies' eyes dart back and forth from Nancy to me. Her face is round like her daughter's. Tramlines streak her forehead.

"This is how you got in trouble in the first place. I didn't accept this kind of behaviour then and I won't accept it now. Like I told you, if you can't live by my rules, you are going to have to move." Nancy's jaw tightens. "One mistake is not enough? You can scarcely care for one child."

Nancy blushes. Her mother slams the front door and walks toward me. I stand.

"Where is Shaun?" Erma Davies demands.

"He is in the bedroom sleeping," Nancy says. "And this is ..."

"And this is how you're looking after a sick child?" her mom interrupts. "And you haven't even cleaned up the mess you left in the kitchen last night."

Erma Davies glimpses at her watch, holds her head high, turns to avoid me and continues down the hallway.

"I want him out of my house right now," she says.

I pick up the partially completed application form from the table.

"But Mom, this is not what you think. This is the welfare worker."

"The what?" Erma Davies stops walking, turns, stares at her daughter and then at me.

"Mr. Maynard is a worker from the welfare office," Nancy says.

Erma Davies squints as she stares at me and starts walking toward us.

"You are a welfare worker."

I nod.

"Have a seat, Mr. Maynard," Nancy whispers.

I glance at Nancy, at the chair, then at her mom.

"I'm sorry," Erma Davies says. "For a moment, I thought you were someone else."

I extend my hand. Erma Davies shakes it weakly. I sit. I unfold the application forms and rest them on the now dry table mat.

"Who did you think I was?"

Erma Davies' voice becomes almost inaudible. "You look somewhat like Shaun's no-good father."

Nancy smiles and then raises her hands to cover her mouth and nose.

"But now that I look closer, he may be a bit thinner and is not as, ah, dark," her mother says.

"That's what I wanted to tell you, earlier," Nancy whispers.

As I uncap my pen, Erma Davies walks toward the table, stands behind my shoulder and looks at the application form. Nancy sits on the other side of the table.

"Does Shaun's dad pay child support?"

Nancy shakes her head.

"Do you have a court order for support for Shaun?"

"I wish," Erma Davies says.

Nancy glares at her mom.

"If she had listened to me, she wouldn't be in this situation. She would still be in school getting an education instead of applying for welfare. I didn't think about getting welfare when I had her. I raised her alone and without asking for or getting a dollar from anyone, not from her father or from the government."

Nancy sighs. She stares at the ceiling. She stares at the unswept floor.

"Shaun's father, what is his name?"

"Jerry Padmore," Erma Davies says.

"Where does he live?"

"Only the good Lord knows," Erma Davies says.

"Mom! He is talking to me, not to you." Nancy says firmly.

I glance from Erma to Nancy. Their eyes lock.

"Excuse me, Ms. Davies," I say. "Nancy has to answer these questions since this is her application."

Erma Davies rests her hands on her hips. Then she points her finger at me.

"Mr. Maynard, you welfare people are part of the problem," she says. "These children learn from an early age that you will give them welfare. This is why they get themselves into all kinds of trouble. If you ask me, you guys make it too easy for them to get money."

A cry comes from the bedroom, "Mom! Mom!" A little boy with a light brown complexion, curly black hair, big dark eyes and sturdy legs, and wearing a Toronto Maple Leafs T-shirt stands in the doorway. He cries. His nose runs and mucus drains into his mouth. The boy looks at his mother, at his grandmother, then at me. Nancy pulls a tissue from the box on the cabinet and walks towards him with outstretched arms.

"Come to Mom, Shaun. Come."

Shaun stops crying. Nancy bends to pick him up, but Shaun circles away from her outstretched arms and runs towards me. He wipes his runny nose with the back of his hand in mid-stride. Drool from his mouth falls onto his chin, onto his already wet T-shirt and onto the floor. His arms flail at his sides.

"Dad-dy! Dad-dy! Dad-dy!" he shouts.

Shaun grabs my knees and climbs onto my lap. His wet hands grab the table, smudging and wrinkling the application forms. They fall to the floor. Lifting him onto my lap, I glance at his mom. Nancy blushes and then rushes towards me. Shaun tightens his already firm grip on my shoulders and cries. The tears rolls down his cheeks and into my shirt. His grandmother stares at me, at him and at the forms that lay scattered on the floor. Erma Davies leans forward and gathers the welfare papers.

"I am so sorry.... I am so embarrassed," she says.

Erma Davies places the forms and my pen on the table and then stares at the ceiling. Nancy stares at the table.

"It's all right," I say as I place my arms around Shaun's back and hug him. He stops crying. His wet face feels warm against mine.

TOPICS FOR DISCUSSION

1. What gender, race, and class stereotypes are exposed through the narrator's encounter with Nancy and her mother?

2. Comment on Erma Davis's words addressed to the narrator: "Mr. Maynard, you welfare people are part of the problem…These children learn from an early age that you will give them welfare. This is why they get themselves into all kinds of trouble…"

3. Explain why the narrator reciprocates the little boy's hug at the end of the story.

Salwa Mohareb Said

*Salwa Mohareb Said has an M.A. in English from the American
University in Cairo, Egypt. She has written short stories for children, pub-
lished in England by Longman's and broadcast by the Egyptian
Broadcasting Service. At present, she is Director of Pensions for the
Canadian Life and Health Association. The story reprinted here first
appeared in the collection* Arab-Canadian Writing: Stories, Memoirs,
and Reminiscences *(1989), edited by Kamal A. Rostom. Like Yeshim
Ternar's story "Ajax Là-Bas" in this unit, "Choices" deals with the plight of
overqualified immigrants who cannot find adequate jobs in Canada.
Nadia and her husband leave behind their privileged social status in Egypt
and choose an uncertain future in Canada. Through perseverance and
tenacity they finally find jobs and start building their life here. However, as
Nadia ponders the differences between her own and her sister's life, she
realizes that success is not without its problems.*

Choices

It was uncommonly cool for a mid-August evening, but Nadia
remained in her chair in the backyard because she did not want to
interrupt the thoughts flowing through her mind. Any movement
would shatter the fragile network of sweet and cruel memories. If
she could pull through those tough times ... surely she could survive the current crisis!

So what if they move to St. John's where she does not know a
soul? So what if they have to sell the house she has grown to love?
She has done all this before. The girls would have to leave their
friends and change schools. Hala will be going to university next
year ... it's too bad she could not stay in her school until gradua-
tion. She wondered how the girls would react to the news ... "Your
father has been offered a promotion if he goes to head the company's operations in Newfoundland. I'm going to resign, and we're
all moving to St. John's." Fear gripped her heart as she rehearsed

what she was going to say to her daughters. She must be getting old. Where is that resilience that carried her through a much bigger move twenty years ago? Surely the risk involved then was far greater than today's. The distance between Toronto and St. John's is but a fraction of the distance between Canada and Egypt, physically, emotionally, and culturally. If she could pull up roots then and come this far, she can do it now. Compared to that major move of twenty years ago, this pales by comparison. Yet the fear and emptiness inside her were overwhelming.

She recalled herself as a young bride in her early twenties, full of drive and ambition. Nothing ever stopped her from going after her dream. She and her husband were two young professionals with a great future ahead of them, by local standards. They had their education, and their families' wealth and social clout to reinforce their claim to success. But they wanted more. They turned their backs on that security to chase a dream all the way across the Ocean. Was it courageous or foolhardy? Her sister, Mona, thought it was foolhardy. But she too was swept by the current of emigration. She did it grudgingly, not by choice, but because she was caught in the tide. Mona had looked around her to find all those she held near and dear leaving ... her best friend was off to Oxford to work on her doctoral dissertation. Her two dearest cousins were in Princeton, and Nadia, her beloved twin sister, was leaving for Canada. So, when Sami came home one day announcing that he had just come from the Canadian Embassy, she knew, in her sinking heart, what her husband was about to announce, and felt powerless to fight the overwhelming tide of departures which was about to engulf her too.

Nadia was all excitement and hope for the future. She looked forward to the challenges of a new life. Mona, on the other hand, looked on the move with dread and fear. The risks were too great! "We're leaving jobs, money, family, and social status to go to an unknown land with different culture, different values ... we'll never belong. We'll always be outsiders with no social position, no status." Nadia had nothing but ridicule for that position. "What great pleasure do you derive from your blessed social status? It's confining and tedious to have your every move watched. I feel like a prisoner of the family name and the social demands. I'd love to go where I can be a drop in the sea ... that would be the ultimate freedom." Little did she know, at the time, how often she would find herself in situations that would make her eat those words.

As she sat in her garden, twenty years later, she recalled those early years of adjusting to being a drop in the sea ... or worse, an outsider, an alien. There were more occasions than she cared to remember, where she had to admit that she really hated being the proverbial drop in the sea. She had the honesty to admit it, but she also had the determination to fight it.

She fought it during those early, miserable cold days, when, as newcomers, she and her husband went looking for work and getting turned down time after time. They were overqualified ... underqualified, or lacked the relevant experience ... and a host of other fictitious reasons to avoid the true reason, they were an unknown, and few are willing to take a chance on an unknown. Having her intelligence and her education discredited was painful. Being distrusted because she looked different and spoke with an accent was painful. Coming back to their tiny apartment to find mail that invariably said "... we regret ..." was painful. But, the most painful of all was a feeling she would never admit to anyone, a feeling that the dream she pursued across the Ocean was unattainable. She refused to admit to those moments of doubt, not even to her husband. She had been a strong force behind their immigration, and felt the full weight of that responsibility and guilt.

Then, after her persistence and tenacity were tested to the limit, small accomplishments started to encourage her to go on. One day she went for an interview for a very junior position with a large organization. She knew that if one of them did not get a job soon, the money they were permitted to emigrate with would run out. She had secretly set a deadline in her own mind that if nothing turned up by the end of that month, they would have to concede defeat and return to Egypt. She went for the interview determined not to let her graduate degrees get in the way of her earning a living. She neglected to mention all her educational accomplishments on the application form. The interview went extremely well and she felt confident that she would be hired. Suddenly, the interviewer asked, "Do you have a university education?" The unexpected question took her by surprise. She hesitated for a moment wondering if she should lie, "y-yes," she stammered in spite of herself, looking down at her cold hands now trembling on her lap. "It's nothing to be ashamed of!" the interviewer said kindly. "Why were you reluctant to tell me?" "Because I really need the job. I can't get work at my real level because I have no Canadian experience. On the other hand, I keep getting turned down for junior jobs because I'm overqualified ..." "Well, the truth is you are. But, I'm prepared to offer you the job anyway. If all works out, you can move up within the company."

Heaven—sheer heaven! She had a job. It didn't matter how low the pay was. Someone finally accepted her. Someone was willing to give her a chance. When her husband had suggested that if things did not open up within another month or two, they should go back, she had resisted. "Yusif! We have to make this work. We always said that we would burn our boats so we wouldn't be tempted to sail right back when the going got tough. We have to think it out." Now that she had a job, she would not have to go back on those words. They can now build a life here. And so they did.

Those were difficult times. A lot of newcomers they knew faced the same problems. Some, like her, were undaunted and tenaciously fought their way up to varying measures of success. Her sister, Mona, was not one of those people. Mona and Sami had their share of problems in adjusting. But Mona cried a lot, and nagged a lot, and never stopped comparing past and present. Her preference was always the past. She had no desire to fight and struggle to create a new life here. It was too hard and required too many sacrifices. She was forever blaming her husband for unsettling her life and forcing her to change.

Sami finally conceded that they would never be happy here. He drove a cab to make a living, while he was studying to qualify for the Canadian equivalent of his engineering degree. Coming home to an unhappy wife and stacks of books to study, day after day, with no relief in sight, was too much to take. So, Sami and Mona made another momentous decision, and returned to Egypt.

Nadia and Mona were fraternal twins. They grew up in the same environment and went to the same schools, had many of the same friends. But their personalities were very different. Their friends used to joke about the disparity in their approaches to life. Mona was gentle, docile, and very conservative, while Nadia relished change and took on every challenge. Their mother used to watch them as they demonstrated their opposing solutions to problems, and shake her head knowingly with only one explanation for the great difference between the two. "The same fire which melts the butter, hardens the egg!"

Mona could not adapt to change, and had no desire to do any-thing contrary to what her mild nature dictated. Adapting required an effort and a fighting spirit. Mona refused to fight. She preferred to go home. For Nadia home was now here. She belonged here in this Suburban Toronto garden. She also belonged to the beautiful skyline she saw every time she looked up from her desk in the office. She would never entertain the delusion that she was absolutely at home or at peace anywhere, but this was as close as she would ever get.

The front door, which she had left open, was blown shut by a sudden gust of wind, and the sound startled her out of her brief encounter with those forgotten memories.

She forced herself out of her reverie and out of her comfortable chair and walked absentmindedly to the kitchen. She poured herself a cup of coffee and reached out mechanically to push the "play" button on the cassette player perched precariously on the edge of the table. There was an old tape in it. An old Egyptian song she had forgotten about. The singer had long since died. But the beautiful voice was still there. Nadia felt a lump in her throat as she remembered the first time she heard that song twenty-five years ago. A simple song from days gone by could still awaken in her feelings … feelings whose intrusion she could not allow too often, or she could not function. Feelings of love and longing for a land and a people she abandoned years ago, but never forgot. She did not want to forget, but just to dampen the pain that accompanied the memory, and to lessen the longing she would always feel. Forgetting was not within her power. The Nile that this voice from the dead was singing about ran in Nadia's very veins. She had no power to change that. There were thoughts and feelings and expressions that came alive in her mother tongue. There was a way of thinking, a tolerance, a sense of humor, a twist of phrase, and a whole view of life that were her birthright, and that no distance, physical or temporal, could possibly erase.

The voice from the scratched old tape rose in a familiar refrain, and Nadia felt warm tears running down her face. The same kind of tears she shed when she first came to this new land and homesickness overcame her. Tears no one knew about, then or now. She was the strong one, the fighter, the one who rose to every challenge and moved ahead undaunted. She never could permit herself such moments of weakness, except when she was alone. She did have an image to preserve. Besides, she always managed to fight her moments of weakness. Mona gave in to hers.

Nadia was a little annoyed with herself for allowing a song to invoke such a sentimental and emotional reaction. She had not reacted that way for years. Yearning, perhaps, but not tears! Was she becoming overemotional and sentimental, or was the thought of uprooting herself again too much to take? The first time she did that she was taking an immense risk, but her youthful enthusiasm overshadowed the magnitude of the step she was taking. With that experience to draw upon, she was approaching this new venture both stronger and weaker. Stronger because she was better prepared for the pain to come, but weaker because she now knew that the pain may recede with time, but it never completely disappears. It was here right now! Something reopened the old wound … a voice from the past, singing in a language she rarely used now, of a river which, though she had not seen it for many years, was a part of her very being. She remembered Shakespeare's "What's gone and what's past help/should be past grief."

She wished it were so. But grief was ever present. She felt like Orestes, destined to be forever pursued by the Furies—never to be at peace. There may be moments of acceptance and even contentment. Moments when logic would convince her that she was as close to being happy as she could ever hope to be. But she knew, even during those brief moments, that her own Furies were lurking in the shadows ready to torment her. They were insidious creatures that manifested their presence in different ways and had a million disguises. Right now, they were in the form of her undying love for the land she chose to leave, for reasons she could no longer remember. It must have been those same Furies that posed as the reasons that made her leave in the first place. She ran then, and continued to be driven all her life. Her own Furies, at times appearing as dissatisfaction, at times as a driving ambition. Whatever their disguise, they always achieved their aim—to keep her running. Running from home and country ... Running in search of a dream ... Running towards success ... always running ... The end result being that she was never allowed to rest or be at peace. She did not believe that some angry creature from the underworld had really set them upon her to punish her. She had made choices in her life that courted them and drew them to her. She had defied the order of things by not accepting anything without questioning it, modifying it, changing it. She had declared herself a challenger to anything and everything that would presume to enter into her life. She had announced that she was in charge, and would change her world to what she wanted it to be, and would not acquiesce and take the easy predetermined route. By choosing to challenge, change and fight, she created the very Furies that would forever haunt her existence.

Nadia shuddered. She was sure it was not from the brisk breeze blowing in from the kitchen door, but from the realization that she had created these monsters, and, given a second chance, she would probably make the same kind of choices that led to their creation.

The girls came in from the movies. "Hi, Mom!" She asked how the movie was. "Boring," said Hala, the youngest. "I thought it was great," was the response from Leila.

Nadia told her daughters about the upcoming move. Hala was full of enthusiasm and wanted to start planning right away. "Great! Absolutely fantastic ... it'll be exciting to live in a new place ..." Leila was quick to interrupt her younger sister, "what do you mean 'Great,' you twit? We'll have to leave all our friends and ..."

Nadia watched the girls arguing and realized that she had really known how her daughters would react to the upcoming change. Their argument reminded her of her arguments with Mona, and of her mother saying, "the same fire that melts the butter, hardens the egg."

Nadia had not melted under the fire. Her youngest daughter was like her. The eldest was definitely the kind that would melt like butter. She would be the kind that always invokes sympathy and protection. She would never be called upon to fight any battles or put out any fires.

Somehow, Nadia felt sorry for the one who appeared to be the stronger and tougher of the two. The youngest would seek out challenges. She would never accept what life hands her down without questioning it. She would never give in to defeat. But, in demonstrating all that apparent strength, she will be inviting perpetual battle. She will appear to be choosing to be in charge of her world. But what she will, in reality, be creating, are her own Furies—who will relentlessly pursue her all her life.

TOPICS FOR DISCUSSION

1. Twenty years earlier Nadia made a big move from Egypt to Canada; today she is facing another major move in her life. What is the difference this time?

2. What motives did Nadia and her husband have for coming to Canada? What were her sister Mona's motives?

3. What are Nadia's recollections of their early immigrant years? Why did she feel that "her intelligence and education" were discredited by Canadian employers?

4. Compare different responses the sisters had to the problem of adjustment to a new life in Canada. How are their differences accounted for?

5. What prospects and experiences in the new land might be determined by the newcomers' expectations and their social backgrounds? Compare on the basis of the stories by Salwa Mohareb Said, Yeshim Ternar, and Katherina Vlassie.

Emma LaRocque

*Emma LaRocque was born in 1949 in a small Métis community in Big
Bay, Alberta. She has a B.A. in English/Communications, an M.A. in
Religion, an M.A. in History, and a Ph.D. in Aboriginal History from the
University of Manitoba, where she is Professor of Native Studies. In 1975,
she published* Defeathering the Indian, *a social commentary on the failure
of the Canadian education system to accommodate the needs of Native students with respect to the curriculum and racist stereotypes propagated
through teaching history and literature. She has published numerous academic essays and is a frequent lecturer on rights, education, racism, colonialism, literature, and women's issues. Her poems and her introductory
essay on Native writing in Canada have appeared in* Writing the Circle:
Native Women of Western Canada, *edited by Jeanne Perreault and
Sylvia Vance (1990). She defines writing as "the art of bringing to birth
the human condition in thought form."*

A Personal Essay on Poverty

Liberalism has made much of poverty in our last decade. Statistics
on poverty have been flying around from all directions. And as I
mentioned before, Native people have been closely associated with
it; so closely in fact that some very significant questions have been
bypassed.

What is poverty anyway? Is it the failure to reach beyond that mag-
ical Poverty Line established by the Economic Council of Canada? Or
is it "…relative to the living standard the rest of society enjoys." And
more important, what is so sacred about what the majority enjoys?

To me it seems obvious that poverty is relative all right; but not
necessarily relative to the wealth of the majority, but rather to one's
own perceptions of material possessions.

My two brothers, one sister and I grew up in a one-roomed but
well-managed log cabin. Many of our clothes were handsewn by my
very resourceful mother. All our wooden furniture (two beds, one
table, a cupboard, several night stands, three chairs and a bench) was

put together by my practical father. Our diet consisted of a large variety of wild meats, berries, bannock, potatoes, some vegetables and herbal teas and so on, all of which were usually cooked with originality and imagination.

At the age of nine, against my father's perceptive advice, I howled my way into school. He knew only too well that sooner or later I would come home with new desires. As predicted, a few months later I wanted juicy red apples, oranges, bananas, trembling jello, bread and even red-and-white striped toothpaste! Once, my father teasingly wondered what I could possibly do with toothpaste and brush because my teeth were falling out! Toothless or not, I found the pictures at school powerfully suggestive.

Other school pictures also played with my mind. I saw Dick, Jane and Sally's suburban home and their grandparent's expansive and, oh, so clean farm. Not for a long time was I to appreciate my home again.

The point is, I had been perfectly content to sleep on the floor, eat rabbit stew and read and play cards by kerosene lamp until my perceptions were swayed at school. Neither had I suffered spiritual want. I had been spellbound by my mother's ability to narrate Cree legends and enriched by my father's dreams, until the teacher out-lawed Cree and made fun of dreams.

From then on I existed in poverty; not with reference to our log cabin, our food and our small wood-stove as compared to the brick schoolhouse, its food and its huge, coal-burning pot-belly stove, but because I was persuaded by my teacher's propaganda and the pic-tures.* The teacher's authoritarianism, coupled with his failure to reinforce whatever world we came from, effectively weakened our respect for our parents.

Still, there is more to poverty than its relativity. Even if I had believed in my home and its simple beauties, it is true that I had no money. And without that commodity, eventually I could not be mobile. And to be immobile in any society is to be quite choiceless. It is at this point that equal opportunity becomes meaningless.

It is psychologically cathartic to know that one has a choice. Ultimately, poverty in the North American context is not having enough money to choose among alternatives. Poverty exacts its toll on people not always because of a mere lack of material possessions, but often because of choicelessness.

Today, there are hundreds of urban dwellers who are suffering from "cabinitis." Come Friday afternoon there is a mass and speedy exodus to the "simple" life of their cabins. These people are often happy there because they are there by choice. They feel a sense of self-direction.

People may be "culturally deprived" perhaps only in that they are deprived of choice. In this sense then, most of us are "culturally deprived" in some area because most of us cannot choose everything we want out of life.

Now I live in a city, and I often see children playing on concrete, at artificial playgrounds and in overcrowded parks or swimming pools. I always feel a profound sense of sadness that these children cannot have what I had as a child. No spruce branch from which to master a Tarzanian swing. No soft moss to land on if you fall. No moonlight rendezvous beside a creek, watching a beaver tirelessly build his dam. No place to build an honest-to-goodness, creaking, but functioning, ferris wheel! No pond or lake or river to try out a self-made raft, row boat or canoe. Or to skinny-dip in. No green space to just run and run and run. No wooded meadow in which to lie and sleepily feel akin to the lethargic clouds. No crocuses, wild roses, tiger lilies or bluebells to sniff.

Cultural depravation?

Yes, we must work towards equal opportunity for all. We must help people reach a sense of self-direction and mobility. We must lift people to the place of choice. But we cannot, we must not, dictate what people should choose.

* It must be said that this teacher meant well. He was by nature a disciplinarian but not malicious. Apparently, he sincerely believed that his ways were for the good of the Native children.

TOPICS FOR DISCUSSION

1. What different definitions of poverty does Emma LaRocque give in her essay? How does her own definition go against the grain of standard definitions of poverty?

2. Jean Jacques Rousseau, eighteen-century French philosopher and advocate of a "return to nature," said that "unhappiness consists in the excess of desire over power." How do personal examples given by Emma LaRocque support this view?

3. Explain LaRoque's claim that "choicelessness" is the greatest cause of poverty in North America.

4. Emma LaRocque, Jeannette Armstrong, and Tomson Highway all seem to be drawing strength and inspiration from traditional Native lore. How are their approaches different?

MAPS/ PLACES/ MEMORY

INTRODUCTION

Travelling across the geographic borders and crossing the thresholds of time, the past is not abandoned. It dwells in memory of places and people, creating an intimate geography of the mind. The past resides in particular images of times past and lives lived then. Sometimes "the map of memory" is all that remains if the actual landscape has been destroyed by violence or utterly transformed by time. Sometimes the people whom we cannot forget exist as an enigma that will never be solved. Those who remember have themselves changed in their journey from the past. Although scenes from childhood revisited in memory might be bathed in a nostalgic glow, when they are confronted with adult perceptions upon real returns, the clash of memory and actuality can be troubling. The maps of memory are alive and constantly edited; they may survey landscapes that never existed or that have been reshaped by time. Without them we could not orient ourselves in the past or retrace the way that has brought us to where we are and has made us who we are.

Michael Ondaatje

*A poet, novelist, critic, editor, photographer, and documentary filmmaker,
Michael Ondaatje was born in Ceylon (now Sri Lanka) in 1943, in a
family of Dutch extraction that had been living on the island for several
generations. He went to school in England and moved to Canada in 1962.
He attended Bishop's University, the University of Toronto, and Queen's
University. He lives in Toronto and teaches English at Glendon College,
York University. His films include* Sons of Captain Poetry *(about the poet
bp Nichol) and* The Clinton Special *(about Theatre Passe Muraille). He
received two Governor General's Awards for Poetry, for his long poem* The
Collected Works of Billy the Kid *(1970) and for* There's a Trick with a
Knife I'm Learning to Do *(1979). His other books of poetry include* The
Dainty Monsters *(1967),* Secular Love *(1984),* the man with seven toes
(1969), and Handwriting *(1998). His novel* In the Skin of a Lion
*(1987) won The Trillium Award and the City of Toronto Book Award.
Another novel,* The English Patient *(1992), won a Governor General's
Award for Fiction as well as the Booker Prize, and was made into an
Oscar-winning movie in 1996. He has also published experimental narratives that defy classification, mixing (auto)biographical narrative, fiction,
and documents, in* Coming Through Slaughter *(1976) and* Running in
the Family *(1982). His most recent novel is* Anil's Ghost.

*The poem "Letters & Other Worlds" deals with the problem of a father
and son relationship. In life, Michael Ondaatje had not had the possibility
of getting to know his father, Mervyn Ondaatje, because Michael had left
home at the age of eleven. His search for a lost father through art, through
his poetic imagination, leads to constructing the elusive image of the father.
In 1981, critic Stephen Scobie called "Letters & Other Words" not only
"the greatest of Ondaatje's poems," but also "the greatest single poem in
Canadian literature."*

Letters & Other Worlds

For there was no more darkness for him and, no doubt
like Adam before the fall, he could see in the dark'

My father's body was a globe of fear
His body was a town we never knew
He hid that he had been where we were going
His letters were a room he seldom lived in
In them the logic of his love could grow

My father's body was a town of fear
He was the only witness to its fear dance
He hid where he had been that we might lose him
His letters were a room his body scared

He came to death with his mind drowning.
On the last day he enclosed himself
in a room with two bottles of gin, later
fell the length of his body
so that brain blood moved
to new compartments
that never knew the wash of fluid
and he died in minutes of a new equilibrium.

His early life was a terrifying comedy
and my mother divorced him again and again.
He would rush into tunnels magnetized
by the white eyes of trains
and once, gaining instant fame,
managed to stop a Perahara in Ceylon
– the whole procession of elephants dancers
local dignitaries – by falling
dead drunk onto the street.

As a semi-official, and semi-white at that,
the act was seen as a crucial
turning point in the Home Rule Movement
and led to Ceylon's independence in 1948.

(My mother had done her share too –
her driving was so bad
she was stoned by villagers
whenever her car was recognized)

For 14 years of marriage
each of them claimed he or she
was the injured party.
Once on the Colombo docks
saying goodbye to a recently married couple
my father, jealous
at my mother's articulate emotion,
dove into the waters of the harbour
and swam after the ship waving farewell.
My mother pretending no affiliation
mingled with the crowd back to the hotel.

Once again he made the papers
though this time my mother
with a note to the editor
corrected the report – saying he was drunk
rather than broken hearted at the parting of friends.
The married couple received both editions
of *The Ceylon Times* when their ship reached Aden.

And then in his last years
he was the silent drinker,
the man who once a week
disappeared into his room with bottles
and stayed there until he was drunk
and until he was sober.

There speeches, head dreams, apologies,
the gentle letters, were composed.
With clarity of architects
he would write of the row of blue flowers
his new wife had planted,
the plans for electricity in the house,
how my half-sister fell near a snake
and it had awakened and not touched her.
Letters in a clear hand of the most complete empathy
his heart widening and widening and widening
to all manner of change in his children and friends
while he himself edged
into the terrible acute hatred
of his own privacy
till he balanced and fell
the length of his body
the blood screaming in
the empty reservoir of bones
the blood searching in his head without metaphor

TOPICS FOR DISCUSSION

1. What personal emotions does the speaker unveil while contemplating the tragic life of his father? What is implied by the contrast between the silence of the father's suffering and the articulateness of his "gentle letters"?

2. There are recurrent images of falling in the poem. Are there any hints as to what had driven the father to self-destruction?

3. How does the poem describe the relationship between the parents?

4. Interpret the connections between the epigraph and the poem.

5. Compare the effect that the father has on his son in Mordecai Richler's memoir and Michael Ondaatje's poem. How is the "mystery" of the fathers portrayed?

Alootook Ipellie

Alootook Ipellie, a talented Inuit writer and graphic artist, was born in 1951 in Frobisher Bay (now Iqualuit, in a new province of Nunavut, until 1999 part of the Northwest Territories). He was educated in Iqualuit, Yellowknife, and Ottawa, where he now lives. Ipellie is one of the generation of Inuit writers caught in a crisis of identity, trying to keep alive their traditions while undergoing profound changes in their lives due to outside influences on their culture. He has worked as a CBC announcer and producer, and has been editor and contributor to different Inuit maga-zines, including Inuit Today *and* KIVIOQ Inuit Fiction Magazine. *His poems and stories have been anthologized in* Northern Voices: Inuit Writing in English, *edited by Penny Petrone (1988), and* Gatherings: The En'owkin Journal of First American Peoples *(1991). The impor-tance of Frobisher Bay, as a crossroads of the north and a crossroads of Ipellie's personal landscape, is the substance of his 1980 essay "Frobisher Bay Childhood." The impact of white culture in terms of money, food, and entertainment is strong, but the values of Inuit culture nonetheless remain sound in this warm and humorous recollection.*

Frobisher Bay Childhood

When anyone asks me where I was born, I usually answer, 'Frobisher Bay,' but I never can tell them exactly where my birth-place was. I always say, 'Somewhere down the bay.'

But Frobisher Bay is the place where I grew up. My most vivid childhood memories are still strongly rooted in this town. It is the place where I suffered my set-backs and experienced my triumphs. Although they may not know it, the people I grew up with are still dear to me. They really are an extension of my own life. For this reason I will always come back to Frobisher no matter where I live on this earth. Sometimes, one's roots are sacred to a person.

I remember the first time I went to school. It was in a small red and white metal building, which was the Anglican Church at that

time. I was about eight years old then, and we had only one teacher—
she was a lady. It was a chilly winter day with the sun shining from
the sky above. I had no idea why we were called together in the
church. The first day we played a few games and it was cold inside, so
we had our parkas on. Round and round we went holding hands
together, until finally the game was all over. It was actually the first
day of my education; the *Quallunaaq* feeling had entered my heart.

I cannot say exactly how I felt at the time, but I am quite sure I
enjoyed it. I remember there was a machine inside the church that
made a noise; I found out later that this sound came from a round
disc inside a box with a top that opened and closed. I learned that
the discs were records and that the box was a 78 r.p.m. record player
with a handle on the side that you had to wind in order to make it
play. This was very new to me at the time and another extraordinary
addition to my knowledge of the new things the white man was
bringing to our little town.

Many of the essentials for living came in by freight ships when
the ice broke up in late July. The sight of these great vessels entering
the world where we lived made thrills go through our hearts. If a ship
came while we slept, the elders wasted no time telling us the news.

'Wake up boys, there is a big umiak anchored in the bay.' We
got up, rushed out the door, and looked at the enormous vessel that
was already unloading its cargo into the barges.

Our ship that came to Frobisher was the Hudson's Bay
Company ship, bringing the year's goods to the stores. When it
arrived, most of the Inuit in town went to help unload the barges.
This was during high tide and everyone worked as a unit, just like a
circus setting up the big tents and other things to get ready for the
opening night. There was laughter among the people, a sign of happiness which never seemed to stop as long as the ship stayed. The
way they worked together was truly beautiful; they reminded me of
a large family. No matter how old or young they were, they were
there carrying things, big or small, both day and night.

At low tide, when there wasn't much work to do, the Hudson's
Bay Company staff members brought out hot tea and pilot biscuits
for everyone. We were hungry by then and as soon as the paper cups
were handed out, we scrambled to reach into the large teapot as if it
was our last chance. It was a thrill to be among these people; my
own Inuit brothers and sisters. I looked at them as truly wonderful
human beings, enjoying their day together. But soon there would be
a time to end all this when the ship left to go to other settlements in
the North. It was time now to get paid.

This was a day of joy, when everyone lined up to receive their
money. It was usually only a dollar for each day and night that they

helped in the unloading of the cargo. Even a few bills satisfied them, although they had worked hard for at least a whole week. There were no feelings of being underpaid or cheated; they merely took what they were given. And the very same day, most of them were completely broke again. They loved to spend money on goods of all kinds. Fascination was in their eyes when they saw certain things for the first time, and they thought to themselves, 'I must buy this thing—it is so beautiful and different.'

In those days I remember that the United States had an Air Force base in Frobisher Bay. We, as Inuit kids, would go over to their base to wait outside their kitchen in hopes of being offered something to eat. We often succeeded and the smell of their food was like nothing that we had ever smelled before.

There came a time when at least once a day I would start to dream of having tons and tons of *Quallunaaq* food right in our little hut. Even if all of the food could not go in, I would think of becoming a genius at storing food and somehow get it all in there.

One day when a group of us were just outside the Hudson's Bay store in the base area, a number of guys came out of the store and got in their jeep. As the jeep started up one of them threw us what looked like paper money. We scrambled for it like hungry pups … only to find out that it was play money made for the game of Monopoly. We looked up at the guys on their jeep and they were laughing their heads off. We nearly cried in disappointment.

I can remember one day I picked a fight with one of the students at lunch hour. The boy was one of those who was always causing trouble with other children and teachers. I distinctly had the feeling that I could beat him easily that day. I was feeling very strong and all my friends cheered me on. It was as if we were fighting for the heavy-weight boxing championship of the world. All the kids made a 'ring' around the two of us and we crashed into each other without a bit of hesitation, fists flying and muscles bulging from our arms! We grabbed each other's parkas and wrestled to the ground and up again. We swung our arms like sledge-hammers towards the opponent's head and made noises like only fighters made! I heard the crowd around us shouting words of encouragement and it was clear that the majority were rooting for me. It was important that I did not suffer a defeat in front of my friends. I fought hard but in the end, I received a bleeding nose and cried. Luck was not with me that day and it was good that my old friends were still my old friends. I never fought again after that.

There was a community hall in Apex Hill, which is about three miles from Frobisher Bay, and I remember they used to have a free movie for everyone on Sunday nights. Those of us who did not have very much money to throw around could not pass up the chance to see a full length movie free. So we would walk to Apex and back to see the shows that were often filled with action.

When the first movies came to our land, a whole new world was introduced to the Inuit. Our eyes would open up in fascination when the lights went out to start a movie. When the first frame appeared on the screen, we started to live in a world of fantasy.

The walks back home were as entertaining as the shows. Everyone got a big kick out of what they saw and amused themselves by reminiscing about the action-filled parts of the movie. Some of us would re-enact the roles of the movie stars and we had fun entertaining each other.

When we got back to Frobisher after the movie we'd find a deck of cards and start playing. My group of buddies played cards at least once a week like 'hard-nosed' gamblers. We would take our places and decide who was to deal the cards first and then go on to the serious business of winning as many games as we could. There was no cheating, and we played until one of us won everything the other players had.

What we were playing for were pictures of Hollywood stars.

Probably every kid in town had a movie idol in those days and pictures of these movie stars were considered as valuable as any good wristwatch or bicycle. So we never missed an opportunity to look through any magazines and newspapers that we could find around town. If we happened to find one good picture of John Wayne or Tony Curtis, it was as if we had found a gold nugget worth at least a couple of hundred dollars. Photographs of stars from western movies were without a doubt the most sought after because they were worth the most at the card table.

Next came the sword-clanking stars like Kirk Douglas or Steve Reeves. And there were the strongmen—like Tarzan, Hercules and Sampson. They were big heroes when I was an Inuit child. The photographs of clowns like Jerry Lewis, Bob Hope and the Three Stooges were also popular. So were Laurel and Hardy, and that timid knee-shaking character, Don Knotts.

The quality and the size of the pictures were very important. A good photo of John Wayne was worth two poor ones of the same star. Colour pictures were worth a few times more than black and white—no matter what condition they were in. The pictures of the stars in newspapers were considered good bargains but they were not as crisp as the magazine pictures and did not last long. Most of us could not get photographs from magazines so we had to resort to movie advertisements in the newspaper and newspapers were very scarce in our town in those days.

I can remember many times when my pockets would bulge with magazine photographs after a successful day of playing cards. They were valuable to me, so I could not afford to leave them around at home where they would not last for two minutes. I took great care not to crumple them. If I did, they would not be worth much when we started playing cards. So they were a bit of trouble to me because I could not move around the way I wanted to, and sitting down was always a problem. If I sat down many times during the day, I would find out that some of the faces of the movie stars were completely wiped out because of all the rubbing they were going through. A picture without a recognizable face was worth not a penny at the card table.

Clipping out photographs of movie stars was 'big business' for us as Inuit children. A good collector would naturally be considered the one to beat at the card games that would last for several hours. If he happened to be a little greedy about his collection we had all the more pleasure when we won his precious pictures.

These are a few memories of my childhood in Frobisher Bay. Life in the Arctic is changing fast and Frobisher has changed along with its people. If Frobisher has a distinct character today, it is that it has become 'home' to many Inuit from other communities in the North. On any given day in Frobisher you might meet an Inuk who had come from a town as far away as Port Burwell in the east or from Tuktoyaktuk in the west. There were Inuit from Northern Quebec, from the High Arctic, from the Central Arctic or the Keewatin. Today there is no surprise in meeting an Inuk from Alaska or even from Greenland, on the streets of Frobisher Bay. Who knows, maybe one day we will begin to see whole families coming in from Siberia to live in Frobisher Bay!

TOPICS FOR DISCUSSION

1. In one of the opening paragraphs the author says that "one's roots are sacred to a person." How does his essay support this statement?

2. How much space in this essay is devoted to showing the contacts between the Inuit and "quallunaat" (white people)? What was the Inuit experience of money? How did the Inuit entertain themselves?

3. Analyze the relationship between the loose structure of this story and the working of memory on which it seems to rely.

4. Compare Alootook Ipellie's reaction to the imposition of white culture with the responses of Pat Deiter-McArthur (Day Woman) and Carol Geddes. How do they differ in tone and method?

Gabrielle Roy

Gabrielle Roy, a distinguished Canadian writer, was born in 1909 in Saint-Boniface, Manitoba, the youngest of eleven children. In 1927, after graduating from Grade Twelve, she enrolled at the Winnipeg Normal Institute where she completed her teacher training. From 1937 to 1939, she lived in England and France, where she studied drama and began writing. She moved to Montreal when she was thirty. She received several literary awards, including the 1957 Governor General's Award for Rue Deschambault *(1955; translated as* Street of Riches*), the Prix David (1971), the Molson Prize (1978), and the Canada Council Prize for Children's Literature (1979). Among her other books are* Bonheur d'occasion *(1945; translated as* The Tin Flute*), the first Canadian work to win a major French literary award, the Prix Fémina;* La Petite poule d'eau *(1950; translated as* Where Nests the Water Hen*);* La Rivière sans repos *(1970; translated as* The Windflower*); and* Ces enfants de ma vie *(1977; translated as* Children of My Heart*). Gabrielle Roy died in 1983. Published posthumously was the first volume of her autobiography,* La Détresse et l'enchantement *(1984), translated as* Enchantment and Sorrow *(1987). "My Manitoba Heritage," first published in the review* Mosaic, *was translated by Alan Brown. She describes Saint-Boniface, her childhood town on the prairies, as a meeting place for immigrant populations. She writes of the "divided love" of the Québécois who have transported their culture to other parts of Canada, but can never forget their roots. She also remembers the landscapes of Manitoba—the hills, the prairie, and the horizon—which have significance for Roy that she cannot abandon.*

My Manitoba Heritage

I

My maternal grandparents came from a little, lost region in the foothills of the Laurentians, north of Montreal. One fine day they left everything that had been their life to answer the call of the West and become homesteaders in Manitoba. They were no longer young—they had reached middle age, in fact—and it was a decision with no return, and a tremendous adjustment in their lives.

They travelled by railway, and then from St. Norbert, which at the time seems to have been a kind of caravanserai for French-Canadian settlers heading south, they started off one spring morning in their wagon filled to the ridge-pole, across the wild plain, following a faintly marked trail toward the rolling Pembina mountains. According to my grandfather, their irregular profile was supposed to console his wife for the loss of her native hills—but the very opposite happened: the sight of these pretentious little humps was to sharpen her regret at ever having left the steep slopes of her youth. This was the beginning of generations of divided love in our family, divided between prairie and mountain: a heartbreak, as I wrote in *The Road Past Altamont*, but also an inexhaustible source of dreams, of confidences, of leavings and "travellations" such as few people knew to the extent we did, a family that was horizon-bound, if there ever was one. And of course it is in their divided loves that artists and others find their hurts and treasures.

At the time of our family epic, my mother was a lively girl with a vivid imagination. Any voyage would have delighted her, for she had never been away from home, except for the occasional jaunt with her father from St. Alphonse to the big market on the square in Joliette. How can one imagine the effect of the prairie opening out before her without end and without reserve, wide as the sky which until then she had seen clipped by the crests of hills like the disconnected curves of a jigsaw puzzle. Now here was a sky that stretched all the way across from one sweet horizon to the other.

She never recovered from her emotions during that trip, and would tell about it all her life. To the point where my own childhood also fell under its spell, as my mother launched again into the old story, holding me on her knees in the big kitchen rocking chair; and I would imagine the pitching wagon and the accompanying rise and fall of the horizon as in a ship at sea.

Later, when I read Chekhov's *The Steppe* I felt myself in exactly the same atmosphere as in my mother's story. Everything was there: the rapture at the sight of the great, flat expanse of land, inviting as an open book and yet obscure to the mind; the touching unexpectedness, in this monotonous unfolding landscape, of the least sign of human presence—in the Russian story the windmill, visible from so far and for so long; in my mother's version, the roof of a house appearing at last in the distance of this uninhabited country—and even the feeling that this elusive horizon, constantly calling, constantly retreating, was perhaps the symbol and image of the ideal in our lives, or of the future as it appears to the eyes of our youth, full of promises that will always be renewed.

Once at their destination, which my grandmother called the "barbarian lands," although a number of her compatriots were already established there, she and my grandfather went about the task common to all settlers: recreating what they left behind.

Soon they had their steep-roofed houses, their sculptured cabinets, their bench beds, their kneading troughs and their spinning wheels; with their speech, still pure and picturesque in those days, their "Jansenist" faith, as people would say now, forgetting perhaps to what extent its severity was tempered by the shy tenderness of their hearts; with the grim cross in dark wood on the bedroom wall, but also the gaiety of their violins; and with all these and their memories and traditions, they built on this land in Manitoba, to the sound of the wind and the high, rustling grass, a new parish similar in all things to innumerable villages in Quebec.

My grandfather, the moving spirit behind this venture, I knew only through stories, which perhaps distorted his true face as much as they revealed it, as each raconteur painted him in his own image. Yet I often find him alive in myself at those odd moments of the soul when we seem to be acting in perfect liberty in our dreams and wanderings, but are really closely in harmony with the spirit of some ancestor. It is perhaps through him that I am still so deeply moved by the great elusive horizon, and especially the setting sun, from which came the clearest call.

My grandmother's tall figure hovers over my first memories like the grain elevators of the west, those towers rich in wheat and aroma and the magic of my childhood.

If she lived now, amid the preoccupation with self-fulfilment for women, my grandmother would likely be director of some big business or heading up a Royal Commission on the status of women. In her day, her talents were fully occupied from dawn till dusk making soap or cloth or shoes. She also concocted herbal remedies, dyes for her cloth and splendid designs for her rugs. I believe there still exist a few pieces of her homespun linen as resistant as her own willpower. In that "barbarous land" she succeeded in ruling, seldom giving in to it but often bending it to her own strong nature, having as little as possible to do with all these foreigners around her, these English and Scots, but re-baptizing in French all things and places they had named before her arrival.

For example, the neighbouring village of Somerset, where she had to go for her more serious shopping: on a fine autumn day she'd be sitting high in her buggy, reins in hand, looking very fine in her black bonnet and wide skirts spread across the width of the seat.

"Well, good-bye. I'm going shopping in *Saint-Mauricette.*"

What would she have thought, she who created saints whenever she felt like it, of this age of ours which has unmade them by the dozen? Or of this ecumenism which has the audacity to bring together what she saw fit to keep asunder?

On second thought, I imagine she would have ended up rejoicing, not at the diminution in the communion of saints but at the growth in that of the believers.

II

The eldest daughter of this proud woman was my mother, and she lived, so to speak, in order to conciliate the opposing tendencies of her parents, from whom she inherited qualities in equal doses, for she was frightened yet infinitely attracted by the unknown. The longer she lived the more her self-confidence won out over her circumspection. In her were best united our family's two fond attachments: for Quebec, where she was born and of which she had the treasury of memories that only a child's ardent imagination could have kept safe; and for Manitoba, where she had grown up and loved and suffered. Perhaps the most successful lives are those that seem destined to bring about a meeting of such neighbouring ways which otherwise would run parallel forever. It seems to me now that her life was spent in trying to bring things together. First and foremost, her poor children who were so different in character; then the neighbours; and, finally, everyone. She lived in love for what was, is and will be.

Toward the end of her life, sick and very old but still full of the great wish of her life to see the sites and beauties of the world, she was anxious to make a farewell visit to Quebec to see some distant cousins again, she said, to call on this one or that one; but I suspect that the real purpose of her trip, perhaps unknown to herself, may have been to climb to the top of a Laurentian hill to listen to the wind in a tall pine, just to see if it sang as it had when she was a child.

In the little cemetery of Saint-Mauricette, I have also seen her, her face sad and serious, suddenly bend down angrily to pull out a weed from the grave of my grandmother, who in her lifetime had never tolerated a weed either in her flower beds or in her existence.

The place to which you go back to listen to the wind you heard in your childhood—that is your homeland, which is also the place where you have a grave to tend. Though I chose to live in Quebec partly because of the love for it which my mother passed on to me, now it is my turn to come back to Manitoba to tend her grave. And also to listen to the wind of my childhood.

Long before it was time for my mother's grave, before marriage, before the time for bearing children, when love was, for her, like the beautiful Manitoba horizon, a prospect of the most delightful mirages, a man was already making his way toward her through the years, following the mysterious paths of fate: he, too, had left Quebec, emigrated to the States, and in a variety of jobs had forged an experience as broad as life. A self-made man, he was now on the verge of returning to Canada, but via Manitoba.

They must have met at one of those evenings when Quebecers got together, evenings loud with singing, with memories, and talk about old Quebec. Perhaps on that first evening my father, who was gifted with a fine voice, charmed the girl with one of those old ballads I myself later heard him sing: *Il était un petit navire*, or *Un Canadien errant*, sad, sweet songs to which he brought a disconcerting sincerity, as if they were a barely veiled admission of his own uprooted state.

They liked each other, this dark-haired girl with the sparkling eyes, the soul of gaiety, and the blond man whose blue eyes were heavy with an indefinable melancholy, as if the struggle to educate himself and rise above the fate of so many like him at the time had made him over-sensitive to unhappiness.

They married, as people did then, for life, for better and for worse, accepting in advance the children God would choose to "send" them. Not only would they accept them, they would exhaust themselves to give them a better life than they themselves had had, richer and more enlightened. What was more, and as if this effort was not enough, they intended to transmit intact to their children the ancestral faith and language which in those days went together.

But against what odds! A material existence which by itself was difficult to ensure; children which it would have been more reason-able not to have; and now this stubborn determination, in the face of common sense in a continent where almost everyone spoke English, to preserve those words that bear from one generation to the next a people's continuity, a people's soul. The surprising thing is that they met this challenge perhaps better than their descendants who are in many ways infinitely better off.

III

My father had become a civil servant, assigned to settling immigrants on the virgin lands of Saskatchewan and, later, Alberta, a task which he carried out admirably, full of a paternal care for these bewildered souls whose confusion he understood from his own bitter times of test and sacrifice before he managed to achieve his present level. My parents had eleven children. Three died young. The elder ones were already scattered when I came into the world, the "last little one," as I was called for a long time. This was in Saint-Boniface, in the short street called Deschambault, whose gentle rusticity I tried to convey in my book *Street of Riches*. Did I succeed? Is it possible to record in a book the spellbinding powers of childhood, which can put the whole world inside the tiniest locket of happiness?

We lived with our backs to the town—a very quiet little town, serious, going about its business, its loudest noise being the church and convent bells—and facing the open spaces. These "open spaces" were nothing but lots which faded off into brushland and, for me, prefigured the truly open prairie. In places it was interrupted by small circles of trees, often stunted oaks which for as long as I can remember made me think of the chance encounter of travellers crossing the plain, who had gathered 'round for a moment to swap their news. The fact that the oaks stayed on the same spot day after day, and that their circle was never altered, did not hinder my fancy: they were people telling their stories of the world and all that they had seen and done.

In fact, Deschambault Street was a place where one lived one-third in France, one-third in Quebec, and to a great extent in our own personal fancies which changed with the seasons or the arrival of a new neighbour, or perhaps took shape from our contemplation of the infinite spaces that began where the street ended.

Saint-Boniface breathed, prayed, hoped, sang and suffered in French, but it earned its living in English, in the offices, stores and factories of Winnipeg. The irremediable and existential difficulty of being French-Canadian in Manitoba or elsewhere!

Yet it was perhaps at this time of my childhood that French life in Manitoba was at its purest, in a fever of discussions, demonstrations and visits of encouragement from Quebec, and a fervour which did not succeed in destroying the obstacles. The draining-off to Quebec of our educated young people, who found no way of living in French, had not yet reached its peak; it was to result later in a cruel impoverishment of our community. On the contrary, we received almost constant reinforcements from Quebec, in small groups: a new notary, a new teacher, a printer, a doctor. Some help also came from France. When, in 1928, I went to take over my first class in the little village of Cardinal, it happened that at least half my pupils were from Brittany or the Auvergne. For me it was as if I had spent that year in the *Massif central* or some retreat in the Morbihan. I had every opportunity to learn certain richly regional expressions. How marvellous, when one went to teach in a village, to receive more than one gave! The same was true of Notre-Dame-de-Lourdes, Saint-Claude and other predominantly French Manitoba villages.

Whether their origins were humble or elevated, these immigrants of French nationality or language, Walloon, Italian, a few Flemings, as they mixed in among us, enriched our French life and culture with vitality and a most distinctive originality.

Strange as it may seem today, I owe to Manitoba the good fortune of having been born and raised in a Francophone area of exceptional fervour. No doubt it was the fervour of a frail group fraternally united in its numerical fragility and its threatened ideal to build a common front.

I suppose that this enthusiasm, like a wick turned too high, could not burn forever. But its light was there—long enough to illuminate some lives.

IV

As soon as the Red River was crossed and we were in Winnipeg, it was another world. Even today the crossing of the Provencher Bridge from Saint-Boniface to Winnipeg is for me like going from the particular to the general. I know that the contrast between the two is less marked; but in those days, almost without noticing it, we made the transition from our life, somewhat turned inward on itself, to the manifold, strange, torrential and nostalgic human flood that made up Manitoba's population and came from all parts of the earth. This was the second marvellous gift I received from that province: to have glimpsed while still very young the pied disparity of the species—along with the realization that we are basically very much alike. Without having to travel, I could see the peoples of the earth parade before my eyes. I had only to stroll through the Canadian Pacific railway station to see women in white kerchiefs, their gaze so distant it was surely fixed on the other end of the world; or whole families with their bundles, their eyes dulled with boredom, sitting in a circle on their trunks, waiting for lord knows what; or patriarchs with long beards, wrapped in strange capes, followed by their families in Indian file along the wide sidewalks, as if they were picking their way through a mountain pass. I have said these things time and again, and can do no more than say them again every time I write about Manitoba, because for me the sight of these bewildered people, which the province offered me when I was very young, has become inseparable from my feelings about life.

At first my mother was startled and fascinated by this motley crowd of humanity that flowed almost past our door. In comparison to their lives, our own now seemed settled and secure, at least with some roots, she liked to emphasize. But the fascination was stronger than her mistrust. Soon she took her youngest children by a Red River cruise boat to see the Ukrainians at St. Andrews, and from the deck we would watch, perhaps a little ashamed, as the women, gleaning, trying to straighten their aching backs, would shield their eyes from the sun to stare at us, the do-nothings who had no better way to spend their time than watching others work. She also took us to see the Icelanders in Gimli; or we would simply cross the narrow River Seine, a stone's throw from home, to hear the mass "in Belgium," as we used to say.

The *Arabian Nights* of my childhood were made up of these excursions into Little Wallonia, Little Ukraine, Little Auvergne, Little Scotland, Little Brittany, wherever they were in Manitoba, and also the nearly exact replicas of Quebec scattered over the plain. This already, no doubt, gave me that un-anchored feeling, the drifting sensation of casting loose from habit which, with the slight anxiety it produces, is unequalled for making us want to see and seize and hold everything new, if only for a moment.

My father, home from long expeditions among the settlers, always brought fresh news about "his" unruly Doukhobors, "his" quiet Ruthenians, "his" devout Mennonites. His settlements now extended almost to Medicine Hat, each more surprising than the last, so that you'd think his tales were taken from certain pages by Gogol. This is perhaps why, when in later years I read *Dead Souls*, I was not as astonished as some western readers. Tchitchikov's adventures seemed somehow familiar to me. What was comical, singular and improbable was just as familiar to me as the dull, believable and everyday aspect of life. I even had to learn to tone down certain elements of the reality that lay behind some stories so that people wouldn't think I was overdoing things shamelessly.

This brings me to the essential thing Manitoba brought me. My father's stories, the little trips we took with my mother, the Manitoba backdrop where the faces of all the peoples of the world were to be seen, all this brought the "foreigner" so close to me that he ceased to be foreign. Even today, if I hear a person living only a few miles away described as a "stranger," I cannot help feeling an inner tremor as if I myself had been the victim of an insult to humanity.

Either there are no more foreigners in the world, or we are foreigners all.

But the most enduring thing Manitoba gave me was the memory of its landscapes. I have travelled quite a lot. Occasionally I have been happy elsewhere and managed for a moment to feel at home in the gentle range of the Alpilles, or, odder still, in a certain small village in Epping Forest, Essex, where I ended up one day by utter chance; and there's a corner of the Isle of Rhodes, in Lindos, where at times I thought I might like to live, among the bougainvilleas and the women all in black seen against the whitest walls in the world, and the little interior gardens made of simple pebbles arranged with such grace that they compose exquisite mosaics.

At last it was the St. Lawrence, the link with our most remote Canadian past, but still a living, moving sea lane, always flowing toward the future. I live near enough to the river to see it from my window at all times, and I never grow weary of it, especially in the country, in Charlevoix, where it is twenty-two miles wide and comes and goes in regular, ample tides like the beating of creation's very heart. The "sea" drops, as they say here, and my own heart knows a kind of letdown; it rises, and my sad being finds a fresh departure.

But all these are adult loves, reflected on and sought after. My childhood love is the silent sky of the prairie, fitting the soft, level earth as perfectly as the bell cover on a plate, the sky that could shut one in, but which, by the height of its dome, invites us to take flight, to fly to freedom. My love encompasses the special silhouette, two-walled, of our grain elevators, their blue shadow like a cutout against a sky blurred with heat, the only thing on a summer day that reveals from afar the existence of the villages on this flat immensity; the mirages of those torrid days when the dryness of roads and fields throws up from the horizon illusory waters trembling between land and sky; the small clumps of trees, the bluffs gathered in a circle as if to chat in the desert about the wide world; and the infinite human variety of that countryside.

When I was young in Manitoba, one of our favourite outings was a trip to Bird's Hill. What was so attractive about it then? From the level plain there arose, for no apparent reason, a singular, long, sandy crest, the shore, one would have said, of some ancient lake, dry for centuries and turned to land, grass and market gardens, except in certain parts where brush allowed the persistence of wild life, and where one heard the plaintive cry of birds. No doubt it was a former strip of water left behind by the Sea of Agassiz since that immemorial time when Manitoba, almost entirely under water, was not even a dream. We would stay there, full of respect and astonishment. Perhaps we had an inkling that this strange crest of sand was uniting ages before our very eyes, the ages we call "past," those yet to come, the new, the old, those that persist, those that overturn, those we think dead, those we call "today," and that all these times were in truth no more than a second on the great dial.

Bird's Hill is perhaps my most sacred memory of Manitoba: on the shore of long-vanished waters, these ancient fossils, these dreams of youth, this unshakeable confidence in the far-off horizon.

You know how it fools us, this Manitoba horizon! How many times, as a child, have I set out to reach it! You always think you're about to arrive, only to see that it has retreated slightly, kept its distance once again. It is really a great signpost of life which an invisible hand mockingly maintains beyond our reach. As we get older, we grow a little discouraged and we even suspect that there is a supreme ruse behind all this, that we will never reach the horizon's perfect curve. Sometimes, however, we feel that others after us will undertake the same mad venture and that this horizon, still so far away, is the circle of mankind, full and united at last.

TOPICS FOR DISCUSSION

1. What is the "divided love" Roy's family has experienced that she considers in her second paragraph? What is the effect of the two images, the prairie and the mountains, on her imagination? How do these two geographic representations reflect the opposing qualities in her grandparents?

2. What cultural features do the Québécois transport with them to Manitoba? How do they recreate "what they have left behind"?

3. What is the "irremediable ... difficulty of being French Canadian in Manitoba or elsewhere"?

4. From what parts of the world did inhabitants of Saint-Boniface come? How has early exposure to a culturally diversified environment changed Roy's attitude to such words as "homeland," "foreigner," or "stranger"?

5. Roy often compares her experiences to literature—her own and others. How do these literary allusions connect Saint Boniface with the scattered cultures of the world? For Roy, what does the horizon symbolize?

Jeannette Armstrong

*Jeannette Armstrong is an Okanagan who was born in 1948, on the
Penticton Indian Reserve in British Columbia. She is the grandniece of
Hum-Ishu-Ma (Mourning Dove, 1888-1936), considered the first Native
American woman novelist. She received a traditional education from
Okanagan elders and her family, and has raised her own two children on
the reserve as well. She speaks the Okanagan language fluently. She
obtained a Bachelor of Fine Arts degree from the University of Victoria in
1978. Armstrong is a poet, fiction writer, teacher, artist, sculptor, and
activist for indigenous rights. She is director of the En'owkin International
School of Writing in Penticton, a Native-run school which grants diplomas
through the University of Victoria. She has published the children's books*
Enwhisteetkwa Walk in Water *(1982) and* Neekna and Chemai *(1984),
the novel* Slash *(1987), and the collection of poetry* Breath Tracks *(1991).
In 1993, she edited* Looking at the Words of Our People: First Nations
Analysis of Literature. *Her visual and artistic works have been recognized
through several awards in Canada. She has collaborated with famous
Native architect Douglas Cardinal on the book* Native Creative Process: A
Collaborative Discourse *(1991). She has also produced video and sound
recordings, of which "Indian Women," on the Cargo Record release* Till the
Bars Break, *was nominated for the Canadian Juno award. She has per-
formed a story-telling mini-series on "Arts Express," Vision TV. Works in
progress include a music art video collaboration of South American and
Okanagan indigenous musicians and artists, and a new novel.*

"This Is a Story" was published in All My Relations: An Anthology
of Contemporary Canadian Native Fiction, *edited by Thomas King
(1990). Kyoti is a traditional shape-shifting trickster figure found in
Native mythologies. He can create, change, and destroy, but usually the
results of his actions are beneficial to people.*

This Is a Story

It came to me one morning early, when the morning star was up
shining so big and bright, the way she does in the summers. It was
during the women's gathering at Owl Rock. It was the same year

that the Red Star came so close to the earth that it was mentioned in the papers.

I had been sitting up with the fire. One woman had to sit up with it at all times during the gathering. One friend had stayed up with me to help keep me awake. It had been cold and I was wrapped up in a Pendleton blanket. It was the second to last night of the gathering. I was getting very sleepy when George said, "Tell me a story." "Okay," I said. "This story happened a long time ago. It's real."

Kyoti was coming up from the river, from the great Columbia River up to the Okanagan River. Kyoti had come up through there before. One time before that I know of. That time Kyoti came up the Okanagan River which runs into the Columbia River. That was the time when Kyoti brought salmon to the Okanagan. Everywhere Kyoti stopped at the Peoples' villages, salmon was left. It made everyone happy. It was a great gift. Kyoti did that a long time ago.

Now, after waking up from an unusually short nap, Kyoti was walking along upstream, wanting to visit with the People in the Okanagan. These were Kyoti's favourite people. Visiting them always meant a real feast with salmon. Kyoti was partial to salmon.

While walking along, Kyoti noticed a lot of new things. A lot of things changed since that last trip through here. There sure were a lot of Swallow people, and they had houses everywhere, but Kyoti couldn't find any People, or even the villages of the People. Things looked very strange.

Eventually, Kyoti came to a huge thing across the river at Grand Coulee. It was so high it stretched all the way across the water and blocked it off. Kyoti stopped and looked at it for a while not having any idea what it might be. It didn't look good, whatever it was. Something was worrisome about it. Kyoti had thought of going up to the Kettle Falls to where the Salmon Chief stayed, but there didn't seem to be any way salmon could get past that thing, no matter how high they jumped. Kyoti was pretty hungry by then, not having seen any People. Just to make sure, Kyoti decided to go up the Okanagan River to where the People had been real happy to get the salmon brought to them.

It was a good thing Kyoti didn't go up to Kettle Falls anyway. Kyoti didn't know yet, that all the People had moved away when the Falls had disappeared under the new lake behind Grand Coulee.

So Kyoti when back down the river and started up the Okanagan. Kyoti kept going along the river and, sure enough, what Kyoti was afraid of came true. There was another one of those things right there at Chief Joseph. But this time there were a couple of People fishing there. They were the first People Kyoti had seen anywhere along the river. They were directly below that huge thing that stretched way up and across the river.

So Kyoti went up to them and waited for a greeting and some show of respect. Like an invite to eat. After all Kyoti was respected in these parts. Kyoti had brought the salmon to these People.

Kyoti waited for a while but neither of the young men said anything. They just kept on fishing. Kyoti got tired of waiting for them to speak first and said, "How is the fishing?"

The both just looked at Kyoti, like they didn't understand.

Kyoti again spoke, slower and louder this time, "Is the fishing good? I bet there are some big ones this time of year."

One of them tried to say in Swallow talk that they didn't know the language.

That was how Kyoti found out that they couldn't understand the language of the Okanagan people!

Kyoti couldn't figure that one out, but since Kyoti knew all the languages, Kyoti talked to them in Swallow talk. Kyoti asked them again how the fishing was.

They looked at Kyoti and one of them answered, "We been here two days, nothing yet."

Well Kyoti was pretty disappointed. Kyoti was hoping to eat a couple of salmon for lunch. Kyoti thought that maybe it wasn't a lost cause after all. People in their village might have food, maybe even salmon, since this was fishing season.

Kyoti waited around for a while and finally asked, "Where are all the People?"

One of them answered by asking what Kyoti meant.

"Well, I would like to talk with your headman," Kyoti said very seriously.

Actually Kyoti just wanted to eat. Kyoti was starving.

The both laughed. "What headman. Hey, man, where'd you come from?" one of them asked.

Kyoti kinda got mad then and answered, "I came walking up the river. I never saw any People. All I been seeing is those Swallows and they sure got lots of houses. Now you talk to me in their talk and laugh at me. I'm hungry and you don't even offer me anything to eat."

Well that shamed them guys out. Even though they weren't quite sure of what Kyoti was talking about. One of them said, "Cheeze, you coulda just said that in the first place. We're Indians. Come on, we'll go over to the house and feed you up."

So that was how Kyoti got to Nespelum. Kyoti got to meet one old person there that talked right. All the rest of the People just talked Swallow talk. They used words in Swallow that didn't have a meaning that Kyoti could figure out.

What was the most surprising was that all the people lived in Swallow houses and ate Swallow food. A whole lot of things were pretty strange.

Kyoti had looked and looked for somebody who could talk in the People's language. Kyoti asked the one person who could talk proper, how this had all happened.

The person was a very old woman. Kyoti recognized her name and knew which family and village her People were from. She was from an old headman family.

She looked at Kyoti for quite a while and recognized Kyoti. Then she cried and cried from a long time. "Kyoti," she said, "I never thought you were going to come back. Things haven't been good for quite a while now. I kept hoping you would show up. Them Swallows came. We don't know what happened. They did lots of things. They built that thing across the river again, like when they were Monster people and you broke their dams to bring the salmon up. I don't think it's made out of spit and clay like that other time, but it's made of something like that. They did lots of other worse stuff. How come you never came back for a long time? Now look what happened."

Kyoti was quiet for a while. "Well I guess I went to sleep for a while. You know sometimes I oversleep a little," Kyoti joked, trying to make her feel better.

Actually Kyoti was well known for oversleeping all the time. And actually Kyoti always used that as an excuse for being too late for something important.

But the old woman just kept crying. She kept on talking, saying, "Nobody listens to me. Nobody knows you anymore. You better go up to Vernon, up there in the North Okanagan. Go see Tommy, he keeps telling people about you. Maybe he can tell you something about what happened."

So Kyoti continued on up the river, stopping at each village. This time they were easy to find, now that Kyoti knew that the People had moved into Swallow homes. They were easy to find because they looked different than the way Swallows kept their houses. The People didn't seem to care to keep the houses the way the Swallows worked at it, day in day out, non-stop until they dropped dead. That was no surprise. They weren't Swallows.

Kyoti tried to talk to some of the headmen. Kyoti would suggest something like, "You should break down them Swallow dams, and let the salmon come back. They know where to come, they never forget. I told them not to. You shouldn't eat that Swallow food. Look at all the sick People."

Actually Kyoti himself was getting pretty sick and gaunt from eating stuff that didn't taste or look like food. Especially real food like fresh salmon.

But the headman would just shake his head and say, "Get out of here, Kyoti. Your kind of talk is just bullshit. If you say them things People will get riled up and they might start to raise hell. They might even try to do something stupid like break the dams. Them Swallows get real mad real easy. Besides, we'll just end up looking stupid. We gotta work with them now even if we don't exactly like what they do. We gotta survive. We gotta get money to buy food and other things. We gotta have jobs to live. That's how it is now, we can't go back to old times. We need them Swallows, they're smart. They know lots that we don't know about. They know how to live right. We just got to try harder to be like them. So get outta here. You're not real anyway. You're just a dream of the old People."

They would say things like that even while they talked right face-to-face to Kyoti. Even when Kyoti was right there in front of them.

Kyoti would walk on feeling real bad. Kyoti had seen lots of People in really bad shape. They walked around with their minds hurt. They couldn't see or hear good anymore. Their bodies were poisoned. They didn't care much for living anymore. They thought they were Swallows, but couldn't figure out why the Swallows taunted and laughed at them. They couldn't seem to see how the Swallows stole anything they could pick up for their houses, how they took over any place and shitted all over it, not caring because they could just fly away to another place. They couldn't seem to see that the Swallows treated them just as they pleased without any respect.

Kyoti could see that them Swallows were still a Monster people. They were pretty tricky making themselves act like they were People but all the while, underneath, being really selfish Monsters that destroy People and things like rivers and mountains. Now Kyoti could see the reason for being reawakened early. There was work to be done. It was time to change the Swallows from Monsters into something that didn't destroy things. Kyoti was Kyoti and that was the work Kyoti had to do.

Eventually Kyoti came to a place were a young one was sitting by the river. This young one greeted Kyoti properly in People talk. He looked at Kyoti's staff and asked politely, "Who are you, old one? I know all the People in the Okanagan. I haven't seen you before, but you look like somebody I must have known before."

Kyoti sat down and then said, "You look like somebody I once knew. An old Chief. He was a really big important chief. He was so important that he took care of People all up and down the whole Okanagan. He never kept a single salmon for himself if somebody needed it. Me, I'm just a traveller. I move around a lot when I'm not sleeping. Never know where I'll be tomorrow. I'm looking for Tommy, I guess."

The young man said, "Tommy? The old man? Yeah you must mean him. Some of us call him our chief now. It was Tommy told my mom to make sure that I was to sit here and watch the river, every day during salmon-run time."

"You see he knows that I'm a chief of the Kettle Falls. I'm a Salmon Chief, but no salmon come up here now, and there is no falls there anymore. My great grandfather was the last Salmon Chief to see the salmon come up the river. The Swallows came after that. Now I wait here and watch the river, like my father and his father before him did. They died without seeing one salmon come up the river."

"I guess I will keep on waiting. I believe Tommy when he says that we got to not give up. Sometimes I think I will see them coming. Shining and in clean water. I close my eyes during salmon-run time, and I see them. Millions of salmon coming up the river. I see my People singing, all coming down to the river to be with me, to eat again what we were given to eat. But then I open my eyes and nothing is ever there. I'm so tired and so all alone here. Nobody else cares."

So that was when Kyoti took out the shining rainbow ribbons and hung them on his staff.

Kyoti walked up to Tommy's door and said, "Tommy, open the door. I have come to talk to you. I'm going to ask you to get the People together. The ones who can hear. Tell them that I am back. You know all of them. I am going to break the dams. I'm hungry and the young one at the river has waited long enough. All my children will eat salmon again"

Kyoti shook the staff and the ground shook, too, as Tommy came out the door facing east. You shoulda seen Tommy's face, when he saw Kyoti and the rainbow ribbons hanging on the staff.

That story happened. I tell you that much. It's a powerful one. I tell it now because it's true.

Sometimes I think of that story and that morning at Owl Rock, when I see rainbow colours in the oil slicks along the river, during salmon-run time in the Okanagan, and I feel the ground shake ever so little.

TOPICS FOR DISCUSSION

1. What changes in the People's way of life does Kyoti notice upon his return to the Okanagan? How is the contrast between the People and the Swallows developed?

2. Armstrong's narrative can be read as a symbolic parable disguising "real" concerns under the surface of traditional storytelling and mythic characters. What are these "real" concerns?

3. What comic effects are achieved in the story? Can we find any traces of orality (that is, traditional oral transmission) there?

4. Compare the importance such authors as Gabrielle Roy and Jeannette Armstrong attribute to the meaning of place in the preservation of cultural heritage. What different writing styles and strategies do they employ to write about Manitoba and the Okanagan respectively?

Dionne Brand

Dionne Brand, born in 1953 in Trinidad, moved to Toronto in 1970. She received a B.A. in English and Philosophy from the University of Toronto, and an M.A in History and Philosophy from the Ontario Institute for the Studies in Education. From 1990 to 1991, she was a writer-in-residence at the University of Toronto. She has published six books of poetry, including Chronicles of the Hostile Sun *(1984),* No Language is Neutral *(1990), which was nominated for the Governor General's Award, and* Land to Light On, *which won this award in 1997. She co-authored* Rivers Have Sources Trees Have Roots—Speaking of Racism *(1986), and edited* No Burden to Carry: Narratives of Black Working Women in Ontario, 1920s to 1950s *(1991). In 1996, she published her first novel,* In Another Place, Not Here; *her second novel is entitled* At the Full Change of the Moon. *Brand is also a documentary film maker, known for her National Film Board's Studio D productions:* Older Stronger Wiser *(1989),* Sisters in the Struggle *(1991), and* Long Time Comin' *(1993). She has published her politically engaged essays in* Bread out of Stone *(1994). She is a social activist involved with Black, lesbian, and feminist communities. She has edited and done research for a number of alternative journals and papers, including* Fuse, Our Lives, Fireweed, Canadian Woman Studies, *and* Resources for Feminist Research.*

The following story comes from her first collection of stories, Sans Souci and Other Stories *(1988). The narrator returns to the scene of her childhood, revisiting the plantation where she was born and where her grandfather had been overseer for twenty years. The contrast between Black poverty and white affluence on this former slave plantation—the workers crowded into slave barracks while the white mansion was used only two months a year—provokes the narrator's resentment and anger. Things have not changed as much as they should have.*

St. Mary's Estate

St. Mary's Estate was further on. Past the two rum and grocery shops, past Miss Dot's, past the savannah, past Miss Jeanne's

parlour—paradise plums in large bottle jars. Then a piece of bush.
Then St. Mary's.

Most of it is still there I notice, as the jeep misses the St. Mary's
entrance and drives a little way on to Schoener's Road, the dried-out
river bed in which duennes used to play all night, or so the story
goes. I tell my sister this is where the spirits of dead unchristened
children used to live, duennes, calling children in the evening to
come and play. Our friend, driving the jeep, asks if I want to write
down the correct spelling of the name of the road. I tell him it does
not matter. I have known that road and that dry river bed for thirty-
four years with a mixture of fear and curiosity, though I've only ever
stood this distance from it. The story might still be true. The trees
and the stones have been preserved in my head with their sign of
silence, yellowness and eerie emptiness. When we look toward the
river bed, the three of us, we look as if we're watching something or
someone. Not emigration, not schooling, not brightly lit cities have
managed to remove the shapes of duennes in the river bed by
Schoener's Road. Not even Schoener, probably a Dutch privateer,
with all his greed and wickedness, debauchery and woman-burning,
not even he could remove the shapes of duennes in this river bed, by
putting his strange name to it. It is still quiet, waiting for dusk for
duennes to come out calling to play whoop.

The jeep turns around. The two male passengers of a truck
leaving Schoener's Road stare at us as the vehicles negotiate passage.
Then the jeep turns right into the gravelled entrance of St. Mary's.
There is still a white sign board on a post, now leaning into the
ditch at the entrance, now woodlice eaten. The letters are worn, but
officious and distant; painted a long time ago, they survive like the
post. A vigilant reminder and a current record of ownership and
property. At this point you can see the sea straight ahead, in back of
the house where I was born. This entrance gives you a sense of
coming home, the same sense I've always had upon seeing it. The
eyes light on the completeness of the scene it guards. There are two
long barracks, one on each side of the gravel road. In front of the
right barracks there is a great tamarind tree, now a little shrivelled
but still protecting the place underneath, dirt swept clean, where
people, mostly men, used to gather and play cards, drink rum and
talk. Of the two barracks this one still houses people. All that is left
of the other are the nine to twelve thick white pillars which it stood
on once and the triangular moving roof under which copra is put to
dry. Bush has overgrown the floors and the walls have been
removed, perhaps from fire, or perhaps from ancient wear, sunk into
the ground. That's where Cousin Johnny used to live. He was deaf
and did not speak. He made beautiful soups and mouth-watering

coconut bakes and saltfish. The whole compound would smell sweetly of his bakes on a Saturday evening.

The jeep eases along for another fifty yards; my eyes rest on the place, old and familiar like watching the past, feeling comfortable and awestruck at once. Then too, resentful and sad. A boy atop the left barracks stops raking the copra to watch us. No one else is about. The air is very still, yet breathing, a breeze, quiet and fresh, blowing from the sea. The sea here, too, is still. A country beach, a beach for scavenging children, thinking women, fishermen. The sea is not rough or fantastic, nothing more stupendous than an ordinary beauty, ever rolling, ever present. The kind of sea to raise your eyes to from labour. This must have been the look toward the sea that slaves saw as they pulled oxen, cut and shelled coconut, dug provisions from the black soil on the north side of the road. This must have been a look of envy.

There used to be a big well near the tamarind tree. Plait Hair and Tamasine used to live over there, in the third place of the back row of the right barracks. She had seventeen children; he plaited his hair, refusing to cut it. He worked hard, always in silence, his cheeks sucked in. Tamasine was a big red woman, as big as Plait Hair was slight and wiry. The walls separating each quarter of the barracks from the other did not go up to the roof, so everyone could hear what was going on in the other. Each quarter was one room. People used to wonder how Plait Hair and Tamasine had seventeen children, since it was difficult to be private. Maybe they'd wait till everyone was asleep, including their children. Even now, I find myself speculating.

There used to be a lagoon on the left, past the left barracks, off into the bush ...

The gravel road slows the jeep, as it edges toward the small wood house where I was born. Set in the centre to observe the two barracks, its back is toward the sea, its legs standing halfway in sand, halfway in dirt. It's the same house, thirty-four years later. The jeep moves even more slowly because of the silence of the place. As it passes the barracks there is no sign or sound of life except the boy on the copra house gone back to his work.

"It's the same house," I say; and to my sister, "Do you remember it?"

"No," she says, "I wasn't born yet."

Two men come out of the house as the jeep pulls to a stop near the front steps. I recognize one of them as the man who took over after my grandfather was fired as overseer of St. Mary's Estate. An emotion like resentfulness rises in me. It is only a memory of my grandfather, in his sixties; after twenty years, he was to be let go and, from what I could pick up at three or four years old, this new man was the cause. The

new man, the overseer, is now an old man. His youth had been thrown
in my grandfather's face and his ability to husband cocoa. I'm amused
that something learned such a long time ago can still call upon the
same emotion and have it come, fresh and sharp like this. I put on a
smile and walk up the steps, my hand outstretched, saying, "Hi, I was
born in this house. I just want to look around." He cracks a smile in
his stern face, as recognition passes over his eyes and confirms, "Oh
you is a Jordann," saying my last name as it has always sounded—like
the name of a tribe, a set of characteristics ranging from criminal to
saint, axe women to shango priestess, obeah woman. My grandfather's
life put the sound into my last name. My grandmother's life put the
silence after it. Jordann, like a bearing, like a drum.

My grandfather had children and outside women and outside
children. He could read and he could write, which made him
valuable. He was the overseer for twenty years at St. Mary's. He had
an ornate hand and was such a strict parent that all his children
wrote exactly like him. He rode two horses, Noble and Buddha.
Noble was white and Buddha was black. Noble for show and
Buddha for faithfulness. He drank rum at the first shop and the
second shop, drinking and gambling out the pittance that he made
tending St. Mary's for a white man. He wrote letters and took care
of everyone else's business. He gave advice freely, he took only advice
which could ruin him. He always walked straight up and stiff, the
length of his six feet. Until the last years which he spent here, he
lived a life of grace, depending on what was not possible, riches, and
escaping payment of the debts he incurred dreaming about it. Grace
only lasts forever with God, not with white men, so papa was
disposed of when age was tired of holding out on his face and when
he was unable to create a vision of acres of rich purple cocoa trees
for the estate owner. Then everything caught up with him, mostly
his debts and we all went to live in town, except he.

He first went to live in a house up a steep cliff which he could not
mount because of his sore foot and then settled into a shack near the
road where he sold ground provisions, callaloo bush, okra and pepper.
Finally he got a job as an agricultural officer, walking miles into the
bush to talk to farmers. The last entries in his diary, the ones before he
died, only said, optimistically, "can't go to work, sick today."

The dirt around the house is mixed with sand and broken bits
of shells. During deep tide, the sea comes in as far as the front yard,
lashing against the pillow tree trunks which the house stands atop.
We get the okay from the new man and head toward the beach. My
sister and our friend follow me as I tell them,

"There used to be a lagoon over there; once it caught on fire.
This is where we used to put garbage. See the shells are better here.

This is a place for a kid to hunt shells and stones. This is where I used to play."

They follow me, looking at me a little strangely or perhaps trying to see what I see. My childhood—hunting up and down the beach for shells, stones, bits of bottles, snails, things washed up by the sea, lagan; the blue red transparent shine of 'garlent'; seeing how far you could walk; pointing to Point Galeoto; swearing we could see Venezuela; digging into crab holes.

"This is a place for a kid," I say. "Every Good Friday, a tree would appear in the lagoon. Mama said it was a sign of Christ."

We move away toward the lagoon. It is the dry season. The lagoon is still there despite the years of garbage throwing. Then we walk back toward the house, along the beach, and I point toward a river's mouth rippling into the sea, two hundred yards to the right of the wooden house.

"It was hard to cross there, the tide was too strong sometimes."

And then I see it, and I feel something in me hesitate to walk toward that side. It is a huge green house, hidden from the wood house by trees but visible on the sea side. It used to be yellow, it seems to me; but I could be mistaken. Rust, brought on by the spray of the sea, swells on its sides. It is empty and it is closed. I turn to my sister,

"That fucking house. Do you see that fucking house!"

My sister looks at me, understanding. I cannot bring myself to move toward the house or that part of the beach.

"That goddamned house. It's still there."

I feel such anger and yet, still, my feet do not move toward it. So angry, I feel nauseous. "Fuckers!" I yell, but the wind and the sound of the sea lift the word and balloon it into a feeble scream. The uselessness of that sound stops me and I explain to our friend who looks perturbed, "That's where they used to live."

In fact, they didn't live there. They came with their children every July. Then we had to be reverential toward them; we could not walk to that side, especially if they were on the beach. They left at the end of August and then, we kids would rush, with my mama who went to clean the house, to see what they had left. Even what they had left we could not touch, thank God, because mama wouldn't allow us. Mostly, we children envied the real doll's head that lay here or there and the shoes discarded. Their children always wore shoes and socks. We ran about like mad things in bare feet and washed-out clothing.

For two months, this wasn't our place. For two months papa bowed and scraped, visibly. And mama warned us grandchildren not to misbehave or embarrass the family.

And still after this long, the imperative of habit and station causes my legs to stand where they are. Do not go near the house. It is the white people's house. It is their place and we are 'niggers'. Reaching back into me, thirty-four years, a command, visceral, fresh as the first day it was given. It still had the power of starvation, whip and ... blood. I turn and we walk back toward the wood house and the stern-faced new man.

This is where I was born. This is the white people's house. This is the overseer's shack. Those are the estate workers' barracks. This is where I was born. That is the white people's house this is the overseer's shack those are the slave barracks. That is the slave owner's house this is the overseer's shack those are the slave barracks.

This estate has been here for hundreds of years. Papa was the overseer. It is the end of the twentieth century and the slave barracks are still standing; one, with people living in it; the other refusing to drop into the earth, even though it has no walls. Tamasine and Plait Hair used to live in the barracks. Uncle Johnny used to live in the one that's half gone. The walls were thin cardboard and the daily gazette was used as wallpaper.

To sleep beneath the raw stench of copra, night after night, for two hundred years is not easy; to hear tired breathing, breathless fucking, children screaming, for five hundred years is not easy. And the big house was always empty, except for two months of the year. The slave barracks whose layers of gazette paper stretched for hundreds of years, was packed with Black humanity, rolling over and over and over without end, and still. This is where I was born. This is how I know struggle, know it like a landscaper. An artist could not have drawn it better.

"Fuckers. Fuckers. Fuckers." I hear myself muttering, under my breath. "Fu-u-ck, they're still there."

I go up the steps of the wood house, asking the new man,

"Sir, who owns this place?"

"Hackens and them, nah," he replies, leaning his now gray head as if I should know or remember, "They always own it."

"Always?"

"Yes." The new man nods as he speaks, "You know, them is big shot."

I must not have remembered about the house; because now, I can see it from the front of the wood house, too. Twenty of us were born in the two rooms of this wood house, while that one stood empty, locked. I'm looking to where I had instinctively not looked before. The house is still there, green, the windows locked, rust bleeding from its joints.

We climb into the jeep saying good-bye to the new man.

Always.

The jeep hobbles up the gravel road past the quiet barracks. The boy on the roof doesn't stop his work this time to look at us. We get to the sign post. "St. Mary's Estate," it says once again, judiciously. Red-eyed, I have a picture of the green house in my head, ablaze.

TOPICS FOR DISCUSSION

1. What do the "duennes" represent for the narrator? How are they symbolically related to her present situation?

2. What gives the narrator "a sense of coming home"? What concrete sensory images enliven the scenes of her visit? Is there any indication early in the story that her attitude to this place has changed since she was a child?

3. What are the main symbols of colonial exploitation that inflame the narrator's anger? What stylistic devices are used to signal the narrator's rage? Why does she use the pronoun "they" rather than the name of the estate owners?

4. How does this visit to the place where she was born affect the narrator? Has anything changed since her childhood? What is the meaning of the word "always" repeated twice at the end of the story?

5. Compare the role of memory in the pieces written by Gabrielle Roy and Dionne Brand. What is the significance of memory for both individual and collective self-definition?

Tomson Highway

Tomson Highway is a Cree, born in 1951 on the Brochet Reserve in Manitoba. At the age of six he was pulled from his culture and sent to a residential school. He studied music and English at the University of Western Ontario and in England. He worked as a social worker in his community before he turned to the theatre. He is Artistic Director of Native Earth Performing Arts, a professional Native theatre in Toronto. He has worked for the theatre as a producer, director, actor, stage manager, and mostly as a playwright. He wrote, produced, composed, and performed in plays such as The Rez Sisters *(1986),* Aria *(1987),* New Song…New Dance *(1988),* The Sage, the Dancer, and the Fool *(1989), and* Dry Lips Oughta Move to Kapuskasing *(1989). The* Rez Sisters *won a Dora award for best new play and a Chalmers Award. His latest play to be staged is* Rose. *In 1998 he published a novel,* Kiss of the Fur Queen.*

   Commenting on his use of women's voices in "The Rez Sisters," Highway says: "There is no gender in Cree…A male/female hierarchy doesn't exist…What I find so flawed about Christian mythology is that it makes room for only two genders…[In the Aboriginal world] the deity permeates all living things and holds the same position of equality in all living things…But there are really three genders in the Aboriginal belief. The third gender is the buffer, the peacemaker, between men and women. These are the people who can speak the same emotional language and, theoretically, can talk and feel like men or women when they choose." In his writing Highway emphasizes a traditional Trickster figure, like Weesageechak in the story below, which embodies Native humour and spirit in the face of all kinds of problems and difficulties.

The Lover Snake

The magazine photograph is of a Sikh. A male Sikh. Male Sikhs wear turbans. It's a tradition that goes back many, many generations, so it is said. You can always tell a Sikh when you see one by the turban he wears. Most, as I recall, also wear beards like this one in the photograph does. Fine beards. A fine-boned people. A fine-looking people. This particular Sikh, the man in the photograph, has, pictured with him, the uppermost portion of a large snake slithering down over the front and center of the bright orange turban he wears, the reptile's diamond-shaped head, with its distended eyes, hovering just centimeters over the man's forehead, its flickering tongue slicing air between his eyes. This is the photograph in the magazine.

Dahljeet has always worn a turban, as I remember. In fact, he has an entire closet full of them at his home in Vancouver. Dahljeet is a Sikh.

Now Dahljeet and I have been friends for many years. An unusual alliance, people would observe from time to time. And between us, Dahljeet and me, we would agree that the friendship was an unusual friendship. I mean, there he was, very much an Indian and here I was, also very much an Indian. Only, we were such totally different kinds of Indian. Worlds apart. So different, it was laughable. And we'd laugh. North Cree hunter ambles down the slope of Robson Street beside north Indian maharajah. An odd pair. To be sure.

And yet, we became close, Dahljeet and I. More than friends, more than brothers, more than lovers, even. It was almost as if, in the midst of certain totally unexpected moments in time we spent together, there would arrive from somewhere a certain buzzing half-sound, a certain inner ringing as perfect in pitch and purity as the tone from a tuning fork. It was beautiful. We met when we were both just short of twenty years of age.

Dahljeet would talk of elephant parades at magnificent royal weddings in the heat and dust of not-so-long-ago north India and of dark women in rainbow-coloured saris, draped in silver and gold and diamonds at summer places in the mountains and at winter places away from mountains. He had stories, too, of cobras that I remember particularly well.

And me? Well, I would talk to him of pure white snow and of rivers that never run dry and of ice-cold lakes from which you could drink by simply dipping your hand through crystal surfaces and cupping and lifting water to your mouth. I talked – not to be out-done by his stories of elephant parades and gold-sprinkled saris – of vast herds of caribou in spring-time, a sea of rolling, shifting, swaying antlers before my hunter father's keen, watchful eye. And of moccasins and belts covered with the most fanciful patterns and designs in glass beads. My sister, Marie-Adele, in particular, I'd confide to Dahljeet, is an artist at the art of applying beadwork to the smoked hide of young caribou. He owned twenty-seven turbans, my friend said in reply, and, later that afternoon, he showed me these twenty-seven turbans in his closet at his home in Vancouver: the colours were fantastic!

There were no snakes where I was born, so Weesageechak, that half-crazed little Cree Indian clown whom no one's ever seen, though he's lived ten thousand years and more among us, I told Dahljeet, this particular Weesageechak, well, he's never seen a snake or done anything with one or ridden one or cooked one and eaten one. He would have danced with one if he'd met one, I laughed. No. No snakes in far north Saskatchewan…which made his stories of maharajas and cobras, yes, cobras in particular, that much more fascinating. I was electrified!

They say, in north India, according to my friend, Dahljeet – he of the twenty-seven multi-coloured turbans and the fine, dark beard – that cobras mate at a certain time in their lives, the male with the female, and that they then sustain this relationship for the rest of their lives, as a couple – unlike sled dogs and caribou and men and women. And there comes a time when the occasional cobra will get killed by some over-zealous hunter, some nervous little man. And when this happens, the surviving cobra, the mate of the snake just killed, will find that man, the killer of his mate, will hunt him down even if it should take him thirty years and more, even if he should have to travel from the pale yellow dust of Punjab province to the border of Nepal or even to North America somewhere, perhaps Vancouver – he will travel there, this other cobra, somehow, even in the realm of the dream world, and he will find that man, and he will kill that man, that over-zealous hunter, that nervous little man. Then, and only then, will that cobra, the lover snake, lie down and die.

Many, many years later, Dahljeet and I ceased to be friends. Something happened. Something died inside of me. I haven't seen him in many years; he and I, we've lost touch. I understand that he lives still in Vancouver and has become even more the academic, the scholar, the thinker he so much was back then, that he teaches at one of the universities, so I've learned only recently, lecturing on the teachings of some obscure Eastern philosopher whose work relies to a great degree on the inner workings of myth and legend. I, on the other hand, now make my home in northwestern Ontario, working in the field of radio broadcasting and helping as much as I can – as poet, writer, thinker after my own fashion – to revive the breathing, the singing, and the shrieking of that half-crazed little Cree clown, Weesageechak, that essential spirit many had thought was on his way to dying, to leaving forever these snow-white landscapes so precious to us all. Now that we're over thirty years of age, we've lost touch, Dahljeet and I. This is the way of things, they say, the natural course of events in the lives of friendships, of love.

But I refuse that explanation. For me, it is a pale, flimsy story, of no consequence, no fantastic substance. I hold, instead, this magazine photograph in front of me and I gaze into it and I wonder if that isn't Dahljeet there in his brilliant orange turban and his fine, dark beard. And the snake? The cobra, the lover snake, come to lay claim to his over-zealous hunter, his nervous little man. And kill him…kill…kill…

Dahljeet and I, we are no longer friends.

TOPICS FOR DISCUSSION

1. What ethnic and sexual-romantic stereotypes are challenged by the story? How is the word "Indian" used?

2. Why does the narrator identify with the "half-crazed little Cree clown, Weesageechak"? Compare this Trickster figure to Jeannette Armstrong's Kyoti.

3. What are different possible symbolic interpretations of "the lover snake"? Compare with the use of the snake symbol in Pauline Johnson's story.

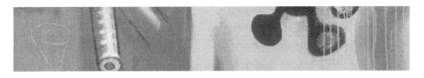

BORDERS/ IDENTITIES/ SELVES

INTRODUCTION

The paradox of "Canadian identity" is that of any identity in the age of globalization and mass migrations of people. As Guy Bédard says, "in all Western societies, identity has become considerably more complex and dynamic, crossing many boundaries." I would add that his statement applies not only to "Western" societies but also to other parts of the globe caught up in transnational networks.

For many Canadians, especially those with recent experience as migrants or a strong ethnic identity, the challenge of multiplicity can be either enriching or bewildering. It is not just the external world that is becoming increasingly diverse; as many authors in this unit show, there is diversity of identities and identifications within one person. Different configurations of factors such as gender, race, class, sexuality, age, ability, religion, and languages we speak complicate simple binaries of belonging and non-belonging. Consequently, rather than looking at identity as the "essence" of who we are, it is useful to view identities as constructs that are not solid and permanent but constantly fragmented and changing, as much as the world around us is changing historically. For the writers whose voices we hear in this unit, different identities may be liberating or constraining, subversive or conservative, or both at the same time. However, since identities can be adopted voluntarily or imposed from without, we have to remember that some of them can be oppressive.

Cyril Dabydeen

Born in 1945 in a family of Indian immigrants, Cyril Dabydeen came to
Canada from Guyana in 1970. He studied English at Lakehead
University and at Queen's University. He lives in Ottawa. From 1984 to
1987 he was Poet Laureate of Ottawa. Dabydeen taught at Algonquin
College and University of Ottawa, and has been a race relations specialist
with community groups, municipalities, and the federal government. He
has published over twenty volumes of poetry and prose dealing mostly with
the problems of reconciliation among ethnic, racial, and religious groups.
He is a strong advocate of multicultural harmony and community. His
books of poetry include This Planet Earth *(1979),* Islands Lovelier Than
a Vision *(1988),* Stoning the Wind *(1994), and* Born in Amazonia
(1995). He also edited anthologies of African Canadian and Caribbean
writing, A Shapely Fire: Changing the Literary Landscape *(1987) and*
Another Way to Dance: Contemporary Asian Poetry from Canada and
the United States *(1996). His two novels,* Dark Swirl *and* The Wizard
Swami, *came out in England in 1989. He has published short story collec-*
tions such as Still Close to the Island *(1980),* To Monkey Jungle
(1988), Jogging in Havana *(1992), and most recently,* My Brahmin
Days and Other Stories *(2000), which draws on Dabydeen's diasporic*
identity as South Asian Caribbean in Canada.

Multiculturalism

I continue to sing of other loves,
Places...moments when I am furious;
When you are pale and I am strong
As we come one to another.

The ethnics at our door
Malingering with heritage,
My solid breath, like stones breaking;
At a railway station making much ado about much,
This boulder and Rocky Mountain,
CPR heaving with a head tax
As I am Chinese in a crowd,
Japanese at the camps,
It is also World War II.
Panting, I am out of breath.

So I keep on talking
With blood coursing through my veins,
The heart's call for employment equity,
The rhapsody of police shootings in Toronto,
This gathering of the stars one by one, codifying them
And calling them planets, one country, really...

Or galaxies of province after province,
A distinct society too:
Québec or Newfoundland; the Territories...
How far we make a map out of our solitudes
As we are still Europe, Asia,
Africa; and the Aborigine in me
Suggests love above all else—
The bear's configuration in the sky;
Other places, events; a turbanned RCMP,
These miracles—

My heritage and quest, heart throbbing;
Voices telling me how much I love you.
YOU LOVE ME; and we're always springing surprises,
Like vandalism at a Jewish cemetery
Or Nelson Mandela's visit to Ottawa
As I raise a banner high on Parliament Hill
Crying "Welcome!"—we are, you are—
OH CANADA!

TOPICS FOR DISCUSSION

1. Who is the I-speaker in the poem? Whom do his shifting identifications reflect?

2. The poem includes a wealth of historical and geographical
   allusions. Is there any principle to their selection?

3. Is the poem a praise or a critique of multiculturalism?

Guy Bédard

*Guy Bédard is associate professor in the Department of Political Science at
the Université du Quebec in Montreal, where he teaches courses in method-
ology, statistics, and political sociology. His doctoral dissertation focused on
the "national question of Quebec." The essay reprinted here was first published in* Talking About Identity: Encounters in Race, Ethnicity, and
Language, *edited by Carl E. James and Adrienne Shadd (2001). Guy
Bédard looks at the historically changing meanings of such identity labels as
"Canadian," "French Canadian," and "Québécois."*

Québécitude: An Ambiguous Identity

*A̶ccepter de réflichir sur les resorts qui sont à l'origine de notre iden-
tité, c'est déjà un peu admettre que celle-ci est une construction de
l'esprit. À tout le moins, c'est reconnaître que ce qui va de soi, ce qui
semble appartenir à l'éternité, être déterminé par les conditions objec-
tives d'existence des individus ou à l'évolution historique des collectivités,
a encore besoin de l'apport de la raison pour voir clairment le jour. C'est
aussi une manière d'échapper aux idées qui façonnent notre être, s'expa-
trier de soi-même.*

All identities are a construction of mind. The emergence on the
Québécois identity is a perfect example. Even though I readily subscribe to this identity, I must admit that, on a philosophical level, I
still have difficulty grasping the concept of Québécois identity and
how it is constructed. Through my life history and experiences,
therefore, I want to explore this identity and how, at this stage in
Quebec's history, it has become increasingly inconsistent and con-
tradictory for me.

For as long as I can remember, I have never identified myself as
other than Québécois. And yet it is only recently that the term has
even appeared in the dictionary. Prior to the 1960s, I would have

said that I was French Canadian. In so doing, I would be defining myself first and foremost as a French-speaking Catholic, and therefore as a member of a community whose demographic boundaries extend beyond the borders of the province of Quebec. My reading of Quebec history also tells me that in another era I would have called myself *Canadien,* but in a particular way that most Canadians today would be completely unable to imagine. Up until the middle of the nineteenth century, the term "Canadian" referred almost exclusively to the descendants of the French colonists.(Jacques Cartier used the word "Kanada" to identify the Aboriginal peoples who lived in the St. Lawrence Valley. Shortly thereafter, it came to signify the inhabitants of French origin born in the colony.) Others preferred to call themselves British subjects: Irish, Welsh, Scottish, and English. So how did the term "Québécois" come about? And why do I feel that I must now identify myself as a Québécois? No book has ever explained this to me.

To be honest, there was a time when I would never have called myself Québécois. This was during my childhood, when the boundaries of my universe did not extend beyond family, the part of the street where we lived, the route I took to school, and the friends I made. After this early period, everything turned upside down.

Three incidents stand out in my mind: the parade down chemin du Roy when Charles de Gaulle travelled the historic route down the St. Lawrence River linking Montreal and Quebec in the days of New France (this happened prior to the now-famous *Vive le Québéc libre!* speech), a visit to Expo '67, and reading *White Niggers of America,* by Pierre Vallières.

I was nine years old at the time of the first two events. I barely remember de Gaulle's visit. However, I do remember that my parents were very proud to have been there when de Gaulle passed through Quebec City. This feeling, and perhaps the crowd's enthusiasm, as well as the obvious interest of my parents in all that spoke of our heritage, contributed to shaping a constant, but not well-defined, identity: an attachment to my roots, to my origins, and to my ancestors.

The second event is much fresher in my memory; it also reveals the ambiguous character of my early identity. Leaving Quebec City to visit Expo '67 in Montreal, I was to discover another country, a foreign land that allowed me to recognize my own. This was not China, or the USSR or Great Britain, or any of the countries that had built pavilions on Île Sainte-Hélène, where the international exposition took place. This was simply Montreal, the metropolitan centre. At nine years old, I had a sense of geography and space that was still quite limited. The never-ending voyage and the turbulence and feverishness of a big city were impressive. At the very least, the distance that separated the two cities, as much a function of their differing lifestyles as the number of kilometres one had to travel between them, was enough to impress upon me the idea of difference. There existed a country called Québec (without a doubt, to avoid confusion, others called it Quebec City) to which I identified and belonged. I became Québécois in the sense that I certainly was not Montréalais.

In retrospect, this anecdote might seem rather insignificant, the simple manifestation of the fertile imagination of a nine-year-old and his ignorance of the basics of geography. However, on further reflection, it brings out the ambiguous and changing character of Québécois identity. The increasing uneasiness that I feel each time I hear nationalists say *Le Québec au Québécois* illustrates this in yet another way. In adhering to this battle-cry, some *indépendantistes* are necessarily forced to admit that there are certain individuals whose status as residents of Quebec is not enough to qualify them as Québécois. Therefore, they adopt a logic of exclusion. But this is not what bothers me most. Is there an identity or a way of thinking that is not ultimately exclusionary? After all, those who call themselves Canadian do not treat other peoples of the world any differently. No! What profoundly embarrasses me about this slogan *Québec au Québécois* is that it forces me to choose between a territorial concept of Québécois citizenship – a perspective that, let us remember, is defended by a good number of *indépendantistes* – and an ethnic definition of Québécitude based on race, culture, and language: social markers for exclusion.

Somehow, I know that to say Québécois presupposes race, culture, and language, or at least one of these elements. It implies that we need to find affinities with a group, a community. There would not be so much commotion about Québécois identity if we were living, as some *indépendantistes* insist, in a "normal country" – that is, an independent state. In other words, there would not be this dichotomy if Quebec were independent. At least, the racism or xenophobia of this ethnic definition of Québécois identity would be completely clear. The problem is that, as things stand, there is a lot of confusion in this respect: it is often difficult to distinguish between the simple act of self-affirmation and racism.

Nor is the territorial criterion of Québécitude sufficient for me. After we agree on the boundaries of the territory concerned, we must then establish a full and complete definition of Québécois citizenship. Using ethnicity as a basis for identifying oneself as Québécois is too dependent on how each one of us envisages the criteria, and on our individual life histories and experiences. Imagine for a moment if I had kept the vision of Quebec that I had when I was nine years old, and you get a sense of the breadth of perspectives on this issue.

For me, the real *prise de conscience* came when I was twelve. During his stay in prison, Pierre Vallières, the presumed head of the *Front de Liberation du Québec (FLQ)*, wrote a book about his childhood and adolescence, *White Niggers of America.* Vallières made me aware of a whole world of oppression, of the *porteurs d'eau*, the francophone proletarians of Montreal subjected to the "Speak White" dictates of the Anglophone bourgeoisie. For the first time I realized that this city, Montreal, was also mine, was in some small way my home too. Oh! To be sure, there were enormous differences with Quebec City: 95 percent of the population in Quebec City is francophone; the English presence is insignificant. But what Vallières described closely resembled my father's life. He had to quit school at the age of ten. He sweated for English bosses who couldn't be bothered to communicate with him in French. I couldn't help but notice that in one of the factories where my father worked for several years and where the overwhelming majority of employees spoke only French, signs were exclusively in English.

I do not know if this vision of my father's lived experiences is totally accurate; it may have been distorted and exaggerated by the eyes of the child that I was. However, it was enough for me to accept Vallières' vision of the world: *Vive le Québec libre!* And socialist to boot. The history books took care of the rest. They recounted a long series of events that marked the relations between the francophone and anglophone communities of Canada: the deportation of the Acadians, the English Conquest, the hanging of Louis Riel and the crushing of the francophone Métis rebellion in western Canada, the implementation of the laws at the turn of the twentieth century prohibiting the teaching of French in schools in the other Canadian provinces, and so forth.

I felt that I belonged to an oppressed and persecuted people. I had the impression that the others, the anglophones with whom I had no contact other than what I read in books, were constantly seeking to annihilate the group to which I identified and belonged. The demographic decline of francophone communities outside Quebec was ample proof.

And yet these beliefs never fully rang true for me. To hold onto this perception of being an oppressed and persecuted minority, I had to appeal to experiences that frankly were foreign to me, that came from a history I had never personally experienced. I was a child of the Quiet Revolution; I lived in an era where the use of French was more prevalent than at any time since the Conquest.

From this point of view, outside of Montreal, you could say that Quebec has been reconquered. Since moving to the metropolitan centre of Quebec – Montreal – I can see that French is well-entrenched here, too. The threat of assimilation has been reduced to the point where it is no longer feared. And if there is still oppression, it certainly does not manifest itself in the same way. Through the years, the Quebec state has encouraged the emergence of a francophone bourgeoisie that knows how to exploit the country's natural resources as well as anyone. So why do I still have the desire to call myself Québécois?

It is perhaps the force of collective habit and the pressure of institutions. In thirty years, the term "Québécois" has become common usage. First affirmed by the poets, novelists, playwrights, and *chansonniers,* the term is today used by virtually everyone. The media are its foremost proponents, where even the news coverage is influenced by its implications (everything that happens outside Quebec gives the appearance of being somewhat foreign). Governments have also adopted it. I cannot think of a single politician who would dare not use the term. Even the members of the communities called anglophone and allophone now demand to be included in that so-named collectivity. The term is celebrated, emphasized, displayed, and asserted.

However, this is not the only vision or perspective of the world here. As in all Western societies, identity has become considerably more complex and dynamic, crossing many boundaries, Certainly, the rise of advanced communication and technology has given birth to the concept of a global village. Moreover, I frequently have the impression that I have more in common with intellectuals in London, New York, or Bangkok that with Quebec workers or the convenience store owner in my neighbourhood. To invoke the weight of habit or the power of institutions to explain why I identify myself as Québécois seems unsatisfying. It is to forget that this identity is in competition with other identities.

I do not know precisely what it is that makes me Québécois. All I know is that occasionally I feel as foreign in Paris or Toronto as I do in Amman when the chanting from the mosques fills the small hours of the morning. It is difficult to understand. However, a number of events in the history of the Québécois community resulted in the construction of a "collective imagination" that distinguishes this community from others, defining it vis-à-vis the rest of the world, whereby my diverse personal experiences have imprinted this "imagination" in my mind. In short, apart from the historical and cultural specificities, the process by which a Québécois identity was born is not much different from the formation of other community identities around the globe.

TOPICS FOR DISCUSSION

1. Explain the author's opening statement that "all identities are a construction of mind."

2. What ambiguities and contradictions are revealed by the history of naming in the use of such terms as "Canadian," "French Canadian," and "Québécois"?

3. The author claims that identity always involves a way of thinking that is exclusionary. What markers of exclusion does he mention in his essay?

4. Explain the differences between a territorial versus an ethnic definition of citizenship? What problems does the author find with both in the case of Québec?

5. Compare the use of foreign words and expressions by Isabel Vincent, Frank G. Paci, Garry Engkent, and Guy Bédard. Portuguese, Italian, Chinese, and French words and phrases appear in their respective texts, usually without translation. What functions do they have?

Helen Bajorek MacDonald

Helen Bajorek MacDonald has an M.A. in Canadian Studies from Trent University. She was on the collective of AVANCER: The Student Journal for the Study of Canada and in 1998 edited New Visions of Nation: Re-Imagining Canadian Culture(s). It included papers from an annual bilingual national student conference at Trent. She has written on Polish Canadian writing and is currently working on a book project based on her thesis dealing with the experiences of Polish survivors of Soviet labour camps during WWII. Her essays and articles have been published in a number of Canadian magazines, papers, and scholarly journals. An auto-biographical piece on her relationship with her Polish grandmother was anthologized in Our Grandmothers, Ourselves: Reflections of Canadian Women, edited by Gina Valle (1999). Helen Bajorek MacDonald says, "I tell [my sons] with pride of their Polish heritage. I also teach them the value of diversity, and the importance of empathy and care for those who struggle every day to stay alive and sane. I remind them how fortunate they are to be Canadian, and how important it is to keep our doors open to those who suffer under the many hands of oppression."

A Canadian Passport

In May 1975, my immigrant parents uprooted their six children to chase my Polish father's dream of being a small business owner. After years of scouting garages, greasy spoons and country stores, they bought the general store with post office and gas pumps located in the tiny village of Kendal, about 40 km east of our home in Oshawa, Ontario.

I was introduced to the village just a few weeks before the move. After a half-hour ride in silence, after watching from the back seat of the real estate agent's car as the landscape transformed from the familiar space of my working class "ethnic" urban neighbourhood to bucolic farms and rolling hills, the village appeared as a cluttered assortment of buildings dropped like Dorothy's house upon the low-lands of the countryside.

The first structure that could be seen from the main road was a little white clapboard United Church located at the edge of the village. It also was the tallest. Like an unattended tollgate, the church separated tobacco fields from houses. It stood mute and unpretentious, without a steeple or chimes or even a parking lot.

The houses were few and modest. As we turned off the side road, the short main street dawdled lazily through the village toward a row of red tobacco kilns that stood as beacons of promise for the season's crop. A mangy little dog levelled a one-eyed glance from his snoozing spot in the shade of a porch.

Being predisposed to the dramatic, I determined the village quiet was as the silence that falls with the dust in the aftermath of an atomic explosion. And being a bookish type with a fondness for history, I imagined we had been transported back to the days of the Loyalists to a place called *Upper Canada*.

And in the tranquility of an instant and with the confident sweep of a critical eye, I judged the place as primitive, protestant, and boring.

A little bell, positioned above the door, jingled as we entered the Kendal General Store. The well-worn hardwood floor told of many customers who trod in and out over the years carrying gossip and mail, food goods, hardware, coveralls, rubber boots, cigarettes, and pop and ice cream: a regular *soup-to-nuts* kind of place.

There is a blur of adults: my parents, the real estate agent, the owners, and some customers hovering at the counter and behind shelves, openly observing and sizing us up. There are smiles, hands are shaken, and the drone of dull polite conversation about the drive and the weather, all set against a backdrop reminiscent of a scene from *Green Acres*: Sam Drucker's General Store, pickle barrel and all.

The scruffy, pipe-smoking, overall-clad man at the counter, a local bachelor farmer and regular customer, smelled as though he'd crawled out of a manure pile. I would come to know a number of such local characters whose regular shopping trips were void of such necessities as laundry detergent and deodorant.

The move of our family of eight was chaotic and overshadowed by emotional turmoil. It also resulted in a significant transformation of our family and it is impossible to say now if all of the bad things could have been avoided or if all of the good things can be linked only to the move.

We left a large solid two-storey brick home built during the post-war immigration and industrial boom fuelled, in part, by Oshawa's automobile industry. The influence of General Motors was evident on signage posted at the city limits along Hwy. 401: "Oshawa: the City that Moto-vates Canada."

Our house was located in a dynamic working class community that had been settled predominantly by post-war immigrants. Mom came from England and was in the minority in our community. Dad came from Poland and like many of our neighbours was a child survivor of the wartime Soviet labour camp experience. There were others who came from Germany, from Ukraine, from Italy, from Malta, from Ireland and elsewhere. My childhood memories percolate with the aroma of fresh-baked bread, spicy sausage and garlic, and glasses filled with vodka and wine.

Across the street from our home was St. Hedwig Polish Roman Catholic Church that dominated the neighbourhood. Several Felician Sisters from the neighbouring convent taught at the Catholic elementary school where many of the children arrived on their first day speaking a language other than English. The neighbourhood bakery catered to eastern European palates.

Our new house, on the other hand, built in the mid-19th Century, was a cramped, crooked, creaking little frame storey-and-a-half structure with insul-brick siding located in a middling protestant, rural village where the general store—attached to our house—was at the centre.

Most of the village and outlying families traced their arrival back several generations and intermarriage through the generations meant almost everyone was kith and kin.

And so in the spring of 1975 our plucky and naïve family surfaced from the ocean of obscurity in an industrious multicultural neighbourhood, to the rustic conservative (big 'C' and little 'c'!) fishbowl.

Although I perceived there to be certain limitations to living in what I termed "hicksville," a part of me recognized that the move would serve as an 'out' from my ethnic constraints. I immediately saw a much-craved opportunity to enter and masquerade within mainstream Anglo culture.

In other words, I could shed my DP roots for a real Canadian life, however backward it seemed. I would learn how to be a real Canadian, not just a hyphenated Canadian, from people who'd been here for generations. I even imagined I'd be free of the dumb Polak jokes that shadowed my childhood. A fresh start, I thought, and I was willing to pay the price, whatever it might be, for entry into the heart of Canadian culture.

Dad took a leave from his trade as a mechanic in the Rejects Department at General Motors to serve Canada Post while Mom left nursing to tend shop. It was a moment of great pride the day we watched the mounting of a new *Coca Cola* sign over the storefront: "Bajorek's General Store." I doubt, however, that my father anticipated that he would enter a small world where his thick distinct accent created a chasm between his sense of self and his ability to garner the respect he so craved and believed was his due as postmaster and merchant. While he dreamed he'd finally made it, he remained an outsider and was seemingly unaware that others perceived him and treated him with great difference.

Removed from the margins of the ethnic enclave, Dad's difference was more evident to me and I became even more committed to the idea of escaping the sting of my 'foreign' roots.

I was fifteen years old and the eldest of six. The social shock was more traumatic than the culture shock. There was no means to communicate with my former high school friends for there was no way of getting back 'home' and phone calls were out of the question because of long distance charges.

Once active in Polish cultural activities and in school sports and clubs, and having a wide social network, I withdrew and became a teenager craving isolation. While my siblings quickly made friends, I resented leaving so much behind.

I put in my share of hours working in the store, helping with the rural mail delivery as well as with regular household chores. Within a year I got a job as a waitress which distanced me from my family as well as from other teenagers in the village who worked for better wages on area tobacco farms.

On July 12th a squawk of music drifted off the steaming main street and through the store windows. I left my post behind the counter to see a small band of sad and outdated folk hobble through the village, fifes and drums lacking both rhythm and harmony.

"Orangemen," I was told.

"I thought they stopped killing Catholics a few hundred years ago," I observed.

"They don't kill 'em anymore. They just celebrate King Billy's victory over the Catholics."

I was at a crossroads. On the one hand, I wanted to 'fit in' as a soapy white-bread 'real' Canadian. I didn't want to feel a pariah, different and out of place. On the other, I rejected the ideology of any group that represented what I considered to be intolerance.

I grew up during the heady days of Prime Minister Pierre Elliott Trudeau's multicultural policies that had captured the imaginations of many post-war immigrant families. The environment my parents fostered was one that stressed tolerance and celebration of all cultures as the only way to live in a diverse community that was home to many new Canadians who set as a goal to shed old world prejudices and animosities. The Orange Parade represented to me a throwback to a time of violence and intolerance. For a histrionic moment, I worried there might arise some hostility against our Catholic and 'foreign' family.

Some long-time area families still maintain the Kendal Orange Lodge and some diluted versions of Orange traditions. But no horror befell our family that day, or any other. And nobody tried to prevent my marriage a few years later to a local fellow whose roots in the area go back seven generations and whose paternal grandfather was for a time during the 1930s Master of a nearby Orange Lodge. However, his small-minded paternal grandmother went to her grave unaware her grandson had set up home with a dangerous "backstabbing Catholic"!

The store was open seven days a week and kept my parents busy and pre-occupied. I obtained my driver's license within months of my sixteenth birthday and often drove the family station wagon to school—so very uncool!—and after classes made trips to wholesalers for store goods.

Village life was notably different from what I had known. There were distinct cultural codes to learn as well as familiarity with local family trees to ensure accurate delivery of the mail and that no offence was made while serving customers. Political lines were drawn firmly and publicly along family lines. There were few secrets in a village where even the trees had eyes and ears.

One day, a local woman came into the store. She was invited by my mother to retire to our kitchen and, over a pot of tea the two women sat in maternal inquisition as they surveyed the landscape of the other's origins, values, and outlook while scrutinizing the virtues of their children. I knew already my mother worried her firstborn "little girl" was seeing "a man," he being nineteen at the time and with limited prospects as he was employed only seasonally in work on the village tobacco farm.

Despite the long hours my parents committed to the business, they lost it. It has been suggested that six children ate them into bankruptcy! In September 1977, broken and broke, they moved back to Oshawa while I entered a two-year college program in another city. I was not quite eighteen and essentially out on my own. I returned 'home' only once when, during the following summer, I was employed in secretarial work at General Motors in the Quality Control Department.

From a distance, I saw only glimpses of our family life and the rapid wreckage that followed the failure of the business. I was busy being a college student, then seeking my first full-time position as a Legal Secretary, and then planning a wedding. I was independent and self-sustaining, and a week after my 20th birthday, I married my country love who was then in the midst of his electrician's apprenticeship.

It was easy, through the act of marriage, to cut my ties with my Polish cultural roots. As I took on a new name, a 'Canadian' name, I knew the world would perceive me as Canadian, not something 'foreign.' And never again did anyone ask, "What are you?" for a MacDonald is 'in,' while a Bajorek is foreign.

There were family tensions when I shunned a formal wedding mass in favour of a private garden ceremony held on a Friday afternoon. A rent-a-minister, who I found in the Yellow Pages, officiated. We invited guests to a dance (not a formal Polish meal) held later that evening. My struggling parents were probably relieved they didn't have to pay for a lavish wedding but there were some disapproving remarks about their first-born defying certain cultural expectations. I didn't know it then, but I was clearing a path for other family members who would also break from cultural and religious tradition.

We moved into a small apartment situated above a liquor store that was located on the one-block downtown of Orono, a small town near Kendal. After a few years marriage, working and saving, we began the hunt for a place to build our nest. There was no question it would be in the country. I fit in. Even my name, changed with marriage, served as signifier of my belonging and as passport into the community where I have been very active and am widely known.

Though I was a newcomer, and would often feel different, my children would never be 'othered.' They come from here.

TOPICS FOR DISCUSSION

1. What differences between rural and urban Ontario did Helen Bajorek MacDonald personally experience after her family moved from Oshawa to Kendal?

2. MacDonald embarks on a quest to become "a real Canadian, not just a hyphenated Canadian." What causes her discomfort with her ethnic roots? Who is "a real Canadian" to her? Does she succeed in becoming one in the end?

3. How was she influenced by her working class immigrant background and by the liberal ideology of multiculturalism? Still living in the country, why is she "at a crossroads" with regard to her identity? Compare her desire to pass and her rediscovery of the value of ethnicity to Isabel Vincent's experiences.

Sun-Kyung Yi

Sun-Kyung Yi was born in 1967 in Seoul, South Korea, and immigrated to Canada in 1976. She studied journalism and political science at the University of Regina. She is a writer, journalist, broadcaster, and film-maker. She has produced radio works for CBC and worked as a reporter for The Globe and Mail *and the* Kitchener-Waterloo Record. *Her articles and essays have been published in* NOW *Magazine, The Toronto Star, and in anthologies. She received honorary recognition from the 1993 Media Human Rights Awards. Her television documentary* Scenes from a Corner Store *(1996) was nominated for a Gemini Award, and won awards at the New York and San Francisco film festivals. In 1997, she published her book,* Inside the Hermit Kingdom: A Memoir, *where she recalls her childhood in South Korea, her life as a young immigrant in the 1970s in Regina, her travel to North Korea in 1994 on assignment for CBC, and her return to her roots in South Korea in 1996. In the essay reprinted below, Sun-Kyung Yi experiences the splitting of her identity by the hyphen in "Korean-Canadian." Although a member of both cultures, she feels that she is "accepted fully by neither."*

An Immigrant's Split Personality

I am Korean-Canadian. But the hyphen often snaps in two, obliging me to choose to act as either a Korean or a Canadian, depending on where I am and who I'm with. After 16 years of living in Canada, I discovered that it's very difficult to be both at any given time or place.

When I was younger, toying with the idea of entertaining two separate identities was a real treat, like a secret game for which no one knew the rules but me.

I was known as Angela to the outside world, and as Sun-Kyung at home. I ate bologna sandwiches in the school lunch room and rice and kimchee for dinner. I chatted about teen idols and giggled with my girlfriends during my classes, and ambitiously practiced piano and studied in the evenings, planning to become a doctor when I grew up. I waved hellos and goodbyes to my teachers, but bowed to my parents' friends visiting our home.

I could also look straight in the eyes of my teachers and friends and talk frankly with them instead of staring at my feet with my mouth shut when Koreans talked to me.

Going outside the home meant I was able to relax from the constraints of my cultural conditioning, until I walked back in the door and had to return to being an obedient and submissive daughter.

The game soon ended when I realized that it had become a way of life, that I couldn't change the rules without disappointing my parents and questioning all the cultural implications and consequences that came with being a hyphenated Canadian.

Many have tried to convince me that I am a Canadian, like all other immigrants in the country, but those same people also ask me which country I came from with great curiosity, following with questions about the type of food I ate and the language I spoke. It's difficult to feel a sense of belonging and acceptance when you are regarded as "one of them." "Those Koreans, they work hard.... You must be fantastic at math and science." (No.) "Do your parents own a corner store?" (No.)

Koreans and Canadians just can't seem to merge into "us" and "we."

Some people advised me that I should just take the best of both worlds and disregard the rest. That's ideal, but unrealistic when my old culture demands a complete conformity with very little room to manoeuvre for new and different ideas.

After a lifetime of practice, I thought I could change faces and become Korean on demand with grace and perfection. But working with a small Korean company in Toronto proved me wrong. I quickly became estranged from my own people.

My parents were ecstatic at the thought of their daughter finally finding her roots and having a working opportunity to speak my native tongue and absorb the culture. For me, it was the most painful and frustrating 2 ½ months of my life.

When the president of the company boasted that he "operated little Korea," he meant it literally. A Canadianized Korean was not tolerated. I looked like a Korean, therefore I had to talk, act, and think like one, too. Being accepted meant a total surrender to ancient codes of behaviour rooted in Confucian thought, while leaving the "Canadian" part of me out in the parking lot with my '86 Buick.

In the first few days at work, I was bombarded with inquiries about my marital status. When I told them I was single, they spent the following days trying to match me up with available bachelors in the company and the community.

I was expected to accept my inferior position as a woman and had to behave accordingly. It was not a place to practice my feminist views, or be an individual without being condemned. Little Korea is a place for men (who filled all the senior positions) and women don't dare to speak up or disagree with their male counterparts.

The president (all employees bow to him and call him Mr. President) asked me to act more like a lady and smile. I was openly scorned by a senior employee because I spoke more fluent English than Korean. The cook in the kitchen shook her head in disbelief upon discovering that my cooking skills were limited to boiling a package of instant noodles. "You want a good husband, learn to cook," she advised me.

In less than a week I became an outsider because I refused to conform and blindly nod my head in agreement to what my elders (which happened to be everybody else in the company) said. A month later, I was demoted because "members of the workplace and the Korean community" had complained that I just wasn't "Korean enough," and I had "too much power for a single woman." My father suggested that "when in Rome do as the Romans." But that's exactly what I was doing. I am in Canada so I was freely acting like a Canadian, and it cost me my job.

My father also said, "It doesn't matter how Canadian you think you are, just look in the mirror and it'll tell you who you *really* are." But what he didn't realize is that an immigrant has to embrace the new culture to enjoy and benefit from what it has to offer. Of course, I will always be Korean by virtue of my appearance and early conditioning, but I am also happily Canadian and want to take full advantage of all that such citizenship confers.

But for now I remain slightly distant from both cultures, accepted fully by neither. The hyphenated Canadian personifies the ideal of multiculturalism, but unless the host culture and the immigrant cultures can find ways to merge their distinct identities, sharing the best of both, this cultural schizophrenia will continue.

TOPICS FOR DISCUSSION

1. What does it mean to be a "hyphenated Canadian"? According to the author, what are the ordeals of people straddling two cultures?

2. Why does the author say that Koreans and Canadians have such difficulty in merging? Why don't some Canadians view Koreans as Canadians? Why doesn't the president of "little Korea" tolerate Canadianized Koreans?

3. Find a few examples of cultural differences mentioned in this article. When talking about cultural differences, what are some ways to avoid cultural stereotyping?

4. What is the ideal of multi-ethnic interactions postulated by the author? What kind of attitude change would it require in both the host culture and the immigrant cultures?

Drew Hayden Taylor

*Drew Hayden Taylor was born in 1962 on the Curve Lake Reserve in
Ontario. He went to Seneca College, where he studied broadcasting. He has
worked as a journalist, author, and director for such media as television,
radio, press, and theatre. His one-act plays* Toronto at Dreamer's Rock
and Education Is Our Right, *as well as the full-length play* The
Bootlegger Blues *were published in 1990. In 1998, he published the play*
Only Drunks and Children Tell the Truth *and in 1999* The Baby
Blues, *which became the winner of the Alaska State University Playwrights
Award. In his writing, he employs social satire and humour, mixed with
elements of traditional Native storytelling. The following piece has been frequently anthologized. It can be found in* Funny, You Don't Look like
One: Observations From a Blue-eyed Ojibway *(1998), a collection of
Taylor's articles that he describes as "the ideas and observations of a Native
person living in this country we call Canada—the good, the bad and the
ugly." As a blue-eyed Ojibway, Drew Hayden Taylor is often mistaken for a
white by his fellow Native people while has to prove to disbelieving whites
that he is Native. He turns this ambiguous position to comic effect and, as
a final gesture of asserting his identity in a culture that judges by appearances, he humorously "secedes" from both the Ojibway and Caucasians and
declares himself to be an "Occasion"—a one-of-a-kind.*

Pretty Like a White Boy: The Adventures of a Blue Eyed Ojibway

In this big, huge world, with all its billions and billions of people,
it's safe to say that everybody will eventually come across personalities and individuals that will touch them in some peculiar yet
poignant way. Individuals that in some way represent and help
define who you are. I'm no different, mine was Kermit the Frog.
Not just because Natives have a long tradition of savouring Frogs'
legs, but because of his music. If you all may remember, Kermit is
quite famous for his rendition of 'It's Not Easy Being Green'. I can

relate. If I could sing, my song would be 'It's Not Easy Having Blue Eyes in a Brown Eyed Village'.

Yes, I'm afraid it's true. The author happens to be a card-carrying Indian. Once you get past the aforementioned eyes, the fair skin, light brown hair, and noticeable lack of cheekbones, there lies the heart and spirit of an Ojibway storyteller. Honest Injun, or as the more politically correct term may be, honest aboriginal.

You see, I'm the product of a white father I never knew, and an Ojibway woman who evidently couldn't run fast enough. As a kid I knew I looked a bit different. But, then again, all kids are paranoid when it comes to their peers. I had a fairly happy childhood, frolicking through the bullrushes. But there were certain things that, even then, made me notice my unusual appearance. Whenever we played cowboys and Indians, guess who had to be the bad guy, the cowboy.

It wasn't until I left the Reserve for the big bad city, that I became more aware of the role people expected me to play, and the fact that physically I didn't fit in. Everybody seemed to have this preconceived idea of how every Indian looked and acted. One guy, on my first day of college, asked me what kind of horse I preferred. I didn't have the heart to tell him 'hobby'.

I've often tried to be philosophical about the whole thing. I have both white and red blood in me, I guess that makes me pink. I am a 'Pink' man. Try to imagine this, I'm walking around on any typical Reserve in Canada, my head held high, proudly announcing to everyone 'I am a Pink Man'. It's a good thing I ran track in school.

My pinkness is constantly being pointed out to me over and over and over again. 'You don't look Indian?' 'You're not Indian, are you?' 'Really?!?' I got questions like that from both white and Native people, for a while I debated having my Status card tattooed on my forehead.

And like most insecure people and specially a blue eyed Native writer, I went through a particularly severe identity crisis at one point. In fact, I admit it, one depressing spring evening, I dyed my hair black. Pitch black.

The reason for such a dramatic act, you may ask? Show Business. You see, for the last eight years or so, I've worked in various capacities in the performing arts, and as a result I'd always get calls to be an extra or even try out for an important role in some Native oriented movie. This anonymous voice would phone, having been given my number, and ask if I would be interested in trying out for a movie. Being a naturally ambitious, curious, and greedy young man, I would always readily agree, stardom flashing in my eyes and hunger pains from my wallet.

A few days later I would show up for the audition, and that was always an experience. What kind of experience you may ask? Picture this, the picture calls for the casting of seventeenth-century Mohawk warriors living in a traditional longhouse. The casting director calls the name 'Drew Hayden Taylor' and I enter.

The casting director, the producer, and the film's director look up from the table and see my face, blue eyes flashing in anticipation. I once was described as a slightly chubby beachboy. But even beachboys have tans. Anyway, there would be a quick flush of confusion, a recheck of the papers, and a hesitant 'Mr. Taylor?' Then they would ask if I was at the right audition. It was always the same. By the way, I never got any of the parts I tried for, except for a few anonymous crowd shots. Politics tells me it's because of the way I look, reality tells me it's probably because I can't act. I'm not sure which is better.

It's not just film people either. Recently I've become quite involved in Theatre, Native theatre to be exact. And one cold October day I was happily attending the Toronto leg of a province-wide tour of my first play, *Toronto at Dreamer's Rock*. The place was sold out, the audience very receptive and the performance was wonderful. Ironically one of the actors was also half white.

The director later told me he had been talking with the actor's father, an older Non-Native type chap. Evidently he had asked a few questions about me, and how I did my research. This made the director curious and he asked about his interest. He replied 'He's got an amazing grasp of the Native situation for a white person.'

Not all these incidents are work related either. One time a friend and I were coming out of a rather upscale bar (we were out YUPPIE watching) and managed to catch a cab. We thanked the cab driver for being so comfortably close on such a cold night, he shrugged and nonchalantly talked about knowing what bars to drive around. 'If you're not careful, all you'll get is drunk Indians.' I hiccuped.

Another time this cab driver droned on and on about the government. He started out by criticizing Mulroney, and eventually to his handling of the Oka crisis. This perked up my ears, until he said 'If it were me, I'd have tear-gassed the place by the second day. No more problem.' He got a dime tip. A few incidents like this and I'm convinced I'd make a great undercover agent for one of the Native political organizations.

But then again, even Native people have been known to look at me with a fair amount of suspicion. Many years ago when I was a young man, I was working on a documentary on Native culture up in the wilds of Northern Ontario. We were at an isolated cabin filming a trapper woman and her kids. This one particular nine-year-old girl seemed to take a shine to me. She followed me around for two days both annoying me and endearing herself to me. But she absolutely refused to believe that I was Indian. The whole film crew tried to tell her but to no avail. She was certain I was white.

Then one day as I was loading up the car with film equipment, she asked me if I wanted some tea. Being in a hurry I declined the tea. She immediately smiled with victory crying out 'See, you're not Indian, all Indians drink tea!'

Frustrated and a little hurt I whipped out my Status card and thrust it at her. Now there I was, standing in a Northern Ontario winter, showing my Status card to a nine-year-old non-status Indian girl who had no idea what one was. Looking back, this may not have been one of my brighter moves.

But I must admit, it was a Native woman that boiled everything down in one simple sentence. You may know that woman, Marianne Jones from 'The Beachcombers' television series. We were working on a film together out west and we got to gossiping. Eventually we got around to talking about our respective villages. Hers on the Queen Charlotte Islands, or Haida Gwaii as the Haida call them, and mine in central Ontario.

Eventually childhood on the Reserve was being discussed and I made a comment about the way I look. She studied me for a moment, smiled, and said 'Do you know what the old women in my village would call you?' Hesitant but curious, I shook my head. 'They'd say you were pretty like a white boy.' To this day I'm still not sure if I like that.

Now some may argue that I am simply a Métis with a Status card. I disagree, I failed French in grade 11. And the Métis as everyone knows have their own separate and honourable culture, particularly in western Canada. And of course I am well aware that I am not the only person with my physical characteristics.

I remember once looking at a video tape of a drum group, shot on a Reserve up near Manitoulin Island. I noticed one of the drummers seemed quite fairhaired, almost blond. I mentioned this to my girlfriend of the time and she shrugged saying 'Well, that's to be expected. The highway runs right through the Reserve.'

Perhaps I'm being too critical. There's a lot to be said for both cultures. For example, on the left hand, you have the Native respect for Elders. They understand the concept of wisdom and insight coming with age.

On the white hand, there's Italian food. I mean I really love my mother and family but seriously, does anything really beat good Veal Scallopini? Most of my aboriginal friends share my fondness for this particular brand of food. Wasn't there a warrior at Oka named Lasagna? I found it ironic, though curiously logical, that Columbus was Italian. A connection I wonder?

Also Native people have this wonderful respect and love for the land. They believe they are part of it, a mere chain in the cycle of existence. Now, as many of you know, this conflicts with the accepted Judeo-Christian i.e. western view of land management. I even believe somewhere in the first chapters of the Bible it says something about God giving man dominion over Nature. Check it out, Genesis 4:?, 'Thou shalt clear cut.' So I grew up understanding that everything around me is important and alive. My Native heritage gave me that.

And again, on the white hand, there's breast implants. Darn clever them white people. That's something Indians would never have invented, seriously. We're not ambitious enough. We just take what the Creator decides to give us, but no, not the white man. Just imagine it, some serious looking white man, and let's face it people, we know it was a man who invented them, don't we? So just imagine some serious looking white doctor sitting around in his laboratory muttering to himself, 'Big tits, big tits, hmm, how do I make big tits?' If it was an Indian, it would be 'Big tits, big tits, white women sure got big tits' and leave it at that.

So where does that leave me on the big philosophical scoreboard, what exactly are my choices again; Indians—respect for elders, love of the land. White people—food and big tits. In order to live in both cultures I guess I'd have to find an Indian woman with big tits who lives with her grandmother in a cabin out in the woods and can make Fettuccini Alfredo on a wood stove.

Now let me make this clear, I'm not writing this for sympathy, or out of anger, or even some need for self-glorification. I am just setting the facts straight. For as you read this, a new Nation is born. This is a declaration of independence, my declaration of independence.

I've spent too many years explaining who and what I am repeatedly, so as of this moment, I officially secede from both races. I plan to start my own separate nation. Because I am half Ojibway, and half Caucasian, we will be called the Occasions. And I of course, since I'm founding the new nation, will be a Special Occasion.

TOPICS FOR DISCUSSION

1. Taylor relates a number of incidents involving misunderstandings about his identity. How do some of these incidents reveal racial tensions between white and Native people? What is the

role of "show business" in creating and maintaining Native stereotypes?

2. What irony is implied in Taylor's talking about being "pretty like a white boy"? What does it tell us about racial self-image among Aboriginal people and whites?

3. What are the advantages of Native culture, according to Taylor? How does he satirize some of the pretensions of white culture? How does humour help to communicate a serious subject matter in this essay?

4. How does Taylor prove the absurdity of exclusionary notions of identity?

5. Compare attitudes to identity in different Native authors (Drew Hayden Taylor, Alootook Ipellie, Carol Geddes, and Pat Deiter-McArthur). How does proximity to white culture affect their self-definition?

David Suzuki

*David Suzuki was born in Vancouver in 1936. He is a writer, educator,
journalist, TV and radio host, environmentalist, and a world-renowned
geneticist. He received a Ph.D. in genetics in 1961 from the University of
Chicago.* He has written several books and many articles in the area of
ecology and has hosted numerous television shows, including *The* Nature
of Things. *He has published* Geoethics: The Clash Between the New
Genetics and Human Values *(1989) and* Time to Change: Essays
(1994). He is co-author, with Keibo Oiwa, of The Japan We Never
Knew: A Journey of Discovery *(1996). The following excerpt comes from
his book* Metamorphosis: Stages in a Life, *published in 1987. David
Suzuki confronts the problem of being perceived as "too Canadian" during
his visit to Japan. Conversely, in another essay, "Last Dance on Racism's
Grave," he is seen as not Canadian enough by white patrons of a bar that
he frequents in his hometown, Vancouver. He is caught between two cultures as a Canadian in Japan and a third-generation Japanese in Canada.
In both cases, identity is imposed from without, based on external traces
and characteristics, and does not necessarily coincide with the subject's own
sense of identity.*

Ancestors—The Genetic Source

My genes can be traced in a direct line to Japan. I am a pure-
blooded member of the Japanese race. And whenever I go there, I am
always astonished to see the power of that biological connection. In
subways in Tokyo, I catch familiar glimpses of the eyes, hairline or
smile of my Japanese relatives. Yet when those same people open their
mouths to communicate, the vast cultural gulf that separates them
from me becomes obvious: English is my language, Shakespeare is my
literature, British history is what I learned and Beethoven is my
music.

For those who believe that in people, just as in animals, genes
are the primary determinant of behaviour, a look at second- and

third-generation immigrants to Canada gives powerful evidence to the contrary. The overriding influence is environmental. We make a great mistake by associating the inheritance of physical characteristics with far more complex traits of human personality and behaviour.

Each time I visit Japan, I am reminded of how Canadian I am and how little the racial connection matters. I first visited Japan in 1968 to attend the International Congress of Genetics in Tokyo. For the first time in my life, I was surrounded by people who all looked like me. While sitting in a train and looking at the reflections in the window, I found that it was hard to pick out my own image in the crowd. I had grown up in a Caucasian society in which I was a minority member. My whole sense of self had developed with that perspective of looking different. All my life I had wanted large eyes and brown hair so I could be like everyone else. Yet on that train, where I did fit in, I didn't like it.

On this first visit to Japan I had asked my grandparents to contact relatives and let them know I was coming. I was the first in the Suzuki clan in Canada to visit them. The closest relative on my father's side was my grandmother's younger brother, and we arranged to meet in a seaside resort near his home. He came to my hotel room with two of his daughters. None of them spoke any English, while my Japanese was so primitive as to be useless. In typical Japanese fashion, they showered me with gifts, the most important being a package of what looked like wood carved in the shape of bananas! I had no idea what it was. (Later I learned the package contained dried tuna fish from which slivers are shaved off to flavour soup. This is considered a highly prized gift.) We sat in stiff silence and embarrassment, each of us struggling to dredge up a common word or two to break the quiet. It was excruciating! My great uncle later wrote my grandmother to tell her how painful it had been to sit with her grandson and yet be unable to communicate a word.

To people in Japan, all non-Japanese—black, white or yellow—are *gaijin* or foreigners. While *gaijin* is not derogatory, I find that its use is harsh because I sense doors clanging shut on me when I'm called one. The Japanese do have a hell of a time with me because I look like them and can say in perfect Japanese, "I'm a foreigner and I can't speak Japanese." Their reactions are usually complete incomprehension followed by a sputtering, "What do you mean? You're speaking Japanese." And finally a pejorative, "Oh, a *gaijin!*"

Once when my wife, Tara, who is English, and I went to Japan we asked a man at the travel bureau at the airport to book a *ryokan*—a traditional Japanese inn—for us in Tokyo. He found one and booked it for "*Suzuki-san*" and off we went. When we arrived at the inn and I entered the foyer, the owner was confused by my terrible Japanese. When Tara entered, the shock was obvious in his face. Because of my name, they had expected a "real" Japanese. Instead, I was a *gaijin* and the owner told us he wouldn't take us. I was furious and we stomped off to a phone booth where I called the agent at the airport. He was astonished and came all the way into town to plead our case with the innkeeper. But the innkeeper stood firm and denied us a room. Apparently he had accepted *gaijin* in the past with terrible consequences.

As an example of the problem, Japanese always take their shoes off when entering a *ryokan* because the straw mats (*tatami*) are quickly frayed. To a Japanese, clomping into a room with shoes on would be comparable to someone entering our homes and spitting on the floor. Similarly, the *ofuro*, or traditional tub, has hot clean water that all bathers use. So one must first enter the bathroom, wash carefully and rinse off *before* entering the tub. Time in the *ofuro* is for relaxing and soaking. Again, Westerners who lather up in the tub are committing a terrible desecration.

To many Canadians today, the word "Jap" seems like a natural abbreviation for Japanese. Certainly for newspaper headlines it would seem to make sense. So people are often shocked to see me bristle when they have used the word Jap innocently. To Japanese-Canadians, Jap or Nip (from "*Nippon*") were epithets used generously during the pre-war and war years. They conjure up all of the hatred and bigotry of those times. While a person using the term today may be unaware of its past use, every Japanese-Canadian remembers.

The thin thread of Japanese culture that does link me to Japan was spun out of the poverty and desperation of my ancestors. My grandparents came to a Canadian province openly hostile to their strange appearance and different ways. There were severe restrictions on how much and where they could buy property. Their children, who were born and raised in Canada, couldn't vote until 1948 and encountered many barriers to professional training and property ownership. Asians, regardless of birthplace, were third-class citizens. That is the reality of the Japanese-Canadian experience and the historical cultural legacy that came down to the third and fourth generations—to me and my children.

The first Japanese immigrants came to Canada to make their fortunes so they could return to Japan as people of wealth. The vast majority was uneducated and impoverished. But in the century spanning my grandparents' births and the present, Japan has leapt from an agrarian society to a technological and economic giant.

Now, the Japanese I meet in Japan or as recent immigrants to Canada come with far different cultural roots. Present-day Japanese are highly educated, upper-middle class and proud of their heritage. In Canada they encounter respect, envy and curiosity in sharp contrast to the hostility and bigotry met by my grandparents.

Japanese immigrants to North America have names that signify the number of generations in the new land (or just as significantly, that count the generational distance *away* from Japan). My grandparents are *Issei*, meaning the first generation in Canada. Most *Issei* never learned more than a rudimentary knowledge of English. *Nisei*, like my parents, are the second generation here and the first native-born group. While growing up they first spoke Japanese in the home and then learned English from playmates and teachers. Before the Second World War, many *Issei* sent their children to be educated in Japan. When they returned to Canada, they were called *Kika-nisei* (or *Kibei* in the United States). Most have remained bilingual, but many of the younger *Nisei* now speak Japanese with difficulty because English is their native tongue. My sisters and I are *Sansei* (third generation); our children are *Yonsei*. These generations, and especially *Yonsei*, are growing up in homes where English is the only spoken language, so they are far more likely to speak school-taught French as their second language than Japanese.

Most *Sansei*, like me, do not speak Japanese. To us, the *Issei* are mysteries. They came from a cultural tradition that is a hundred years old. Unlike people in present-day Japan, the *Issei* clung tightly to the culture they remembered and froze that culture into a static museum piece like a relic of the past. Not being able to speak each other's language, *Issei* and *Sansei* were cut off from each other. My parents dutifully visited my grandparents and we children would be trotted out to be lectured at or displayed. These visits were excruciating, because we children didn't understand the old culture, and didn't have the slightest interest—we were Canadians.

My father's mother died in 1978 at the age of ninety-one. She was the last of the *Issei* in our family. The final months of her life, after a left-hemisphere stroke, were spent in that terrible twilight—crippled, still aware, but unable to communicate. She lived the terminal months of her life, comprehending but mute, in a ward with Caucasian strangers. For over thirty years I had listened to her psychologically blackmailing my father by warning him of her imminent death. Yet in the end, she hung on long after there was reason to. When she died, I was astonished at my own reaction, a great sense of sadness and regret at the cleavage of my last link with the source of my genes. I had never been able to ask what made her and others of her generation come to Canada, what they felt when they arrived, what their hopes and dreams had been, and whether it was worth it. And I wanted to thank her, to show her that I was grateful that, through them, I was born a Canadian.

TOPICS FOR DISCUSSION

1. Why does Suzuki question the validity of the "biological connection" in determining individual identity? How does environment override genes?

2. Although Suzuki resembles them physically, he cannot communicate with his relatives in Japan. He is a *gaijin* (a foreigner). How does being a *gaijin* exclude Suzuki?

3. How have the different generations of Japanese Canadians responded to the experience of the new land? How do people of Suzuki's generation (*Sansei*) view their immigrant ancestors (*Issei*)? Why are the hopes and motives of *Issei* still a "mystery" to Suzuki?

4. Suzuki takes a pragmatic stance towards the question of immigrant adaptation, cutting off the "link with the source of one's genes" if required. Both he and Sun-Kyung Yi have opted for an identity determined by culture rather than the genes. What difficulties do they encounter?

C. Allyson Lee

*A third-generation Chinese Canadian, Corinne Allyson Lee was born in
1950 in Calgary. Feeling singled out as "visible minority," she grew up
with "internalized racism" that she describes as "fear or hatred of one's own
ethnic heritage or prejudice against one's own race." After she finished
school, she moved to Vancouver, where she was gradually healed of her
"sinophobia" and managed to come to terms with her ethnic background.
She has been involved in the lesbian community and has worked as a coun-
selor for Native street kids. In 1994, she was one of the organizers of the
Vancouver "Writing Thru Race" conference, a meeting of writers of colour
from across Canada that stirred a lot of controversy and divided the
writing community on the issue of race. Lee has published poems and essays
in literary journals such as* Fireweed, The Capilano Review, Angles, *and*
Kinesis. *Her works are included in several anthologies of queer writing,
that is, writing by lesbian, gay, bisexual, and transgendered people:* Piece of
My Heart: A Lesbian of Colour Anthology *(1991),* Out Rage: Dykes
and Bis Resist Homophobia *(1993), and* The Very Inside: An
Anthology of Asian and Pacific Islander Lesbian and Bisexual Women
(1994). Lee has co-edited, with Makeda Silvera, Pearls of Passion: A
Treasury of Lesbian Erotica *(1995).*

An Asian Lesbian's Struggle

B y virtue of the shape of my eyes and the colour of my hair, I am
considered by Canadian society to have membership in a "visible"
minority, and am also called a "woman of colour." This means that I
could never "pass" for white, even if I tried. It has long been
regarded as a privilege, to be able to be thought of as white, to have
no physical characteristics which could set one apart for looking different. After all, in Canada, a white person can walk down any street
and not be called a "jap," "chink" or "nigger" and not be asked
"where do you come from – originally?" or "where were you born?"

Aside from the obvious racism generated from external sources, many people of colour often suffer from a more concealed form of oppression: internalized racism. This could be described as fear or hatred of one's own ethnic heritage or prejudice against one's own race. For myself, it has taken decades to get to the point of claiming ownership of such feelings. For most of my life, I belonged to the "Don't Wanna Be" tribe, being ashamed and embarrassed of my Asian background, turning my back on it and rejecting it. I did not want to be associated with, let alone belong to a group which was stereotyped by whites as being noisy, slanty-eyed rice gobblers, "gooks" or chinks.

In spite of my being born and raised on the prairies, in a predominantly white neighbourhood with all white friends, my father tried his best (albeit unsuccessfully) to jam "Chineseness" down my throat. He kept telling me that I should be playing with Chinese kids – there were none in our neighbourhood. He chastised me for not being able to speak Chinese – by the time I entered Grade One public school, I was fluent in both English and Chinese, but my parents, worried that I might not develop good English skills, stopped conversing with me in Chinese. And my father warned me ominously, "You'd better marry a Chinese. If you marry a white, we'll cut you out of our will." All of this succeeded in driving me further away from my roots, leading me to believe that if I acted white enough, i.e. not chatter noisily in Chinese and not hang around in groups, I would actually not look Chinese.

Throughout my home life it was unacceptable for me to embrace my father's traditional Chinese culture and values unconditionally, because, in my mind, I would be accused by others of "sticking to my own kind" and would therefore be set apart from whites. But along with my father's wish for my awareness of cultural identity came along his expectation that I grow up to be a "nice Chinese girl." This meant that I should be a ladylike, submissive, obedient, morally impeccable puppet who would spend the rest of her life deferring to and selflessly appeasing her husband. He wanted me to become all that was against my nature, and so I rebelled with a fury, rejecting and denying everything remotely associated with Chinese culture.

When I moved away from the prairies to the West Coast, I remained somewhat colourless and blind. Still denying any association with my ethnic background, I often voiced, along with others, utter contempt for Hong Kong immigrants who were, in our minds, nothing but repugnant, obnoxious, spoiled rich kids. And it was in this city that I first experienced being called chink and gook on the street.

The connection between my sinophobia (fear or hatred of anything or anyone Chinese) and rebellion against my father did not become obvious to me until years later. Moving into another province meant that there was no longer daily contact with my father, the object of my defiance. I was becoming a little less resistant to Chinese culture, as I busied myself with the task of forming a new life in the city. Seeing new places, meeting new people and taking in new experiences left me a little less time to practice this form of self-hate.

Becoming a lesbian challenged everything in my upbringing and confirmed the fact that I was not a nice, ladylike pamperer of men. Somehow I must have know from an early age that I would never fit into this conformation. My friendships with women had always been more satisfying and intense than those with men. I had grown up with a secret morbid fear of marriage, and I did not know why until I became involved with a woman.

By coincidence, my first lover was a woman of colour, someone who was proud of her own heritage. She became interested in mine, and through her support and love, I began to look more positively at my culture and see that it did hold a few interesting qualities. Her heritage and mine, although distinct and separate, had some notable and fascinating similarities. Both celebrated yearly festivals. And both cherished the importance of higher education and the formation of a solid family structure. She helped me see that it could be fun to explore the various aspects of my culture, but at this point I still did not claim it as my own.

Years later, white women lovers came into my life, teasing me and calling me a "fake" Chinese because, after all, I did not even speak the language. This helped to bring back the old feelings of sinophobia again, and it did not occur to me then that certain white people would seek me out and be attracted to me because of my ethnic background. I had heard of "rice queens," white men who go after Chinese men. But there was no such term for white women who felt a strong affinity towards Chinese women. It would be much later that I would coin the phrase "Asianophile," my own description of such women.

Another woman entered my life, and by another coincidence, she was Chinese, born in Canada, and proud of her heritage. This I found to be both mystifying and affirming at the same time. She had not developed an attitude of sinophobia in her childhood, and as a result never felt contempt or derision for her background or her association with it. It felt like a bonus to be able to talk with her without having to explain little idiosyncrasies of our common culture and language. I no longer felt ashamed of it. She was starting to help me reclaim a heritage I had previously denied.

I felt certain that we were the only two Chinese lesbians in the world, until I began to meet others from different Asian backgrounds. At an Asian lesbian conference in California, I learned that there were indeed others who shared similar stories of struggles against externalized and internalized racism. Meeting Asian lesbians in my own city was like taking a course in Anti-Racism 101, which helped to raise my political awareness. These special women made me realize that it was fine to get upset over injustice and oppression, great to speak out about it, and necessary to fight against it. Gradually my awareness of my background was no longer the source of my shame, but the beginning of my empowerment. My attempts at conquering my sinophobia continues to be an uphill struggle, as I deliberately seek out to meet other Asian lesbians and maintain friendships with them. Years ago I would have shunned them, or at best, ignored them. There is still as sense of discomfort, however, when I go out socially with a group of Asian women (and I find myself looking around the room hoping not to catch contemptuous racist stares from white patrons), or when my white friends tell me that they feel left out or uncomfortable around a large group of my Asian women friends.

As I go through this struggle, however, there are many bonuses in my life. I am enriched by the company of some very supportive and loving friends: Asian women, other women of colour, white women and men. I have reached a point of understanding about the origins of my previous self-hate and how it has pervaded my life and magnified the dysfunctional relationship with my father. And there is always that private joy in knowing that my father (who doesn't even know it) won't have to worry about my marrying a white boy.

TOPICS FOR DISCUSSION

1. Why does Lee perceive "whiteness" as a privilege to be desired?

2. Lee's "sinophobia" has its roots both in her rejection of gender traditionalism and in internalized racism. Explain how she developed her "sinophobic" attitude.

3. Why did coming out as a lesbian help her to accept the ethnic part of her identity?

4. Compare the relationship between a young girl and her parents in Lee's autobiographical narrative and in Anne Jew's story "Everyone Talked Loudly in Chinatown." Why did they both have to hide their sexuality from their parents? Discuss the problems with homophobia (hostility and fear of homosexuality) that young people who identify themselves as gay, lesbian, or bisexual may face with their family and friends.

Camille Hernandez-Ramdwar

*Camille Hernandez-Ramdwar was born and raised in the prairies, and
currently lives in Toronto with her son and daughter. She graduated from
York University in 1991, and she continues her graduate work at the
University of Toronto. Her writing, both creative and academic, explores
issues of race, multiracial identities, and interracial relationships. She says
that she has been writing about her experiences as a Canadian woman of
colour for most of her life, and that she tends to identify with and find
strength in her Caribbean roots. She describes herself as "a TrinCan of
Trinidadian/Ukrainian-Canadian heritage." Her works have appeared in*
Sharing Our Experience *(1993) and a special 1994 issue of* West Coast
Line *devoted to Canadian First Nations Writers and Writers of Colour. In
"Ms Edge Innate," she records her difficult search for a sense of belonging
and identity. Because of her mixed heritage, she feels deprived of any right
of cultural inheritance. The experience of racism has profoundly influenced
her perception of what it means to be Canadian. She reveals the hidden
presumption of whiteness in the definition of a Canadian; she also reveals
the racist and sexist stereotypes that Black women are bombarded with. In
the end, defining herself as Ms Edge Innate, she chooses to situate herself on
the borders of society that has become ever more "divided, departmentalized, tribalized."*

Ms Edge Innate

Do you know who I am? I'm the one you can't leave alone. The
one who puzzles you, intrigues you. I am the original definition of
"exotic." Acceptable in many ways, the café au lait of life, more
palatable because I am diluted. Not as offensive, not as threatening—
you think. Certainly not as obvious. But hard to ignore.

They call me white, they call me black—they've called me
everything in between. Honestly, if one person could claim global
citizenship, it would be me, because who could dispute it? But then

again, looks count for everything, and I *know*, people see what they want to see. If they're looking for a new member, I'm it. If they're looking for a scapegoat, I'm it. If they're looking for a specimen, I'm it. If they're looking for an excuse, I'm It. I'm It I'm It I'm It—a glorious game of tag and everyone wants to participate.

I don't think my parents realized the complexity of what they were getting into. Like most interracial couples, they just closed their eyes and ears and hoped for the best. Of course the children would be beautiful, of course both sides would ooh and aah over the benefits—the dark (but not too dark) complexion, the wavy (not too curly) hair, everybody should have been happy, everyone should have been satisfied. Those large dark eyes, like the eyes of orphan poster children: "Is she adopted? Where did you get her?" Looks of bewilderment as my mother tries to explain her husband is "foreign," "dark." Dark like the night? Like tar? Like a rapist? Oh dear, you didn't marry one of *those*?

I went to my mother's family reunion when I was sixteen. I guess I went out of respect for my mother, because I didn't go for myself. There was no reason for me to be there, as far as I could see. I didn't resemble anyone in the crowd, and there were over three hundred people there. I remember leaving in the middle of the big barn dance, because I couldn't relate to anyone, and was tired of being asked whose (half-breed bastard darkie nigger) offspring I was.

My mother raised me, she loved me, but upon reaching adulthood, I've realized that there was something very important my mother could never give me—a culture which matched my colour. If women are the bestowers and the keepers of culture, the ones who pass on language, nuance, myth, food, spiritual teachings and values to children, then I have been culturally malnourished. It wasn't my mother's fault. In fact, through many years of struggle, I have learned that there is no one to blame. I could have blamed my parents—my mother for wanting an "exotic" experience, my father for coveting a white woman, but they made their choices, and now I am the one who must deal with the consequences of their actions.

Because I was raised in my mother's homeland, and not my father's, I grew up with my mother's culture. And my parents wanted it that way. If there were women who could have taught me things about my "other" culture—my paternal grandmother and aunts—I was removed from them by an entire continent and a sea.

My mother loved me, she raised me, but she could never quite understand me. She did not live in my skin. In fact she seemed oblivious to my colour, as my father had become oblivious to his. These issues to them were irrelevant, or, in retrospect, too painful.

Ms Edge Innate 379

They hoped my acculturation would make up for my colour. They hoped I would automatically assimilate—perhaps even marry white, continue the dilution of our blood, whiten the grandchildren. They never spoke of this, but it was inferred in their actions and statements. I, having no choice, subjected to the isolation of an all-white community (save for the few foster children sprinkled amongst the middle class white families), almost made their wishes a reality.

Because I grew up in this country, because I can speak the language, understand the nuances, the not-saids, the thought patterns, because I can decipher the white response, I am considered Canadian. But I hate this indefinable term. "Oh Edge, you're so Canadian!"

You know what Canadian is to me? A Canadian is someone who likes hockey, likes the winter, the whiteness. A Canadian is someone who spends every summer going to "the lake" ("a pool of stagnant water" my father used to call it). A Canadian is someone who thinks this is the greatest country on earth. Someone who wants to perpetuate the status quo. Someone who travels to the Third World and hangs out with other (white) Canadians, Australians, Brits and occasionally Americans. Someone who thinks of Third World women and men as "an exotic experience." Someone who is ignorant of world history, geography, and is profoundly culturally ignorant. All black people are "Jamaicans" or "from Africa." All South Asian people are "Pakis." East Asians are invariably "Chinese." First Nations people are drunks, or militant troublemakers.

My friend's brother said that the Mohawks at Oka had no right to pick up guns. Oh? I've heard this since many times—they have no right to be angry, no right to defend their land, no right to seek retribution. Canadians have become so accustomed in their psyches to the docility of people of colour that it is reprehensible to them that these "non-whites" are no longer behaving like children, accepting what is thrown at them.

But I digress. It is obvious that, to me, a Canadian is not a person of colour, nor an aboriginal person. A Canadian is white— one of the "two founding nations" or one of the following stream of later immigrants—Jewish, Ukrainian, German, Italian, Portuguese, etc. Therefore, upon meeting black Canadians, I am heard to say "Well, you are black first, then a Canadian by fault of birth," to which they reply, no, my people have been here for five generations and you'd better damn well believe I'm Canadian. To which I counter-attack—oh yeah? When was the last time you WEREN'T asked where you are from? How many of "your people" are represented in government—at *any* level? Why are there race riots in Halifax, where black people have been living as long as white people have? Why are black people being shot by police?

Because I could not identify with my mother's culture, and because I could not acquire whiteness, I strongly adopted my father's culture. I wonder how much of this was choice, how much necessity, and how much instinct. I know I gravitated towards things black and Caribbean long before I knew what those two intertwined yet distinct cultures represented. Everything else (literally) paled in comparison.

When I was small, I would go to parties with the other kids, and someone would put on a record, and I would get up and dance— perfect rhythm, hips, feet—and everyone would stare in amazement and ask—where did you learn how to dance? Who taught you? How do you do it? No one taught me, I would respond—and then think, Edge, you're different. I would sit down to play "Peanut Man" on the piano with my Jewish friend, try to teach her the syncopated beat, but no matter how many times she rehearsed it, it just wouldn't come out right. And I'd think, doesn't she hear what I hear? It's so simple! Again—"I'm different."

And boys—white boys—fascinated by some myth of my sexual powers—dark, musky, hypnotic—would taunt me and tease and abuse me. In Grade One I was called "sex maniac" by gangs of six-year-old boys...and in later years, acquired the trappings of that myth—the oversexed mama, the hot tamale, hot Latin blood, ball-busting black woman who could fuck you in half. They bought it, I dished it out—desperate for love and acceptance and to be considered beautiful in the era of Farrah Fawcett and Cheryl Tiegs. Because black women were to fuck, not to love, because I was a nymphomaniac *anyway,* it was alright to sexually abuse me.

And I've paid a price for all this acting, this "assimilation" if that's what it's called. A Trinidadian man told me years ago that people like me were schizophrenic, would always be schizophrenic because we are living in a world that does not allow us to integrate ourselves, our psyches. I don't know about this—there may have been a time in my life when I truly had a hard time feeling whole, but I now know who I am, what I am and where I fit in the scheme of things. Other people may have a problem defining me, but that is their problem. I know where I stand.

(Oh the words of the strong, of the self-knowing—where have I gained such courage? How long have I envied people who simply look into the mirror and state "I Am"? People who can point to one nation on a map, or even continent, and say "This is where I/my people are from." The urge for Wholeness, Completeness in a world that consistently denies it.)

I watch couples on the street very carefully, mixed couples, interracial couples, and I always think of the children. If you make children, who will be raising them? Who will be teaching them? Are these white women who mother children of colour really prepared for the struggles that child will endure? Are they willing to accept that they can not and have not walked in that child's shoes? Are they prepared to confront their own ignorance? Can they truly offer support and guidance to that child?

I watch with interest the conflicts over black children placed in white foster homes. The whole movement to end this, to end the assimilation, the "loss of the race," and I can't help but think, yes, but what about those of us who grew up in a mixed race home and *still* did not get culturally nourished? Does it really matter if you are raised by your "blood" parents or not when the issue is culture? That is to assume that your parents' culture is always your own—which isn't necessarily the case. I know I had to fight for my culture; I had to wade and sift through endless genetic memories; I had to tune into ancestral voices and dreams; I had to see myself in eyes that easily reflected my own because they were similar. Eyes that knew richness, pain, history, joy, rhythms of life. I had to seek that, and it was a long journey. I had to leave icicle stares and snow-capped schooling, literally and figuratively, in order to see myself in my natural habitat.

And they call me Ms Edge Innate, precipice girl, riding on the wave of something wholly internal, a calling I can't explain save to say it is in my soul. Innate: i.e., inborn, not acquired. I had to revert back to myself. I had to struggle to claim what was already mine. Something that explains myself to me, something that makes sense.

But I can not expect you to understand—not yet. I watch as people become further divided, departmentalized, tribalized … and I wonder on the choices I will have to make—again—and that my children will have to make. There is no camp for us to fit easily into, there never has been, and we are always asked to choose, but by reason of our appearance the choice is often made for us.

I am tired of choosing; I long to be whole. The mirror lies, it confuses—appearances are so deceptive and so subjective. My inner voice tells the truth. Ms Edge Innate—here I am, on the periphery of *your* world, but knowing that what is mine is wholly and soully my own.

TOPICS FOR DISCUSSION

1. How does Camille Hernandez-Ramdwar define a Canadian? Why does she feel excluded from the definition of a Canadian? How does she justify her identification with her father's culture rather than her mother's culture?

2. How has she been affected by sexist stereotypes about Black women? To what degree did she internalize these stereotypes when she was at school? According to her, what are the reasons why some Black women may feel insecure in their self-esteem?

3. What specific grievances does she have against her parents? Why is she concerned about the future of children born to mixed couples? In what way is these children's situation similar to (or different from) the situation of Black children placed in white foster homes?

4. Compare the cultural alienation of Sun-Kyung Yi with that described by Camille Hernandez-Ramdwar. How different are their respective responses to their identity crises?

5. Compare different strategies of shocking the reader that are used by Drew Hayden Taylor and Camille Hernandez-Ramdwar. How effective are these strategies? How does the subject matter justify the use of shock and surprise in each case?

SELECTED BIBLIOGRAPHY

Begamudré, Ven and Judith Krause. *Out of Place: Stories and Poems.* Regina: Coteau Books, 1991.

Birbalsingh, Frank. *Jahaji Bhai: An Anthology of Indo-Caribbean Literature.* Toronto: Tsar, 1988.

Black, Ayanna. *VOICES: 16 Canadian Writers of African Descent.* Toronto: Harper Collins Publ., 1992.

Black, Ayanna. *Fiery Spirits: Canadian Writers of African Descent.* Toronto: Harper Collins Publ., 1994.

Byrne, Nympha and Camille Fouillard, eds. *It's Like the Legend: Innu Women's Voices.* Toronto; Women's Press, 2000.

Camper, Carol, ed. *Miscegenation Blues: Voices of Mixed Race Women.* Toronto: Sister Vision, 1994.

Ciatu, Angelina Nzula et al. *Curaggia: Writing by Women of Italian Descent.* Toronto: Women's Press,1998.

Clarke, George Elliott. *Fire on the Water: An Anthology of Black Nova Scotian Writing.* 2 vols. Porters Lake, N.S.: Pattersfield Press, 1991.

_____. *Eyeing the North Star: Directions in African-Canadian Literature.* Toronto: McClelland & Stewart, 1997.

Conway, Sheila, ed. *The Faraway Hills are Green: Voices of Irish Women in Canada.* Toronto: Women's Press, 1992.

Fife, Connie. *The Colour of Resistance: A Contemporary Collection of Writing by Aboriginal Women.* Toronto: Sister Vision, 1993.

Grant, Agnes. *Our Bit of Truth: An Anthology of Canadian Native Literature.* Winnipeg, Manitoba: Pemmican Publication, 1990.

Grouev, Ivaylo. *Bullets on the Water: Canadian Refugee Stories.* Montreal-Kingston: McGill-Queens University Press, 2000.

Harris, Claire and Edna Alford. *Kitchen Talk: Contemporary Women's Prose and Poetry.* Red Deer, Ab: Red Deer College Press, 1992.

Hutcheon, Linda & Marion Richmond. *Other Solitudes: Canadian Multicultural Fictions.* Toronto: Oxford UP, 1990.

James, Carl E., ed. *Experiencing Difference.* Halifax: Fernwood Publishing, 2000.

James Carl E. & Adrienne Shadd, eds. *Talking about Identity: Encounters in Race, Ethnicity, and Language.* Toronto: Between the Lines, 2001.

Kadi, Joanna, ed. *Food for Our Grandmothers.* South End Press, 1994.

Kamboureli, Smaro, ed. *Making a Difference: Canadian Multicultural Literature.* Toronto: Oxford University Press, 1996.

King, Thomas. *All My Relations: An Anthology of Contemporary Canadian Native Fiction.* Toronto: McClelland & Stewart, 1990.

Lee, Bennett & Jim Wong-Chu. *Many-Mouthed Birds: Contemporary Writing by Chinese Canadians.* Vancouver: Douglas & McIntyre, 1991.

McGifford, Diane. *The Geography of Voice: Canadian Literature of the South Asian Diaspora.* Toronto: TSAR, 1992.

Moses, Daniel David & Terry Goldie. *An Anthology of Canadian Native Literature in English.* Toronto: Oxford UP, 1992.

Mukherjee, Arun. *Sharing Our Experience.* Ottawa: Canadian Advisory Council on the Status of Women, 1993.

Oiwa, Keibo. *Stone Voices: Wartime Writings of Japanese Canadian Issei.* Montreal: Vehicule Press, 1992.

Perreault, Jeanne & Sylvia Vance. *Writing the Circle: Native Women of Western Canada.* Edmonton, Alberta: NeWest, 1990.

Petrone, Penny. *Northern Voices: Inuit Writing in English.* Toronto: University of Toronto Press, 1988.

Pivato, Joseph, ed. *The Anthology of Italian-Canadian Writing.* Guernica, 1998.

Rafiq, Fauzia, ed. *Aurat Durbar: The Court of Women, Writings by Women of South Asian Origin.* Toronto: Second Story, 1995.

Rostom, Kamal A. *Arab-Canadian Writing: Stories, Memoirs, and Reminiscences.* Fredericton, N.B.: York Press, 1989.

Scheier, Libby , Sarah Sheard & Eleanor Wachtel. *Language in Her Eye: Writing and Gender. Views by Canadian Women Writing in English.* Toronto: Coach House Press, 1990.

Silvera, Makeda. *Piece of My Heart: A Lesbian of Colour Anthology.* Toronto: Sister Vision, 1991.

Swartz, Sarah Silberstein and Margie Wolfe, eds. *From Memory to Transformation: Jewish Women's Voices.* Toronto: Second Story Press, 1998.

The Telling Book Collective. *Telling It: Women and Language Across Cultures.* Vancouver: Press Gang Publishers, 1990.

Tiessen, Hildi Froese & Peter Hinchcliffe. *Acts of Concealment: Mennonites Writing in Canada.* Waterloo, Ont.: University of Waterloo Press, 1992.

Tracey, Lindalee. *A Scattering of Seeds: The Creation of Canada.* Toronto: McArthur & Company,1999.

Valle, Gina, ed. *Our Grandmothers, Ourselves: Reflections of Canadian Women.* Vancouver: Raincoast Books, 1999.

Waddington, Miriam. *Canadian Jewish Short Stories.* Toronto: Oxford UP, 1990.

Warkentin, Germaine, ed. *Canadian Exploration Literature: An Anthology.* Toronto: Oxford University Press, 1993.

Wolf, Kirsten, ed. *Writings by Western Icelandic Women.* University of Manitoba, 1997.

The Women's Book Committee and Chinese Canadian National Council. *Jin Guo: Voices of Chinese Canadian Women.* Toronto: Women's Press, 1992.

COPYRIGHTS AND ACKNOWLEDGEMENTS

We wish to thank the publishers and copyright holders for permission to reprint the selections in this book, which are listed below in order of their appearance.

UNIT ONE:
FIRST CONTACT/BEGINNINGS/MIGRATIONS

THE IMMIGRANTS from *Selected Poems* 1966–1984 by Margaret Atwood. Copyright © Margaret Atwood 1990. Reprinted by permission of Oxford University Press Canada.

AS IT WAS IN THE BEGINNING by Pauline Johnson. From *The Moccasin Maker* (Tucson: University of Arizona Press, 1987).

A VISIT TO GROSSE ISLE by Suzanna Moodie.

BITS AND PIECES OF THE PAST reprinted with permission of Key Porter Books from Double Vision by Lyse Champagne. © Lyse Champagne, 1990.

MY DEAREST CHILD by Dr. Joy Mannette. Reprinted by permission of the author.

From THE CONCUBINE'S CHILDREN by Denise Chong. Copyright © 1994 by Donna Morrissey. Reprinted by permission of Penguin Books Canada Limited.

BREAKING THE BARRIERS: REFUGEE WOMEN IN CANADA by Dr. Helga Mills. This article originally appeared in *Canadian Woman Studies, Les Cahiers de la femme* (Spring 1989). Reprinted by permission of the author.

UNIT TWO:
CHALLENGES/RACISM/DISCRIMINATION

YO WHITE BOY by Michelle La Flamme. "White Boy" first appeared in 1992 as spoken word on the CD entitled VOID to VOICE, which was a compilation of African-Canadian and First Nations' Resistance songs set to music. It has also appeared in the

UNIT FOUR:
EDUCATION/DIFFERENCE/POWER

WHO ARE YOU? by Rita Joe, from *Poems of Rita Joe,* published by Abanaki Press, Halifax, Nova Scotia. Reprinted by permission of the author.

GROWING UP NATIVE by Carol Geddes. Reprinted from *Homemaker's Magazine* vol. 25, no. 7 (1990). Reprinted by permission of the author.

NEWCOMER by Mehri Yalfani. Material from *Parastoo: Stories and Poems.* Copyright © 1995 by Mehri Yalfani. Reprinted by permission of Women's Press.

FINDING A NATIONALITY THAT FITS by Isabel Vincent. Reprinted from *The Globe and Mail,* December 3, 1990. Reprinted by permission of *The Globe and Mail.*

THE OTHER FAMILY by Himani Bannerji. Reprinted by permission of the author.

RETURN OF THE FROGS by David Arnason. Reprinted by permission of Turnstone Press © David Arnason, 1994.

UNIT FIVE:
GENDER/FAMILIES/RELATIONSHIPS

THINGS UNSAID by Bernice Lever. Reprinted by permission of Black Moss Press.

MY FATHER'S LIFE from *Home Sweet Home* by Mordecai Richler, copyright © 1984 by Mordecai Richler. Used by permission of Alfred A. Knopf, a division of Random House, Inc.

TO EVERY THING THERE IS A SEASON by Alistair MacLeod. Printed by permission of McClelland & Stewart.

MANCUSO'S AND SONS. The excerpt from *The Father* by F. G. Paci is reprinted by permission of Oberon Press.

A WEDDING IN TORONTO by Austin Clarke from *When He Was Free and Young and He Used to Wear Silks,* copyright © 1971 by Austin Clarke. Published in Canada by House of Anansi Press Ltd. Reprinted by permission of the author.

UNIT EIGHT:
BORDERS/IDENTITIES/SELVES

INDEX